# Auctioning Public Assets

In many countries all over the world, governments are privatising firms that were previously under public control. This is happening, for example, in public utility sectors such as gas, water and electricity, in transport sectors such as rail and metro and in radio and telephony. This book provides an overview of the economic issues that are involved in this transfer of ownership of public assets. Combining a theoretical framework with a set of case studies of recent sales of state-owned assets from Europe and the USA, it asks which sort of allocation mechanism can a government adopt? Which is most suited to a particular sale? And how will the choice of allocation mechanism affect future market outcomes? With contributions from international experts, this book offers an accessible introduction to auction theory and an invaluable, non-technical analysis of existing knowledge. It will be of interest to students, non-specialists and policy-makers alike.

MAARTEN JANSSEN is a professor of microeconomics at Erasmus University Rotterdam. His main research interests are in game theory and the economics of information. His research has focused on co-ordination games, consumer search and adverse selection. He has been advising firms and government bodies on issues related to market structure.

# Auctioning Public Assets

*Analysis and Alternatives*

*Edited by*

Maarten Janssen

CAMBRIDGE
UNIVERSITY PRESS

PUBLISHED BY THE PRESS SYNDICATE OF THE UNIVERSITY OF CAMBRIDGE
The Pitt Building, Trumpington Street, Cambridge, United Kingdom

CAMBRIDGE UNIVERSITY PRESS
The Edinburgh Building, Cambridge, CB2 2RU, UK
40 West 20th Street, New York, NY 10011–4211, USA
477 Williamstown Road, Port Melbourne, VIC 3207, Australia
Ruiz de Alarcón 13, 28014 Madrid, Spain
Dock House, The Waterfront, Cape Town 8001, South Africa

http://www.cambridge.org

First published 2004

Printed in the United Kingdom at the University Press, Cambridge

*Typeface* Plantin 10/12 pt.     *System* LATEX 2ε    [TB]

*A catalogue record for this book is available from the British Library*

*Library of Congress Cataloguing in Publication data*

Auctioning public assets: analysis and alternatives / Maarten Janssen (editor).
  p.   cm.
Includes bibliographical references and index.
ISBN 0 521 83059 1 (hb) – ISBN 0 521 53757 6 (pb)
1. Telecommunication – Great Britain.   2. Telecommunication – Netherlands.
3. Government auctions – Great Britain.   4. Government auctions –
Netherlands.   I. Janssen, Maarten Christiaan Wilhelmus, 1962–
HE8094.A93   2003
352.5'54 – dc21   2003055155

ISBN 0 521 83059 1 hardback
ISBN 0 521 53757 6 paperback

# Contents

# Figures

# Tables

# Contributors

LUISA AFFUSO is a senior consultant at National Economic Research Associates Ltd (NERA) in London, and is affiliated to the London Business School. She was previously at the Department of Applied Economics of Cambridge University. Her main area of expertise is in competition and regulation, and her knowledge spans a wide range of industries, with a special focus on transport and telecommunications. Her experience includes projects for the European Bank for Reconstruction and Development and the World Bank. She has written several papers on railways, franchising and vertical restraints in retailing.

ROGER VAN DEN BERGH is a professor of law and economics at the Erasmus University Rotterdam. From 1987 until 2001 he was president of the European Association of Law and Economics. He has published widely on economic analysis of competition law, the economics of tort law and consumer protection, as well as the economic aspects of harmonisation of laws.

TILMAN BÖRGERS is a professor of economics and director of the Centre for Economic Learning and Social Evolution, both at University College London. His research interests are the foundations and the applications of game theory. He has published on knowledge and learning in games in journals such as *Econometrica*, the *Journal of Economic Theory*, and the *Review of Economic Studies*. Most recently, he has completed a survey of the European UMTS spectrum licensing process, which will appear in *Economic Policy*.

ERIC VAN DAMME is a research professor in economics at CentER and director of the Law and Economics Centre (TILEC), both at Tilburg University. His main area of expertise is game theory and its applications, including auctions, antitrust and regulation. He is a fellow of the Econometric Society and secretary and treasurer of the Game Theory Society. He is on the editorial board of several journals and he contributes to popularising the field by writing a bi-weekly column for the *Algemeen Dagblad*.

MAURICE DYKSTRA is a senior researcher at SEOR and a fellow of the Erasmus Competition and Regulation Institute. Before joining SEOR he worked for the Netherlands Ministry of Economic Affairs, CPB (Netherlands Bureau for Economic Research) and IOO (Institute for Research on Public Expenditure). His main research experience is in energy economics and productivity and efficiency analysis. He has worked as a consultant for regulators, ministries and other governmental organisations.

MAARTEN JANSSEN is a professor of microeconomics at Erasmus University Rotterdam. His main research interests are in game theory and the economics of information. His work focuses on co-ordination games, consumer search and on dynamic adverse selection models. He has published in journals such as the *International Economic Review*, the *Journal of Industrial Economics* and the *Journal of Economic Theory*. Recently, he has been consulting in issues concerning industrial organisation and auctions.

JAAP DE KONING has a background in econometrics. He is a director of SEOR, a research institute with close ties with Erasmus University Rotterdam. He is also a professor of labour market policy at this university. Formerly he was director of the labour research department and a member of the management team of the Netherlands Economic Institute (now Ecorys). His main fields of research are labour economics and the economics of education.

EMIEL MAASLAND is a researcher at SEOR and a fellow of the Erasmus Competition and Regulation Institute. His current research focuses on auction theory and the analysis of bidding behaviour in auctions. He has advised the Dutch government on the design of several auctions, including the auctions of petrol stations and radio broadcasting frequencies. He has advised the Czech government on the design and implementation its UMTS auction, and consulted to Wind in the Italian UMTS auction. He has also been on a research team that on behalf of the Dutch parliament evaluated the Dutch UMTS auction.

TANGA MORAE McDANIEL is an economist at the Department of Applied Economics of Cambridge University. Her primary academic interests include applied microeconomics and experimental economics. Her recent research has addressed market design and regulation in the gas and electricity industries of England and Wales. Papers relevant to this research have been or will be published in the *Journal of Regulatory Economics, Fiscal Studies, Utilities Policy* and the *CRI Regulatory Review*.

BENNY MOLDOVANU holds the chair of economic theory at the University of Bonn. He previously taught at Mannheim, and held visiting positions at Michigan, Northwestern, University College London, Tel-Aviv and Jerusalem. His research focuses on the theory and applications of auctions and mechanism design. He serves as an associate editor for leading professional journals such as *Econometrica*, the *Journal of Economic Theory* and *Games and Economic Behavior*. In 2001 he was awarded the Max Planck Research Prize. He has advised large industrial firms and European governments on auction design. His work has been published in *Econometrica*, the *American Economic Review*, the *Journal of Economic Theory* and the *Review of Economic Studies*.

YVES MONTANGIE is a researcher at the Erasmus Competition and Regulation Institute in Rotterdam, professor of business law at the Lessius Business School in Antwerp and a member of the Brussels bar. He previously worked as an assistant professor and project researcher in EC law at the University of Antwerp. He specialises in competition law and has published exhaustively on this subject in national and international journals.

KARSTEN NEUHOFF is a PhD student at Cambridge University. He has written several working papers on the industrial organisation of markets embedded in network industries. These provide a rich setting for the analysis of markets characterised by very high fixed costs, spatial interactions over the networks, scarcity of transmission capacity and dynamic effects due to R&D, learning and investment. Using empirical analysis from the UK, continental Europe and Korea he aims to provide theoretical tools for market design and regulation.

DAVID NEWBERY is a professor of applied economics at Cambridge University. A fellow of the Econometric Society and of the British Academy, he was president of the European Economic Association in 1996. He has led research projects on electricity and telecommunications privatisation and regulation, transition economies, tax reform and road congestion charging. He has published extensively in academic journals on these and other topics. His most recent book is *Privatization, Restructuring and Regulation of Network Utilities* (MIT Press).

TIMOTHY C. SALMON is currently an assistant professor in economics at Florida State University. He began working on the problems associated with the design of mechanisms for allocating public resources when he was an economist with the Federal Communications Commission's Auctions and Industry Analysis Division working on the design and conduct of the FCC's spectrum auctions. His current research combines theoretical, experimental and empirical approaches to issues in the design of auctions as well as issues in behavioural economics.

JOSEPH SWIERZBINSKI received his PhD in applied mathematics from Harvard University and is currently a senior lecturer in economics, a research fellow at the Centre for Economic Learning and Social Evolution (ELSE) and course director for the MSc in Environmental and Resource Economics, all at University College London. His research interests include environmental economics, experimental economics and the design of markets and other incentive mechanisms. His publications include articles in the *Journal of Political Economy*, the *Economic Journal*, the *Journal of Environmental Economics and Management*, and the *International Journal of Game Theory*.

NICO VAN DER WINDT is a director of SEOR. He studied economics and econometrics at Erasmus University Rotterdam. As director of different divisions of the Netherlands Economic Institute he was previously responsible for research and advice in the field of macroeconomic policy and sector modelling for a large variety of countries. He also spent three years as adviser to the Indonesian government. His main current research interests are economic policy modelling and competition policy.

# Preface

At the beginning of the twenty-first century, many European governments have allocated the right to use third-generation mobile telephony (UMTS) frequencies to private telecommunications parties. The allocation mechanisms that were adopted differed widely among countries. Some countries chose to use one or other form of auction for allocating the rights, whereas others chose a Beauty Contest in which market players were selected on the basis of the proposals they had submitted for how to use the frequencies. Some allocation procedures were considered successful, while others were heavily criticised. The first auction, the one in the United Kingdom, was declared a big success as there were many interested parties participating in the auction, one of the licences was won by a newcomer and the government raised a very large sum of money. The second auction, the one held in the Netherlands, was termed a failure by many commentators. The revenue was only a fraction of the revenue in the UK, even when calculated per head of the population. Moreover, all licences were won by incumbent parties and only one newcomer showed up for the first bidding round, indicating that newcomers were not interested in participating in the auction.

The mixed experience, together with the changing prospects for profitability of the UMTS technology, has led to the question whether, and under what circumstances, auctions are appropriate allocation mechanisms. Are auctions where firms have to pay large sums of money to acquire a licence at least partially responsible for the current state of the telecommunications sector? This general question is particularly important because governments throughout the world will face circumstances in which they want to have private companies performing operations that have some public-interest aspect to them. Examples include: the allocation of airport slots, (commercial) radio frequencies, different forms of public transport operations (such as metro, high-speed trains, buses, etc.), petrol stations, etc.

The potentially large benefits and possible pitfalls of auctioning government assets led to a decision by the Dutch government to ask a group

of civil servants to write a report comparing auctions with other allocation mechanisms. This group was mainly concerned with issues related
to the allocation of rights to operate in a market. The recent UMTS
auction may serve as an illustrative example. Market parties need to have
the right to use certain frequencies to be able to provide consumers with
UMTS services such as mobile internet access. In the auction, the available frequencies were clustered into lots and the highest bidder for a lot
won the licence to operate in the market using the frequencies of that lot.
The group focused on two central questions:

(1) What mechanisms could a government use, in principle, to allocate
    rights to operate in a market and which mechanism is to be preferred
    under what circumstances?
(2) What are the important design issues once a particular allocation
    mechanism has been chosen?

The civil servants worked from October 2001 to March 2002. This group,
formally under the supervision of the Ministry of Economic Affairs, asked
the Erasmus Competition and Regulation Institute (ECRI) to guide the
research work of a group of academic economists on these two questions.
The research consisted of case studies and more theory-oriented studies
surveying the relevant literature, and served as background material for
the working group. The present book is based on the research that was
initially carried out for the Dutch Ministry of Economic Affairs. The
book is also divided into a theory-oriented part and a part devoted to
case studies. I should like to thank the Dutch Ministry of Economic
Affairs for permission to let a wider audience become acquainted with
the work we have done.

   When preparing this book we had two types of audience in mind. The
first type consists of people who professionally have to deal with the question of how to allocate government rights to parties. This group consists
of government agencies, bureaucrats working in different ministries, private companies and lawyers who act on behalf of interested parties. The
second type of audience consists of advanced undergraduate students
in economics and MBA students who are interested in assessing recent
auction outcomes without going into the more technical journal articles.

   There are two reasons why most journal articles on auctions and the
few available textbooks on auctions are not especially helpful to these two
types of audience. First, the majority of the literature is quite technical
and the audiences we have in mind are either not able or do not have
the time to delve into the technicalities. Second, most of the auction
literature looks at auctions as independent events, i.e. all the relevant
information concerning the auction can be summarised in the number of
bidders that show up for the auction and their valuations for the object

that is sold. Such a description is relevant in many art auctions and other types of auction where the participants do not interact before or after the auction is held. One of the important questions that this book deals with is whether such a description is also relevant when a government wants to allocate a right to operate in a market.

The chapters in the book are written in such a way that the main insights of recent literature are discussed by means of simple, sometimes numerical, examples. The relevant theory is discussed in the first part of the book, while the case studies in the second part illustrate how the theoretical insights can be used in practice in a wide variety of different sectors.

Finally, I should like to thank Cor Guijt and Marcella Petri for helping me with the last stages of preparing the book.

*Rotterdam, February 2003*                                    MAARTEN JANSSEN

# Introduction

*Maarten Janssen*

Governments own many assets that are of genuine importance to society and that, for one reason or another, they do not want to exploit on their own. Examples include: mobile telephony frequencies, radio frequencies, airport slots, public infrastructure, land for different uses, high-voltage electricity cables, etc. In all these cases, a government needs to choose one or more private companies to use these assets in a proper way: it needs to select mobile telephony companies, (commercial) radio stations, airlines, rail (or other transport) operators, oil companies (if the land is designated for use as a petrol station). What all these cases have in common, besides the fact that the government has to choose who can use the public assets, is that the assets to be allocated are used to serve consumers in a market type of environment.

There are potentially many ways a government can allocate these assets. It can use auctions, Beauty Contests, first-come-first-served, grandfather rights and lotteries, to mention just a few of the most common allocation mechanisms. In *auctions*, firms typically have to make one or more financial bid(s) and the company with the highest bid wins the object to be allocated. In a *Beauty Contest*, firms have to submit a plan of how they will use the asset in the future and they have to provide credentials that make their plan trustworthy. A committee typically determines who wins the contest. In the *first-come-first-served* mechanism, firms who are the first to mention their interest in using the asset, get the right to do so. *Grandfather rights* are conservative in nature: they basically determine that the company which has used the asset in the past will continue to use it (unless it has badly performed). Grandfather rights are typically used to allocate airport slots. *Lotteries* assign the right to use the asset to one of the interested companies at random. In the Netherlands, the scarce places to study medicine at universities are allocated by means of a lottery among interested students. In certain cases, a government may also allocate heterogeneous demand and supply by means of a matching

I would like to thank Eric van Damme for helpful comments on an earlier version.

algorithm, as studied in chapter 10 of this book. There, Benny Moldovanu discusses how medical doctors in the United States are matched to hospitals.

In this book, we are mainly interested in the question of which mechanism is to be preferred under what circumstances? And, if a particular allocation mechanism is chosen, of what the important design issues are. In other words, we are interested in mechanisms that have certain desirable properties for the seller, in our case the government. As there are no clearly defined considerations forming the basis of the latter three allocation mechanisms (first-come-first-served, grandfather rights and lotteries), it seems obvious that all of them are dominated either by a Beauty Contest or by an auction. Therefore, in what follows we shall mainly consider these two types of mechanism. The difference between the two mechanisms will be explained in more detail below.

This introductory chapter discusses most of the general issues that are involved in choosing between auctions and Beauty Contests and it places the remaining chapters in perspective. Here, and in most of the chapters that follow, we start from the observation that answers to the above questions crucially depend on the objectives the government wants to achieve. Section 1, therefore, discusses possible goals and the relationships among them. A government will typically aim, among other things, at a well-functioning product market. The working of the product market depends to a large extent, however, on how the government has chosen to shape the licences (what is allocated?) and how many licences are allocated. Section 2, therefore, deals with these two issues. I then proceed to the how-to-allocate question. Section 3 argues that there are many different forms of Beauty Contests and auctions. The section attempts to provide criteria that help to demarcate Beauty Contests from auctions. Section 4 then provides a list of properties on which the two prototypes of different allocation mechanisms can be scored. Sections 5 and 6 discuss important design issues that are relevant to either auctions or Beauty Contests. Finally, section 7 sketches the plan of the rest of this book. All references in this Introduction are to the chapters that follow.

## 1    Goals

There are different goals that a government may want to achieve when allocating the right to operate in a market. I mention here the following six, but there may be others. The first three goals refer to the outcome of the allocation process, while the last three goals refer to the process itself.

(1) Efficient operation of the aftermarket
(2) Market that provides publicly desirable goods
(3) Revenues
(4) Value-maximising allocation process
(5) Efficient allocation process
(6) Transparent selection process

I will explain each of these goals in turn. The first thing a government should realise is that the allocation procedure is *not* an isolated event. By determining what is allocated and to whom to allocate, the government fixes important ingredients that shape the aftermarket. Hence, it may attempt to design the allocation mechanism in such a way that the market after the players are selected operates efficiently. Efficiency can be measured in terms of Pareto-efficiency or in terms of total surplus. In both cases, consumer welfare plays an important role.

The second potential goal differs from the first in the sense that consumers and producers may, according to the public authority, underestimate the importance of certain goods. The second goal explicitly states that the government may take a paternalistic stance in the situation where its preferences differ from those of consumers and producers. This is the classic case of merit goods. For example, in the case of radio broadcasting the government may want to ensure that there is a wide variety of radio stations.

As the assets to be allocated usually have an economic value, the government may also use the allocation procedure to raise revenues. These revenues can be used to alleviate difficulties in the government's financial situation. The government may also use these revenues to reduce some forms of tax or in general expenditure.

The last three objectives are more concerned with the allocation mechanism itself (who gets the right to operate on the market) than with the outcome of the allocation procedure. A value-maximising allocation process is a mechanism in which the firms with the highest valuations win the licences. One way to measure the efficiency of the allocation process is by looking at the total surplus of the seller (the government) and the (winning) buyers of licences. An allocation procedure is transparent if the criteria are formulated in such a way that, given the bids or the plans of the participating companies, the winning parties are chosen in an unambiguous manner.

It is important to distinguish goals 1 and 4 and 5: given a certain market design, firms individually try to figure out how much money they will make in the market. Based on these estimates, they determine their valuation for the licence. The difference between a value-maximising allocation process and an efficient allocation process is that the objectives of the seller are also taken into account. The first objective, *efficiency of the market*, means that the market allocation is such that the sum of consumer, producer and government surplus[1] is maximised (if total surplus is taken as the welfare measure). The allocation mechanism can be efficient without the aftermarket being efficient.

In chapter 5, Janssen and Moldovanu show, by means of examples, that the different goals can contradict each other. For example, an efficient (competitive) market implies that the profits of firms are negligible so that they are not willing to pay very much for a licence. As a result any allocation mechanism where licences to operate in a competitive market are sold will lead to low revenues. Also, a value-maximising allocation mechanism may not lead to an efficient market and vice versa. This is, in a sense, easy to see as value maximisation only looks at the valuation of firms, whereas the latter notion also takes consumer surplus into account. If differences in cost structures are the only difference between firms, i.e. if they have the same market power, the same customer base, etc., then the two objectives coincide: low-cost firms will typically have the highest valuations and the market will be more efficient with low-cost firms.

An important lesson of the above is that it is not enough just to state the different objectives governments may want to achieve. Rather, one should also consider the relations among the objectives and in cases where the objectives contradict each other, choices concerning objectives have to be made.

The extent to which revenues should be an important goal on its own is open to discussion. A first thing to note is that from the perspective of total surplus, higher revenues means lower producer surplus. So, in a very first rough approximation total surplus does not depend on the size of the revenue. It may, of course, be true that there are important indirect effects: it may be that a euro in the pocket of the government is spent more efficiently (from the point of view of total surplus) than the same amount of money in the pocket of a private firm. High revenues may be a good alternative to distortionary taxes (another way to raise government income). However, there does not seem to be any country where tax rates have been lowered after high (auction) revenues have been obtained. It seems more likely that governments use (auction) revenues to provide (more distortionary) subsidies or to lower the amount of government debt financed through the issuing of bonds (see, on the latter, chapter 9 by Tilman Börgers and Joe Swierzbinski). In short, the welfare impact

---

[1] Government surplus measures the amount of money the government is willing to give up in exchange for the outcome that is obtained.

of high revenues may be positive, but the size of this effect may be quite small.

It is important to define the goals of a privatisation exercise properly. Properly defined goals provide guidelines for the design of the allocation mechanism. It is also important when it comes to evaluating the success of the exercise afterwards. Defining goals also implies an understanding of the relations among the different goals one may want to pursue and of the ranking of the goals in the case of inconsistencies. Sometimes, in formulating the goals it may be important to give some attention to the origin of the issues at hand. Usually, the question of allocating rights to operate in a market arises when (groups in) society feels uncomfortable with the existing situation. Publicly run firms may be inefficient or may not have the right incentives to innovate. New technologies may come about that need to be exploited. It may be easier to formulate the goals of the privatisation exercise if its origin is well understood.

Having said that it is important to formulate the goals explicitly, I realise that it is not always easy to do so. Governments consist of many people with differing objectives. There are government bureaucrats, ministers and deputy ministers, and different (members of) political parties in Parliament. All of these want to have a say about what the goals of the allocation mechanisms should be and it may very well happen that many (sometimes inconsistent) goals are considered in order to reach a compromise among the different players. Without properly formulated goals, it is, however, impossible to decide what decision concerning the allocation mechanism should be made.

## 2    What and how many will be allocated?

The most important question to be answered when putting a certain task in the hands of the private sector is how the market should be *designed*. Given technological and legal constraints, the government is in the position to think of market conditions that best guarantee that the desired goals are achieved. Quite often, the market is *not* there, but is constructed by the government itself.

Looking at some of the case studies, it is clear that most of the interesting questions arise at the market design stage. For example, in chapter 12 Luisa Affuso and David Newbery look at the way rail services can be privatised. Roughly speaking, there are two models: the Swedish model, where there is a vertical separation between infrastructure and operation – the infrastructure is in public hands and a private firm is responsible for the trains and the train schedule; and the Argentinian model, where the country is split into regions and within each region a single firm is responsible for both infrastructure and railway services. In principle, in both systems, there is also an issue of how many competitors there should be in the market: one, two or more? Of course, given the fixed costs of building infrastructure, it probably does not make much sense to have more than one local operator in the Argentinian system, whereas one may consider two or more operators in the Swedish nationwide system. Markets work in quite different ways under the two systems and it is important to consider the pros and cons of each system *before* a mechanism is chosen to allocate the right(s) to operate a service within the already chosen system.

Another example in this context is the way reintegration services are being privatised in the Netherlands (see the contribution by Maurice Dykstra and Jaap de Koning in chapter 11). The right to help a certain 'lot', consisting of a certain number of unemployed people, to find a job is offered to private companies and the companies can 'bid' how, and for how much money, they are going to do this. The groups are very heterogeneous, consisting of both men and women, handicapped and non-handicapped, people of various ages, and so on. The people themselves do not have the choice of which company they prefer to have to reintegrate them. This means that the licence is defined in such a way that it rules out the existence of a market where firms compete for individual clients. Other ways that could have been chosen are simply to have a certain number of reintegration firms in each region and allow unemployed people to choose the firm they prefer best,[2] or to have sector-specific or age- or handicap-specific reintegration firms. It is not the point to argue here that one system would have been necessarily better than another. What is argued is that it is important to consider the different possibilities for designing the market and to choose the market design that best guarantees that the aims of the privatisation process are reached.

Another case study that clarifies the issue of what needs to be allocated and how many need to be allocated is the UMTS case (by Emiel Maasland and Benny Moldovanu in chapter 7). This may seem a little strange at first sight as the issue of what to allocate seems to be quite obvious: a certain amount of spectrum. Delving a little deeper makes it clear, however, that in this case too there are many (important) issues to be settled. A first issue is whether firms are obliged to serve a whole country or only the most profitable areas and, if the whole country has to be served, what is the time frame in which this has to be done. A second issue is whether firms that

---

[2] This may be achieved by giving unemployed people 'vouchers' that can be used to buy reintegration services. This is similar to the situation found in Australia, the authors mention.

are granted a licence have to provide roaming conditions for firms that do not have a 2G network. A third issue concerns the length of the contract. Public goals (the whole country needs to be covered by a network) may be achieved by defining the objects that will be auctioned in a proper way. Also, the nature of competition in the market may depend on the roaming conditions, as it will be more attractive for potential suppliers to enter the market when they know that they can roam on an existing network. Finally, it is, of course, important to specify how many licences are to be awarded as this determines the number of competitors in the market.

Studying these three cases makes clear that it is important to think about what and how many (licences) to allocate, as this will determine how much competition in the market there will be. These issues have to be faced *prior to* the choice of an allocation mechanism. They are relevant no matter whether the allocation of the licences is done by means of an auction or in any other way, such as a Beauty Contest.

## 3      Which mechanisms can be considered?

Auctions and their alternatives are ways to select the private parties that are granted a licence to operate in the market. The efficiency of the market, one of the most important goals from an economic point of view, depends to a large extent on the way the market is designed (how the licence is defined and how many licences are allocated). From the point of view of the *efficiency of the market*, the choice of allocation mechanism (and the subsequent design) is important as it co-determines whether low-cost firms will operate in the market (see the discussion above) and whether newcomers will have a chance to obtain a licence. That is, given any market design (see section 2) and the associated efficiency of the market a government can choose between different allocation mechanisms to determine who will operate in the market. The choice of mechanism determines how the *competition for the market* will take place.

A first, maybe trivial, point is that it is important to ensure that the government can make a *choice of which allocation mechanism to use*. To make the best choice, all options should be considered. In practice, however, it may be difficult to get all options on the table as various parties may have an interest in limiting the option set.

### 3.1      *What are the options?*

If it is important to consider the different options, can we then determine and characterise what these options are? The main distinction is between auctions on one hand and Beauty Contests on the other. The main difference between these two types of allocation mechanism is that the latter always contains an element that cannot be easily quantified or otherwise made objective. Auctions, on the other hand, are allocation mechanisms where a pre-defined algorithm determines who has the best bid. What is certainly not the case is that prices do not play a role in Beauty Contests, or that in a Beauty Contest prices have to be exogenously fixed. A Beauty Contest can very well incorporate bidders specifying the amount they are willing to pay for the licence. Accordingly, in a Beauty Contest 'price offered' can be one of the items on which parties are scored.

Auctions can be categorised into either single- or multi-attribute auctions. Multi-attribute auctions are auctions where a bid has more than one dimension, i.e. bidders do not only bid on price, but also on (for example) quality dimensions. Traditional auctions, such as first- and second-price sealed-bid and open cry, are single-dimensional as bidders only bid on price. The distinction between single- and multi-attribute auctions is important in relation to Beauty Contests. The distinction makes clear that in auctions quality considerations (if they can be objectively measured) can play a role in three ways: as an imposed minimum requirement on the bidder, and/or as a way the licence that is auctioned is defined (that is before the bidding process during the auction takes place), and/or as part of the bidding process. In the latter case, when quality is an integral part of the bidding process, there should be an objective measure to translate quality bids into price bids.[3]

Beauty Contests can be categorised as either unweighted or weighted contests. In an unweighted Beauty Contest, bidders do not know in advance how their bids will be evaluated. A weighted Beauty Contest is an allocation mechanism in which bidders know in advance the criteria on which they will be assessed and the weights on the different criteria. Even though the maximum score on a certain criterion is known, it remains (somewhat) ambiguous, even in a weighted Beauty Contest, how to score different bidders on that criterion. Prices that are bid can play a role in both types of Beauty Contest. One advantage of having bidders bidding prices, even in a Beauty Contest, is that it becomes clear how much money the government is willing to give up in the situation where a licence is not awarded to the bidder with the best price. One may, in a weighted Beauty Contest, try to give objective criteria for scoring on a certain item. In this book, we continue to call this a Beauty Contest as long as at least one item is scored in a subjective way.

---

[3] Of course, such quality bids only make sense when quality can be easily verified and when companies can credibly commit to providing a certain quality.

Theoretically, one can think of different ways to combine auctions and Beauty Contests. One way is to have bidders make a proposal of how they are going to use a certain licence. The auctioneer determines the ranking of the proposals and this ranking is translated into a bidding handicap. After the bidding handicap is made public an auction is held. A second way is to first organise an auction where the right to participate in a later Beauty Contest is sold. Finally, one can think of the bidders in an auction being determined by a Beauty Contest.

## 4    Properties of the mechanisms

Comparative analyses of the extreme forms of the two instruments have already been made on several occasions (see, for example, Binmore and Klemperer (2002) and Janssen, Ros and van der Windt (2001)). Criteria with respect to the design that are usually used in these reviews are:
• value revelation and efficiency of the bidding instrument
• transparency and lobbying
• speed
• quality
• consumer interests, and
• revenue.
In the literature comparing the two allocation mechanisms, an auction always comes out better: it appears to be efficient, clear and fast and, in addition, if well designed, it raises a fair amount of revenue. In a world in which the parties in the market are much better informed than the government with respect to the economic value of the goods offered (in this instance, the lots), an auction compels the parties 'to put their money where their mouths are'.

Although the choice of an auction can be easily rationalised in this way, it is necessary to mention a number of important reservations. First of all, when evaluating the auction mechanism as being 'efficient, clear and fast', one must not ignore the fact that the auction also has to be designed. Much too soon, however, the evaluator looks only at the few weeks during which the auction itself takes place and easily forgets that a period of months or years has been spent in designing the auction. Speed is therefore a relative notion. The proclaimed transparency also loses much of its appeal if one considers the fact that the market parties, naturally, employ their know-how and relationships to try to adjust the auction model to their own advantage. The efficiency of an auction can be warranted only if its design is adequate, offering to all interested parties more or less equal chances of securing a licence.

Scoring the alternative mechanisms on the other objectives mentioned above, we also get a picture that tends to favour auctions. Apart from the case where bidding prices are an integral part of a Beauty Contest, it seems that auctions score better on the revenue objective as it is difficult to determine a fixed price for other types of Beauty Contest.[4] Also on the aspect of value maximisation and efficiency of the allocation mechanism, auctions score better. One important concern is, however, whether the European legal system allows asymmetric or coloured auctions to be organised, as such auction mechanisms are sometimes necessary to reach the first two objectives concerning the efficient operation of the market. *Asymmetric auctions* (see chapter 4 by Emiel Maasland, Yves Montangie and Roger van den Bergh) are required to create a level playing field between entrants and incumbents. In situations where incumbents have more knowledge about the market than entrants and where they have already invested and this investment is a sunk cost, entrants typically have lower valuations than incumbents. On the other hand, it may be judged that entrants in the market are important as they have more incentives to actively compete in the market to acquire clients. *Coloured auctions*, where a certain number of licences are set aside for specific purposes, may be necessary to serve public interests when for example some cultural group would be easily outbid by others.[5] At the moment it remains unclear whether these types of auctions should be regarded as providing state support for economically weaker companies.

Despite the advantages of auctions, there are important cases, such as artistic competitions, where Beauty Contests are inevitable. It is difficult to imagine that in the case where a government wants to design a new building, it would select an architect by means of an auction. More generally, when the seller wants to get information out of the market about innovative business concepts, it is impossible to define in advance what the object should look like. In such cases, it is necessary to look for alternative allocation mechanisms such as a Beauty Contest. In the case of asymmetric information about quality, where the government does not have the information that private companies have, it may also be

---

[4] There is the danger of fixing the price too high (as France did in the UMTS case) or too low. In certain auctions, it is also important to determine reserve prices, as noted by Tanga McDaniel and Karsten Neuhoff in chapter 8 on auctions of gas transmission access. They also question the appropriateness of running auctions to decide on network investments.

[5] Commercial radio frequencies may be a case where this is true. If the government thinks there should be a classical music radio station or a station for minority groups and if these stations cannot compete on equal grounds with other stations, a coloured auction, where one or more frequencies are reserved for specific types of broadcasting, may be a good alternative.

problematic to run an auction, as shown by Manelli and Vincent (1995). If it is more expensive to provide quality, auctions typically will result in low-quality firms getting a licence.

Another potential disadvantage of an auction is that only minimum requirements are taken into account regarding the use of a licence. A regular auction reduces competition among companies to prices only, given certain minimum quality conditions. In contrast a Beauty Contest offers the possibility that business plans are also judged on quality aspects. Whether or not this quality issue is of importance depends to a large extent on the question of whether or not the market itself is organised in such a way that a socially optimal set of prices and qualities will pertain. If the market can be expected to provide this optimal mix, then this potential disadvantage of auctions should not be taken too seriously. If the market cannot be expected to provide the optimal price/quality mix, then a Beauty Contest may be considered if the quality that is bid in the contest can be enforced by contract.

Concerning consumer interests, it is important to note that neither in auctions nor in Beauty Contests are the interests of consumers directly represented. In designing the allocation mechanism this problem has to be taken into account. One way of doing this is by the choice of the number of lots. Another way in which this problem can be tackled is by staging a contest in which firms bid in terms of the price they set in the market. This mechanism has been used in, for instance, privatisations of gas, electricity and water utilities. Bidding on the price in a market can be applied if the concession sale relates to well-established markets in which services and technologies evolve relatively slowly, as in the examples given above. Obviously it is not possible in a market that does not even exist yet, such as the one for UMTS services.

## 5   Aspects of auction design

There are many aspects of auction design that are important when auctioning the rights to operate in a market. The main features of common auction formats such as open cry and sealed-bid auctions and first- and second-price auctions are discussed in chapter 1 by Tilman Börgers and Eric van Damme. These different auction formats can have an important impact on:

- collusion
- winner's curse
- level playing field/entry deterrence.

*Collusion* may be a real problem in auctions as it lowers the bids of individual bidders and, hence, revenues. As explained by Tim Salmon in chapter 3, collusion may occur when the same bidders appear in different auctions that are held one after the other. It may, however, also occur in a simultaneous multi-unit auction as these auctions allow bidders to form strategies that effectively imply that they will share the licences between them. Collusion can take the form of signalling, when bidders indicate with, for example, the last numbers of their bids which licence they would like to obtain. Salmon also describes the different mechanisms the FCC has used in order to try to prevent firms from colluding.

The *winner's curse* may arise in common value auctions where the bidders' valuations of the object are strongly correlated and uncertain. A famous example is the auctioning of the right to exploit a certain oil field. In this case firms use seismological research to estimate the amount of oil in a certain location. On the basis of this research, the firms can calculate what the field is worth. Some estimations are, of course, more optimistic than others. A bidder who wins an auction may infer from the fact that he made the winning bid that he was too optimistic about the value of the oil field. This is the winner's curse. Another application may be the market for UMTS services, as at the moment the auction is held, nobody has an idea about the way the market will develop.

A last issue is whether all participants have equal chances of obtaining a licence. In quite a few instances, the licences that are to be allocated and the market that is to be designed are in one way or the other related to already existing markets. This is the case for UMTS, where the existing 2G market offers somewhat comparable services and the 2G network may be upgraded to make it suitable for UMTS services. Upgrading a network is cheaper than building a completely new network. Another example is the high-speed train, where the national train operator has superior information about the market potential, in addition to having cost advantages in maintenance. When incumbents have advantages over potential entrants, entrants are confronted with the question of whether they should take part in the auction at all as preparing for an auction may cost the firm a significant sum of money. If the number of licences is (much) larger than the number of incumbents, this question does not arise as newcomers have enough chances to secure a licence. If this is not the case, it may very well be that very few entrants participate in the auction. One way to overcome this problem is to introduce asymmetries in the auction design. This issue is further studied in chapter 4 by Emiel Maasland, Yves Montangie and Roger van den Bergh from an economic and a legal perspective. Different types of asymmetries can be introduced:

- reserving a licence for newcomers
- reserving a licence for a specific purpose (a coloured auction)
- introducing bidding handicaps.

From an economic point of view there may be good reasons to introduce one of the above types of asymmetry. Reserving a licence for entrants is advisable when an entrant can stimulate competition in the market. A similar argument can be made for bidding handicaps. A coloured auction can be defended when there is a clearly specified public goal and the firms that are needed to realise this goal do not have a chance to win a regular auction. One problem with bidding handicaps is that it is difficult to determine how small or large the handicap should be.

## 6 Aspects of Beauty Contest design

The economic literature on Beauty Contest design is (almost) non-existent.[6] Academic economists typically have little to say on what seems to be more of a bureaucratic procedure than an economic process. An important practical issue in Beauty Contest design is how to overcome the ambiguity that is inherently associated with evaluating the proposals. One potential solution is to attempt to make a very detailed list of how proposals will be scored well in advance. However, in the cases where a Beauty Contest is most desirable, i.e. when the seller wants to get information from the market about innovative business concepts, one simply cannot prepare such a precise evaluation scheme in advance. Some degree of ambiguity cannot be avoided if a Beauty Contest is held.

There are, nevertheless, a few general issues to be considered when designing Beauty Contests. A first issue is the degree to which scores on different criteria are substitutable for each other. In a standard weighted Beauty Contest, proposals are scored on different criteria, the scores on all these criteria are summed and the winner is the proposal with the highest score. Alternatively, one can think of a procedure in which on certain criteria a proposal has to get at least more than a minimum score to be considered acceptable (see chapter 2 by Maurice Dykstra and Nico van der Windt for more detail).

A second issue is how to score on the different criteria. Sometimes, the quality of a proposal (firm) is judged on the basis of the quality of the people who work for the firm at a certain date. This is, for example, the case in the research assessment of universities in the United Kingdom. When it is easy for people to change jobs, it is questionable whether this measurement really measures the quality one is interested in. The measure may also lead to side-effects such as the hiring of people just before the relevant date.

---

[6] The chapter on Beauty Contest design is, therefore, based on practical experience rather than on existing literature.

A third issue concerns whether the proposed 'beauty' of a proposal is also fixed in a contract. There are two related points here. The first is that if a proposal wins because of certain aspects in the proposal, then these aspects have also to be fixed in a contract with the winning organisation. In the Dutch reintegration case (see chapter 11), this was only partly done, as most of the contracts with the reintegration firms were standard and not directly related to the bids that were made. The second point is that it is advisable not to score a proposal on 'beautiful aspects' that cannot afterwards be verified (and hence cannot be the subject of a contract).

A last point concerning Beauty Contest design is that in some cases it may make sense to have an initial qualification phase, in which a limited number of firms are selected, before the full contest takes place.[7] This two-stage procedure may have advantages if organisations are requested to provide a very detailed plan. Knowing that there are a limited number of competitors, firms have higher chances of winning the contest and therefore better incentives to make significant effort in writing the proposal, i.e. limiting the number of competitors may increase the quality of the proposals. Second, a two-stage procedure may also reduce the time it takes for government authorities to evaluate the different proposals. A two-stage procedure was followed in some of the Dutch contests among reintegration firms, but not in all of them.

## 7    Plan of the book

In the rest of this book, the issues that are discussed above are considered in much more detail. The book has two parts. In the first, relevant theoretical issues are discussed, whereas the second is of a more applied nature and has many case studies.

Part I starts off with two chapters providing an overview of the relevant design issues in auctions and Beauty Contests, respectively. Two of the common problems that are encountered in designing allocation mechanisms, namely collusion and entry deterrence, are the focuses of chapters 3 and 4 respectively. Legal issues are also considered in chapter 4 on how to create a level playing field. Chapter 5 shows how traditional insights from auction theory may not hold true when participants in the auction continue to interact with each other in a (future) market environment.

Part II considers different types of case study. Chapters 6 and 7 consider the two best-known auctions ever held: the FCC auctions in the United States and the UMTS auctions for 3G mobile telephony in Europe. Two other types of auction form the content of the subsequent two chapters.

---

[7] In certain cases, a pre-qualification phase may also be considered for auctions.

Auctioning gas transmission access in the United Kingdom is the subject of chapter 8, while chapter 9 compares different auction procedures that are used to sell government bonds in a variety of countries. Chapters 10 and 11 concern non-auction mechanisms. The first of these studies the way medical interns are matched with (allocated to) hospitals in the United States, while the second evaluates the way in which reintegration agencies in the Dutch labour market are selected. The book concludes with a chapter on the different ways in which rail franchises are allocated.

### References

Binmore, K. and P. Klemperer 2002, 'The biggest auction ever', *Economic Journal* 112: 74–96.

Janssen, M., A. Ros and N. van der Windt 2001, 'De draad kwijt? Onderzoek naar de gang van zaken rond de Nederlandse UMTS-veiling' (Research into the proceedings of the Dutch UMTS auction), Erasmus University Rotterdam.

Manelli, A. and D. Vincent 1995, 'Optimal procurement mechanisms', *Econometrica* 63: 591–620.

*Part I*

# Theory

# 1     Auction theory for auction design

*Tilman Börgers and Eric van Damme*

## 1    Introduction

In this introductory survey we review research papers on auction theory that may be of relevance to the design of auctions of government assets in general, and of spectrum licence auctions in particular. We focus on the main intuitions emerging from these papers, and refer to the original papers for technical details.

We begin in section 2 with a discussion of why economists typically favour auctions over other methods for allocating licences to operate in a market. In section 3, we have a first discussion on auction design, stressing the fact that a seller will typically face a much more complicated problem than just what auction form to use; he also has to think carefully about what to sell, whom to allow as bidders and when to sell. Of course, the solution to these problems will also depend on what goal is to be achieved. Assuming these problems are solved, we turn, in section 4 to an exposition of auction formats. We start the discussion with the simple case in which the seller has just one indivisible object for sale, for which we describe the four basic auction forms: two open auctions – the English (or ascending) auction and the Dutch (or descending) auction – and two sealed-bid formats, the first-price auction and the second-price (or Vickrey) auction. In the second part of the section, we show how these auction formats can be extended to deal with the situation in which the seller has available multiple units of the same object, or multiple objects. In this process, we will encounter a large variety of auction formats. In section 5 we discuss these various auction formats from the bidders' perspective: what strategies could one expect the competitors to follow and how should one bid oneself? We also discuss the implications of rational bidding strategies for the variables which the seller probably cares about,

We are grateful to Maarten Janssen for inviting us to write this survey. Preparing it has made us painfully aware of the gaps in our knowledge of the auction literature and we apologise for all errors and omissions. Tilman Börgers gratefully acknowledges financial support from the Economic and Social Research Council (UK).

such as efficiency and revenue. In section 6 we pull our insights together, and ask which policy lessons our analysis suggests. Section 7 concludes.

At the outset, we wish to stress the limitations of this chapter: the reader should be aware that it is a theoretical study. Theory alone has no policy implications; it needs to be combined with empirical analysis (of field data, or experimental data) before policy recommendations can be derived. In this chapter, empirical or experimental evidence is cited where it is particularly prominent, but it is not surveyed systematically. Therefore, what we say here does not in itself provide a basis for policy recommendations. Put differently, any policy implication that is derived from the theory exposited in this chapter should be prefaced with the qualification: 'if the theory captures practice well, then policy should be . . .'.

## 2    Why auctions?

Governments allocating spectrum licences to mobile telephony companies or, more generally, licences to operate in a market, have a variety of methods at their disposal. The traditionally most popular method has been the Beauty Contest, where companies are invited to submit business plans, and a government agency selects those companies whose business plans seem most credible, and which are most likely to deliver services that the government believes to be valuable. In recent years, auctions have been the more popular method. What is the rationale for using auctions?

To answer this question, we wish to make a distinction between auctions as used in the private sector and auctions used by the government. We first discuss why a private-sector seller may prefer to dispose of an item by means of an auction. Next, we consider which of these arguments also apply when it is the government that acts as a seller.

A seller of a unique item would typically want to get the best price for the item; hence, the question is what selling mechanism would result in the highest expected price. If the seller knew what each interested buyer would be willing to pay for the item, his problem would be trivial: he would simply make a 'take-it-or-leave-it' offer to the buyer with the highest willingness to pay. Of course, in practice, the seller does not have the required information, and in these circumstances he may either set the price too low, in which case he would not expropriate what the market could bear, or set the price too high, so that he would not succeed in selling the item.

An ascending auction provides an attractive alternative. In such an auction, each potential buyer is willing to bid as long as the price is lower than the bidder's reservation value. Hence, bidding will continue until the second highest reservation value is reached, and the ultimate price will be this second highest value. The seller thus does worse than with complete information, but typically he does better than by making a 'take-it-or-leave-it' offer. Moreover, when the number of bidders is large, the auction performs almost as well as the seller could have performed had he complete information. This is the main reason why auctions are attractive mechanisms for private sellers: they extract good prices even if the seller is poorly informed about individual buyers' willingness to pay.

As a possible selling mechanism, a private-sector seller may also consider negotiating with potential buyers. He might hope to learn buyers' true willingness to pay by observing their strategic moves in the negotiation. But, of course, buyers will anticipate that they will be closely watched in the negotiation. They will be very wary of giving too much away too early. Bids in an auction might also give information away, but as long as the seller's commitment to the auction mechanism is firm, bidders know in advance how their bids are going to be used in the allocation process. They do not have to worry about concealing information. Therefore, auctions encourage more information revelation by buyers, and it is this information revelation that is needed for a successful sale. Furthermore, auctions may attract more interested parties than negotiation processes, and Bulow and Klemperer (1996) have shown that, under certain assumptions, an auction without a reserve price, as long as it attracts at least one more bidder than a negotiation, raises more expected revenue than any negotiation procedure.

In the context described above, the ascending auction has another very attractive property: it results in an efficient allocation, i.e. the auction allocates the object to the bidder who values it most. It is this property that also makes auctions an attractive selling mechanism for governments. As for a seller in the private sector, a government seller typically is uncertain about how much bidders are willing to pay for the items that it sells, but, in contrast to private sellers, governments may not be primarily interested in raising revenues, but in achieving an efficient outcome of some sort. (See section 3 for a brief discussion on the goals of the government and for why a government might also be interested in raising revenues.) The above argument suggests that it still might be a good idea to auction as the auction may produce an efficient outcome. Indeed, the case for using auctions to sell licences has usually been based on the twin arguments that an auction is an efficient procedure (i.e. it is quick, transparent, not very susceptible to lobbying, and reasonably proof against legal action) that produces an efficient outcome; see McMillan (1994).

One should point out, however, that the efficiency argument in favour of auctions is not as strong as it might appear at first. First of all, when there are 'frictions', the efficiency property need not hold; for example, if the person with the highest value faces a binding budget constraint at a level lower than the second highest value, the bidder with the second highest value will win; see Krishna (2002) for some results on auctions in which bidders are budget-constrained. Second, and in particular in the case of a government seller, one should be very careful with what one means by 'efficiency': one should be aware that 'economic efficiency' is not equivalent to 'the licences ending up in the hands of those that value them most'. As Janssen and Moldovanu show in detail in chapter 5 in this book, the reason lies in all kinds of externalities that exist in licence auctions. The main externality is that a benevolent government will sell the licences (also) having consumer welfare in mind. Consumers, however, are not participating directly in the auction and, as a result, the outcome in which the licence is put in the hands of the firm that values it most, may not be the one that consumers prefer. In fact, the preferences of the consumers may be exactly opposite.

As a specific example, based on Gilbert and Newbery (1982), suppose that a government sells a second licence to operate in a market in which one player is already active. For a newcomer, the licence represents the right to compete, while for the incumbent it offers the opportunity to maintain a monopoly. Since the incumbent's profit loss from losing the monopoly is typically larger than the entrant's gain in profit from being allowed to compete, the monopolist will win an auction for the second licence. Therefore, an auction will allocate the licence to the monopolist and will not produce a competitive outcome. As a competitive outcome yields higher economic efficiency (total welfare) than a monopolistic outcome, an ordinary auction will not achieve the efficiency goal.

Thus, in order to reach an efficient outcome in this asymmetric situation, the government might use an auction variant; for example, the government might simply ban the incumbent from the auction of the second licence. In this case, one of the entrants is sure to win and this 'asymmetric auction' might attract more bidders and might result in higher revenue than the auction in which the incumbent is allowed to bid and in which entrants know that they cannot win. More sophisticated 'discriminatory auctions' can have the same effect (see chapter 4 by Maasland, Montangie and van den Bergh for further discussion, in particular about whether such auctions might violate basic EU principles by involving discrimination or state aid). The point here, however, is more general: if an ordinary auction does not produce the desired result, then one may adjust the auction rules to obtain an outcome that one likes. Auctions are an extremely flexible allocation mechanism, and they allow a government considerable freedom of action.

Just as price-setting or negotiations are alternative selling mechanisms for private-sector sellers, the Beauty Contest is typically the alternative selling mechanism considered by governments for the allocation of government assets. In such a Beauty Contest, bidders describe in detail what they plan to do with the licence, with the government then selecting the best plan. There are, perhaps, two main concerns which economists have about Beauty Contests. One is that the commitments made by bidders in Beauty Contests are hard to enforce. If bidders anticipate this enforcement problem, then they can promise arbitrary things, and there is no guarantee that the winners are really those who make best use of the objects for sale. The second concern is that, given the discretion used and the subjective elements in a Beauty Contest, there might be more potential for corruption of government officials in a Beauty Contest than in an auction. See the Introduction to this book for more details on this issue.

Summarising the above, we may state that auctions have certain desirable properties that alternative allocation mechanisms do not have and that, therefore, an auction may be preferred whenever allocation by this means is feasible. This, however, does not imply that any auction will do and that auctions do not have any drawbacks. In the remainder of this chapter, we will show that the choice of auction may be of great importance and that 'side constraints' in the auction may be needed in order to ensure that a desirable outcome is reached.

## 3        Pre-auction decisions

When a government is selling assets or licences, a large number of design questions have to be addressed. First of all, the government should be clear about the *goals* that it wants to achieve. For example, should the government try to maximise revenue, or should it aim for market efficiency? One argument for suggesting that governments might be concerned about auction revenues is that such revenues might allow governments to reduce more distortionary taxes elsewhere in the economy. However, efficiency is typically the dominant goal of governments.

The efficiency goal is sometimes identified with the objective of 'placing licences into the hands of those that value them most'. This is not always the same as efficiency, though. For a general discussion on this important point, see Janssen and Moldovanu (this volume, chapter 5). One example has already been given in the previous section. As another example, think of a government selling licences to operate radio stations. Under quite natural and general conditions, stations that broadcast 'middle of the road' music will be willing to pay most for these licences; however, an outcome in which all stations broadcast similar music will normally not be efficient. In such a case, if the government wants to achieve an efficient outcome, it should impose conditions on some of the licences, which will typically reduce revenue. This example again shows that the different goals that the government may want to pursue (efficiency and revenue) may be in conflict.

Once government objectives are clear, the next important question is one of *what* will be sold. An example where this clearly mattered was the recent European UMTS auctions. There the question was: 'How large (in terms of spectrum) should a UMTS licence be?' It was not clear how much spectrum a UMTS operator would need, and therefore how many licences could be fitted into the available spectrum. Thus, it was not clear how many players there would be in the resulting market. While most countries simply fixed this number in advance, Germany and Austria dealt with this difficulty in a different way. These countries decided not to auction licences, but rather abstract blocks of spectrum, and bidders could themselves choose the number of blocks for which they wanted to bid. The key idea behind these auction designs was that the mechanism not only helped governments to discover which companies should hold licences, but also how much spectrum was actually needed for third-generation spectrum licences, and thereby discover for how many companies there was space in the spectrum.

An interesting objection has been raised in the academic literature against this innovative approach. It is that companies' bids in these auctions will not primarily reveal to governments how much companies value extra spectrum, and thus what the optimal size of a licence is, but rather how much companies value monopoly power (see Jehiel and Moldovanu (2000b)). This is because bidders will understand that the future market structure emerges endogenously from the auction. By buying up spectrum a bidder can reduce the amount of spectrum available to others, and, in particular, a bidder can prevent others from entering the market. Thus, bids in these auctions might not be related at all to the true value of the spectrum, and instead might indicate what value the bidder attaches to a reduction in the number of competitors in the market. If this argument is accepted, then it appears better to make a possibly imperfect judgement about the optimal size of licences, and to let the auction determine only who gets which. It should be added that in practice this argument has not appeared to be of much relevance to the German and Austrian auctions. The precise reasons for this are unclear, and it is worth keeping this argument in mind for future auctions.

The above example also indicates that relatively frequently a government may need to build additional regulatory constraints into the auction.

This need arises especially in the situation of franchise bidding where the government awards the right to provide a service to that party that is willing to do it for the lowest compensation, and where the auction results in the licence winners enjoying market power in the ensuing market. In these situations, part of the compensation is paid before any service is delivered and the government has to ensure that the service is indeed delivered and is of the quality that has been promised and agreed upon. Elaborate contracts and extensive monitoring may be needed in this case of 'moral hazard'; Williamson (1976) gives a good overview of the difficulties and the trade-offs involved.

Another issue to be considered before an auction is who should be allowed to participate. For bids in an auction to be credible, bidders must be financially respectable, and most government auctions include an appropriate screening of bidders. Requiring deposits forms another safeguard against non-serious bids. In some cases one may go further in restricting the set of admissible bidders. For example, if licences to operate in a particular industry are auctioned, then one may wish to exclude incumbents from the auction, either to ensure that the post-auction market is more competitive, or simply to attract more entries into the auction.

The timing of auctions is also important. Consider again the experience with the European UMTS auctions. Governments that were early in auctioning their licences have typically earned (much) higher revenue per capita than those that were late. The UK was the first country to auction its licences and, therefore, the UK was, in effect, not only auctioning a licence to operate in the UK, but the option to construct a pan-European network. This option might have made the UK licence more valuable, so it might have attracted more bidders to the UK auction, with higher revenues as a natural consequence. Similarly, if the German UMTS auction had taken place later in time, the tide might have turned and the Sonera/Telefonica consortium might have realised that a six-player German market was not viable and not profitable for them; in that case, German revenue could have been much lower. While it might have been beneficial for revenues to hold auctions earlier, it might have been beneficial for efficiency to hold them later. As time progressed, more information about UMTS technology, and the corresponding handset technology, became available, and thus efficiency became more feasible.

In essence, all of the above arguments amount to saying that the outcome is determined by supply and demand conditions, and that the government can influence both of these. Perhaps less obvious at first is the fact that the outcome will also depend on the market mechanism – the auction format – that is used. Therefore, we now turn to a discussion of auction formats.

## 4     Auction formats

We now assume that the questions 'what to sell?', 'when to sell?' and 'whom to allow to bid?' have been answered, and we focus on the question 'how to auction?'. While our main interest is in describing auction mechanisms that can be used for selling multiple identical or heterogeneous objects, we start with the simplest case in which there is just one object for sale.

### 4.1     Selling a single object

Two types of auctions can be distinguished: sealed-bid or open. In *sealed-bid formats*, bidders simultaneously and independently submit a bid, possibly in a sealed envelope, or perhaps using a more modern communication technique. These bids are then opened and the auction outcome is determined following some rules that have been announced in advance. In *open auction procedures*, bidding proceeds in stages in real time. In each round, bidders act simultaneously and independently; at the end of each round, all bidders observe the outcome of that round, and then adjust their bids on the basis of what they have seen so far.

The best-known open procedure is the ascending, or English, auction, in which the price is raised until just one bidder is left. This bidder then wins the object at the price at which the ultimate competitor dropped out. In practice, one observes a large diversity of English auction forms: the auctioneer may announce successive prices, or the initiative for calling out prices may lie with the bidders themselves; bidders may know which competitors are still in the race, or they may be denied this information, etc.

A second open procedure is the descending, or Dutch, auction in which the auctioneer lowers the price until one of the bidders shouts 'mine' or pushes a button on his computer terminal. The (first) bidder to stop the auction clock wins the object and pays the price at which he stopped the clock. Note the important difference from the English auction: in the English auction, the winner pays a price that is determined by his strongest competitor; in the Dutch auction, the winner pays a price determined by himself.

In *sealed-bid procedures* bidders bid only once; they simultaneously communicate their bids to the auctioneer. Any reasonable auction format will allocate the object to the bidder who has made the highest bid; however, there is a variety of ways in which the price can be determined, with different corresponding auction formats.

The easiest rule for determining the payment by the winning bidder is, of course, that he has to pay his own bid. This is also the most common sealed-bid procedure, and we will refer to it as the 'first-price sealed-bid auction'. The reader may notice that this procedure bears a strong resemblance to the Dutch auction procedure. After all, in the Dutch auction, each bidder also has to decide on just one number: the price at which he will stop the auction clock. Calling the latter price the player's 'bid', we see that, in the Dutch auction, the highest bidder wins and pays his bid. Consequently, the Dutch auction is equivalent to the first-price sealed-bid auction.

There is, however, at least one important alternative to the 'pay your bid' rule: the successful bidder may be required to pay the highest unsuccessful bid. This sealed-bid auction format is called the 'second-price auction', or the Vickrey auction, after William Vickrey, a winner of the Nobel Prize in Economics, who proposed it; see Vickrey (1961). As in both this auction and the English auction, the winner pays a price that is determined by his strongest competitor, these two formats are related to each other. The 'second-price sealed-bid' format, however, is not fully equivalent to the English auctions that are being used in real life; a crucial difference is that the ascending price format allows bidders to observe the drop-out points of other bidders, which might be valuable information. Therefore, one needs to study the ascending price auction separately from the second-price sealed-bid auction.

Of course, open auctions and sealed-bid auctions are only two extreme types of auction and it is easy to conceive of intermediate forms. One important intermediate form is the 'Anglo-Dutch' format (see Binmore and Klemperer (2002)). Under this format, an open ascending auction takes place first, until the number of remaining bidders reaches a certain threshold. Then a 'first-price sealed-bid' auction is conducted among the remaining bidders. This auction format bears a certain resemblance to the way real estate is auctioned in the Netherlands. Usually this is done by means of a pair of auctions: an English auction followed (a week or so later) by a Dutch auction. In contrast to the Anglo-Dutch format, however, the first auction in this case only stops when one bidder is left, and everybody can participate in the second auction. The price resulting from the first auction determines the reserve price of the second auction and, if the price resulting in this second auction is higher than in the first, the winner of the first auction receives a certain percentage of the winning bid.

## 4.2     Selling multiple units of one object

When selling multiple units of the same object, a first choice to be made is whether the units will be sold sequentially, i.e. one after the other, or simultaneously, i.e. all at the same time. When using a sequential auction, one has to decide which auction form will be used at each stage. This might be any of the auction forms that have been discussed above. For example, in the Dutch flower auction in Aalsmeer, flowers are sold by means of a sequence of Dutch auctions.

Our emphasis here will be on simultaneous auctions. As before, one may distinguish between open and sealed-bid auctions. Two prominent open formats are the descending price format and the ascending price format. An ascending price format involves a gradually increasing price, with bidders indicating how many units they want at each price, and the auction closing once the number of units requested by the remaining bidders is equal to the number of available units. All bidders then have to pay the price at which the auction closed. As in the single-unit case, the price at which a bidder reduces his demand may reveal important information to the competing bidders.

Formally, in the ascending, or English, auction, the auctioneer gradually and continuously raises the price. At each price $p$, each bidder $i$ indicates his demand $d_i(p)$, i.e. he informs the auctioneer about how many units he would like to have at this price. The auctioneer then calculates total demand

$$d(p) = \sum_j d_j(p) \tag{1}$$

and compares total demand with total supply $s$. Prices are increased until a price $p^*$ is reached where $d(p^*) = s$ and each bidder $i$ is then allocated $d_i(p^*)$ units at a price $p^*$ for each. Hence, all units sell at the same price. In practice, different variants may be distinguished: bidders may, or may not, know the demand as expressed by their competitors; they may, or may not, be prevented from increasing their demand again after they have previously reduced it, etc.

In the descending, or Dutch, auction, the price starts at a relatively high level and is then gradually lowered. At each price $p$, bidders will be informed about the supply $s(p)$ that is still left and they have to indicate when the price has reached a level at which they are willing to buy one or more units. The auction closes when as many bidders have indicated their willingness to bid as there are items available, i.e. when $s(p) = 0$. Each bidder has to pay the price at which he indicated that he was willing to buy. In this case, when bidder $i$ buys three units, say at prices $p_1$, $p_2$

and $p_3$, he pays a price $p_1$ for the first unit, $p_2$ for the second unit and $p_3$ for the third unit. Hence, this auction form is discriminatory: different units (might) sell for different prices.

Each of the above auction formats has a related sealed-bid version. In sealed-bid auction formats, bids take the form of demand curves: bidders indicate separately how much they are willing to pay for the first unit they acquire, how much they are willing to pay for the second unit, etc. Typically the outcome of the auction is determined by finding first the price at which demand equals supply. All bids made above this price are satisfied, with a tie-breaking rule specifying which bids at the market-clearing price will be satisfied as well. Various sealed-bid auction formats differ with respect to the precise rules that determine bidders' payments. In a 'uniform price auction' the market-clearing price is also the price that all bidders have to pay for all units that they have been allocated. In a 'discriminatory price auction' bidders have to pay for each unit exactly the amount they bid.

Formally, in the uniform price auction, each bidder $i$ communicates his entire demand curve $d_i(.)$ directly to the auctioneer. The auctioneer then computes total demand $d(.)$, as well as the market-clearing price $p^*$ for which $d(p^*) = s$. Each bidder $i$ is then allocated $d_i(p^*)$ units for which he pays $p^* d_i(p^*)$ in total. When the number of units is an integer, say $n$, two variants may be distinguished: the market-clearing price may be the lowest one of the accepted bids, or it may be the highest one of the rejected bids, i.e. in the latter case is the highest price $p$ for which $d(p) = n + 1$. In the former case, the uniform price auction is related to the ascending price open auction.

In the discriminatory auction, the bidders also communicate entire demand functions to the auctioneer. The auctioneer calculates the market-clearing price just as before, but now each bidder pays his bid for each unit that he is awarded. For example, if bidder $i$ indicates that he wants five units and that he is willing to pay $p_1, p_2, \ldots, p_5$ respectively for these units with $p_1 > p_2 > p_3 > p_4 > p_5$ and the market-clearing price $p^*$ satisfies $p_3 > p^* > p_4$, then bidder $i$ will be awarded three units and he will be requested to pay $p_1 + p_2 + p_3$ in total. Obviously, this discriminatory auction is closely related to the descending price auction. However, in contrast to the single-unit case, there is now one important difference. It is that all bidders except the first one to bid can observe some bids by previous bidders. This additional information may be useful to them.

In his seminal 1961 article, Vickrey noted that, in the case where bidders are interested in buying multiple units, both the uniform and the discriminatory auction have important drawbacks and he proposed an auction form that does not suffer from these drawbacks. In a multi-unit

Table 1.1. *An example to illustrate the multi-unit Vickrey auction*

|   | 1st | 2nd | 3rd | 4th |
|---|-----|-----|-----|-----|
| 1 | 50* | 47* | 40* | 32 |
| 2 | 42* | 28  | 20  | 12 |
| 3 | 45* | 35* | 24  | 14 |

'Vickrey auction' the highest bids are again accepted, but the pricing rule is more complicated: bidders have to pay for the $k$th unit which they gain the value of the $k$th highest losing bid placed by the other bidders. This pricing rule is a direct generalisation of the single-unit Vickrey rule and it has a clear economic interpretation. In the single-unit case, the winner of the auction pays the value that the strongest competitor expresses for the item. To phrase this slightly differently, the winner pays the externality that he exerts on the competing bidders, that is, the value that they could have generated had he not been present in the auction. In the multi-unit case, the units are allocated to those bidders that express the highest values, and each winner pays the value the other bidders could have generated had he not been present.

An example may illustrate this. Suppose six identical units are for sale, and there are three bidders each of whom is interested in at most four units. The bidders' marginal values are given in table 1.1. (The table should be read as follows: bidder 1 expresses a value (bid) of 50 for the first unit that he gets, 47 for the second unit, etc.). The Vickrey auction allocates three units to bidder 1, one to bidder 2 and two to bidder 3, as indicated by the entries marked * in the table. In this way the highest possible total value is realised. How much should bidder 1 pay for his units? If he were not there, we could allocate three units more to bidders 2 and 3. Of these we would give two units to bidder 2 (values 28 and 20) and one unit to bidder 3 (value 24). Consequently, bidder 1 should pay 28, 24 and 20 for his units, a total of 72. Similarly, bidder 2 should pay the externality he exerts on bidders 1 and 3, i.e. he should pay 32. Finally, bidder 3 receives two units and he should pay 32 for the second and 28 for the first, or a total of 60.

The reader may now wonder whether this Vickrey auction has an equivalent open variant. The answer is in the affirmative, as has recently been shown by Ausubel (2003). In Ausubel's auction, as bidding progresses, bidders 'clinch' units sequentially. The price to be paid for each unit is the price at which the auction stood at the time the unit was clinched. More formally, the price is gradually increased from 0. At each price $p$, each player expresses his demand $d_i(p)$ and we compute $d(p)$ just as before. In addition, for each price, we calculate the total demand of the opponents

$$d_{-i}(p) = \sum_{j \neq i} d_j(p) \tag{2}$$

as well as the supply that is available to satisfy the demand of player $i$ after his competitors have satisfied all their demand

$$s_i(p) = s(p) - d_{-i}(p). \tag{3}$$

As we increase $p$, total demand $d(p)$ will fall and at a certain $p$ we will have

$$d_{-i}(p) < n \tag{4}$$

where $n$ is the total number of units that is available. Let $(p_1, i)$ be the first combination where this happens. At this price, the competitors of $i$ demand one unit less than is available; hence, $i$ has 'clinched' one unit, and the Ausubel auction indeed allocates one unit to bidder $i$ at this price $p_1$. We thereby reduce supply by one unit (hence $s(p) = n - 1$ for $p > p_1$), we also reduce the demand of bidder 1 by one unit and we continue the process. We repeat this process, always allocating one unit to a bidder $k$ as soon as the residual supply that is available for this player $s_k(p)$ is strictly positive, until total residual supply becomes zero.

We can illustrate the Ausubel auction by means of the values given in table 1.1. If one increases $p$, one sees that residual demand remains at least 7 as long as $p < 20$. When $p = 20$, the total demand of bidders 2 and 3 drops to 5 and bidder 1 can be allocated his first unit at this price. We now cross out 50 from the first row in the table and reduce the supply to 5. Next, at $p = 24$, bidder 3 drops a unit and we have $s_1(p) = 1$ so that bidder 1 can be awarded a second unit at price 24. And so on.

### 4.3    Multi-object auctions

We now allow for the possibility that the objects on offer are non-identical. For example, spectrum licences sold by auction may differ in size, or in their location in the electromagnetic spectrum. These objects may have different values, and so will fetch different prices.

When heterogeneous objects are sold, both sequential and simultaneous sales are again possibilities. In the case of a sequential auction, an important decision is the order in which the objects are sold: should the object with the highest expected price be sold first or last? Or is it preferable to adopt a random order? The sequencing may also be determined endogenously, i.e. the buyers may determine which object is sold

Table 1.2. *Description of the state of a*
*simultaneous ascending auction*

| $A_1$ | $A_2$ | $\ldots$ | $A_n$ |
|---|---|---|---|
| $B_1^t$ | $B_2^t$ | $\ldots$ | $B_n^t$ |
| $b_1^t$ | $b_2^t$ | $\ldots$ | $b_n^t$ |
| $m_1^{t+1}$ | $m_2^{t+1}$ | $\ldots$ | $m_n^{t+1}$ |

first. For example, the seller can initially auction the right to choose first from the set of all objects; the highest bidder wins and chooses an object from the set. The bidders are then informed which objects are still left, and the process repeats itself.

When the Federal Communications Commission planned to sell multiple, non-identical spectrum licences at the beginning of the 1990s, the auction theorists McAfee, Milgrom and Wilson devised the 'simultaneous ascending auction' by means of which the licences could be sold simultaneously (see Milgrom (2000)). In this auction, all objects are sold simultaneously using an English auction procedure in which prices on each object are increased until there is no more bidding for any of the objects. At that point, the auction ends and the bidders that have made the highest bids receive the objects. As always, variants are possible: prices can be raised continuously or in discrete steps, for example, and bidders may receive full or incomplete information about which bidders are standing high at a certain point in time. We now describe one variant in more detail.

Label the available objects as $A_1, A_2, \ldots, A_n$ and let there be $m$ bidders, $i = 1, \ldots, m$. The auction will proceed in a number of rounds and, in each round, it will be in a certain state. The state of the auction includes a description of (i) who has made the highest bid on each item up to that round, (ii) the value of that bid and (iii) the minimum that has to be bid on each object in the next round in order for the bid to be valid. Hence, the state of the auction at time $t$ may be represented as shown in table 1.2. The columns of this table correspond to the various lots; $B_j^t$ denotes the bidder that is standing highest on lot $j$ at the end of round $t$ and $b_j^t$ is the corresponding highest bid; $m_j^{t+1}$ is the minimum bid that has to be made in round $t + 1$. The auction starts in round 1 with the minimum bids $m_j^1$ having been chosen by the auctioneer. In each new round, the auctioneer sets new minimum prices, which typically are a certain percentage increment, say 5 or 10 per cent, above the previous highest bids.

Table 1.3. *Player's bidding rights in round* t
*in a simultaneous ascending auction*

| 1 | 2 | $\cdots$ | M |
|---|---|---|---|
| $R_1^t$ | $R_2^t$ | $\cdots$ | $R_m^t$ |

In addition to information on the lots, bidders also have information about the number of 'bidding rights', $R_j^t$, that each bidder $i$ still has in round $t$. The bidding rights provide an upper boundary for the number of objects for which bidder $i$ may seek to become the leading bidder in round $t$. Thus, if bidder $i$ has $R_j^t$ bidding rights in round $t$ and this bidder is currently having the highest bids on $k$ lots, then, in round $t + 1$, this bidder is allowed to bid on at most

$$\max\left(0, R_j^t - k\right) \tag{5}$$

lots on which he is not standing high. The auction rules will determine how the bidding rights evolve, so, in addition to table 1.2, in each round the table of remaining bidding rights will also be available to players (table 1.3). The rules may, for example, reflect concerns about competition in the aftermarket, so that bidders are not allowed to acquire more than a certain maximum number of objects. On the other hand, in order to speed up the auction, if a bidder would like to receive $k$ objects, then we would like to force him to bid on $k$ units, or at least we would not want him to bid for too long a time on a substantially smaller number of objects. The rules may then say that a bidder loses bidding rights if he does not bid for a sufficiently large number of objects.

Let us give an example. Suppose that we want bidders to bid seriously from the start and that each bidder could possibly acquire all $n$ objects. In that case we will have $R_i^1 = n$ for each bidder $i$. Second, the number of bids that bidder $i$ will make in this round will determine his number of bidding rights in round 2: if bidder $i$ bids on only $l$ lots, then $R_i^2 = l$. Subsequently, if in round $t$ bidder $i$ is standing high on $l_1$ lots and he bids on $l_2$ lots on which he currently is not standing high, then in round $t + 1$, we will have $R_i^{t+1} = l_1 + l_2$. Note that, as a consequence, $R_i^{t+1} \leq R_i^t$ for all $i$ and $t$.

In each round, bidders, having access to the tables, such as those in tables 1.2 and 1.3, will simultaneously decide on which lots to bid and how much to bid. Of course, bidders will have to take into account the restrictions on the minimum bids and the bidding rights. As a result of the bidding, the auctioneer will adjust the 'bid table' and the 'activity table' and provide the updated information to the bidders. The process will continue until a round $t^*$ is reached in which no more bids are made. The bidders that are standing high at $t^*$ receive the lots and pay the price they have bid, and lot $j$ is sold to bidder $B_j^{t^*}$ for the price $b_j^{t^*}$. Note that all auctions close simultaneously; as long as there is bidding on at least one lot, it is (theoretically) possible that in some future round there might still be bidding on other lots. Also note that the simultaneous auction allows bidders a lot of flexibility: a bidder who is bidding only on lot $j$ at first, might switch to a different lot $j'$ if he has been overbid on $j$, and if he finds that $j$ is getting too expensive. Because of this flexibility, one may expect that, in this auction, similar objects will be sold at similar prices. This property is not guaranteed when the objects are sold in a sequential auction, and this is one of the reasons why a simultaneous format is preferred to a sequential one.

Finally, note that, in this simultaneous ascending auction, bidders bid on individual lots; there is no possibility of bidding directly on packages. As we shall see in the next section, when different objects are comple-ments, i.e. when the value of a pair of objects together is larger than the sum of the individual values, allowing such package bidding might im-prove the efficiency properties of the auction. In that section, we will also briefly discuss how package bids can be included and whether allowing for package bidding has drawbacks as well.

## 5      Bidding behaviour

To find out which auction format is optimal for the seller, one first has to ask how bidders will bid under different auction formats. In this section, we will describe and explain some aspects of bidding behaviour, and we will examine their implications for the choice of auction format. We will not provide a full overview of the results that are available, but limit ourselves to a couple of salient features with high practical relevance. As in the previous section, we move from the simplest to the more complicated situations.

### 5.1      *Single object; own value is known*

Let us write $v_i$ for the value that bidder $i$ assigns to the object that is for sale. Consequently, if player $i$ wins the object for a price $p$, then his net gain is $v_i - p$; if $i$ does not win the object, he does not have to pay and his utility is normalised to 0.

In the English auction, as long as the price is below the own value, it is optimal to stay in the auction: if one quits one is sure to lose, while one might make a positive profit if one stays in. On the other hand, if the price is above the personal value, it is optimal to drop out, since winning would confer a loss. We can conclude that rational bidders will remain in the auction until their value is reached and that the bidder with the highest value will win the auction: the auction outcome is efficient.

A similar conclusion is reached in the Vickrey auction: bidders should submit bids that are equal to their true valuation of the object (Vickrey, 1961, 1962). The reason is that under the second-price rule the bid only determines *whether* the bidder wins the object, but not *how much* he has to pay when he wins. A bid that is exactly equal to the true value ensures that a bidder wins whenever the price determined by the auction is below the bidder's value, and that he loses otherwise. Formally, for each bidder it is a (weakly) dominant strategy to bid truthfully: if my value is $v_i$, then, for any possible combination of bids of my opponents, bidding $b_i = v_i$ yields at least as much profit as any alternative bid, and sometimes the truthful bid yields strictly more.

Note that the above conclusions do not depend on the risk attitudes of the players, nor on the information that they have about their competitors' values. The simplicity of the optimal bidding strategy in the English and in the Vickrey auctions can be regarded as one important advantage of these formats. However, it turns out that student subjects in experiments often do not discover the optimal bidding strategy in the Vickrey auction, even if they are given the opportunity to gather experience and learn (see Kagel (1995)). Thus, it seems that, perhaps, not too much weight should be attached to the strategic simplicity of the Vickrey auction.

The situation is fundamentally different in the Dutch and first-price auctions. Under such a format, the only way for a bidder to achieve a positive surplus is for him to bid less than his true value. The issue now is by how much bidders will shade their bids, and this is a difficult problem: the longer a bidder waits, the more profit he makes if he wins, but the larger the risk that he will lose the auction. Hence, a bidder is facing a risk–return trade-off and his decision will depend on his beliefs about the competitors' values and his risk attitude. The more risk-averse he is, or the more intense he expects the competition to be, the higher he will bid.

Let us assume that bidders are risk-neutral, so that they only care about expected gains, an assumption that will be maintained throughout most of this chapter. Suppose also for the present that each bidder knows not only his own value, but also the values of all competitors. In that case, the bidder with the highest value knows that he can safely wait until the clock reaches the second highest value: no competitor will bid at such a price since he would make a loss when winning at that price. Consequently, in this case, the bidder with the highest value will win and he will pay (approximately) the second highest value, just as in the English auction.

One of the results derived by Vickrey (1961) was that this equivalence of auction forms generalises to certain settings in which bidders are uncertain about their opponents' values. Consider the so-called symmetric independent private values (SIPV) model, in which bidders are risk-neutral, and consider their values as independent draws from the same distribution. If the seller does not impose a minimum bid, then, in an equilibrium each bidder will bid the value that he expects his toughest competitor to have, conditional on his own value being the highest

$$B_i(v_i) = E\left(\max_{j \neq i} v_j \,\middle|\, \max_{j \neq i} v_j \leq v_i\right). \tag{6}$$

As a consequence, in this benchmark case, the bidder with the highest value will win the object, so the auction outcome is efficient. Furthermore, the above equation shows that bidders will shade their bids exactly so that on average the payment will be equal to the second highest value and, therefore, the expected price will be equal to the expectation of the price paid in the equilibrium of the Vickrey auction. It also follows, therefore, that a risk-neutral seller will be fully indifferent between any of the four auction forms (without minimum bids) that have been discussed: they all yield an efficient allocation and the same expected revenue.

Let us briefly illustrate how an equilibrium as in (6) can be derived. Imagine that there are two bidders, that each bidder $i$ knows his own value $v_i$, but that he considers his competitor's value $v_j$ to be an (independent) draw from the uniform distribution on [0,1] and that the first-price auction is used. Since the situation is symmetric, a strategy $B(.)$ (a map that translates values into bids) that is good for one player should also be good for the opponent. We are looking for a bidding strategy $B(.)$ such that $<B(.),B(.)>$ is a symmetric Nash equilibrium, i.e. given that my opponent bids according to $B(.)$, it is in my best interest to bid according to $B(.)$ as well. Bidders with higher values are more eager to win the object; hence, they will be willing to bid more, and, consequently, we will assume that $B(.)$ is an increasing function. Assuming that player 2 bids according to $B(.)$, let us check under what conditions player 1 finds it optimal to bid $B(x)$ for any possible value $x$ that he might have. If player

1 bids $B(y)$ instead, then, if his competitor bids according to $B(.)$, his payoff would be

$$u(y \mid x) = \begin{cases} x - B(y) & \text{if } v_2 < y \\ 0 & \text{if } v_2 > y \end{cases} \tag{7}$$

which would yield the expected payoff

$$Eu(y \mid x) = [x - B(y)]y. \tag{8}$$

Here we have used the assumptions, first, that $B(.)$ is increasing, so that the bid $B(y)$ is winning if and only if $y > v_2$ and, second, that $v_2$ is uniform on [0,1] so that $y = \text{Prob}[v_2 < y]$. Player 1 wants to maximise his payoff, so he wants to choose $y$ such that $Eu(y \mid x)$ is maximal. The first-order condition is

$$\frac{\partial Eu(y \mid x)}{\partial y} = x - B(y) - B'(y)y = 0 \tag{9}$$

and, to have an equilibrium, this condition should be satisfied for $y = x$, or

$$B(x) + xB'(x) = x. \tag{10}$$

We can conclude that the equilibrium strategy $B(.)$ should be a solution to this differential equation. Fortunately, the differential equation is simple to solve, yielding

$$B(x) = x/2 + C/x \tag{11}$$

for some constant $C$. This integration constant is determined by the minimum bid that the seller requires in the auction. If there is no minimum bid, then a buyer will participate no matter what his value is and we will have $B(0) = 0$. In this case $B(x) = x/2$, and the result confirms equation (6): assuming that player 2's valuation $v_2$ is less than $x$, $v_2$ is uniformly distributed between 0 and $x$, and thus the conditional expected value from the right-hand side of (6) is just the midpoint between 0 and $x$, that is $x/2$.

We now generalise these observations to an SIPV model with $n$ bidders where values are independent and identically distributed with distribution function $F$. Consider any symmetric equilibrium of any symmetric auction format. Given his value $x$, a bidder can calculate upfront his probability of winning the auction, $P(x)$, as well as the expected transfer, $T(x)$, he will have to make to the seller. Furthermore, the buyer can calculate the corresponding quantities resulting from his pretending that his value would be $y$. If a bidder plays as if his value were $y$, his expected payoff would be

$$U(y \mid x) = xP(y) - T(y). \tag{12}$$

In equilibrium, pretending to have a different value does not pay, because otherwise a bidder with value $x$ would prefer the bid of a bidder with value $y$ to his own bid, and we would not have an equilibrium. Hence, we must have

$$\frac{\partial U(y \mid x)}{\partial y} = 0 \quad \text{for } y = x. \tag{13}$$

If we write $U(x) = U(x \mid x)$ for the equilibrium expected utility for a bidder with value $x$, we therefore have $U'(x) = P(x)$, hence

$$U(x) = U(0) + \int_0^x P(z)dz \tag{14}$$

where we have assumed, without loss of generality, that 0 is the lowest possible value of $x$. From this it follows that any two auction mechanisms that have the same $P(.)$ function and that both satisfy $U(0) = 0$ have the same expected utility for the buyers. Moreover, we have that the seller's expected revenue is given by

$$R = n \int T(x)dF(x) \tag{15}$$

and since $T(x) = xP(x) - U(x)$, it also follows that the seller must be indifferent between any two auctions that have the same $P(.)$ function and that satisfy $U(0) = 0$. In summary, the seller, and all the buyers, are indifferent between auction formats which imply the same rule for allocating the object (the $P(.)$ function) and which imply the same utility for a bidder of the lowest conceivable type. This result is known as the *Revenue Equivalence Theorem*.

Without a reserve price, the four standard auction formats defined above imply that, in equilibrium, the object is allocated to the bidder with the highest value (hence, they have the same $P(.)$ function) and that the bidder with the lowest value has zero expected utility, i.e. $U(0) = 0$. Therefore, the Revenue Equivalence Theorem implies that all players are indifferent among these auction formats.

Let us now ask the question of which auction format the seller should choose? The Revenue Equivalence Theorem implies that this reduces to the question of which function $P(.)$ to choose, and what value for $U(0)$. If the seller is only interested in the efficiency of the allocation rule, then the four auction formats discussed above, with zero reserve price, are obviously optimal. In the case where the seller wishes to maximise expected returns, Myerson (1981) has solved the problem. He has shown that the seller will optimally set $U(0) = 0$, and will allocate the object to the bidder with the highest value, except if this highest value is below some reserve price $m^*$, in which case the seller does not sell at all. The optimal value of $m^*$ turns out to be independent of the number of bidders. It is equal to the 'take-it-or-leave-it' price that the seller would ask when faced with one bidder, with a value drawn from the distribution $F(.)$; hence, if the seller's value of the object is zero, $m^*$ is found by solving

$$\max_m m(1 - F(m)). \tag{16}$$

Which auction rules implement this format? Analysing equilibria of auctions with reserve prices along the lines indicated at the beginning of this subsection, one finds that any of the standard auction formats, with optimal reserve price $m^*$, implies the desired allocation rule, and yields zero expected utility for the bidder of the lowest conceivable type. Therefore, any such auction is optimal. The seller is indifferent among all four standard auction formats with this reserve price.

The results which we have described in this subsection are well known, but they do not directly apply to licence auctions because the circumstances in which these auctions are conducted differ from those assumed in the theorems. The next subsections discuss several ways in which spectrum auctions deviate from the assumptions underlying the Revenue Equivalence Theorem and Myerson's optimal auction analysis, and why, given these deviations, the choice of auction format matters.

## 5.2    Asymmetries

In the previous subsection we assumed that all bidders regarded their valuations as independent draws from the same distribution. This means that bidders regard all competitors *ex ante* as equally strong. In many practical situations, however, some bidders might be known in advance to be stronger than others. We can describe such a situation formally by assuming that some bidders' valuations are drawn from a distribution which typically yields higher values.

As a simple example, consider the extreme case in which there are only two bidders, and bidder 1's value is drawn from a uniform distribution between 0 and 1, while bidder 2's value is drawn from a uniform distribution between 2 and 3. Thus, it is known in advance that bidder 2 can make much better use of the object than bidder 1. What will happen if one of the four standard formats is used to auction the object? The analysis of the English auction, and the second-price auction, will not change. As we noted above, that analysis is independent of the symmetry assumption. Thus, bidders will bid their true values, bidder 2 will always win, and he will pay bidder 1's value. In the first-price and Dutch auctions, by contrast, one equilibrium will be that bidder 1 bids his own value, perhaps recognising that he has no chance of winning. Bidder 2 will then find it optimal to bid the maximum value of bidder 1, that is to make a bid equal to 1, and thus not risk any probability of not winning the auction. This holds for any value which bidder 2 might have. If this equilibrium is played, then a first-price, or Dutch, auction will guarantee the seller a revenue of 1, whereas a second-price, or English, auction will only give a revenue equal to the true value of bidder 1. *Revenue equivalence* between the standard auction formats no longer holds, and the seller has a preference for a first-price auction. Vickrey (1961) has already shown that in general no unambiguous statement about the revenue ranking of the standard auction formats is possible if bidders are asymmetric. (See also Maskin and Riley (2000) for a recent investigation.)

### 5.3    The winner's curse and the linkage principle

Bidding becomes more difficult when a player does not know his own value, which will be the case in many real-life auctions. In particular, bidders will typically have different pieces of information about the true value of licences, and each bidder would revise his own valuation of the licences if he had not only his own information, but also the information of the other bidders. While the information of competitors is not directly available, a bidder might be able to infer it from their behaviour. For example, if bidder 1 sees that bidder 2 bids very aggressively on one particular licence, he might infer that this licence is more valuable than he previously thought. Alternatively, if a bidder sees other bidders drop out early, then he might revise his own valuation downwards. In open auctions, one can thus learn from the bidding behavior of other players: their bids may reveal some of their information and may allow a bidder to make a better estimate of his own value. The Revenue Equivalence Theorem abstracts from such informational issues.

If informational considerations of this sort play a role, then successful bidders run the risk of suffering from the *winner's curse*. This refers to the fact that the winner of an auction is the bidder who has the highest estimate of the value of the licence, and that this estimate and the corresponding bid may be overly optimistic. Other bidders apparently have had information that gave reason for more caution, and had the winning bidder had access to other bidders' information at the time of bidding, he would probably have revised his own valuation of licences downwards. A winner who does not think these issues through in advance will suffer from the winner's curse, i.e. he will pay more than the licences are worth.

To illustrate the possibility of the winner's curse, let us consider the following question: in the case in which one is not sure about the value and the Vickrey (second-price) auction is used, should one bid the expected value of the object? Let us assume that the situation is symmetric and that the value of the object is the same for each player. As a specific example, think of bidders bidding for the right to drill for oil in a certain location; the amount of oil that can be extracted is (to a first approximation) independent of the winner of the auction, so the right to drill has the same value for all bidders. Indeed, the study of the winner's curse originates from analysing these situations (see Capen, Clapp and Campbell (1971)). If bidding the expected value is the optimal strategy for one bidder, then it would also be followed by the other players and in that case the winner of the auction would be the one who has estimated the highest expected value. In being told that he has won the object, this bidder is also being told that all other bidders have estimated the value to be lower than he has, which is bad news. Furthermore, the winner has to pay the estimate of the second most optimistic bidder and this may be above the actual value as well. In short, if one bids the expected value, one risks having to pay more for the object than it is actually worth, and thus falling prey to the winner's curse.

A rational strategic bidder in a second-price auction will anticipate that a winner's curse might arise, and will adjust his bid downwards. He will therefore bid conservatively. The result of such downward adjustment of bids will, of course, be lower average revenue for the auctioneer. If a bidder wins, he is told that he has the highest estimate; hence, a conservative way of bidding would be to bid the expected value of the object, conditional on all opponents estimating this value to be lower. It turns out that this is too conservative; one may allow for the possibility that at least one of the opponents is as optimistic as one is oneself. If we write $X_j$ for the stochastic signal received by player $j$, it can be shown that, in the Vickrey auction, player $i$ should bid

$$B_i(x_i) = E\big(v_i \,\big|\, x_i = \max_{j \neq i} X_j\big). \tag{17}$$

To illustrate our discussion, suppose there are three bidders who bid in an ascending auction for an object that is worth

$$v = (x_1 + x_2 + x_3)/3 \tag{18}$$

to each of them. Here $x_i$ is a signal that player $i$ has received about the value; player $i$, however, does not know the signal $x_j$ received by the competitor, which he considers to be drawn from the uniform distribution on $[0,1]$. A naïve bidder would bid the value of his own signal: $b_i(x_i) = x_i$. Such a bidder would suffer from the winner's curse. The naïve correction for the winner's curse, which conditions on the event that both other signals are below one's own, results in a bid of: $b_i(x_i) = (1/3)x_i + (2/3)\,(x_i/2)$. This is because the expected value of a signal, conditional on being less than $x_i$, is $x_i/2$. However, the equilibrium bid is larger than this, and conditions on the event that one of the other bids is the same as $x_i$. Thus, it is: $b_i(x_i) = (2/3)\,x_i + (1/3)\,(x_i/2)$.

Efficiency of auctions where bidders do not know their own value becomes an issue when, unlike in our example, valuations have a common as well as an idiosyncratic component. Under symmetry conditions, the bidder with the highest signal will have the highest value and will make the highest bid, so the Vickrey auction will also result in an efficient allocation in this case. Under these same conditions, also the Dutch (first-price) auction will also yield an efficient outcome, and the equilibrium bidding strategy is given by a similar, but slightly more complicated formula. However, if individual signals are, unlike in our example, affiliated, the seller will usually not be indifferent among these auctions: the Dutch auction results in lower (or at least not higher) expected revenue than the Vickrey auction, which in turn yields expected revenue no higher than the English auction. In other words, the loss which the auctioneer suffers because bidders adjust their bids in anticipation of the winner's curse is typically lower in second-price auctions than in first-price auctions, and it is lower in the English auction than in the Vickrey auction.

A popular intuition for these results, which is, however, only partially correct, is that the more information a bidder has, the smaller the chance of falling prey to the winner's curse and the more aggressively a bidder can bid. The result is an application of a more general idea (originally derived in Milgrom and Weber (1982)), which in auction theory is known as the 'linkage principle': it works, at least on average, to the auctioneer's advantage if he can link the price paid by winning bidders to signals that are correlated with the signals of winning bidders. An excellent exposition of the linkage principle is in chapter 7 of Krishna (2002). His proposition 7.1 formulates the linkage principle for a general setting in which bidders' valuations are not necessarily common. The linkage principle is often related to the winner's curse, but the connection is only loose. In particular, there are common value settings where individual signals are independent, and therefore the linkage principle does not apply, even though the winner's curse is clearly relevant.

In a first-price auction, conditional on being told that he has won, a bidder does not have more information than the information he used when he made his bid; in particular, the auction price just depends on his own bid. In contrast, in the Vickrey auction, the payment made by the winner is linked to the information of one of the losers of the auction. In a common value environment, if the signal of the loser is correlated to the signal of the winner, the linkage principle implies that the second-price auction offers the auctioneer higher average revenue than the first-price auction .

As a further application of the 'linkage principle', we obtain the classic argument in favour of open auction formats. These formats allow bidders to observe other bidders' decisions, such as these bidders' decisions to exit from the auction. If other bidders' signals contain information about the value of the object, and a bidder's own signal does not include this information, then bidders will have an incentive to learn from others' decisions, and to revise their own plans continuously. This will tighten the link between other bidders' signals, and the price paid by the winning bidder. If signals are correlated, then the linkage principle implies that an open format leads to a higher expected revenue for the seller than a closed format.

To conclude, under natural assumptions, the four basic auction forms still all generate an efficient outcome, but they typically do not yield the same expected revenue for the seller. The English auction yields at least as much expected revenue as the Vickrey auction, and the Vickrey auction yields at least as much as the Dutch auction. If the seller can avoid collusion among the bidders (see below), he is thus advised to organise an open ascending procedure as this provides the tightest link between the price paid by the winning bidder and the signals observed by other bidders.

## 5.4    Bidding in multiple unit auctions

We emphasise from the outset that the literature on auctions with multi-unit demand is much less developed than the literature on auctions with single unit demand. Multi-unit demand is, in fact, one of the areas on which current research in auction theory is concentrating. At this stage, though, the question on which we focused in previous subsections, i.e. 'What is/are the equilibrium/a of a given auction format under certain assumptions about values and information?', has not been answered at any level of generality for multiple-unit auctions. We can thus only point out some intuitions, but we cannot present any general results.

Since a sequential auction is easy to organise, a seller will find it tempting to sell multiple units sequentially. For a bidder, a sequential auction presents considerable strategic complexity, however. For example, there might be a reason to hide true values in early auctions so as to induce other bidders to bid lower in later auctions. In addition, supply/demand conditions change during the auction. On the one hand, there is an incentive to bid *more* aggressively in later auctions because fewer items remain for sale; on the other, some bidders, possibly those with the highest valuations, have already won a licence and have left the auction. Thus, there is an incentive to bid *less* aggressively. How these intuitions interact, and what is optimal bidding behaviour in sequential auctions, has only been resolved in some special cases (see chapter 15 of Krishna (2002)). For sequential auctions in which each bidder is interested in just one item, it turns out that the effects exactly cancel each other out, irrespective of whether the auction format is first-price or second-price, sealed-bid: the expected price for which item $l + 1$ will be sold is exactly equal to the price for which item $l$ is sold. However, it is also well known that in practice bidders' behaviour deviates from the predictions derived for these special cases: in many real-life auctions, prices display a downward drift; see Ashenfelter (1989).

The situation gets even more complicated if bidders are interested in multiple units, and especially so when there are complementarities and players' values are superadditive ('$1 + 1 = 3$'). For example, if bidder 1 has already won one item, he may need a second one in order to generate value from the first. He may, therefore, need to bid very aggressively on a second unit, with two effects. On the one hand, his competitors know that it is unlikely that they can win the second unit, which may discourage them from bidding; on the other, they know that bidding is relatively riskless for them, so they may bid to drive up the price for bidder 1 and weaken him in that way. To put it differently, bidder 1 is liable to a 'hold-up' problem in this case. Of course, if a player foresees this, and considers the risks to be too large, he may decide not to participate in the first place. As a consequence, it does not seem a good idea to use a sequential auction in situations like these, and the consensus view is that it is better not to confront bidders with the complications of a sequential format.

Moving to simultaneous auctions, we report three interesting intuitions emerging from the literature. The first two relate specifically to uniform price auctions, to which we will mainly restrict ourselves.

We note, first of all, that the uniform $(n + 1)$-auction (in which all winning bidders pay the highest losing bid) does not share the desirable properties of the second-price auction from the single-unit case, at least not in the situation where bidders are interested in more than one unit. The reason is simple: if a bidder can demand more than one unit, he can influence the market price and he will profit from a lower market price on all the units that he gets. Thus, there is the possibility of players engaging in *demand reduction*: bidders understate their true value of different units (Ausubel and Cramton, 1996; Engelbrecht-Wiggans and Kahn, 1998). While demand reduction implies that a bidder will not win some units that he would have liked to win, it is advantageous because it reduces the price which the bidder has to pay for all those units which he will win. When demand goes down, the equilibrium price at which the market clears goes down too. Demand reduction is a source of inefficiency in uniform price auctions, and it reduces sellers' expected revenues.

To give a very simple example, suppose that there are two units and two bidders, with bidder 1 wanting to have two units and player 2 interested in just one unit. Bidder 1 will realise that his demand for the second unit might set the price; if he pretends not to value this second unit (bids 0 for it), then he is guaranteed to get one unit for free, and this will frequently be better than to compete head-on with bidder 2 in an attempt to acquire two units. As a second example, assume that there are two bidders who each want two units and that supply is also equal to two units. Furthermore, suppose that each bidder knows his values and that it is known that all (marginal) values are in the order of 50. If bidders bid truthfully and compete head-on, price will raise to approximately 50 and each bidder will have utility close to zero. If the ascending English auction is used, it is, however, much better to reduce demand to one unit immediately. If one bidder does this, the other notices immediately that he can stop the auction by also reducing his demand. In this case, each bidder will get one item and the price will be close to zero. In equilibrium, therefore, bidding will stop immediately at price zero. Grimm, Riedel and Wolfstetter (2002) illustrate that a demand reduction strategy was successfully followed in the German DCS-1800 auction. In a simplified model of that auction, these authors also show that the unique 'sensible' equilibrium will result in demand reduction.

The second intuition that emerges from the literature on sealed-bid auctions with multi-unit demand is that uniform price auctions offer an opportunity for a particular form of implicit collusion. The strategies adopted by bidders for this form of collusion involve overstating the willingness to bid for the first few units, and understating the willingness to bid for later units. Values are overstated for those units that the bidder is sure to win. What the bidder bids for these units is certain not to influence the market price directly. Understatement occurs for those units that the bidder regards as 'marginal', i.e. he might win them, or he might not win them. Understatement of values for these units goes beyond the demand reduction effect described in the previous paragraphs; see Binmore and Swierzbinski (2000).

The logic behind these strategies, first pointed out by Wilson (1979), is that each bidder's demand function is very steep around the equilibrium price. The effect of this is that each bidder also faces a very steep residual demand. That will mean that an increase in demand will lead to a very sharp rise in the market-clearing price. This in turn deters all bidders from raising their demand. Note that this form of implicit collusion assumes that bidders can predict the market-clearing price relatively well. If there is large uncertainty regarding this price, then this form of collusion cannot be implemented.

Discriminatory price auctions create other, more subtle inefficiencies, but we will not discuss these here. One advantage of the more complicated pricing rule adopted in the Vickrey auction is that similar problems do not arise there. Vickrey(1961) showed that the auction that he proposed inherits the desirable properties of the Vickrey auction in the single-unit case: it is a dominant strategy for each player to report his values truthfully to the auctioneer. Consequently, the Vickrey auction is easy to play, honesty is the best policy and bids coincide with actual values. As a result, therefore, this Vickrey auction is a robust mechanism that produces an efficient outcome: it is impossible to generate higher total surplus. Note that this does not imply that this auction format also raises the highest possible revenue for the seller; on the contrary, the revenue in the Vickrey auction can be quite low. Of course, since demand reduction also harms revenue, it is not clear that a uniform auction will result in higher revenue.

The third intuition emerging from the literature concerns the case in which bidders do not know their own value, and each bidder believes that other bidders hold private information that is potentially relevant to their own valuation. We explained above that in the case of single-unit auctions the winner's curse arises. In the case of multi-unit auctions, there is also a loser's curse. This refers to the fact that losing at the margin now implies good news about the value of the good: the winners of the non-marginal units must have had better information (Pesendorfer and Swinkels, 1997). This leads bidders to bid more aggressively.

The linkage principle which we explained above for single-unit auctions fails in the case of multi-unit auctions (Perry and Reny, 1999). There is no clear ranking of different auction formats in terms of their expected revenue. An intuitive explanation of this may be seen in the presence of the loser's curse.

Table 1.4. *Increasing marginal values (for player 1)*

|   | 0 | 1 | 2 | 3 |
|---|---|---|---|---|
| 1 | 0 | 0 | 60 | 99 |
| 2 | 0 | 0 | 80 | 90 |

We conclude this subsection by pointing out that additional problems arise when the bidders' values are superadditive, that is, when marginal values are increasing over a certain range. To illustrate, consider the situation represented in table 1.4. There are two bidders and three units; each bidder requires at least two units to generate value, with bidder 1 valuing two units at 60 and three units at 99, etc. The efficient allocation is that bidder 1 obtains all three units. Assume that the ascending English auction is used to allocate these units. Notice that the demand of player 1 is given by

$$d_1(p) = \begin{cases} 3 & \text{if} \quad p \le 33 \\ 0 & \text{if} \quad p > 33 \end{cases} \tag{19}$$

whereas the demand of player 2 is given by

$$d_2(p) = \begin{cases} 3 & \text{if} \quad p \le 10 \\ 2 & \text{if} \quad 10 < p \le 40 \\ 0 & \text{if} \quad p > 40. \end{cases} \tag{20}$$

These demands are such that there is no market-clearing price, i.e. $d_1(p) + d_2(p) \ne 3$ for all $p$. If the English auction is used to sell the units, then the auction will stop at $p = 34$, where player 2 will buy two units. This English auction does not produce an efficient outcome.

In this example, the problem is caused by the non-convexity; to give player 1 a chance of winning and of reaching an efficient outcome, player 1 should be allowed to make package bids. If he could make package bids, he would bid 91 in total for three units (without having to specify a specific price per unit) and he would win the auction, thus inducing an efficient outcome. We shall discuss package bidding again in the next subsection.

### 5.5    Multi-object auctions

It must be emphasised that the literature on this subject is incomplete. The best-understood auction format is the simultaneous ascending auction format (see Milgrom (2000)). In the simple case in which each bidder can buy at most one licence, and in which informational considerations do not play a crucial role, this simultaneous ascending auction is reasonably well understood. A simple extension of truthful bidding, called straightforward bidding, can be shown to be rational. The key idea here is that each bidder bids for that licence which currently offers the highest surplus, i.e. the highest difference between value and price. A proof that straightforward bidding is an equilibrium strategy can be constructed using earlier results of Leonard (1983) and Demange, Gale and Sotomayor (1986).

We now turn to multi-object auctions in which bidders may demand more than one unit. In this case, several of the problems that we have already encountered in the previous subsection reappear. In this subsection, we discuss two of these in greater detail: the exposure problem, and the free-rider problem.

*5.5.1    The exposure problem*    In the previous subsection, we mentioned that a bidder may be liable to hold-up in a sequential auction in which he needs to acquire multiple units in order to generate value. The same happens in multi-object auctions. Imagine that two objects are for sale by English auction and that bidder 1 needs to acquire both to generate value. If he has already bought the first object, for price $p_1$, then, in the second auction, this price, having been paid, is a sunk cost and it will be completely irrelevant for bidding. If the bidder attaches value $v$ to the pair of objects, then in the second auction he will be willing to bid up to $v$ and, if the competition for the second object is intense, for example because some bidders are only interested in this second object, the total price paid, $p_1 + p_2$, may well exceed the value. Of course, a player will be aware of the risks involved and he may decide that they are so large that it is better not to participate in the auction at all. Sequential auctions, therefore, may attract few bidders and may generate low revenue. It may, therefore, not be a good idea to set up the auction as a sequential one. In van Damme (2002b), this argument was used to criticise the decision of the government to use a sequential auction to sell licences to operate petrol stations, the aim of which was to bring new entrants into the market.

The exposure problem is not avoided by the simultaneous ascending auction (SAA) format. Consider the values in table 1.5, where the lots A and B are complements for player 1, but substitutes for player 2. Hence, player 2 is satisfied with one unit, and he is indifferent to which lot he gets, while player 1 is willing to pay more for the second object if he has already bought the first one.

Table 1.5. *The exposure problem*

|   | A | B | AB |
|---|---|---|----|
| 1 | 4 | 4 | 10 |
| 2 | $v$ | $v$ | $v$ |

If the SAA format is used, prices on both lots will rise to 4 at which point player 1 is facing a difficult decision: he is willing to pay up to 5 for each object, provided that he obtains both of them, but he cannot be sure that he will win these two items for a total cost no greater than 10. If player 1 continues bidding and $v > 5$, the price of each object will rise above 5 and player 1 is sure to make a loss. Several possibilities now arise. If player 1 does not take the risk, he quits at 4, each bidder wins one licence and, if $v < 6$, the outcome is inefficient. If player 1 continues bidding at $p = 4$, then he might win both lots and force an efficient outcome, but he cannot avoid making losses.

The literature contains only a very few results about rational bidding if an exposure problem is present. See Krishna and Rosenthal (1996) for an example. For a practical example of the relevance of the exposure problem, see the discussion in van Damme (1999) on the Dutch DCS-1800 auction.

*5.5.2    Package bidding and the free-rider problem*    Bidding in multi-object auctions becomes more complicated when there are complementarities among licences. Complementarities exist if a bidder values some particular licence, A, more if he already holds another licence, B. In this case, bidders would like to submit two separate bids for A, one applying if the bidder wins A only, and another applying if the bidder wins A and B at the same time. In such cases, it is desirable to expand bidders' strategy sets and allow them to make mutually exclusive bids for different packages of licences without the bidder having to specify prices for individual items in the package. Auctions allowing for these possibilities are called 'package auctions' or 'combinatorial auctions' and their great advantage is that they avoid the exposure problem. For a long time, economists have regarded such auctions with some scepticism because of the complexity involved. The recently increased popularity of combinatorial auctions derives to a significant extent from experimental research with student subjects in which such auctions have been shown to perform well. The relevant experiments have been undertaken at the University of Arizona, and are documented in a report for the Federal Communications Commission of the United States (Cybernomics, 2000).

Table 1.6. *The free-rider problem*

|   | A | B | AB |
|---|---|---|-----|
| 1 | $x_1$ | 0 | $x_1$ |
| 2 | 0 | $x_2$ | $x_2$ |
| 3 | 0 | 0 | 10 |

The successful experimental work with combinatorial auctions has now triggered additional theoretical research in this area. As is the case with many other auction formats, there are static and dynamic versions of such auctions. In fact, the Vickrey auction can easily be extended to include package bids: each bidder expresses a value for each possible package, the auctioneer determines which partition of the objects maximises total value and he asks each bidder to pay the externality that he imposes on others, i.e. the loss in value that they incur because of his getting some of the objects. Formally, let $N$ be the set of items and let $S$ denote any subset. A bid of player $i$ now specifies the amount $b_i(S)$ that $i$ would want to pay for each set of items that he might want to have. Given such bids for all players, the auctioneer can calculate which partition of $N$ maximises value (as expressed by the bids) and he can allocate items accordingly. If each bidder has to pay the opportunity cost of the items that are allocated to him, i.e. the loss of value to the competitors because these objects are then not available to them, it is a weakly dominant strategy of each bidder to report the value truthfully, and the auction generates an efficient allocation. While this efficiency property is desirable, an obvious drawback is that bidders have to communicate a lot of information to the auctioneer and the computational burden may be considerable. (If there are ten objects, then a bid can specify up to 1024 numbers for each bidder.)

Recently, Ausubel and Milgrom (2002) have proposed a dynamic combinatorial auction which allows very flexible package bidding. They show that an extension of honest, 'straightforward' bidding creates efficiency in their design, and achieves efficient outcomes. We will not discuss that auction form in detail, but confine ourselves to showing that allowing package bids is not a panacea. Suppose there are three bidders and two objects, with values as in table 1.6. Here, only bidder 3 is interested in the pair, while bidders 1 and 2 are each interested in only one of the items Suppose that bidder 3 has made a package bid of 10 on the combination AB. Suppose also that players 1 and 2 know that the structure of the values is as in the table (thus, player 1 knows that player 2 is only interested in B), but that the actual values are private information. In this case, players 1 and 2 face a co-ordination problem: they have to bid up the prices and they will win only if $p_1 + p_2 > 10$; if they jointly outbid player 3, then the net revenue of player $i$ is $x_i - p_i$; hence, each player wants the total bid to be higher than 10, but each wants to contribute as little as possible to the common good of winning. Consequently, there is a co-ordination problem (which is exacerbated by the fact that the values are private) and the players may not be able to solve this problem. As a result, even though it may be that $x_1 + x_2 > 10$ and that it would be efficient for the players 1 and 2 to win the items, the outcome may be that prices are not raised sufficiently to outbid player 3.

### 5.6    Collusion

Up to now, in this section, we have assumed that the bidders behave non-cooperatively. It is, however, easy to see that, in auctions, the incentives to collude are very strong. Suppose there are two bidders for one item and the values are $v$ and $V$, with $v < V$. If both players participate in an English auction, the price will be $v$, but if players collude, identifying the bidder with the highest value before the auction, and agree that the weaker bidder will not compete, then the price will drop to 0. Consequently, the gains to collusion are $v$. As these gains can be considerable, there are strong incentives for bid-rigging. A simple method for collusion which aims at lowering the price that the winning bidders have to pay is a so-called 'bidding ring' (see Graham and Marshall (1987)). A bidding ring first establishes internally, in a preliminary auction, who should win the object. The bidding ring then only lets the winners of the preliminary internal auction submit serious bids in the official auction. While bidding rings are typically illegal, they are not always easy to detect. Therefore, the possibility of bidding rings needs to be taken seriously.

The issues that arise in this context are similar to the issues that arise in general cartel behaviour: what market structures (auction forms) are most conducive to cartels? How can the cartel identify the efficient outcome? Can it agree on division of the gains achieved from bid-rigging? How can the cartel agreement be enforced? We now discuss these questions in greater detail.

Because bidding rings are normally illegal, the underlying agreements among bidders cannot be enforced through the courts. It is therefore important whether bidders can enter into bidding ring agreements that are self-enforcing in the sense that once the agreement has been established, no party has an incentive to deviate, provided that they believe that the other parties to the agreement will stick to it. A general theoretical insight which is relevant in this context is that cartel enforcement is simpler in more transparent markets in which players interact repeatedly. The argument is simply that, in a more transparent market, a deviation from the collusive agreement can be detected more easily, while the repeated interaction provides the opportunity to punish those that deviate from the agreement, thus making deviation less attractive.

As an application of this insight, we can see that collusive agreements can most easily be enforced in English ascending auctions. Indeed, in the above example, suppose that the two bidders have reached an agreement and that the weaker bidder is supposed to stay out. Does this weaker player have an incentive to deviate? Well, if he does and participates in the auction, the opponent will notice immediately and counter with a higher bid; bidding will then enter a competitive phase, which the weaker bidder cannot win as he has the lower value in the first place. Consequently, there is no incentive whatsoever to deviate and the collusive agreement is stable.

Bidding rings in second-price auctions are typically also self-enforcing. Suppose bidders have formed a bidding ring and they have identified the bidder that has the 'right' to win the auction. In a second-price auction, this bidder can simply enter his value as a bid, and the price will be the maximum of the seller's reservation value and the highest bid of the bidders that are not members of the ring. The ring successfully lowers what the lead bidder of the ring has to pay since typically the highest losing bid will be lower. If the cartel works efficiently, another ring member has no incentive to bid: he has a lower value than the ring member that has the right to bid; hence, he can never win, unless he overbids his value. Non-lead bidders could increase the price that lead bidders have to pay, but, of course, they have no incentive to do so.

A first conclusion, therefore, is that English and Vickrey auctions are even more susceptible to collusion than other markets. In other industrial markets, cartels operate by restricting supply, which confers a positive externality on non-cartel members: they benefit from the higher price, but, unlike cartel members, they are not hindered by a production quota. Therefore, in industrial markets, there is a free-rider problem: one prefers to have a cartel in the market, but one also prefers not to be a cartel member. In an English or second-price auction, however, outsiders, do not directly benefit from the existence of an efficient cartel: such a cartel will be represented by the most aggressive member and any non-cartel member will face exactly the same competition as if there were no cartel. Consequently, in such auctions, there is an incentive to form all-inclusive cartels.

In a first-price sealed-bid auction, the situation is somewhat different. In this case, the cartel bidder will shade his bid, and the larger the coverage of the cartel, the more he will shade it; this offers cartel members the opportunity to outbid the designated bidder. As a simple example, suppose the cartel is all-inclusive and the seller sets no reserve price. In this case, the designated bidder will bid almost nothing and bidding a small amount suffices to outbid him. As a consequence, bidding rings can be expected to be more stable in second-price auctions than in first-price auctions.

A second conclusion, therefore, is that open auctions are more susceptible to collusion than sealed-bid auctions and that second-price auctions are more vulnerable to collusion than first-price auctions. It follows that, when we take into account the possibility of collusion, the seller's ranking of auctions is exactly opposite to the ranking we derived under non-cooperative behaviour. While under non-cooperative behaviour, the English auction is preferred to the Vickrey auction and the Vickrey auction is preferred to the Dutch auction (on the basis of the seller's expected revenue), we now see that the English auction is more susceptible to collusion than the Vickrey auction and that the Vickrey auction, in turn, is more susceptible than the Dutch auction.

The above paragraphs discussed the issue of enforcing the cartel agreement. But will a cartel be able to conclude such an agreement and will it be able to identify the most efficient bidder in the cartel? An efficient cartel must allocate the right to bid to the strongest bidder in the cartel and it must adequately compensate the other cartel members for giving up their right to bid. One way of achieving these objectives is to organise a pre-auction knockout in which this right is sold. McAfee and McMillan (1992) analyse such pre-auction knockouts. They distinguish between the situation in which the cartel participates in a sequence of auctions so that the books of the cartel office have to balance only on average and the situation in which transfers among the members have to balance in each possible instance. In the former case, the additional degree of freedom makes the problem easier to solve. In 2002, a Dutch parliamentary investigation uncovered a bidding ring in the construction sector, which, allegedly, operated in just this way.

Market transparency also helps the cartel in reaching an efficient agreement: the better the information about the players' values, the easier it is to see which bidder should win and by how much the others should be compensated. In this respect, the Dutch UMTS auction provides interesting lessons. See van Damme (2002a) and Janssen, Ros and van der Windt (2001) for further discussion on this point.

## 6    Which auction form to adopt?

We now return to the question of which auction form will best serve the seller's interests? As already indicated in the Introduction to this chapter, the answer will depend not only on theoretical insights, but also on empirical evidence. Here, we confine ourselves to some general theoretical considerations.

In this chapter, we have mainly limited ourselves to standard auction formats. In subsection 5.1, we briefly discussed 'optimal' auctions, i.e. auctions which maximise the seller's expected revenue. There we saw that, if the SIPV assumptions apply, any of the standard auctions is optimal, provided that the reserve price is chosen appropriately. Once the SIPV assumptions are relaxed, optimally designed auctions are often highly implausible in practice, and require detailed prior knowledge of the agents' subjective beliefs as well as strong precommitment power by the auctioneer; see McAfee, McMillan and Reny (1989). Consequently, we will here restrict ourselves to standard auctions. We discuss various design issues that arise and point out the trade-offs that exist in resolving them.

## 6.1    Sequential or simultaneous auctions?

This issue arises when the seller has multiple units for sale. It was extensively discussed in the 1990s when the United States was working towards the design of the spectrum auctions. We have also given it ample attention in this chapter. The only argument we have given for why a seller might choose to adopt a sequential auction is that such an auction appears easier to organise. We have also seen, however, that frequently this argument is not convincing: this simple solution for the seller results in a very complicated problem for the bidders. We have given several arguments for why a simultaneous auction should be preferred, and we have not identified drawbacks, at least drawbacks that could not be remedied. The clear advice is to sell related licences simultaneously as far as possible.

## 6.2    Open ascending auctions or sealed-bid auctions?

Open auctions sometimes appear to be strategically simpler than sealed-bid auctions. Compare the English auction and the related second-price, sealed-bid (Vickrey) auction. We have seen that, in the SIPV model, staying in the auction until the value is reached is the optimal strategy in the English auction, and that similarly, in the Vickrey auction, it is optimal to bid one's own value. Experimental research with student subjects as bidders has shown that bidders often do not realise the simple logic behind this result if the auction is conducted in a sealed-bid format. By contrast, if the auction is conducted as an open ascending auction, bidders easily understand that they should drop out once bidding has reached their reservation value.

Why is strategic simplicity desirable? Bidders are more likely to play equilibrium strategies, and if the choice of an auction format is based on equilibrium predictions, then it is more likely to be successful if bidders recognise equilibrium. Transparent auctions are also less liable to legal challenge, and they reduce the chance that bidders place bids on which they later have to default.

A different argument, this time in favour of sealed-bid auctions, can be constructed from our discussion of asymmetries in subsection 5.2. If some bidders are known *ex ante* to be 'weak', then these bidders have a better chance of winning in first-price sealed-bid formats than in English ascending format. Thus, weaker bidders may have a stronger incentive to participate in the first place (Klemperer, 2002). This might raise revenue, but this gain comes at the expense of efficiency.

As explained in subsection 5.3, winner's curse effects may imply that open formats lead to higher expected revenue. But, as shown in subsection 5.4, in multi-unit settings the effect is no longer clear.

An argument against ascending auctions is that these are more vulnerable to collusion than sealed-bid and descending formats. In open auctions it is easier to detect whether members of a cartel ring deviated from the agreed bidding strategy, which makes it easier to implement some form of punishment for such deviators. From the auctioneer's point of view, this is undesirable, as it might reduce revenues.

Overall, therefore, there is no unambiguous theoretical case, either in favour of sealed-bid auctions, or in favour of ascending auctions.

## 6.3    *Reserve prices*

Any auction will typically involve a reserve price, i.e. only bids above a certain minimum are allowed. In a sealed-bid auction, a reserve price can be implemented simply by ignoring bids that are below the reserve price. In open ascending price auctions, bidding can simply start at the reserve price. In descending price formats the auction can close at the reserve price even if the number of bids is still below the number of units for sale.

A seller might be tempted simply to set the reserve price equal to the value that unsold licences have for him. However, revenue considerations suggest that a higher reserve price should be set, as in equation (16). This may appear at first paradoxical because it implies that the seller risks not selling all objects even though there are some bidders whose value is above the auctioneer's own value. However, the existence of the reserve price encourages more aggressive bidding, and this more than compensates for the risk of not trading when trade would be efficient. Equation (16) shows that a revenue-maximising seller should always set a reserve price that exceeds his value.

If a reserve price is set, it is important that it is credible and that the auctioneer does not later reduce it. Sellers, of course, face a temptation to lower their reserve price, if they see that at the reserve price they cannot sell everything that they want to sell. It is important that sellers do not give in to this temptation. If bidders believe that the auctioneer might later lower the reserve price, then they will bid lower, and the crucial advantage of the reserve price will be lost.

Related to this issue is the question of whether the reserve price is secret or known. A secret reserve price (i.e. bidders know that there is a limit, but they do not know its value) offers the seller an easier opportunity to renege and to sell even if the actual price is below his reserve price. Hence, a secret reserve price is less credible than a public reserve price, and bidders will take this into account in their strategies. Because of these considerations, the literature advises a revenue-maximising seller to announce publicly the reserve price.

A reserve price can make it more difficult for bidders to collude successfully in an auction, especially if the reserve price is secret. With a secret reserve price, the situation is less transparent, which makes it more difficult for bidders to identify the gains from collusion, and consequently what side payments the strongest bidder should make to induce his competitors to stay out of the auction. If the seller adopts a public reserve price, this should be higher the more bidders he expects to participate in the cartel; see Krishna (2002, ch. 11).

Reserve prices can be problematic, however, when entry is an issue. In general, it appears to be that entry issues should be given more weight than the effects described in the previous paragraphs. If additional bidders enter the auction, then all bidders will raise their bids, and this effect seems to be more important than the incentive to bid higher which reserve bids provide (see Bulow and Klemperer (1996)). In the SIPV model, when the number of bidders is endogenous, it is optimal not to set any reserve price at all; see McAfee and McMillan (1987) and Levin and Smith (1994).

### 6.4    What should bids look like?

Our discussion of superadditive valuations and complementarities indicated that auction formats which do not give bidders the opportunity to express these by placing package bids create complicated strategic problems for bidders, and inefficiencies. Thus, it seems desirable to offer bidders an opportunity to express in their bids such key aspects of their preferences. On the other hand, excessive flexibility seems to make the strategy space too large. For example, when a multi-object auction calls for package bids for arbitrary combinations of objects, then the strategy space may very soon become too large to be manageable for bidders.

### 6.5   How much information should be revealed?

In the case of single-unit auctions the linkage principle suggests that it is good for revenues to reveal at each stage of a multi-round auction each bid, and the bidder who placed it. On the other hand, the more public bids are, the easier it becomes for bidders to collude in multi-unit or multi-object auctions.

### 6.6   What should be the pricing rule?

It is usually a good rule that the highest bidders win an auction. It is less clear how prices should be determined. However, in general a good rule for determining prices seems to be that each winning bidder should pay for the externality that he imposes on other bidders by winning. The price should therefore be the highest valuation of the other bidders. This idea underlies not only the auction formats proposed by Vickrey, but also the Ausubel auction in the multi-unit case, and the Ausubel–Milgrom auction in the multi-object case. In this context, it is important that the seller can commit himself not to use for other purposes the information that is revealed in such Vickrey auctions. Indeed, bidders in these auctions are willing to bid truthfully only because this information will not be used for pricing purposes. Rothkopf, Teisberg and Kahn (1990) have argued that, in practice, Vickrey auctions are rare since governments will not be able to enter into such commitments. In particular, bidders will fear that the information they reveal in the auction might be used against them after the auction. Furthermore, truthful revelation might also present the government with a problem; when, in New Zealand, the Vickrey auction was used for selling telecommunications licences, the government suffered political trouble because it was revealed that the winning bidder was willing to pay much more than the price he had to pay (see McMillan (1994)).

### 6.7   Risk aversion

Bidders are often averse to risk. This leads to different bidding behaviour from the ones discussed so far in some auction formats, and therefore some of the results explained above no longer hold. Consider the comparison between the first-price sealed-bid auction and the Vickrey auction in the case where bidders have symmetric private values but are risk-averse.

Bidding behaviour in the Vickrey auction will not change: bidding one's true value remains the best strategy, by the same argument that was used in subsection 5.1. However, equilibrium bids in the first-price sealed-bid auction will increase. This can be explained as follows. By raising his bid, a bidder reduces the uncertainty to which he is exposed in return for an additional payment that is to be paid in case of winning the auction. The risk reduction is more valuable to a risk-averse bidder than to a risk-neutral bidder. The marginal incentives to raise his bid are therefore higher for a risk-averse bidder, and risk-averse bidders will bid more in equilibrium than risk-neutral bidders. Because with risk-neutral bidders the Vickrey and the first-price sealed-bid auction yield identical expected revenue, it follows that with risk-averse bidders expected revenues are higher under the first-price sealed-bid format than under the Vickrey format.

Often it is the case that the seller is also risk-averse. In the case of spectrum auctions, for example, it seems plausible that government agencies which sell spectrum would like to avoid as much as possible any uncertainty about the revenues which they receive. In this case, too, the first-price auction is preferable. The intuition is related to the intuition explained above. The first-price auction removes part of the uncertainty about the returns. Conditional on the identity of the winner, and the winner's true valuation of the object, there is no further uncertainty about returns in the first-price auction, but there is such uncertainty in the second-price auction.

### 6.8    Externalities

It has been argued that, in spectrum auctions, bidders' valuations of licences reflect so-called allocative externalities, i.e. that a bidder's valuation of a licence depends on which other bidders get a licence. If bidders' valuation structure incorporates allocative externalities, it becomes much harder to analyse optimal bidding behaviour in standard auctions. Important contributions to this literature are due to Jehiel and Moldovanu (1996, 2000a, 2001). Situations in which such externalities are present can represent formidable strategic complexity for bidders; in fact, equilibria in the standard game-theoretic sense need not exist.

Revenue-maximising mechanisms in the case of positive externalities turn out to be very sophisticated. They require substantial precommitment power by the auctioneer, and seem in practice implausible. If attention is restricted to more simple mechanisms, however, then Jehiel and Moldovanu (2000a, sect. 4.1) obtain an interesting result which is of potential practical relevance: if there are strong negative externalities, and bidders are afraid that licences will fall into the hands of particular competitors, then it might be in the interest of the auctioneer to set a very low reserve price, or to pay for participation. This will intensify bidders' fears that the competitors will obtain licences, and will therefore induce them to bid more aggressively.

Maasland and Onderstal (2002a, b) consider the case of financial externalities, in which auction losers prefer the auction winner to pay more. One reason for such a preference might be that losers meet winners in other markets and that, because of budget constraints, the winner might be a less fierce competitor in these other markets if he has paid more in the auction. The authors show that if such externalities are present, bidders will bid more aggressively in the first-price auction than in the second-price auction, so the seller's expected revenue is higher in the former.

### 6.9    *Fighting collusion*

Bidding rings lower the expected revenue of the auctioneer and, from his point of view, they are, of course, undesirable. The arguments from subsection 5.6 indicate that second-price auctions are more in danger of being manipulated by bidding rings than first-price auctions, and that English auctions are even more vulnerable to collusion. This general argument is also relevant in the case when multiple objects are for sale, but simultaneous ascending auctions are vulnerable to further types of collusion (see Brusco and Lopomo (2002) and chapter 3 in this volume by Salmon). Bidders can agree to share licences in a particular way, and to place very low bids without challenging each other. If any bidder deviates from this agreement, then bidders revert to a more competitive equilibrium. These bidding strategies are self-enforcing. The envisaged collusion relates to market-sharing and differs from the collusion which a bidding ring practises in that all bidders who are participating in the collusion are present in the auction. By contrast, in a bidding ring, only certain members of the bidding ring enter the auction.

The vulnerability of the simultaneous ascending auction to collusion strengthens the case for a sealed-bid format. However, it is unclear how a sealed-bid format could address all the complex issues that this case raises.

### 6.10    *Asymmetries among bidders*

Which auction format should the auctioneer choose when he knows that bidders are asymmetric? The issue is complicated and arguments can be constructed which go either way, in favour of a first-price format, or in favour of a second-price format (see Krishna (2002, sect. 4.3)). However, probably the most important consideration in the context of spectrum auctions is entry. If weaker bidders know in advance that they have a low chance of winning a licence, they will not be willing to participate in the auction. There are a variety of costs associated with participation in the auction. Weak bidders will give these costs more weight than the prospect of winning a licence.

A further interesting intuition regarding asymmetries among bidders is that optimal auction designs will typically seek to favour the weaker bidders, for example by offering them 'bidding credits' (see Myerson (1981) and Maskin and Riley (2000)).

## 7     Conclusion

What lessons can be drawn from the material in this chapter? Frequently, people complain about the advice that economists give, arguing that, if one asks ten economists for advice, one will get eleven different opinions. This complaint is understandable, but probably not always justified. In this specific case, the questions 'What auction should I use as a seller?' and 'How should I bid in this auction?' do not allow for a unique answer, i.e. the answer will be context-dependent and cannot be determined by theory alone.

Economic theory offers two types of general theorems that are very useful. The first type of 'useful' theorem is the 'equivalence theorem' that informs us that it really does not matter what one does. The Revenue Equivalence Theorem falls within this class, as does the Modigliani–Miller Theorem in the area of finance. Such theorems are useful as a theoretical benchmark, as a starting point: if certain conditions hold, it really does not matter what one does. In practice, the conditions underlying these theorems need not hold and this invites further theoretical development about what happens when one of the maintained assumptions is violated. A detailed investigation may then show what is the best thing to do. Since Vickrey started the theoretical study of auctions, this is exactly what has happened in the academic literature of the subject.

This study has shown that the answer of what to do does not admit an easy and uniform answer: the 'optimal' auction depends on the details of the situation. As Paul Klemperer has said: 'Good auction design is not "one size fits all"' (Klemperer, 2002, p. 184). This brings us to the second type of 'useful' theorem that economics offers. These are the so-called impossibility theorems that inform us that it is impossible to find a mechanism that satisfies all the properties that one wants. The best-known impossibility theorem is Arrow's Theorem about the impossibility of aggregating individual preferences into a consistent welfare function. In the field of auctions, there is a similar theorem: there is no single auction that is always best. The auction to use depends on the circumstances of the case and, as several examples in this chapter have shown, getting the details of the auction right may influence whether or not the auction will be a success. The material from the previous sections may be helpful in putting some structure on these details, so that the auction designer can distinguish the forest from the trees, allowing him to implement a better design.

### References

Ashenfelter, O. 1989, 'How auctions work for wine and art', *Journal of Economic Perspectives* 3: 23–36.

Ausubel, L. 2003, 'A generalized Vickrey auction', *Econometrica*, forthcoming.

Ausubel, L. and P. Cramton 1996, 'Demand reduction and inefficiency in multi-unit auctions', mimeo, University of Maryland.

Ausubel, L. and P. Milgrom 2002, 'Ascending auctions with package bidding', *Frontiers of Theoretical Economics* 11, article 1, Berkeley Electronic Press.

Binmore, K. and P. Klemperer 2002, 'The biggest auction ever', *The Economic Journal* 112: C74–C96.

Binmore, K. and J. Swierzbinski 2000, 'Treasury auctions: uniform or discriminatory', *Review of Economic Design* 5: 387–410.

Brusco, S. and G. Lopomo 2002, 'Collusion via signalling in simultaneous ascending bid auctions with multiple objects and complementarities', *Review of Economic Studies*, 69: 407–36.

Bulow, J. and P. Klemperer 1996, 'Auctions versus negotiations', *American Economic Review* 86: 180–94.

Capen, E., R. Clapp and W. Campbell 1971, 'Competitive bidding in high-risk situations', *Journal of Petroleum Technology* 23: 641–53.

Cybernomics 2000, 'An experimental comparison of the simultaneous multiple round auction and the CRA combinatorial auction', Report to the Federal Communications Commission.

Damme, E. van 1999, 'The Dutch DCS-1800 auction', in F. Patrone, I. García-Jurado and S. Tijs (eds.), *Game Practice: Contributions from Applied Game Theory*, Kluwer Academic Publishers, Tilburg.

2002a, 'The Dutch UMTS-auction', *Ifo Studien, Zeitschrift für Wirtschaftsforschung* 1/2002: 175–200.

2002b, 'Pompen en verzuipen' (Pumping and drowning), *Economisch Statistische Berichten* 87–4354: 271–3.

Demange, G., D. Gale and M. Sotomayor 1986, 'Multi-item auctions', *Journal of Political Economy* 94: 863–72.

Engelbrecht-Wiggans, E. and C. Kahn 1998, 'Multi-unit auctions with uniform prices', *Economic Theory* 12: 227–58.

Gilbert, R. and D. Newbery 1982, 'Preemptive patenting and the persistence of monopoly', *American Economic Review*, 72: 514–26.

Graham, D. and R. Marshall 1987, 'Collusive behavior at single-object second-price and English auctions', *Journal of Political Economy* 95: 1217–39.

Grimm, V., F. Riedel and E. Wolfstetter 2002, 'Low price equilibrium in multi-unit auctions: the GSM spectrum auction in Germany', Discussion Paper SFB 373, Humboldt University, Berlin.

Janssen, M., A. Ros and N. van der Windt 2001, 'De draad kwijt? Onderzoek naar de gang van zaken rond de Nederlandse UMTS-veiling' (Research into the proceedings of the Dutch UMTS auction), Erasmus University Rotterdam.

Jehiel, P. and B. Moldovanu 1996, 'Strategic non-participation', *RAND Journal of Economics* 27: 84–98.

2000a, 'Auctions with downstream interaction among buyers', *RAND Journal of Economics* 31: 768–91.

2000b, 'A critique of the planned rules for the German UMTS/IMT-2000 licence auction', mimeo, University College London and University of Mannheim.

2001, 'The European UMTS/ IMT-2000 licence auctions', mimeo, University College London and University of Mannheim.

Kagel, J. 1995, 'Auctions: a survey of experimental research', in J. Kagel and A. Roth (eds.), *The Handbook of Experimental Economics*, Princeton University Press.

Klemperer, P. 2000, 'What really matters in auction design', Working Paper, http://ideas.repec.org/p/wpa/wuwpmi/0004008.html.

2002, 'What really matters in auction design', *Journal of Economic Perspectives* 16: 169–89.

Krishna, V. 2002, *Auction Theory*, Academic Press, San Diego.

Krishna, V. and R. Rosenthal 1996, 'Simultaneous auctions with synergies', *Games and Economic Behavior* 17: 1–31.

Leonard, H. 1983, 'Elicitation of honest preferences for the assignment of individuals to positions', *Journal of Political Economy* 91: 461–79.

Levin, D. and J. Smith 1994, 'Equilibrium in auctions with entry', *American Economic Review* 84: 585–99.

Maasland, E. and S. Onderstal 2002a, 'Auctions with financial externalities', CentER Discussion Paper 22, Tilburg University.

2002b, 'Optimal auctions with financial externalities', CentER Discussion Paper 21, Tilburg University.

Maskin, E. and J. Riley 2000, 'Asymmetric auctions', *Review of Economic Studies* 67: 413–38.

McAfee, P. and J. McMillan 1987, 'Auctions with entry', *Economics Letters* 23: 343–47.

1992, 'Bidding rings', *American Economic Review* 82: 579–99.

McAfee, P., J. McMillan and P. Reny 1989, 'Extracting the surplus in a common value auction', *Econometrica* 57: 1451–60.

McMillan, J. 1994, 'Selling spectrum rights', *Journal of Economic Perspectives* 8: 145–62.

Milgrom, P. 2000, 'Putting auction theory to work: the simultaneous ascending auction', *Journal of Political Economy* 108: 245–72.

Milgrom, P. and R. Weber 1982, 'A theory of auctions and competitive bidding', *Econometrica* 50: 1089–122.

Myerson, R. 1981, 'Optimal auction design', *Mathematics of Operations Research* 6: 58–73.

Perry, M. and P. Reny 1999, 'On the failure of the linkage principle in multi-unit auctions', *Econometrica* 67: 895–900.

Pesendorfer, W. and J. Swinkels 1997, 'The loser's curse and information aggregation in common value auctions', *Econometrica* 65: 1247–81.

Rothkopf, M., T. Teisberg and E. Kahn, 1990, 'Why are Vickrey auctions rare?', *Journal of Political Economy* 98: 94–110.

Vickrey, W. 1961, 'Counterspeculation, auctions and competitive sealed tenders', *Journal of Finance* 16: 8–37.

    1962, 'Auctions and bidding games', in *Recent Advances in Game Theory*, Princeton University Press. Reprinted in R. Arnott *et al.*, *Public Economics: Selected Papers by William Vickrey*, Cambridge University Press (1994).

Williamson, O. 1976, 'Franchise bidding for natural monopolies: in general and with respect to CATV', *Bell Journal of Economics* 7: 73–104.

Wilson, R. 1979, 'Auctions of shares', *Quarterly Journal of Economics* 94: 675–89.

# 2    Beauty Contest design

*Maurice Dykstra and Nico van der Windt*

## 1    Introduction

Beauty Contests are very common in the procurement of goods and services in the public and private sectors. The public sector has also frequently used Beauty Contests for allocating rights to the private sector to produce goods and services, such as the right to exploit radio frequencies for several purposes or the right to exploit railways or other networks. Although the basic principles of Beauty Contests in both applications are the same, the discussion in this chapter focuses on Beauty Contests as an allocation mechanism.

A Beauty Contest is just one mechanism in a range of allocation modalities, such as lotteries, first-come-first-served allocations, Beauty Contests, auctions, etc. It can be argued that among these modalities Beauty Contests are best suited for projects where there is scope for innovation and different approaches by developers and where authorities hope to elicit imaginative proposals for projects. According to this argument, Beauty Contests permit developers to be creative and to tailor projects to the particular needs of the government since the terms are mostly not fully fixed beforehand. For example, procurement of research projects is for this reason virtually always decided by means of a Beauty Contest.

Despite Beauty Contests' widespread use in procurement and allocation, the economic literature on their design is (almost) non-existent.[1] This chapter is therefore based on practical experience, rather than on existing literature.

The main objective of this chapter is to explain the place of Beauty Contests in the context of allocation mechanisms. Against this background it provides a description of the core characteristics of a Beauty Contest (section 2); discusses the reasons for applying a Beauty Contest to the sale of concessions (section 3); and discusses the pros and cons of several practicable Beauty Contest formats and summarises the main features

---

[1] Cabizza and De Fraja (1998) and De Fraja and Hartley (1996) are two examples of exceptions.

of Beauty Contests in the light of the criteria usually applied in judging various allocation mechanisms, such as transparency, value revelation, etc. in section 4.

## 2  Allocation mechanisms

### 2.1  Typology

In practice, a wide variety of different forms of Beauty Contest can be observed. The differences concern both the ways in which the process of the Beauty Contest is organised and how the various substantive elements are treated. The process can consist of several phases, from pre-qualification to the adjudication stage during which the final bids are submitted and judged (as, for example, in the case of a restricted tender). In other cases the process is a single-step procedure in which essentially anybody is allowed to participate (for example, in the case of an open tender procedure). The elements that are taken into consideration to determine the 'beauty' of the bids also differ between one contest and another, even when it concerns the same or similar products and services. Despite these differences Beauty Contests can be characterised by two main dimensions:
• the attributes on which the bids are judged: quality and price; and
• the score function applied in the contest.
In general, both quality and price can be either exogenous or endogenous to an allocation mechanism. In a lottery both are treated exogenously. In most auctions price is endogenous to the allocation mechanism while quality is determined exogenously. And although the name suggests that in Beauty Contests only beauty (quality) is the endogenous attribute in the process, practice shows that often both quality and price are treated endogenously.

Beauty Contests can be divided into two main groups: weighted and unweighted Beauty Contests. In weighted Beauty Contests it is clear from the start how the various quality aspects and price are weighed. A formal algorithm gives weights to the price and quality attributes. In contrast, in an unweighted Beauty Contest the ways in which the various aspects of the bid are treated is not clear, at least not *ex ante*. In other words the bidders have to prepare their bids under uncertainty about how the elements are weighed by those who judge the bids.

The awarding authority cannot directly observe what quantity the concessionaire will produce, at what price and at what quality level, prior to selling the concession. What it does observe is a plethora of bid data in the form of observable characteristics and attributes of the bid, and it is these that must ultimately determine the authority's assessment of the value of the bid. In both the weighted and unweighted Beauty Contests the initial ratings of each quality attribute are determined judgementally. These ratings reflect the subjective views of the awarding authority. In the weighted contest the ratings are subsequently 'summed up' using given *ex ante* weights, while in the unweighted Beauty Contests the summing up is done judgementally.

## 2.2     Quality

Before embarking on a discussion of the various Beauty Contest mechanisms it is essential to say something about what quality often means in the context of a Beauty Contest. Quality can be characterised along the lines of structure, process and performance.

*Structural attributes* refer primarily to characteristics of the bidder. How far can he guarantee that the bid made is upheld? Characteristics are, for instance, a proven track record in a certain line of business, the experience and expertise of the workforce, certification, company finances, etc. One can even question to what extent quality is at stake here. These characteristics are rather signals of quality than actual quality. Spence (1976) describes signals as 'activities or attributes of individuals in a market which alter the beliefs of, or convey information to, other individuals in the market'. The signaller tries to 'create a favourable impression or, more precisely, to affect the [receiver's] subjective probabilistic beliefs'.

*Process attributes* refer primarily to characteristics of the implementation phase of the project for which a bid is made. Bidders submit detailed business plans with information on the proposed investment plan, promised additional investments, organisational plan, roll-out plans, speed of deployment, delivery time etc.[2]

*Performance attributes* refer primarily to characteristics of the product or service as such. Characteristics are, for instance, types of service, technology used to supply services, reliability of service, speed of service etc.

Although an awarding authority should have clearly expressed in the specification what they require to be delivered, a Beauty Contest can allow bidders to add value by suggesting alternative deliverables. These alternatives could include, for example, the delivery of different requirements or different bases for measuring the aspect of performance required. It has to be decided in advance whether the awarding authority should be open

[2] Changing market conditions after the award of a contract often require operators to make significant (and justifiable) modifications in their business plans and investment programmes. These changes reduce the meaningfulness of the evaluation process to the extent that it relied heavily on the assessment of the proposed business plans. See also Affuso and Newbery (chapter 12 in this volume).

to such alternatives and – in as far as may be legally permissible – should conduct the Beauty Contest in such a way that alternative proposals from bidders can be considered.

In the practice of Beauty Contests the attribute quality is usually sub-divided into say four or five different sub-attributes, which in turn consist of a number of characteristic features. This leads to a hierarchy of criteria.

Finally, in order to make an assessment of the quality of a bid, quality attributes and criteria must be measurable, in the sense that it must be possible to assess, at least in a qualitative sense, how well a particular option is expected to perform in relation to a criterion.

### 2.3    Weighted or unweighted

For the transparency of the selection process, it would be beneficial if beforehand it could be made clear how the various quality aspects and price are to be weighed in the Beauty Contest. However, for various reasons it is quite difficult to define the weights *ex ante*.

First of all, in a Beauty Contest (but also in other allocation mechanisms) the bidding parties are usually better informed about the properties of the (object of the) transaction than the awarding authority. Therefore, an important characteristic of this bidding mechanism is the extent to which it reveals information. The awarding authority may make inferences from the information provided by the more informed party, the bidders. As a result it is often easier to compare concrete bids *ex post* than to devise all-encompassing formal definitions, rules and procedures *ex ante*. Therefore, the uneven distribution of information over awarding authority and bidder makes it difficult to specify how the bids will be judged.

Since quality plays an important role in the comparison of the various bids, and quality is usually difficult to quantify, it can be argued that a quantitative evaluation scheme simply cannot accurately represent the value of differing bids in a Beauty Contest. It should therefore not be used as a substitute for the necessary exercise of informed judgement when attempting to address the necessary trade-off between price and quality and suggesting that it is possible to apply a quantitative measure. Following this argument, awarding authorities should be prepared to be flexible and open to proposals. This is especially the case when the awarding authority is interested in alternative innovative ideas for the product or service to be delivered. A clear benefit of weighting is that it disciplines the awarding authority. It makes it much more difficult to favour a certain bidder on the ground of, say, a single attribute – which happens to be the hobby-horse of one of the evaluators – on which the bidder has a high score.

## 3    When should a Beauty Contest be held?

Below we list a number of economic reasons underlying the decision of a government to conduct the sale of a concession by means of a Beauty Contest.

(1) *Price is not a relevant item.* An architectural design competition can be considered as the archetype of a pure Beauty Contest. Such competitions are often intended to create new innovative concepts along which lines the building will later be designed in detail. In the design competition the price of the building plays little or no role at all. In the context of concessions, an example might be a competition for a permit for experimental research of certain gene technologies with the simultaneous prohibition of experimentation by other research groups.

(2) *Not all relevant information is contained in the price.* This may be the case when equity, fairness or externalities are part of the objective function of the awarding authority or when valuation of the item is incomplete due to the existence of missing markets. (see chapter 5 by Janssen and Moldovanu in this volume).

Failure to use the price system as a screening device in the allocation of resources may not be entirely irrational. Sometimes one cares about individual attributes other than marginal rates of substitution of income for whatever it is that is being offered. In some traditional marriage markets the presumptive lover is required to spend uncomfortable hours on the doorstep in order to gain access to the young woman's company. This is intended to screen out the less serious suitors. The girl's family is not interested in the suitor's marginal willingness to pay money as such, unless they are profit-maximisers. Willingness to pay in any medium is a signal and not a measure of what the person is interested in (Spence, 1973, p. 657)

If the concession under sale has some merit character (e.g. public television or public radio), government may wish to take a 'paternalistic' approach to quality. The quality at stake is then not what the consumers perceive as such, but what reflects the television authority's tastes. If the seller of the franchise and the consumers have the same tastes, then quality would be chosen as reflected in the consumer's willingness to pay, and the authority can leave the choice of quality to the winning firm.[3]

---

[3] Additionally the regulator will have to take measures to prevent welfare loss arising from the monopolist setting too high a price and too low a quality.

(3) *Integrated assessment.* The awarding authority wants to make a trade-off between quality and price (e.g. in the procurement of military equipment, or the procurement of research activities). When goods or services are heterogeneous, some projects require to be evaluated on several dimensions and not only on price.

(4) *Minimum quality cannot be set.* The cost of quality is unknown to the awarding authorities or it can only be gathered at prohibitively high cost. This may be the case when potential bidders do not wish to show their cards beforehand or if business is so new that government has insufficient information to set a cost figure on the various quality levels (see Dykstra and de Koning (this volume, chapter 11). Setting minimum quality standards may be prohibitively expensive for all save a few companies. This could inhibit bidding competition.[4]

To have a fair bidding process, one has to specify precisely what is being bid for. Even fairly simple commodities may require pages upon pages of specifications. Compliance with bidding regulations can become so difficult that relatively few bidders can partake in the competition. This may inhibit the competition in itself.

The awarding authority may not wish to set a minimum quality out of fear of setting too high a quality level, which might limit consumer choice.

(5) *Minimising transaction costs.* There may be a trade-off between the activities of the awarding authority and that of the regulator of the concession. Issuing a concession is usually done for a relatively long time period. One thing that government will wish to avoid is the unsatisfactory operation of the concession by the concessionaire. To prevent this, costs related to error avoidance, such as search, bargaining and negotiation, monitoring and enforcement costs, will have to be incurred. The failure to bear these transaction costs can produce a wholly unsatisfactory outcome, one that can often be corrected only at great expense (cost of errors). Minimising transaction costs means minimising the sum of the cost of errors and the cost of error avoidance. This points to the issue of credibility: bids have to be credible. In a Beauty Contest there is scope for assessing credibility on the basis of certain quality criteria.[5]

---

[4] In the competition rules, a clause could be included that allows the possibility of not proceeding with the contest, or of proceeding in a different manner, if the number of bidders is too small.

[5] Another possibility is that the overall judgement of the bid is that the bid is not credible. This may, for instance, be the case if the awarding authority believes that their financial bids are so high that they would not have enough left to pay for their quality commitments.

## 4      Bidding mechanisms

### 4.1      *Valuation of quality: minimum or score*

Before the awarding authority can fix the total quality score the various quality attributes of the bids have to be judged and scores attached to them. Multi-criteria analysis (MCA) provides a large range of techniques for constructing scores and assigning weights, and methods for making overall quality judgements.[6] Below we present only a few basic notions on how to aggregate quality scores.

Although in principle many aggregation schemes are possible, in practice (quasi-)linear models are usually observed, for example

$$Q = \sum w_i Q_i$$

where $Q$ is the total quality score, $Q_i$ are the scores for the separate quality attributes and $w_i$ are the weights of the quality attributes.

Notice that in this case all attributes can compensate for one another. Lower scores on one criterion can be offset by higher scores on other criteria, i.e. trade-offs are modelled. It is possible, for instance, that a bidder who offers a low-quality product, but is very experienced, could win the competition. One way to remedy this is by giving experience a low weight. Another way is by defining thresholds for each attribute. If a bid fails on one of these attributes the bid is disqualified, no matter how good the bid is on other attributes.

The general form of the score function of this type is thus

$$Q = \sum w_i Q_i \quad \text{if } Q_i > Q_{i\,\text{min}}; \text{ otherwise } Q = 0.$$

---

A signal for this may be that the financial bids are far out of line from the other bids. In the Beauty Contest rules, a clause perhaps could be included which allows the possibility that bidders who have made the highest bids are, none the less, not designated as winners.

[6]  In the allocation of concessions, conducting a formal multi-criteria analysis can be very beneficial to the decision-making process. DTLR (2001) lists as advantages of MCA over informal judgement unsupported by analysis:
  • it is open and explicit;
  • the choice of objectives and criteria that any decision-making group may make are open to analysis and to change if they are felt to be inappropriate;
  • scores and weights, when used, are also explicit and are developed according to established techniques. They can also be cross-referenced to other sources of information on relative values, and amended if necessary;
  • performance measurement can be subcontracted to experts, so need not necessarily be left in the hands of the decision-making body itself;
  • it can provide an important means of communication, within the decision-making body and sometimes, later, between that body and the wider community; and since scores and weights are used, it provides an audit trail.

The question of the extent to which the model should be compensatory also again brings to mind the important question of which quality dimensions should be included in the adjudication phase. Should quality characteristics, which are signals of quality rather than measures of actual quality, such as proven track record or expertise of workforce, be substitutable for product quality, for example? If the answer is negative, the signalling quality characteristics should be excluded from the adjudication stage and instead be included in a pre-qualification stage.

If one does wish to include such an attribute in the adjudication stage, as an extra check on the credibility of bids, it is possible to do so simply in the form of a threshold.[7] An example: if experience is subject to a quality threshold, only bids that pass the threshold qualify. The score on experience is not included in the final score. Thus

$$Q = \sum w_i Q_{i \neq e} \quad \text{if } Q_e > Q_{e\min}.$$

Above we have presented a few alternatives for the scoring rule.

Obviously, different scoring rules can lead to different winners. Three examples are presented in Box 1.

---

**BOX 1. EXAMPLES OF SCORING RULES**

**A. EC procurement tender for research**

For each of the five areas, a brief description of the qualitatative award criteria is given together with the area's weighting in terms of a maximum number of points.

(1) Overall quality, methodology and exhaustive nature of the analysis proposed for performance of the study (20 points).
(2) Proven track record in relation to the distribution sector and quality of human resources to be made available for the conduct of the study (studies, publications) (20 points).
(3) Expertise in the field of statistical analysis (20 points).
(4) Level of knowledge of the legal framework and functioning of the internal market (20 points).
(5) Ability to cover the Member States of the European Union in a uniform and consistent manner (20 points).

A bid with less than 10 points on any one of the criteria is disqualified. In addition the bidder has to offer a price for which he is prepared to conduct the research. The winning bid is the one with the highest number of points per euro.

*Source:* http://ted.eur-op.eu.int/

---

[7] This rule consequently functions as a second pre-qualification.

**B. Demonstration project for a wind park in the North Sea**
In the field of procurement an interesting project is that of a demonstration wind park. The principal was the Netherlands Ministry of Economic Affairs. Criteria related to the quality of the bidder, the quality of the project plan, the financial underpinning of the project and the demonstration value of the project. There is no limit to the price that may be offered, but if the bid sum exceeds €9.1 million there is a reduction of the points available.
*Source*: Press release by the Netherlands Ministry of Economic Affairs, 29 October 2001.

**C. Beauty Contest for a second GSM licence in Morocco**
In this Beauty Contest an explicit weighting was made between quality on the one hand (the technical rating) and price on the other. The total score was the sum of the score for the total technical rating and the score for the price offered. The maximum number of points for the technical rating was 40. The highest-price bid was set at 60 points. The valuations of the lower price bids were proportionately lower. So a bid 25 per cent lower than the highest-price bid received 45 points ((100–25)%*60). The winner was the one with the greatest number of points. Given the large weight placed on the price element, this Beauty Contest came close to being a first-price sealed-bid auction.
*Source:* http://www.itu.int/itudoc/itu-d/publicat/ma_ca_st.html (accessed at 24 February 2003).

## 4.2    'Adding up' of quality and price

As with the difficulties of aggregating quality aspects, it is difficult to specify general rules for weighing quality with price.

In a weighted Beauty Contest the score function brings the price and quality elements together into a comprehensive ranking. The score function $S = S(Q, p)$ is one or other form of a utility index. It gives an exact representation of the relationships between the attributes. The bidders know the algorithm (functional form and parameter values). They do not however know the value of the attributes they have included in their bid. In practice the functional form of the score function is usually linear:

$$S = aQ + (1 - a)p.$$

Without loss of generality we can stipulate that for both quality and price a maximum of 100 points can be scored. The highest-price bid equates to 100 points irrespective of the height of the bid. The total maximum score is then also 100.

Similar to the problems involved with putting weights on various quality attributes, setting explicit weights for quality versus price can be arbitrary

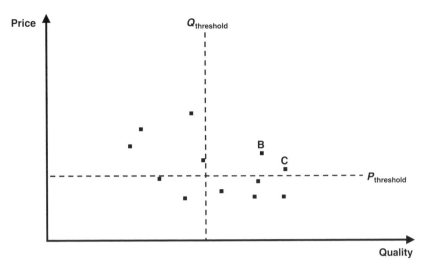

Figure 2.1. Different procedures can lead to different outcomes.

and difficult. By using a two-step procedure this explicit choice can be partly circumvented.

*First quality, then price.* In the first step the bids are evaluated on a pass/no pass basis. Only the bids that offer the highest quality (for instance, the bids which score 80 points or more, or the top 40 per cent) pass on to the second step. In step two the winning bidder is then strictly selected on price. The highest-price bid is then winner, irrespective of the quality offered, given that the bidder has passed the quality threshold.

*First price, then quality.* A similar procedure can be followed, but in this case the pass/no pass test is on price. Only the bids that offer the highest price, say the top 40 per cent, pass on to the second step. In step two the winning bidder is then strictly selected on quality. The highest-quality bid is then winner, irrespective of the price offered, given that the bidder has passed the price threshold.

The different rules may lead to different outcomes.[8] Figure 2.1 shows an example of a number of imaginary bids, where for illustration purposes it is assumed that the bids are not dependent on the procedure followed. Following the linear score function rule, bid A would be the winner if

---

[8] For instance, this may be the case when framing is an issue. The idea of framing is that different phrasings of the choice problem call to mind different possibilities, or lead to different ways of considering the problem. The experimental work on framing effects clearly shows that the phrasing of the choice problem can affect the decision in a non-trivial fashion. See, for example, Shafir, Simonson and Tversky (1993).

Table 2.1. *Bidding rules*

|  | Sealed/bid | Open bid |
|---|---|---|
| Simultaneous | I | II |
| Sequential: first a quality bid is made. Score of bid is made open to all bidders. | III | IV |
| Sequential: first a price bid is made. Score of bid is made open to all bidders. | V | VI |

a relatively high weight was placed on price relative to quality. Using the 'first quality, then price' procedure, bid B is the winner, while if the 'first price, then quality' procedure was followed, bid C would be the winner.

### 4.3    Combining quality and price in sealed and open formats

An important theme in the relationship between the quality bid and the financial bid is what bidders know of one another at the moment the financial bid is placed. In relation to this issue in auctions, one distinction that is made is that between sealed and open formats. For Beauty Contests the same distinction can be made. With regards to information availability to bidders the important difference is that in closed Beauty Contests – in contrast to open Beauty Contests – bidding parties do not know from each other (unless collusion is taking place) what the others are offering and which bid may have to be overbid. This characteristic of being open or sealed can be combined with another one: the order in which bids on quality and price are made. Bids can be made either simultaneously or sequentially. In the sequential version one first makes a quality bid and then a price bid, or the other way around. This means that there are six possible variants, as depicted in table 2.1.

For various reasons, not all variants are likely to come about in practice. The areas I, III and IV designate the formats we believe to be practicable. Below we briefly explain the six variants.

(I) In this format each bidder places only one bid. The bid contains offers on both quality and price. Beyond knowing which parties are partaking in the bidding, the bidders know nothing of what others are bidding on quality and price. In procurement tenders the contest is usually a sealed-bid one.

(II) A quality bid and a price bid are placed simultaneously. Besides the fact that parties may know who is partaking in the bidding, they also at least know what the highest prevailing bid (on quality and price) is.[9]

One can hardly imagine that this format could be used in practice. The scope for raising the quality bid is quite limited. Structural quality features (see subsection 2.2) such as past performance are *de facto* unalterable. It may be possible to raise a bid marginally with regard to some process features or performance features. However, doing so would mean altering the business plan of the bidder in the event he won the bid. Changing a business plan involves substantial time, effort and cost. If the quality bid could be altered significantly this would also raise questions concerning the credibility of the bidder.

Raising the bid will thus be nearly entirely accounted for by the price element. It would then strongly resemble an auction and come close to bidding variant IV (see below).

(III) Besides knowing which parties are partaking in the bidding, the bidders also know how the others have scored on the quality dimension. This knowledge can be used in the one-off financial bid. This system resembles a closed-bid auction with a bid handicap. One's quality score in relation to the highest quality-score bid determines the bid handicap. In the case where the quality score is used as a threshold and the final score includes only price, the competition is no longer a Beauty Contest but an auction.

(IV) For the bidding parties this is the most transparent situation. They know how others have scored on quality and they know the bids during the second stage. It is not the case that the highest-price bid wins, but at any moment everyone can ascertain who the highest bidder is and what the highest bid is. This resembles an English auction with a bid handicap, in which the quality score determines the bid handicap. In the case where the quality score is used as a threshold and the final score includes only price, the competition is in fact no longer a Beauty Contest but an auction.

(V) Besides knowing which parties are partaking in the bidding, the bidders also know how the others have scored on the price dimension. This knowledge can be used in the one-off quality bid. This system resembles a closed-bid auction with a bid handicap, in which one's bid handicap is determined by the price one has bid in relation to the highest-price bid.

---

[9] Here variants are conceivable. The question is what is made public at which moment: all bids or only the highest one; the combination of identity and bid of each bidder or only of the highest bidder.

Table 2.2. *Evaluation of bidding rules*

| | Simultaneous sealed bid (I) | Sequential sealed bid (III) | Sequential open bid (IV) |
|---|---|---|---|
| Winner's curse | − | −/+ | + |
| Externalities | − | −/+ | + |
| Value revelation | − | − | −/+ |
| Transparency for bidder | − | −/+ | + |
| Transparency for awarding authority | + | + | + |
| Costs and time span of implementation | + | −/+ | − |

One can hardly imagine that this format could be used in practice. For a bidder to set an appropriate price without knowing the associated quality level is a bridge too far. One can only set a well-argued price after choosing a certain quality level.[10] In addition the scope for varying the level of quality is quite limited (see bidding variant II).

(VI) In this format, bidders first place a price bid and then can sequentially place higher bids on quality. Bidders can submit bids as often as they want to, and they have knowledge of all previous bids. For the reasons mentioned under variants II and V this format does not seem to be viable.

This leaves us with three feasible formats: the simultaneous sealed bid, the sequential quality-then-price sealed bid and the sequential quality-then-price open bid.

In the rest of this section we compare the three formats in terms of a number of criteria used in the discussions on auction formats: winner's curse, externalities, value revelation, transparency for both the bidder and the authority and cost of implementation.[11] Table 2.2 summarises our qualitative judgements of the three formats in terms of these criteria.

*Winner's curse* In the sequential open-bid format (IV), a bidder can retrieve information from the bidding behaviour of the other bidders about the value of the concession. Bidders thus run a lesser chance of bidding too high a quality and/or paying too much for the

[10] Unless quality and price are unrelated. This would be the case if expected profit does not vary with quality.
[11] For example, Janssen Ros and van der Windt (2001) or OECD (2001).

licence (the so-called winner's curse). Therefore the open-bid mechanism (IV) scores a '+'. The simultaneous sealed-bid format (I) does not have this information-generating feature, and consequently scores a '−'. The sequential sealed-bid format (III) occupies an intermediate position. Bidders retrieve information on the quality bids made. Building on this information they provide the sealed price bid.

*Externalities*   The problem of externalities arises when the value of the concession to a bidder depends on the identity of the competitors. In a sealed-bid competition a bidder has little notion who the winner will be. It is accordingly extremely difficult to hand in a bid, because the value of the concession to the bidder depends on something that is unknown at the time of making the bid. The simultaneous sealed-bid format (I) therefore scores a '−'. In an open competition the parties can more easily monitor who is still participating in the bidding. This makes bidding much easier so that in general the outcome will lead to a more efficient result. The sequential open-bid format (IV) thus scores a '+'. The sequential sealed-bid format (III) again holds an intermediate position. Bidders retrieve information on the quality bids made. Building on this information they can provide a sealed-price bid, which is better informed than in the sealed-bid setting, but less informed than in the open format.

*Value revelation*   In the simultaneous sealed-bid format (I) bidders will bid less than their true value, because they make the trade-off between their price-quality bid and the probability of winning the competition. Their true values are thus not revealed. The open format also delivers much information about the values of the bidding parties. Not all values, however, are revealed. For instance, if the second stage has the format of an English auction the value of the winner is not revealed. The open format (IV) thus scores a '−/+'.

The sequential sealed-bid format (III) may have a slight edge over the simultaneous sealed-bid format (I) on account of its quality-revealing properties. However, in this format bidders will likewise bid less than their true value, because they make the trade-off between their price bid and the probability of winning the competition. We score the sequential sealed format the same as the simultaneous sealed format: a '−'.

*Transparency for bidder*   The more information is provided, the more transparent is the contest. The second stage of the sequential open-bid format may be considered to have strong private-value features given that each bidder has previously made his own quality bid. In the private-value context, bidding in an open format (IV) is relatively easy. One can simply continue bidding until one's true value is reached given the quality one has bid. This format thus scores a '+'. In the simultaneous sealed-bid format (I), bidding is more difficult since there is little 'hard' information on the bids of one's competitors; it consequently scores a '−'. The sequential sealed bid (III) holds an intermediate position.

*Transparency for awarding authority*   We see no obvious reasons why one format is more transparent for the awarding authority than the other. This is of course conditional on the mechanisms being well designed with clear and unambiguous rules. Accordingly all variants score a '+'.

*Costs and time span of implementation*   The costs for both the awarding authorities and the bidders will presumably be lowest in the simultaneous sealed formats and highest in the open format, with the sequential sealed format taking an intermediate position. Likewise, the period of time necessary to run the competition will be lowest in the closed-bid formats and highest in the open format.

*Total*   The final choice, of course, depends on the weights placed on the various elements. The sequential open bid scores highest on all counts save the costs and time span of implementation. In contrast, the simultaneous sealed bid is nearly the exact opposite: it scores lowest on all counts save the costs and time span of implementation.

## 5     Conclusion

In this chapter we have tried to characterise Beauty Contests, with an emphasis on the informational aspects relating to allocation mechanisms.

We mentioned several reasons why a Beauty Contest may be an appropriate allocation mechanism. The validity of these reasons in practice depends strongly on the specifics of each case. These reasons relate especially to informational aspects surrounding the allocation procedure such as, for instance, whether or not all relevant information is contained in the price bid, whether or not the awarding authority can set minimum quality *ex ante*, and minimising transaction costs.

A major challenge in designing a Beauty Contest is how to weigh quality and price. We described several aspects of the design which entail different informational demands on the format design, such as weighted or unweighted score functions, and the adding up of scores or the use of thresholds.

Depending on the properties of the mechanism, a Beauty Contest resembles an auction to a lesser or greater extent. Obviously the Beauty Contest that least resembles an auction is one in which a price element is not incorporated, such as in an architectural design competition. A format that strongly resembles an auction is the sequential open-bid format. This type is very similar to an English auction with a bid handicap, in which the quality score determines the bid handicap. In fact, if the quality score were used as a threshold the format would be an open auction with a pre-qualification stage.

## References

Cabizza, M. and G. De Fraja 1998, 'Quality considerations in auctions for television franchises', *Information Economics and Policy* 10: 9–22.

De Fraja, G. and K. Hartley 1996, 'Defence procurement: theory and UK policy', *Oxford Review of Economic Policy*, 12(4): 70–88.

DTLR (Department for Transport, Local Government and the Regions) 2001, *Multicriteria Analysis: A Manual*, http://www.dtlr.gov.uk/about/multicriteria/ (accessed at 26 February 2003).

Janssen, M., A. Ros and N. van der Windt 2001, 'De draad kwijt? Onderzoek naar de gang van zaken rond de Nederlandse UMTS-veiling' (Research into the proceedings of the Dutch UMTS auction), Erasmus University Rotterdam.

OECD 2001, 'Spectrum allocation: auctions and comparative selection procedures', DSTI/ICCP/TISP(2000)12/FINAL, Paris.

Shafir, E., I. Simonson and A. Tversky 1993, 'Reason–based choice', *Cognition* 49, Reprinted in D. Kahneman and A. Tversky (eds.), *Choices, Values, and Frames*, Cambridge University Press (2000).

Spence, A. M. 1973, 'Time and communication in economic and social interaction', *Quarterly Journal of Economics* 87: 651–60.

1976, 'Informational aspects of market structure: an introduction', *Quarterly Journal of Economics* 90: 591–7.

# 3    Preventing collusion among firms in auctions

*Timothy C. Salmon*

## 1    Introduction

Collusion among bidders in auctions is a serious concern for those interested in designing procedures to allocate public assets whether the goal of the process is efficiency or revenue maximisation. In either case, bidders acting collusively can seriously impair an auctioneer's ability to accomplish their goal. There has been a wide variety of examples of collusion discussed in the economic literature, including collusive bidding for school milk contracts (Pesendorfer, 2000), in cattle auctions (Phillips, Menkhaus and Coatney, 2001), in timber auctions (Baldwin, Marshall and Richard, 1997) and, of course, in spectrum auctions, which will be the focus of this study. We will present a brief survey of recent literature on collusion problems mostly in ascending auctions and then go on to discuss the Federal Communications Commission's (FCC) experience in dealing with collusion in their auctions as a case study in how the lessons from this literature can be applied.

We will be discussing both ascending and sealed-bid auction formats and the incentives for collusion embedded in each, but the focus will be on ascending auctions. Ascending auctions are the primary focus of the literature on collusion in auctions owing to the fact that ascending auctions are more susceptible to 'in-auction' collusion than sealed-bid auctions. The term in-auction collusion is used to refer to collusion that can emerge and be enforced inside a single auction. While sealed-bid auctions are less susceptible to in-auction collusion they are still susceptible to forms of collusion stemming from interactions among the bidders outside of the auction itself. Similarly, our focus will be on multi-unit auctions rather

The author of this survey was formerly an economist with the Auctions & Industry Analysis Division of the FCC and many of the details of the FCC case-study section were learned during that time. The opinions expressed on why the FCC made various decisions, however, are not necessarily those of the FCC or any other employee of the Commission past or present. Thanks to Emiel Maasland and Maarten Janssen for many helpful comments on early drafts.

than single-unit auctions as collusion is more likely in the former than the latter for similar reasons.

Ascending auctions have become quite popular as mechanisms for allocating public resources, as clearly demonstrated by their widespread use in spectrum licence allocations in many countries around the world. The primary reasons for adoption in most cases are that they are generally thought to deliver highly efficient allocations and it seems quite simple for most bidders to figure out how to bid in them. An example of this reasoning is found in Binmore and Klemperer (2002) in which they note exactly these reasons in describing why the UK decided to adopt this format for its UMTS auction. Ascending auctions are thought to be easy to bid in because when there is a single unit of the good available for auction, the bidders know what the object is worth to themselves and if the clock, or Japanese, version of the ascending auction is used, it is a well-known result that the dominant strategy of the game for each bidder is simply to stay in the auction until the price reaches the level of what the bidder believes the object is worth to them and then drop out.[1] Equilibrium strategies in multi-unit auctions are more difficult to derive, but an extrapolation of the single-unit strategy called 'straightforward bidding' is thought to be a reasonable and simple way bidders might approach bidding in such auctions. This strategy involves bidders bidding on the objects that would yield the most surplus to the bidder, given the current prices, so long as the prices are less than their value for the objects. Such a strategy is easy to learn and follow and it has been shown by Demange, Gale and Sotomayor (1986) and Milgrom (2000) that if bidders were to follow such simple strategies, it would lead to approximately efficient outcomes.

If bidders always did engage in straightforward bidding, these results would provide a strong foundation upon which to argue for the use of ascending auctions. Bidders, however, do not always follow this strategy. As we shall discuss below, there are a number of alternative strategies bidders can and do pursue in multi-item ascending auctions that can lead to the bidders achieving a greater level of expected utility, while leaving the auctioneer with less revenue and perhaps the social planner with less efficiency than if the bidders had bid straightforwardly. These strategies

---

[1] The Japanese, or clock, version of the ascending auction involves the auctioneer using a continuous clock to slowly raise the price, with all bidders who are currently 'in' indicating by, for example, standing up in the room. As the price rises, bidders can choose to irrevocably exit the auction by sitting. The winner is the last bidder standing and they pay the price on the clock when the last bidder dropped out. The bidding strategy for the non-clock version of the ascending auction, in which bidders are allowed to submit bids to top a standing-high bidder, is a little more complex although sharing some of the same general properties, and can be found in Isaac, Salmon and Zillante (2002).

represent various approaches to bidders colluding among themselves to end up with an outcome they prefer to the competitive outcome. In situations in which such collusion seems likely, it is definitely important for auctioneer to understand how and why collusion can impact their auctions.

Towards this end, the next section will review some of the recent theoretical, experimental and empirical literature to see what types of collusive strategies exist in these auctions, how likely they are to be played, as well as how one might design auctions either to minimise the possibility of collusion or to minimise its impact. The third section of the chapter will discuss a case study of the FCC's auction programme to see what types of collusion have been experienced in their auctions, how the FCC has dealt with them and how the FCC has altered its rules over time in an attempt to minimise future collusion. We use the FCC as a case study for this purpose because it is an ongoing auction programme that has evolved its approach to dealing with collusion over time in response to specific instances of attempted collusion. These examples and the public nature of the discussion around them make this an excellent environment in which to study the auction design problems arising from collusion. It is also the case that the FCC's experiences with collusion have inspired much of the recent theoretical and empirical literature on collusion and so, in discussing these papers, it is a natural follow-up to discuss their impact on the FCC's programme.

## 2    Review of literature on collusion

### 2.1    *Strategies for collusion*

There has been a large number of papers developing the types of collusive strategy inherent in multi-unit ascending auctions. One of the more important forms of collusion that can exist in either multi-unit or single-unit repeated auctions was formally introduced by Robinson (1985), though of course the subject had been discussed previously, who developed models of bidder cartels or rings in auctions. A bidder cartel is a group of bidders that decides to bid as a single entity rather than as independent bidders. If we assume that there are $n$ bidders involved in an auction and $k \leq n$ of them are involved in a cartel, then the cartel works by having the cartel member with the highest value for the item in that particular auction bidding as they would in a normal auction while the others in the ring submit non-competitive bids or stay out entirely. This will usually allow the cartel member to win the item at a lower price than if they had to bid against the other members of their cartel. Robinson (1985) shows that such cartels are stable in ascending auctions but unstable in first-price sealed-bid auctions without repeated interaction. Stability in this case means that all members of the cartel achieve higher expected utilities by remaining members of the cartel rather than attempting to compete against it.

The reason cartels are stable in ascending auctions is that, at least in the single-unit private values setting, a bidder will always be willing to bid up to their value. Since all other bidders in the cartel would lose the auction anyway to the member with the highest value, they do just as well by not bidding competitively. In a first-price sealed-bid auction, however, bidders submit bids lower than their value, and the smaller the number of bidders they believe they are facing, the farther below their value they bid. For example, if we assume a standard single-unit auction with private values such that bidder values are uniformly distributed on the range 0 to 100, and let $n$ represent the number of bidders in the auction and $v_i$ the value of winning to bidder $i$, the symmetric-equilibrium bid function is $b(v_i) = v_i(n - 1)/n$. For a two-bidder auction, this means a bidder bids half of their value, while for a three-bidder auction, a bidder bids 2/3 of their value. The potential benefit of participating in the ring should be obvious as bidding against one rival and winning will be much more profitable than bidding against two.

Since the designated cartel member is bidding below his value though, another cartel member has an incentive to bid competitively against him. Consider two cartel members, A and B, with values of 80 and 60. If there is only one non-cartel member involved in the auction and the cartel works as it should, then A would bid 40 in the auction thinking he faces only a single competitor. B, however, can look at this situation, see that A will be bidding 40 and realise they can bid 41 and make a profit if they beat the non-cartel member. B's ability to do this relies on having clear knowledge of A's value but in order for A to be given the priority in the cartel to bid in the auction, B would have had to be informed of it. In anticipation of this cheating by B, A would have to bid enough to win against B, which would ultimately make the cartel of little value. Thus the incentive of cartel members to 'cheat' in this manner means that such a ring may break down without repeated interaction. Note that in an ascending auction, bidder A will be willing to bid up to 80 which means that B could never win (without making a loss) by bidding competitively. Therefore B has no incentive to do so and the cartel remains stable.

Cartel or explicit collusion like this usually involves formal communication and agreements between firms. Examples of it are studied by Pesendorfer (2000) and Baldwin, Marshall and Richard (1997).

Table 3.1. *Bidder values*

|        | Bidder A | Bidder B   |
|--------|----------|------------|
| Item 1 | 100      | 80         |
| Item 2 | 100      | 80         |
| Both   | 200      | 80 or 160  |

Collusion that results from repeated interaction is not typically studied as an explicit auction design problem as it is based upon the same principles of collusion that appear in the general literature concerning collusion among firms and must be dealt with in that manner rather than as an auction design issue.

The types of collusion that can be addressed by auction design were first discussed in Vickrey's (1961) seminal paper on auction theory when he explicitly noted that the multi-unit versions of ascending or second-price auctions include very different incentives from those found in the single-unit versions:

It is not possible to consider a buyer wanting up to two units as merely an aggregation of two single-unit buyers: combining the two buyers into one introduces a built-in collusion and community of interest, and the bid offered for the second unit will be influenced by the possible effect of this bid on the price to be paid for the first, even under the first-rejected-bid method. (Vickrey, 1961, p. 27)

This idea is what has come to be known as 'strategic demand reduction' in more recent papers, such as Weber (1997) and Ausubel and Cramton (2002). It is important to distinguish between two forms of demand reduction. The first is not a form of collusion yet its impact on the outcome of an auction is quite similar. The second form of demand reduction involves tacit or explicit co-ordination by firms to settle upon lower prices than would be reached without such agreements.

We can explain both types of demand reduction phenomena through a simple framework. Consider an auction environment in which there are two bidders and two items. In the first situation we will assume that one bidder is interested in winning both items, while the second bidder is interested in winning either of the items but not both. In the second situation, the second bidder will be interested in winning both. Their values for the items are as in table 3.1.

To analyse this example we need to develop two fundamental concepts. The first is the idea of equilibrium in an auction. We will use the game-theoretic concept of Nash equilibrium, which defines equilibrium as a set of strategies such that no bidder could improve their outcome through unilateral deviation. We will also use the term efficiency, which refers to the proportion of the possible value to society that has been achieved by an allocation. If the bidder or bidders who value the items most win the items,[2] then the most efficient, or 100 per cent efficient, outcome has been achieved. If the items end up being assigned to other bidders, then a less efficient outcome has been be achieved.

Considering either case of the preferences bidder B has for winning the items, if the bidders participate in a simultaneous ascending auction, the efficient competitive outcome is for bidder A to win both items, paying 80 for each item and resulting in total revenue to the seller of 160, total surplus of 40 to bidder A and 0 to bidder B. This is the outcome that would be approximately achieved if bidders followed the straightforward bidding strategy described previously, as bidder B would always be willing to bid on item 1 or 2 whenever the price is below 80 and would therefore drive up the prices of both to that level before dropping out.

The non-collusive sort of demand reduction could occur in the situation in which bidder B is only interested in a single item. In that case, once bidder B has placed a bid of 1 on item 2, bidder A could place a bid of 1 on item 1 and cease bidding. Bidder B has no interest in bidding further as he is currently winning one item at a substantial profit and that is all he wanted. If bidder A continues by bidding back on item 2, B will then bid back and continue doing so until the competitive outcome is reached. If bidder A stops bidding, or reduces his demand to a single object, then he ends up with a surplus of 99 rather than a surplus of 40. While this leads to substantially less revenue than the competitive outcome, this should not be termed collusive as this requires no co-ordination or co-operation among bidders. This simply involves one firm reducing the number of items they are bidding on to reduce the price on the items that they win.

Demand reduction outcomes in the second case where bidder B is interested in both items can, however, be considered as collusive. It is possible to achieve the exact same outcome as before in which bidder A wins item 1 for a price of 1 and bidder B wins item 2 for a price of 1. Again, both bidders prefer this outcome to the competitive one, as bidder A would have a surplus of 99 and bidder B a surplus of 79 compared to 40 and 0 respectively.

The important distinction between the two cases is based on what is required for this outcome to be supported as an equilibrium of the ascending auction. To construct an equilibrium that leads to this outcome

---

[2] This analysis, of course, ignores the situations described in Janssen and Moldovanu (this volume, chapter 5). The analysis could be extended to do so, but it is useful to begin with this simpler initial setting.

we need to define strategies for each bidder that deliver it and show that neither bidder would prefer to deviate from them. The strategy for bidder A in this case would involve placing a bid of 1 on item 1 and then committing to bid according to their non-collusive straightforward strategy of bidding until they reach their value if bidder B ever places a bid on 1. This is known as a 'trigger' strategy as bidder A is promising to behave cooperatively unless bidder B does not, and the first instance of non-cooperative play by bidder B triggers immediate punishment from bidder A. If bidder B adopts a similar 'trigger' strategy in regard to item 2, then neither bidder would choose to deviate by bidding on the other's item. Deviation from these strategies would involve something like bidder A choosing to bid on item 2. If he did that, bidder B would punish him by bidding up to his value of 80 on both items. Bidder A would win both items but the outcome would be the non-collusive outcome already described in which bidder 1's surplus is 40. This is significantly lower than his surplus from not deviating, 99. The same can be verified for bidder B. Thus these strategies constitute a Nash equilibrium of the game. The key element that allows this collusive outcome to be supported as an equilibrium is the ability for one bidder to punish the other bidder if they try to cheat from the collusive agreement. This agreement need not be explicit and could well be just tacitly observed and agreed to by both bidders. Such agreements or trigger strategies were not necessary in the case in which bidder B was only interested in a single item, but they are necessary when he is, and it is the presence of these agreements, even when they are only tacitly observed, that makes the latter sort of demand reduction equilibria collusive in nature even though they are equilibria of non-cooperative games.

Using this same example, we can examine an important difference between ascending and sealed-bid auctions. If we think instead of a first-price sealed-bid auction for both of these items simultaneously, then this demand reduction equilibrium disappears. If the bidders were to try to strike an agreement before the auction, either explicitly or tacitly, to bid only 1 on their respective items, this agreement would be unenforceable during the auction as both would have an incentive to deviate from it. If bidder B went ahead and bid a price of 1 on item 2 and nothing on item 1, then bidder A could bid 1 on item 1 and 2 on item 2 and significantly improve the outcome for himself. Once bidder B realised that A had cheated on their agreement, he would have no recourse to punishment as he would in the ascending auction. Without this punishment capability to enforce the collusive agreement, it should no longer be effective.

This example should not, however, be taken as an indication that collusion is not possible in sealed-bid auctions. If the bidders expect to be competing in a series of auctions or even in some repeated interaction outside of the auction environment, they can adopt strategies that involve punishing a deviator in future auctions or business dealings. The key to supporting collusive equilibria as possible outcomes of an auction is the ability of the bidders to punish someone who deviates from a collusive agreement, and such opportunities can arise in any situation involving repeated interaction among firms. This is an application of what is known as the 'folk theorem' among game theorists.[3] This is a general class of theorems which state that collusion can occur in games which are repeated an infinite or unknown number of times assuming players possess sufficient patience. The strategies that support collusion in these cases will take the form of a collusive agreement, with punishment strategies used to enforce the agreement should anyone deviate from the agreed-upon course of action. With such strategies in place, no one would choose to deviate and collusion will be stable.

This allows us to make one very important point, which is that in a situation involving firms that are generally collusive in nature, i.e. they tend to collude on most of their dealings, they will of course collude in any auction in which they are involved. Anything an auction designer proposes to do inside the auction to eliminate collusion will have little success. This type of intrinsic collusion among a group of bidders will also almost certainly involve the explicit structure discussed above and again must be dealt with as a standard anti-trust issue, not as an auction design issue. Collusion can therefore exist under either auction format, but the ascending auction will be significantly more susceptible to it as the agreements can be made and enforced tacitly inside of a single auction.

There are a variety of papers such as Engelbrecht-Wiggans and Kahn (1999) and Brusco and Lopomo (1999) that develop other strategies leading to collusion inside a single auction that are quite similar to the collusive demand reduction example just discussed. Ausubel and Schwartz (1999) and Engelbrecht-Wiggans and Kahn (1999) make the situation for ascending auctions look particularly grim as they show that the collusive strategy is in fact the only strategy that proves to be a subgame-perfect Nash equilibrium of an ascending auction.[4] Anton and Yao (1992), Ausubel and Schwartz (1999), Brusco and Lopomo (1999) and Grimm,

---

[3] A deeper explanation of the idea of folk theorems for repeated games can be found in most game theory textbooks, such as Osborne and Rubinstein (1994) for high-level development or Watson (2002) for a simpler explanation. The particular type of folk theorem applied here was first developed by Fudenberg and Maskin (1986).

[4] A subgame-perfect Nash equilibrium is a stronger version of a Nash equilibrium that places additional restrictions on off-equilibrium path behaviour for sequential move games of this sort. It is generally considered to be the most reasonable equilibrium concept for use in these types of games.

Riedel and Wolfstetter (2001) describe similar collusive equilibria in which bidders signal collusive splits of the objects in the auction early and come to a sort of negotiated agreement about how to divide up the objects in the auction most profitably. These papers paint a very dismal picture of ascending auctions by showing that the collusive equilibria are very damaging to the auction and that it is very reasonable to expect that bidders will be able to agree upon them.

A deeper look at the issue displays some key reasons why the picture for ascending auctions is not likely to be quite so bad in practice as it is in theory. Most of the very pessimistic results about bidder collusion in these papers are derived from very simple two-bidder models. In Ausubel and Schwartz (1999), the authors reframe an ascending auction as a bargaining game in which the two bidders are attempting to bargain over how to split up the items in the auction. They find that the unique subgame-perfect Nash equilibrium of the game involves the bidders splitting the items between themselves at prices well below the competitive level. In a two-bidder game, it seems entirely reasonable that bidders would be able to come to such an accommodation relatively easily. The problem comes in attempting to extrapolate such results to cases involving more than two bidders. As is found in most empirical or experimental studies of collusion or the provision of public goods in non-auction contexts, the difference between a situation involving two agents trying to collude and one involving $n > 2$ agents is very significant, as described in more detail in Isaac and Reynolds (2002). In two-agent situations, the agents can typically collude but this becomes more difficult and less likely as the number of agents grows to even just four or five.

There are both theoretical and practical reasons for the difficulty encountered by more than two agents colluding in auctions. One can understand the issue intuitively by first imagining the difference between two people bargaining over how to achieve an amicable split and the corresponding situation with three or more. Even in a standard bargaining situation where bidders can freely communicate, the difficulty will be increased. This is so because as the number of parties increases, so too does the possibility that two or more of them will have mutually exclusive interests that cannot both be satisfied. Also, the practical details involved in forming an agreement among more and more parties become increasingly complex even in situations where an agreement is possible. Now imagine that all parties have to communicate through potentially difficult to interpret signals such as bids in an auction. Since effective collusion requires that all bidders be able to interpret the signals correctly, the more bidders are involved, the greater is the chance that at least one is unable to understand the signals being sent by the others. While it is certainly still possible for larger numbers of bidders to collude, it will be substantially more difficult.

The technical support for the decrease in collusion as the number of bidders increases is contained in Brusco and Lopomo (1999). It contains the standard two-bidder results indicating that collusion is a serious problem, as is found in other papers, but then extends the analysis to more bidders. They find that the possibility for collusive outcomes diminishes as the number of bidders rises relative to the number of items. The reason is similar to the explanation given above. As the number of bidders grows, the possibility of the bidders finding amicable splits diminishes. Brusco and Lopomo go even further to show that the presence of significant externalities or synergies across items also diminishes the prospects for collusive outcomes.

The intuition behind these results can be explained by examining two different situations. In situation A, imagine two bidders in a spectrum auction, one of whom has a business plan which requires obtaining all licences on the western side of the United States to operate a PCS business. This bidder would like the East Coast licences as well, but does not see these as vital. The other firm has the inverse preferences, which means it wants to operate primarily on the eastern side of the country. In situation B, consider adding a third firm which has a business plan for the centre of the country requiring half of the licences from the eastern and western regions in order to be viable. In situation A, a collusive outcome will almost certainly emerge, with the bidders dividing the country in half and agreeing not to bid on each other's region. In situation B, no bidder will be willing to reduce demand below the half of the country they require and, without side payments, there is no way to split up the licences in a way that would be agreeable to all three. In this case, bidding might continue until the eastern and western bidders have outstripped the willingness to pay of the middle bidder and only then would those two bidders engage in a demand reduction strategy not to bid on the other's half. By then, though, the prices of the licences would be much higher than would result in situation A, diminishing the harm resulting from any collusion that emerges.

There is both experimental and empirical evidence to support the Brusco and Lopomo (1999) results. Kwasnica and Sherstyuk (2002) test these predictions by conducting experimental auctions involving both small and large numbers of bidders and varying sizes of complementarities across items. They find that increasing the number of bidders and/or the presence of large complementarities across items reduces collusion, as predicted by Brusco and Lopomo (1999). They also find an interesting side result arising from the fact that their experiments involved a series of auctions, which is that moderate complementarities lead to winner rotation schemes being used more often as a collusion device by the bidders. Of course, winner rotation schemes only work for repeated auctions as they involve cartel-like behaviour in which bidders with low values in a particular period refrain from bidding while those with higher values bid, and then exchanging roles when their positions are reversed. In a single-shot auction, such strategies could not emerge.

A careful study of different spectrum auctions, including those from the United States, Canada and Australia, is likely to reveal many cases of such behaviour, but Klemperer (2002b) gives a very clear explanation of a sequence of events from the German 3G spectrum auction to demonstrate that such behaviour also occurs in field auctions. In this case, one of the firms in the auction, T-Mobil, appeared unable to interpret, or unwilling to agree to, the demand reduction signals being sent by another bidder, Mannesman. This inability to interpret signals, or unwillingness to agree to the split, led T-Mobil to drive up the prices by €2.5 billion before achieving the same allocation Mannesman initially signalled at a much lower price. This example is particularly interesting since earlier in the same paper and in Grimm, Riedel and Wolfstetter (2002) those exact same two firms are described as having come to a very rapid accommodation in an earlier 1999 German DCS-1800 spectrum auction. In Klemperer (2002b) the reason indicated for the breakdown in collusion is that T-Mobil just did not understand the way a collusive signal would be sent in the second auction, and in fact he appears to criticise the advisers of T-Mobil for this failure to collude. It is worthwhile noting that the 1999 auction involved just two credible bidders while in the later 3G auction six were still in the auction at the time the original collusive signal was sent. Exactly why the collusive outcome was not realised in the second case is uncertain, but what is not in doubt is that the 3G auction with a large number of bidders resulted in greater than expected revenue while the earlier auction with only two credible bidders resulted in a quick collusive agreement and lower than expected revenue.

The indication from these results is that while collusion can be a problem in ascending auctions, and indeed a devastating one in particular cases, theory and empirical evidence tell us that it is primarily a problem of small numbers of bidders. Small numbers of bidders will tend to find it relatively easy to signal collusive outcomes to other bidders and to come to quick accommodations. Larger numbers of bidders and bidders whose interests overlap more and/or involve more complementarities will be significantly less likely to collude effectively. This differentiation between smaller and larger numbers of bidders is mostly absent from the majority of the theoretical analyses of collusion and accounts for the overwhelmingly negative results the literature contains. It is therefore quite important to examine the results from Brusco and Lopomo (1999) and Kwasnica and Sherstyuk (2002) to see the degree to which these problems exist when more than two bidders are involved. This argument, however, is in no way intended to minimise the definite problem of collusion that exists in ascending auctions with a small number of bidders whose interests are relatively mutually exclusive. In such cases, an auctioneer who ignores the possibility of collusion does so at the risk of achieving a very poor outcome.

## 2.2    Proposed solutions

Proposals for how to solve or minimise problems coming from collusion all involve different ways of trying to modify the design of the auction either to limit the possibility of bidders colluding or to limit the harm from the collusion if it is going to exist. It is important to realise that all of these proposals are designed to work against in-auction collusion. This type of collusion will only be an issue in auctions involving multiple units when bidders are allowed to win more than one item and are interested in doing so. In single-unit auctions or auctions in which bidders can win only single items, the only type of collusion that can exist is the general market collusion that we have already pointed out, which cannot be dealt with through the design of an auction.

Several fundamental changes to the design of an ascending auction have been proposed at various times to deal with the problem of collusion. The most basic proposal is to abandon the ascending auction in favour of a sealed-bid design, which, as described previously, is less susceptible to in-auction collusion. The reason it is less susceptible is that a sealed-bid auction removes the ability of bidders to punish other bidders inside the auction for deviating from some proposed collusive split. One might see this as the implicit recommendation of Robinson (1985) and it is also suggested in Engelbrecht-Wiggans and Kahn (1998), who go further to suggest that in a multi-unit auction, the objects might be best auctioned in sequential sealed-bid auctions.

An alternative to getting rid of the ascending auction format entirely would be to have an auction that begins as an ascending auction and then at some point switches to a final sealed-bid round. A simple version of this was proposed by Cramton and Schwartz (2000), but Klemperer (2002a) proposes a more sophisticated version of this approach, calling it the Anglo-Dutch hybrid auction. The way such a design would work is that if there are $k$ objects in the auction and $N > k + 1$ bidders in the auction when it begins, the auction starts as an ascending auction.

This continues so long as there is significant excess demand for the objects, but when the number of bidders drops down to $k + 1$ then the ascending portion of the auction is ended and the remaining bidders participate in a sealed-bid round to conclude the auction. The proposed benefits of this design is that it eliminates the possibility of punishment strategies and therefore destroys any of the collusive equilibria we discussed previously, while preserving many of the advantages of ascending auctions.

Another version of this idea of a final sealed-bid round is described by Ausubel and Milgrom (2001). They propose a final round of proxy bidding be added to the end of an ascending auction, or even using a proxy bid auction in place of an ascending auction. Under their proposal, instead of submitting bids, the bidders would send in a value function to the auctioneer and bidding would be done by a proxy bidding agent in an ascending auction that would place bids according to the straightforward bidding strategy. The reason for this proposal is that it has been shown that if bidders were to bid according to such a strategy, then an efficient outcome would be achieved. This design is an attempt to force them to do so. In the context of a single-unit auction, this is equivalent to e-Bay's proxy bidder design and should be expected to work quite well. Implementing such a design in a multi-unit context appears more problematic and will be discussed in more detail in section 3.

Albano, Germano and Lovo (2001) present a different idea for removing collusive equilibria in ascending auctions which involves using a Japanese, or clock, version of the auction instead of the non-clock versions more commonly used. The difference is that in the clock version, prices rise at the discretion of the auctioneer and bidders are only able to agree to pay the price or drop out. In the non-clock auction, bidders submit specific bids as they choose. The results of Albano, Germano and Lovo (2001) show that using the clock version of the auction does eliminate certain types of signalling equilibria because bidders are no longer able to send signals with their bids, but demand reduction equilibria will still exist. The result of not allowing bidders to submit specific bids is to make collusion more difficult for bidders but not to eliminate the possibility completely.

Yet another novel change to the ascending auction is given by Ausubel (2002). This paper describes an ascending auction design for multiple homogeneous items in which bidders can 'clinch' items as the auction progresses when the demand reaches a point at which it becomes clear that they will win at least one item. When that occurs, the price of that item becomes fixed but the auction continues for the other items. The result is that continuing to bid on other items cannot increase the price of clinched items. This effectively eliminates the incentive to engage in demand reduction.

There have been several experimental studies aimed at investigating this auction design and they are summarised by Sherstyuk (2000) along with other experimental studies of collusion in auctions. The different studies have taken quite different approaches to evaluating the mechanism and their results indicate that the performance of the mechanism depends crucially on the environment and the implementation. In Kagel and Levin (2001) and Kagel, Kinross and Levin (2001), human bidders were placed into auctions of this type, bidding against computer bidders that were programmed to play the equilibrium strategy. The results of the evaluation show that the auction design performs well in comparison to a uniform-price auction in terms of eliminating demand reduction and improving efficiency, but occasionally yields less revenue than expected. Grimm and Engelmann (2001) evaluate Ausubel's dynamic Vickrey auction against five other formats, with each auction involving two objects being auctioned between two human bidders with a demand for two units each. Their findings show again that the dynamic Vickrey auction produced higher efficiency and less demand reduction than the other mechanisms evaluated.

A perhaps more telling examination is found in Manelli, Sefron and Wilner (2000) in which the authors compare Ausubel's dynamic Vickrey auction to the standard Vickrey auction in a more complicated environment involving three items and three bidders, each of whom is interested in winning only two units. The study reports some unexpected behaviour in the dynamic Vickrey auction in which the bidders would bid quite aggressively by bidding on all three objects even though they would receive no value from winning the third item. Subjects would engage in bidding on all three objects until they had clinched the two objects they wanted, which typically led to inefficient outcomes. This strategic gaming of the Ausubel mechanism is certainly not part of the equilibrium strategy and may not even always be beneficial, but the authors report that its use by the subjects was quite robust to variations in the environment. This could indicate that such strategies will be persistent or, at a minimum, that bidders would need significant experience with the mechanism before they learned to bid according to the 'right' strategy. In the short term, such aggressive disequilibrium bidding could lead to inefficient outcomes. The results from all of these experimental studies suggests that in simple environments, the Ausubel dynamic Vickrey auction may work as intended, but in larger and more complex environments it may run into difficulties.

In addition to these large changes to the mechanism, there have been several proposals to modify slightly the rules of specific ascending auctions. One of the more common proposals is to allow only anonymous listings of bids in round results. In most current ascending auctions used for spectrum licence auctions, the identities of those who placed the current standing-high bids and even all past non-winning bids are available for all to see. Under this proposal, those identities would be hidden. The effect of such a change would be to make it impossible for one bidder to tell if another bidder had deviated from some collusive arrangement. They might see that some bidder had bid on a licence they were interested in, but they would not know if it was the bidder they had the arrangement with or another and thus would not know whom to punish. Without the ability to monitor each other's behaviour, both parties to any collusive agreement have the incentive to deviate from the agreement. This suggestion has been made in several FCC proceedings and also by Cramton and Schwartz (2000) and Klemperer (2002a).

Another common suggestion is to raise reserve prices. If bidders are going to be able to agree to collusive splits early in the auction and revenue is a concern of the auctioneer, then using high reserve prices can minimise the harm from those agreements. This too is quite a common suggestion and it has been made by Graham and Marshall (1985) Cramton and Schwartz (2000) and Klemperer (2002a). This proposed 'fix', however, has a very serious potential downside. As noted, the problem of collusion is primarily one of small numbers of bidders. If reserve prices are set too high, this may discourage potential bidders from entering and actually make collusion more likely to occur. This remedy must therefore be used with great care.

Most of the standard approaches to combating collusion we have discussed have been designed to limit the ability of bidders in an auction to punish a deviator. There is another way to break up collusive equilibria of this sort, as suggested by Brusco and Lopomo (1999): additional bidders. If the auctioneer attracts more bidders to an auction, there will be less of a possibility that the bidders could agree, without using side payments, on a split of the items that is mutually agreeable. In the ascending version of the auction, bidders will tend to bid competitively until the values of enough bidders have been surpassed that the remaining bidders can agree to collusive splits. The remaining bidders may still be engaging in demand reduction, but the position of the auctioneer has been made significantly stronger by the addition of the additional bidders.

One issue to note with this, though, is that the additional bidders must be willing and active participants. Some have suggested that problems in some of the European UMTS auctions have occurred as a result of some bidders assuming they would be likely to lose the auction given the relative strengths of the other participants and choosing to bow out of the auction early or even not entering at all. The presence of such weak bidders is certainly not helpful. What is helpful is the existence of additional bidders who believe they have a legitimate chance of winning the auction even against a competitor deemed stronger. This suggests that pro-competitive measures such as giving smaller bidders bidding credits, which allow them to compete against larger firms, may also work against collusion.

## 3    Case study of FCC experience with combating collusion in spectrum auctions

There are two facts about the history of collusion in the FCC's spectrum auctions that explain why this is an important case study to consider. First, there have been a large number of instances of bidders attempting to collude in FCC auctions. Second, these attempts have been largely unsuccessful and to date no one has been able to identify more than a negligible loss in revenue in these auctions resulting from collusion.[5] The reason for this lack of successful collusion is in part the FCC's attempts to minimise collusion, but these attempts have been made far more successful by the large number of competitors that are usually involved in each auction. We will begin this case study by cataloguing some of the more common or well-known types of collusion that have been attempted in FCC auctions and then go on to explain how the rules of the auctions have evolved to deal with these issues. Before reading this case study it might be helpful to study the rules of FCC auctions; these are explained in detail in Salmon (this volume, chapter 6).

### 3.1    Types of collusion in FCC auctions

There are many forms of collusive strategy that have been attempted over the history of the more than thirty spectrum auctions conducted by the FCC. All have shared the same basic structure discussed in section 2. That is, they have involved attempts to settle upon demand reduction equilibria supported by punishment strategies. The interesting part of these attempts is the varied approaches bidders have used to communicate such intentions to other bidders.

The most basic attempts at collusion which have been observed have taken the form of simple punishment strategies. These involve situations

---

[5] The possible exception to this is the DEF block PCS auction. This auction saw the highest level of collusive activity in any FCC auction and there is reason to believe that this led to lower than optimal prices.

such as bidder A, who is interested in licence 1, bidding on licence 2, one they may well not be interested in, in an attempt to convince bidder B, who does want 2, to cease bidding on licence 1. This is sometimes referred to as 'retaliatory bidding' and instances of such behaviour are quite common throughout the FCC auctions. The difficult part of using a strategy such as this to signal another bidder to co-ordinate on the collusive outcome is to find a way to make the other bidder aware of what the signal means.

Perhaps the most creative and well-known approach to solving this communication problem has come to be known as 'bid signalling with trailing digits', which was used during the FCC's early PCS auctions. At that time, bidders were allowed to enter their own bid amounts so long as they were greater than some specified minimum. Since the prices of these licences were in the millions and hundreds of millions of dollars, the last three digits in the bids were of no real consequence. The licences themselves in these auctions were identified by a two- or three-digit code identifying the geographic location of the licence. Imagine a situation in which bidder A is interested in licence 242 while bidder B is interested in licences 105 and 242. If bidder A wants to signal bidder B to stay away from licence 242, he might submit a bid on licence 105 of $5,000,242. The last three 'trailing digits' are used to refer to the licence on which bidder A wants bidder B to cease bidding. Using such trailing digits, bidders could send coded messages back and forth to try to settle upon a collusive outcome.

One problem with the trailing digits approach is that some bidders might not look closely enough at a rival's bid to notice them. This prompted some bidders to make their intentions even more obvious using strategic withdrawals. In an attempt to alleviate the exposure problem in their auctions[6] the FCC allows bidders to withdraw standing-high bids in the auction. When a bidder withdraws their standing-high bid on a licence, the new minimum accepted bid becomes the amount of the previous highest bid on the object. In the early auctions, withdrawals were submitted after a round of bidding had concluded and standing-high bidders declared. In the same scenario as above, assume that bidder B has a bid of $4,500,000 on licence 105. Bidder A could submit a bid of

---

[6] See my general FCC case study (this volume, chapter 6) for more information on the exposure problem. This refers to a situation that can occur when a bidder needs a group of, say, five licences for their business plan and if they win only four they are worth little or nothing to the firm. In that case, the bidder can be 'exposed' to a significant loss if they bid on the package intending to win the entire group and another bidder then bids more on one of the licences than the first bidder is willing to pay. The bidder could end the auction having promised to pay a large sum of money for four licences that are now of little value to him.

$5,000,242 for licence 105 and then withdraw it in the same round. Such a sequence would not only call attention to the bid but also constitutes an explicit offer to bidder B since they can simply resubmit their previous bid of $4,500,000 to regain the standing-high bid on licence 105. Such a withdrawal serves as a very clear signal of bidder A's intent.

Without these two mechanisms, signalling collusive intent is more difficult but it can still be done using retaliatory bidding, which requires a little more effort on the part of the bidders to communicate intent. As an example of one such attempt, in auction 18, the 220 MHz auction, there were three nationwide licences, denoted as K, L and M blocks, in addition to a large number of smaller regional licences. It was well known that one particular bidder, referred to here as bidder 1, had to win one of these three licences but only wanted one. There were four other bidders interested in these licences, with two or three of those being interested in more than one licence. Bidder 1 tried on repeated occasions to signal a collusive equilibrium by following a set pattern of bidding. They bid on licence M in one round and in the next they would bid on all three licences, K, L and M. In the following period, they would bid again on licence M, regardless of whether or not they already held the high bid on that licence. They continued this pattern so long as one of the other bidders bid on licence M.[7] This was a very clear retaliatory signal that bidder 1 would refrain from bidding on the other two licences if the other bidders stopped bidding on licence M. This auction continued for fifteen rounds with bidder 1 following the described strategy and the other bidders bidding more or less evenly across the three nationwide licences, apparently ignoring the collusive offer being made. One bidder dropped out in round 8, while two of the other three dropped out of the competition simultaneously after round 15. At that point bidder 1 stopped bidding, as did the remaining nationwide bidder. Bidder 1 ended up winning licence M and the remaining bidder won the other two.

It seems quite clear that this was an attempt by bidder 1 to collude with the other bidders. The interesting question is whether or not the outcome that emerged was a collusive outcome or a competitive outcome. On the basis of the evidence, it seems more likely to have been a competitive than a collusive outcome. Since the last two bidders dropped out of the auction at the eventual price level, it seems likely that the prices were more than they were willing to pay, rather than that they were agreeing to reduce demand. The remaining bidder could have reduced demand

---

[7] It was possible for multiple bidders to bid on licence M in one round with bidder 1 maintaining the high bid. This is because most of the bids were made at the minimum increment and the FCC's rules state that the bidder who bids first is made the standing-high bidder.

for collusive reasons from three licences to two, but this seems unlikely as well. One thing about the outcome is certain though: by following this strategy, bidder 1 was driving up the price on licence M faster than the prices of the other two items. Consequently, they ended up paying approximately 20–27 per cent more for the license they won than the other two bidders paid for identical items.[8] This example demonstrates a rather clever signalling approach that can be used even in the absence of trailing digits and strategic withdrawals, but it also shows why such collusion attempts are not necessarily effective. Competing bidders are not always willing to go along with the collusive offer being made by another, and pursuing a collusive strategy and failing can be quite costly.

### 3.2     FCC attempts to deal with collusion

The FCC has had some fairly simple anti-collusion rules in place since the auctions began. Their basic requirement is found in Section 1.2105(c)(1) of the Commission's rules:

After the short-form application filing deadline, all applicants are prohibited from cooperating, collaborating, discussing or disclosing in any manner the substance of their bids or bidding strategies, or discussing or negotiating settlement agreements, with other applicants until after the down payment deadline, unless such applicants are members of a bidding consortium or other joint bidding arrangement identified on the bidder's short-form application pursuant to § 1.2105(a)(2)(viii).

The interpretation of this is that bidders can talk among themselves, and form whatever co-operative arrangements they choose, prior to the start of the auction process, which is considered to be when the bidders submit their applications to be bidders. These pre-auction discussions, however, must satisfy two conditions. The first is that any co-operative agreements must be disclosed at the application stage. Second, the agreements must not violate any relevant anti-trust laws dealing with collusion between firms. So long as these conditions are satisfied, bidders can talk as much as they want before applications are submitted, but once that occurs bidders are not allowed to communicate about the auction.

It is interesting to note that this rule allows for the formation of bidder cartels or rings prior to the start of the auction. At first glance, this might seem to be an odd characteristic of an anti-collusion rule. The reasoning behind it is that it would be difficult, if not impossible, to forbid any such discussions and alliances among firms prior to the start of the auction. What the rule does, however, is to ensure that any agreements that are made are publicly viewable so that they can be more easily reviewed in the

---

[8] $3.9 million compared to $3.2 and $3.0 million.

light of standard anti-trust laws. In the previous section we showed that using an auction design to fight any such endemic collusion or concentration of market power in a market will be ineffective. This rule allows for the easier enforcement of standard regulations to combat collusion and concentration of market power.

This prohibition on communication during an auction was one of the reasons bidders were forced to send signals through their bids instead of talking directly. These signals are also technically violations of the anti-collusion rule, but the violation is not as clear and legally actionable. There have been only two cases in which the Justice Department/FCC has prosecuted bidders for violating the anti-collusion rule. One violation was based upon bid signalling, while the other was based on direct communication between two bidders.

In the course of the DEF block PCS auction, High Plains Wireless accused a competitor, Mercury PCS, of using trailing digits to try to signal a warning to High Plains to cease bidding on a particular licence. Mercury's main initial defence was that they believed that bid signalling with trailing digits was a common practice and therefore did not violate the FCC's anti-collusion rules. After an extensive investigation by the FCC and the Justice Department, this case was resolved when Mercury agreed to settle with a consent decree. In general terms, the company had to agree to little more than that they would not engage in similar actions in future auctions. Unfortunately, this was not a strong message to future bidders about the consequences of such behaviour. The reasons the Justice Department settled the case in this manner were never made public, but it seems to have occurred because of the perceived difficulties in convincing a jury that such signalling was collusive in nature and because of the likely low level of provable damage from the incident.

Parallel to the Department of Justice investigation, High Plains had filed a lawsuit against the FCC protesting against the award of licences to Mercury. This lawsuit led to a very long series of appeals, with the most recent decision (11 January 2002) coming from the US District of Columbia Circuit Court of Appeals. High Plains was challenging the award on several grounds, all of which the court dismissed. On the specific charge that the award of licences should be rescinded because of Mercury's violation of the anti-collusion rule, the court ruled that since the language of the rule had not specifically mentioned and forbidden this sort of bid signalling and retaliatory bidding in general, the FCC was not violating its authority to award the licences to Mercury.

The second case of bidder collusion occurred in the same auction and involved one bidder, US West, actually calling another bidder, Western PCS, on the telephone during the auction. The purported intent of the call was to 'apologise' for a mistakenly placed bid on a licence Western had the high bid on. Even if the intent was benign, this still constituted a direct breach of the auction anti-collusion rules. The communication was reported by Western PCS and the outcome was a fine of $1.2 million levied against US West, although they were able to reduce the fine to $800,000 in subsequent negotiations. Western PCS also ended up paying a smaller fine because they waited until well after the auction to report the incident.

In the original FCC auction design there were few design features intended to mitigate collusion beyond this general prohibition on communication. Since those first auctions, many rule changes have been proposed but only two have been implemented, while a third is in the final stages of implementation. As a means of eliminating the possibility of bid signalling, the FCC has changed over to a system of increment bidding. In this system, instead of bidders typing in the specific amounts they wish to bid, they can simply choose to bid some multiple of the minimum increment over the previous standing high bid. If the standing-high bid is $5,000 and the minimum increment is $500, then bidders are allowed to bid by choosing an integer $x$ in the range 1–9' so their new bid will be $5000 + x*\$500$. This makes it impossible for someone to use trailing digits to signal a collusive offer.

Similarly, the FCC has limited the number of withdrawals bidders can place. In the PCS auctions, for the DEF block in particular, bidders were submitting a large number of withdrawals throughout the auction as signalling devices. Not long after this auction, bidders were limited to to submitting withdrawals in only two rounds during the auction. That is, any bidder can choose two rounds in the auction in which to submit withdrawals, but those two rounds can be different for every bidder. This makes withdrawals relatively more expensive to use as signalling devices and has virtually eliminated their use in such strategies.

### 3.3    *Alternative rules that have been considered by the FCC*

The FCC has considered a number of other possible rule changes to reduce further the possibility of collusion in its auctions. Most have been rejected. It is useful though to review some of the more common proposals and explain why the FCC has rejected them. It is important to keep in mind that just because these proposals were rejected in the FCC's case does not mean that they are necessarily bad ideas, just that in the FCC's determination they are not appropriate to adopt in its situation. Therefore this subsection will attempt to describe where, when and why some of these proposals should or should not be adopted, using the case of the FCC as a background example.

Perhaps the most common rule change suggested is to move to anonymous bidding and/or reduce the amount of information published during each round of the auction. The current approach in the FCC's auctions is to publish every bid submitted at the end of every round together with the identity of the bidder. Some propose publishing only the highest bid and the name of the bidder, while others go so far as to suggest that the highest bid only should be published without mentioning the bidder. The reasoning behind such a proposal was discussed above.

There are two main reasons why the FCC has not adopted this proposal. One is something of a philosophical commitment to making the auctions as transparent as possible. This is thought to increase confidence among the bidders that the FCC is conducting the auction in a fair and legitimate manner. If bidders believe the auctioneer to be untrustworthy, this can adversely affect the outcome in many ways, ranging from potential bidders choosing not to participate to actual bidders altering their bidding behaviour in unforeseen ways that could lower revenue and/or efficiency. Full publication of all information represents an attempt to foster that trust.

In many of the FCC's auctions there is a second and more solid economic argument for publishing the information. For many of the services, the value a bidder has for a licence may legitimately depend on which other bidders are bidding on the adjacent licences. One reason for such preferences might be to ensure technological compatibility between providers in a certain region so that they can settle upon roaming agreements later on. Publishing bidder identities can then be very important to obtaining an efficient outcome from the auction. The FCC has continued to publish identities in the belief that the efficiency-enhancing aspects of the information outweigh its potential to be used for collusive purposes. One can argue that bidders are using the information to engage in 'good collusion' as they are using it to co-ordinate on the efficient allocation. In cases such as this in which co-ordination among bidders is necessary to achieve an efficient allocation, an auctioneer should be careful that the desire to eliminate 'bad' collusion does not also lead to the elimination of 'good' collusion.

It is important to realise that the situation of interrelated values described here goes beyond the standard view of affiliated values as developed in Milgrom and Weber (1982) and therefore the value of information revelation goes beyond the standard notion of the linkage principle. Value affiliation refers to the idea that if the value one bidder has for a Boston licence (say) is high then the values other bidders will have for Boston are also likely to be high, and the linkage principle suggests that in such cases, information revelation in an ascending auction can increase revenue. While it seems believable that values in spectrum auctions are affiliated in the Milgrom and Weber sense, the relationship noted above is quite different. The preferences described above involve complementarities between bidders and across licences. In other words, the value a bidder has for winning the Boston licence may depend on the identity of the bidder who wins the New York licence. For situations in which such preferences exist, publishing the identities of standing-high bidders is necessary for achieving efficient outcomes. For other situations in which such cross-bidder linkages do not exist, the economic reason for publishing information will not be applicable and may indicate that anonymous bidding is a viable rule to counter possible collusion.

Another proposal that has been made on many occasions and in many different forms is to end the auction with a final sealed-bid round. Again, the reasoning behind this has been discussed above. Theoretically this sounds like an easy fix, but there are a very large number of problems with it depending on how it is implemented. One possible approach is just to declare that the auction will last $x$ rounds as an ascending auction and that round $x + 1$ will be a sealed-bid round. This implementation leads to a strong incentive for the bidders to engage in parking behaviour. Parking refers to a bidder bidding on licences in which they have little or no interest to draw attention away from the licences in which they are interested. Such behaviour already occurs in the FCC's auctions but the uncertain end-point gives the bidders an increasing incentive to move away from this strategy as the auction progresses. If they know there is a defined end-point, there is no reason to stop parking until then. If that occurs, then all of the information revelation that is the reason behind using the ascending format is eliminated as no useful information is revealed until the sealed-bid round and by then it is not possible to take advantage of it. A final sealed-bid round then is quite likely to have a significantly negative effect on efficiency, and perhaps revenue, although it would break up the collusive equilibria.

An alternative would be to implement an unknown switchover point based on a rule derived from excess demand as in Klemperer's Anglo-Dutch auction, though this specific proposal has not been made to the FCC. This idea is superior but when an auction has perhaps 400 market areas it would be difficult to determine how to implement any such variable switchover rule. In an auction with a small number of roughly homogeneous items, as in the case of most of the European 3G or UMTS auctions, for which it was really proposed, this design might work quite well. In auctions with a large number of heterogeneous objects and markets, it is uncertain how to implement such a design properly.

The proxy bidding suggestion contained in Ausubel and Milgrom (2001) and discussed above has similar implementation problems for large auctions. One of the most significant problems would be constructing an interface through which bidders could send in such a value function. Since values in these auctions are very complex and interdependent, for a proxy auction to have a chance of reaching an efficient outcome, such interdependencies must be accounted for in the system. More problematic still, bidders would have to be able to quantify their values for all combinations of items, which is something they typically cannot do when asked in such a manner. It would also probably need a fair amount of technical sophistication for the bidders to be able to know how to programme their values into the system, as a table simply listing all combinations of licences is not feasible for large numbers of items. These are all very difficult tasks and there is little reason to suspect the problems could be overcome for complex auctions. Unless these problems are solved, this approach is again likely to lead to inefficient outcomes and to bidders being faced with very serious exposure problems. In much simpler scenarios, such as when values are not related across bidders and/or interdependent across items, as well as when the number of items is small, such an approach might work just as it does for e-Bay. In the FCC's case and other complex environments, this should not be expected to be a workable solution.

A final proposal that attempts to deal with collusive behaviour, which was not mentioned in the previous subsection, involves adopting a combinatorial auction design. In such a design, bidders would be able to send in a single bid that would be an 'all-or-nothing' bid on a group or package of items. This is in contrast to the FCC's current system in which bidders must send in one bid per item and they could well end up obtaining only a few items from the group or package in which they are interested. The primary motivation behind switching to such a design is discussed in Salmon (this volume, chapter 6), which is to reduce the exposure problem bidders face. A side benefit is that it can also lower the incentive to reduce demand.

Imagine a situation in which there are two bidders bidding on two items for which their values are as shown in table 3.1 indicating that bidder B sees the two items as perfect substitutes (i.e. the value of both to bidder B is 80). These values indicate that bidder B wants either 1 or 2 but not both, while bidder A wants both. The non-collusive outcome of a standard ascending auction would involve bidder B always being willing to place a bid on either 1 or 2 so long as the price were less than 80. This would result in bidder A obtaining both items for a price of 80 each, resulting in a total cost of 160 and a surplus of 40. If, however, he were to reduce his demand to only a single item he could end up with a much larger surplus, 99, with both bidders bidding a price of just 1 on different items. This is essentially the same example as that discussed earlier.

In a combinatorial auction, this demand reduction strategy is no longer an equilibrium. Winner determination in a combinatorial auction is performed by finding the set of mutually exclusive bids that yield the highest revenue. For example, if bidder A submitted a package bid on 1 and 2 of 20, in order for bidder B to submit a bid for 1 that would win, it would have to be at least 21. What this means is that in order for bidder A to win both items, he only has to submit a package bid for both that is higher than bidder B would be willing to bid for either item individually.

Since the highest bid that B is willing to submit for either 1 or 2 individually is 80, the equilibrium in this case would involve bidder A placing a package bid of $80 + \epsilon$ on both items. Bidder B would not be willing to bid more and bidder A would end up with a surplus of 120. Since bidder A's surplus of 120 is greater in this outcome than under the collusive outcome, the collusive outcome will no longer be an equilibrium of this game. This shows an example of a general phenomenon that the cases in which demand reduction equilibria exist are significantly fewer in combinatorial auctions. We should note that this does lead to less revenue than the competitive outcome in the non-combinatorial design, but it seems unlikely that the competitive outcome is the one that would emerge in the non-combinatorial case.

We can note further that if bidder B possessed additive values for both items, that is, if his value for the package were 160 instead of 80, there would now be a demand reduction equilibrium. So combinatorial bidding does have some advantages in removing certain types of collusive equilibria but it will not remove all of them and may make those easier for the bidders to settle on. As a collusion-fighting device, a combinatorial mechanism alone is insufficient, but its other benefits may lead to it being a desirable mechanism in cases involving significant cross-licence complementarities.

## 4    Conclusion

It should be clear that collusion in auctions can represent a serious obstacle to an auctioneer raising significant revenue or ensuring an efficient allocation. Finding ways to combat collusion in the rules of an auction is therefore a very important task for a designer. It is unfortunately not always an easy problem to solve and it is definitely not a problem for which either the academic or applied auction design literature has developed a complete solution. It is, however, possible to learn from past mistakes and to identify from the academic literature some principles of good collusion prevention in auction design.

The first principle is that if the pool of bidders that will be participating in an auction interact repeatedly outside of the auction and tend to collude in those dealings, there is little an auctioneer can do to prevent collusion inside the auction. Such situations are beyond the domain of auction design and one must approach them from a policy standpoint, the same as for any other case involving collusion among firms.

If collusion is not quite so endemic to the bidder population, the auctioneer has several tools available for limiting the possibility of the development of in-auction collusion. The first step to dealing with collusion involves understanding the environmental characteristics that make it more likely to occur. These include:

(1) Auctions involving multiple items in which bidders are allowed to win, and are interested in winning, more than a single item. This would include repeated single-unit auctions for related goods.
(2) A small number of bidders relative to the number of objects for sale.
(3) Bidders with preferences that are diverse in terms of the items in which they are mainly interested and possess a low degree of complementarity across items.

In situations that do not meet these criteria, it is significantly less likely that bidders would end up colluding. Consequently an auctioneer may be able to design an auction with less concern for collusion-fighting, allowing them to concentrate on other aspects. If these criteria are met, an auction designer must be very careful in designing an appropriate mechanism to fight collusion. The point is that the needs of fighting collusion in an auction design must be balanced against revenue and efficiency concerns. Designing an auction to fight collusion may, in some cases, be counterproductive as, in doing so, other valuable qualities of the auction may be sacrificed. For example, running a sealed-bid auction to fight collusion in a complex case involving interdependent values, where collusion might be expected to be unlikely, may well sacrifice efficiency and/or revenue. That may not be a good trade-off. In a situation in which collusion is more likely, however, the collusion-fighting properties of the sealed-bid auction may dominate and make the sealed-bid auction worthwhile.

Many of the solutions discussed above seem up to the task of minimising collusion in auctions for small numbers of relatively homogeneous goods. For example, using a properly designed first-price sealed-bid auction, instead of an ascending auction, is perfectly appropriate in simple environments of this sort. If the environment is a little more complex and the auctioneer decides that there are some benefits to the ascending process, concealing the identities of the bidders during an auction would allow the retention of much of the positive value-discovery properties of the ascending auction without allowing the use of effective punishment strategies to support collusive equilibria.

These simple collusion-fighting techniques may not be suitable for use in more complex environments involving such things as value linkages across items and bidders, where they would impair the ability of non-collusive bidders to achieve an efficient competitive outcome. Other approaches involving the encouragement and perhaps even subsidisation of marginal bidders to enter the auction, combinatorial auctions and so forth may be required. It is these situations that pose a true challenge to the auction designer and there is more still to learn about the best techniques for cases such as these.

## References

Albano, G., F. Germano and S. Lovo 2001, 'On some collusive and signaling equilibria in ascending auctions for multiple objects', Working Paper, University College London.

Anton, J. and D. Yao 1992, 'Coordination of split award auctions', *Quarterly Journal of Economics* 107: 681–701.

Ausubel, L. 2002, 'An efficient ascending-bid auction for multiple objects', mimeo, University of Maryland.

Ausubel, L. and P. Cramton 2002, 'Demand reduction and inefficiency in multi-unit auctions', Working Paper, University of Maryland.

Ausubel, L. and P. Milgrom 2001, 'Ascending auctions with package bidding', Working Paper, Stanford University.

Ausubel, L. and J. Schwartz 1999, 'The ascending auction paradox', mimeo, University of Maryland.

Baldwin, L., R. Marshall and J. Richard 1997, 'Bidder collusion at forest service timber sales', *Journal of Political Economy* 105: 657–99.

Binmore, K. and P. Klemperer 2002, 'The biggest auction ever', *Economic Journal* 112: 74–96.

Brusco, S. and G. Lopomo 1999, 'Collusion via signalling in open ascending auctions with multiple objects and complementarities', Working Paper, Stern School of Business, New York University.

Cramton, P. and J. Schwartz 2000, 'Collusive bidding: lessons from the FCC spectrum auctions', *Journal of Regulatory Economics* 17: 229–52.

Demange, G., D. Gale and M. Sotomayor 1986, 'Multi-item auctions', *Journal of Political Economy* 94: 863–72.

Engelbrecht-Wiggans, R. and C. Kahn 1999, 'Low revenue equilibria in simultaneous auctions', Working Paper, University of Illinois.

Fudenberg, D. and E. Maskin 1986, 'The folk theorem in repeated games with discounting or with incomplete information', *Econometrica* 54: 533–54.

Grimm, V. and D. Engelmann 2001, 'Bidding behavior in multi-unit auctions – an experimental investigation', mimeo, Humboldt University, Berlin.

Grimm, V., F. Riedel and E. Wolfstetter 2001, 'Low price equilibrium in multi-unit auctions: the GSM spectrum auction in Germany', Working Paper, Humboldt University, Berlin.

Isaac, R. and S. Reynolds 2002, 'Two or four firms: does it matter?', in C. Holt and I. Mark (eds.), *Research in Experimental Economics*, Kluwer Academic Publishers, Norwell, Mass.

Isaac, R., T. Salmon and A. Zillante 2002, 'A theory of jump bidding in ascending auctions', Working Paper, Florida State University.

Kagel, J. and D. Levin 2001, 'Behavior in multi-unit demand auctions: experiments with uniform price and dynamic vickrey auctions', *Econometrica* 69: 413–54.

Kagel, J., S. Kinross and D. Levin 2001, 'Comparing efficient multi-object auction institutions', mimeo, Ohio State University.

Klemperer, P. 2002a, 'What really matters in auction design', *Journal of Economic Perspectives* 16: 169–90.

2002b, 'Using and abusing auction theory: lessons from auction design', Working Paper, Oxford University.

Kwasnica, A. and K. Sherstyuk 2002, 'Collusion via signaling in multi-unit auctions with complementarities: an experimental test', Working Paper, Pennsylvania State University.

Manelli, A., M. Sefton and B. Wilner 2000, 'Multi-unit auctions: a comparison of static and dynamic mechanisms', Working Paper, Centre for Decision Research and Experimental Economics, University of Nottingham.

Milgrom, P. 2000, 'Putting auction theory to work: the simultaneous ascending auction', *Journal of Political Economy* 108: 245–72.

Milgrom, P. and R. Weber 1982, 'A theory of auctions and competitive bidding', *Econometrica* 50: 1089–122.

Osborne, M. and A. Rubinstein 1994, *A Course in Game Theory*, MIT Press, Cambridge, Mass.

Pesendorfer, M. 2000, 'A study of collusion in first price auctions', *Review of Economic Studies* 67: 381–411.

Phillips, O., D. Menkhaus and K. Coatney 2001, 'Collusive practices in repeated English auctions: experimental evidence on bidding rings', Working Paper, University of Wyoming.

Robinson, M. 1985, 'Collusion and the choice of auction', *Rand Journal of Economics* 16: 141–5.

Sherstyuk, K. 2000, 'Some results on anti-competitive behavior in multi-unit ascending price auctions', in C. Plott and V. Smith (eds.), *Handbook of Experimental Economics Results*, Elsevier, Amsterdam.

Vickrey, W. 1961, 'Counterspeculation, auctions and competitive sealed tenders', *Journal of Finance* 16: 8–37.

Watson, J. 2002, *Strategy: An Introduction to Game Theory*, W.W. Norton & Company, New York.

Weber, R. 1997, 'Making more from less: strategic demand reduction in the FCC spectrum auctions', *Journal of Economics and Management Strategy* 6: 529–48.

# 4    Levelling the playing field in auctions and the prohibition of state aid

*Emiel Maasland, Yves Montangie and*
*Roger van den Bergh*

## 1       Introduction

In order to enhance competition in markets which are not functioning well, governments may decide to assign new rights to supply (licences) in an auction. Because of differences in market power and financial strength, the starting positions of incumbent firms and newcomers are not the same (the playing field is not level). As an ordinary auction, in which all firms are treated symmetrically, may not do very well in creating a more competitive market when the playing field is not level, governments may wish to introduce asymmetries in the auction design (levelling the playing field among firms participating in the auction). This chapter discusses some devices to level the playing field and the conformity of such instruments with EC law.[1] A detailed analysis of the conditions under which a level playing field should be created lies outside the scope of this chapter. However, the essence is well formulated by McMillan (1994, p. 157):

> Theory says that auctions usually produce efficient outcomes: in most cases the winner is the bidder with the highest use-value for the license. This argues for laissez-faire . . . Favoring certain bidders is justified, on the other hand, if bidders' willingness to pay does not reflect social value, because of externalities or capital-market imperfections, or for distributional reasons.

In other words, favouring disadvantaged bidders is only justified when it would prove helpful to economic efficiency, i.e. the sum of consumer and producer surplus.[2]

A possible hindrance to the introduction of asymmetries in the auction design – even in cases where it would contribute to economic efficiency – is

We are grateful for valuable comments from Tilman Börgers.

[1] This chapter will not deal with other possible legal obstacles to these devices, such as the non-discrimination principle as found in national public law.
[2] Consumer surplus is the value that consumers in the aggregate assign to the market outcome. Economists define this notion as the difference between what consumers are prepared to pay and what they actually have to pay. The producer surplus corresponds to the profits producers in the aggregate make.

the prohibition of state aid in European law. Article 87(1) of the EC Treaty prohibits aid granted by a Member State or through state resources, in any form whatsoever, which distorts or threatens to distort competition by favouring certain undertakings, insofar as it affects trade between Member States. If asymmetric auctions come within the definition of state aid, they must be notified to the European Commission and will only be allowed if they fall within categories of state aid which are deemed compatible with EC law, or exempted by the Commission on an individual basis.

The structure of this chapter is as follows. Section 2 summarises a number of ways to favour disadvantaged bidders. One of the ways is to level the playing field. We will distinguish different types of affirmative action, such as setting aside licences for weaker parties (potential entrants) and bidding credits. In section 3 we argue that introducing asymmetries does not need to cost money and may even increase the revenues of the Member States. This insight is particularly relevant for the analysis in section 4, which contains a discussion of the prohibition of state aid. To qualify as state aid, advantages must be granted through state resources on a selective basis. At first blush, asymmetric auctions thus seem to fall within the definition of prohibited state aid, whereas symmetric auctions seem to escape the prohibition because of the absence of specific measures favouring bidders. We will investigate whether affirmative action can be legalised by arguing that it may yield additional revenues and thus not cost money. Section 5 illustrates the main findings of the chapter by offering a discussion of the asymmetries introduced in the British UMTS auction. Section 6 concludes.

## 2    Methods to favour disadvantaged bidders

Asymmetries in auctions may jeopardise the government's task of establishing economic efficiency. The fact is that, without compensating measures, auctions may fail to create a competitive market or raise high auction revenue. Fierce competition is important as it implies a high consumer surplus. High auction revenue is a good alternative to distortionary taxes (another way to raise government income). Governments may therefore want to favour disadvantaged bidders. Broadly speaking, there are three ways of doing this.

(1) *Levelling the playing field.* The government makes the auction rules asymmetric in favour of the disadvantaged bidders.[3]

---

[3] In our definition, the playing field in an auction is level when all bidders have the same *ex ante* probability of winning the object. Economists are divided over the appropriate definition of this notion though. See Onderstal (2002) for a discussion of this topic.

(2) *Changing the auction type* (e.g. simultaneous multiple round auction, sealed-bid auction).

(3) *Corrective measures outside the auction.* The government takes corrective measures before or after the auction, so that differences are levelled out.

Let us start by discussing the first possibility: *levelling the playing field.* There are at least six forms of asymmetry which can be introduced to the auction design (a combination of these forms is, of course, possible too):

- *Full (partial) exclusion,* i.e. forbidding certain bidders to bid on all (certain) licences. In the British UMTS auction, for example, the incumbent firms were not allowed to bid on the largest lot; this was set aside for a newcomer.

- *Making the maximal number of licences to be acquired dependent on the existing market situation.* For instance, firms with greater market power are not allowed to acquire as many licences as firms with less market power.

- *Directly favouring certain bidders financially,* for example by giving certain bidders 'bidding credits'. A bidding credit of $x$ per cent means that if a disadvantaged bidder should win a licence, he has to pay only $(100 - x)$ per cent of his bid. This form of asymmetry was used, for instance, in the United States, where Congress commissioned the Federal Communications Commission (FCC) to ensure that businesses owned by members of minority groups and women were given the opportunity to participate in the mobile telecommunications auctions. These 'designated entities' received bidding credits ranging from 10 per cent to 40 per cent.

- *Indirectly favouring certain bidders financially,* for example by giving disadvantaged bidders the possibility of instalment payments.

- *Allowing certain bidders to withdraw their bids (or to make package bids).* The rationale behind this form of asymmetry is to preclude a newcomer from acquiring an inefficient number of licences.

- *Allowing certain bidders to form bidding alliances for joint bidding.* When small firms are given the opportunity to co-operate, they may be able to achieve economies of scale they would not have realised when bidding alone.

When introducing these kinds of asymmetries governments have to be careful. We mention two reasons. First, asymmetric auction rules open up possibilities for arbitrage. A bidder who satisfies the criteria for preferred treatment can bid, and then sell to a bidder who does not satisfy the criteria. Second, asymmetric auction rules create incentives for bidders not belonging to the favoured group to artificially become a bidder of this group. Both these strategic moves were observed in the British UMTS auction (see section 5).

Let us now discuss the second possibility: *changing the auction type.* The choice of a particular auction type is important. One auction type may do much better than another in creating a competitive market and in raising high revenue. For example, in case of *ex ante* asymmetries among the bidders, auction theorists have argued that it may be desirable to have a first-price sealed-bid auction rather than an ascending auction (see, for example, Klemperer (2002)). The intuition underlying this argument is as follows: in an ascending auction, low-valuation bidders (entrants) know that they will ultimately lose to the bidders with the highest valuations (incumbents). They therefore have no incentive to participate. In a first-price sealed-bid auction, low-valuation bidders win with positive probability at favourable terms and this may induce them to participate. In other words, a first-price sealed-bid auction may encourage participation by lower-valuing bidders, which in turn may lead to a more competitive market structure and higher auction revenue. The European UMTS auctions provide good examples of the importance of this insight. In both the Netherlands and Denmark, the number of licences sold was equal to the number of incumbent mobile phone operators. The Netherlands opted for an ascending auction, Denmark for a sealed-bid auction. In line with the above insight, the Danish UMTS auction turned out to be a success and the Dutch UMTS auction a fiasco. In Denmark, one newcomer succeeded in winning a licence, and revenue far exceeded expectations. In the Netherlands, the auction did not attract entrants, and revenue was relatively low (see, for example, van Damme (2002)).

The third possibility is to take *corrective measures outside the auction.* Let us focus on the incumbent/entrant asymmetry. Incumbents have two important advantages over potential entrants. First, incumbents are better informed as they already know existing market conditions. This informational advantage for the incumbent can be (partly) counteracted by the government by its providing as much relevant information as possible (provided the government has information the entrant does not have). Second, incumbents have an investment lead over potential entrants. In the context of the UMTS auctions, some countries mandated incumbents to give entrants, when winning a licence, the possibility of roaming on their networks and of sharing sites. Such an obligation has the effect of decreasing the investment costs of entrants substantially.

In the rest of this chapter we investigate the question whether the asymmetric treatment of the first type (levelling the playing field) involves state aid. The treatment of the second type (changing the auction type) seems to escape the prohibition of state aid because of the symmetry in the rules of the auction. It seems even more likely not to involve state aid when one realises that the true reason why the government has chosen a particular auction type may not be known *ex post*. We will not deal further with the preferential treatment of the third type (*corrective measures outside the auction*) as these specific measures seem to raise a different legal problem from the one we analyse in this chapter.

## 3    Asymmetric auctions and increased revenue

In this section, we illustrate that affirmative action (through set-asides or bidding credits) does not need to cost money and may even increase revenue.[4] This observation is crucial to the analysis of whether affirmative action implies state aid (see section 4). We would like to stress here that gauging *ex ante* the right level of set-asides and/or bidding credits is extremely difficult, and that when the level of set-asides or bidding credits is chosen incorrectly, it would probably have the effect of decreasing revenue.

### 3.1    Set-asides

Auction revenue can be increased by setting aside certain licences for weaker parties (e.g. potential entrants). The argument is simple: by setting aside licences for the weaker parties the number of licences on which the stronger parties (e.g. incumbents) are allowed to bid is restricted, which will intensify the competition. The intensified competition will lead to a higher price. This higher price can compensate for the lower price on the set-aside licences, so that, in total, higher revenue arises. A simple example may illustrate the argument.

**Example 1:** Consider six bidders competing for four identical licences. Each bidder desires at most one licence. Four of the bidders (who are strong) are willing to pay up to 25 for any licence; and two of the bidders (who are weak) are only willing to pay up to 5. Without any preferential treatment, each of the strong bidders would need to bid only slightly more than 5 to outbid the weaker bidders for each licence. The seller collects 20. But if the seller gave preference by setting aside one licence for the weaker bidders, the four strong bidders competing for one of the three remaining licences would bid close to 25, and the weaker bidders would

---

[4] These examples are borrowed from van Damme (1998).

bid close to 5 for the set-aside licence. This asymmetric auction format lifts the seller's expected revenue by 400 per cent, to 80.[5]                    □

Setting aside licences for weaker bidders can also increase revenue in another way, namely when this increases the number of bidders. In example 1, the number of bidders was exogenously given. If the auction had been symmetric, it is questionable whether bidders with a lower value would have wanted to participate in the auction anyway: for they would not have had a chance to acquire a licence. If they did not participate, the symmetric auction revenue in this example would have been zero. The weaker bidders would only have had a chance if the auction had been asymmetrically designed, as in example 1. As we have seen, this auction format generates revenue of 80.

### 3.2    Bidding credits

Likewise, handicapping the stronger bidders or, equivalently, giving bidding credits to weaker bidders could increase auction revenues. A strong bidder might be willing to bid more because he must now compete with subsidised bids. The extra revenue the seller gets from the strong bidders can more than offset the subsidy to the weaker bidders.[6] Essentially, this system is a generalisation of the above-mentioned system of set-asides, which corresponds roughly with the case in which the bidding credit is close to zero. The system with bidding credits has more degrees of freedom and therefore its revenue, if the bidding credit is chosen appropriately, can be higher in general than in a system with set-asides.

**Example 2:** Consider two bidders competing for one licence. One of the bidders is willing to pay up to 10, the other bidder to 20. In an ordinary ascending auction the second bidder will acquire the licence for a price of 10. However, if the rule is that the second bidder only wins the auction if he bids at least twice the price of the first bidder, he will be forced to bid up to 20 and the revenue will be 20. The factor 2 in this example is optimal from a revenue perspective. With a factor $x$ smaller

---

[5] If the seller knows who is willing to pay 25, then he can collect an even higher revenue by making each of them a 'take it or leave it' offer of (just under) 25. In general, however, a seller will not be so well informed.

[6] This happened, for example, in autumn 1994 when licences for narrow bands of the radio spectrum were awarded for advanced paging services networks. Subsidised bids by a minority-controlled company substantially increased the price a concern paid (see Ayres and Cramton (1996)).

than 2, the second bidder will acquire the licence for a price of $10x$. In this case the revenue is not maximal. With a factor $x$ larger than 2, the first bidder will acquire the licence for a price of $20/x$. In this case the revenue is not maximal either and, moreover, the auction outcome is not efficient (i.e. the bidder who is willing to pay most does not acquire the licence).    □

Example 2 illustrates the importance of choosing the correct bidding credit. A factor which is too high favours one party too much and can lead to an inefficient outcome; a factor which is too low stimulates the competition insufficiently and is to the advantage of the party with the highest value. The factor should be chosen in such a way that a level playing field is provided; the factor should compensate the *ex ante* difference between the values of the bidders exactly: when one bidder assigns on average twice as high a value to a licence than the other, then the latter should be given a bidding credit of 100 per cent, i.e. he should only need to pay 50 per cent of his bid.

In Example 2 the optimal bidding credit was easy to determine since the values were known. In general, this will not be the case. Myerson (1981) has shown that in the case where values are not known, a revenue-maximising seller will also want to make use of an asymmetric auction in which the weaker parties are presented with a certain bidding advantage. This result is illustrated with the following example.

**Example 3:** Suppose that there are two bidders for one licence. The first bidder assigns a low value to the licence, which is not known exactly but can be estimated at somewhere between 0 and 10. (Formally, we assume that all outcomes are equally likely, so we assume a uniform distribution.) Bidder 2 assigns a higher value to the licence, estimated at somewhere between 10 and 30, again with a uniform distribution. In an ascending auction, the second bidder will always acquire the licence for an expected price equal to 5. This bidder realises a large surplus (15 on average) and the revenue of the auction is low. An easy way to increase the revenue is by requiring a minimum bid. With a minimum bid of 10, he always sells the licence and the revenue is 10. A required minimum bid of 15 gives him even higher expected revenue. Now the licence sometimes (with probability $\frac{1}{4}$) remains unsold; however, in all other cases the revenue is 15, and the expected revenue is thus $11\frac{1}{4}$. A seller can realise even higher expected revenue. Myerson shows that the following asymmetric auction maximises the revenue for the seller.[7]

---

[7] The expected revenue of this auction is $13\frac{1}{3}$.

(1) Both bidders are asked to make a bid (sealed bid); $b_i$ is the bid of bidder $i$.

(2) If $b_1 + 10 \geq b_2$ (bidder 2 bids less than 10 more than bidder 1), then the licence will not be sold to bidder 2; bidder 1 gets the licence for the price of max $\{5, b_2 - 10\}$ provided that $b_1 \geq 5$; if $b_1 < 5$, the licence remains unsold.[8]

(3) If $b_2 > b_1 + 10$ (bidder 2 bids at least 10 more than bidder 1), then the licence will be sold to bidder 2 for the price of max $\{15, b_1 + 10\}$, provided that $b_2 \geq 15$; if $b_2 < 15$, the licence remains unsold.

This auction favours bidder 1 with a view to inducing more aggressive bidding by bidder 2. Note that if bidder 1 is not favoured, bidder 2 would never bid more than 10, resulting in an auction revenue of at most 10, while in this auction the payment of bidder 2 to the seller can be up to 20.                                                                          □

In conclusion, if the potential buyers are in asymmetric positions, a revenue-maximising seller will use an asymmetric auction format for the following two reasons.

(1) By doing this he creates a level playing field; he corrects for the *ex ante* given asymmetry, intensifying the competition, and this leads to higher bids.

(2) He gives the weaker bidders an incentive to participate in the auction; the potential demand will be increased by this, which also has a price-increasing effect.

Given an asymmetric starting situation, a symmetric auction generates lower revenue than an (optimal) asymmetric one. Only in the case where the bidders are fully symmetric is an ordinary auction (with an optimal chosen minimum price) revenue-maximising.

## 4    Asymmetric auctions under EC state aid rules

In this section, we investigate the legality of asymmetric auctions under the EC rules on state aid. We will give a short description of these rules and will observe that there are no clear guidelines on their applicability to asymmetric auctions. We will argue that a careful case-by-case approach is required to assess the possible impact of the state aid regime on a particular asymmetric auction and expose a number of legal uncertainties that make it difficult to meet the legal burden of proof.

---

[8] Thus, in a revenue-maximising auction the object will not always be assigned to the highest bidder; to maximise the revenue it is sometimes necessary not to accept the highest bid.

## 4.1     Overview of state aid rules

The EC Treaty includes, according to Article 3(1)g, 'a system ensuring that competition in the internal market is not distorted'. To that end, the EC Treaty contains not only a set of rules aimed at private undertakings,[9] but also provisions on measures of the Member States that may have the effect of distorting competition by granting advantages to certain undertakings.

Article 87(1) of the EC Treaty prohibits, with certain exceptions, any aid granted by a Member State or through state resources, in any form whatsoever, which distorts or threatens to distort competition by favouring certain undertakings or the production of certain goods, insofar as it affects trade between Member States. Article 87(2) enumerates certain categories of state aid that are deemed compatible with the EC Treaty and will automatically be exempted from this prohibition by the European Commission. Article 87(3) mentions some categories of state aid, which are not automatically exempted but can be exempted by the European Commission at its discretion.

Article 88(3) requires that any state aid measure a Member State plans to adopt be notified to the Commission. Member States may not put their proposed aid measures into effect until the Commission has approved them. The Commission examines the compatibility of the aid with the EC Treaty not in terms of the form which it may take, but in terms of its effect. It may decide that the Member State must amend or abolish aid which it finds to be incompatible with the common market. The primacy of EC law over the national law of the Member States, as laid down in established case law of the European Court of Justice, implies that the state aid rules will apply whether or not the measure is allowed by national law.

Where aid has been implemented in breach of the procedural rules, i.e. without a formal notification to the Commission having been made, the aid is illegal and the Member State must in principle recover it from the recipient. Third parties may have this aid declared null and void before a national court of law and, when they have suffered damages from the aid having been granted to other parties, claim damages.

Article 89 of the EC Treaty allows the Council of Ministers of the EU to adopt any appropriate regulations for the application of Articles 87 and 88 and in particular to determine the conditions under which

---

[9] Namely, Article 81 (prohibition of all agreements between undertakings, decisions by associations of undertakings and concerted practices which may affect trade between Member States and which have as their object or effect the prevention, restriction or distortion of competition within the common market) and Article 82 (prohibition of the abuse by one or more undertakings of a dominant position within the common market or in a substantial part of it insofar as it may affect trade between Member States).

Article 88(3) will apply and the categories of aid exempted from this procedure. To this end, the Council has adopted a Regulation which empowers the Commission to exempt certain categories of aid from the prohibition.

### 4.2    Applicability of Article 87 to asymmetric auctions

In the light of the foregoing, it is clear that it may be necessary to assess whether an asymmetric auction, which by its very nature entails granting advantages to certain undertakings, may qualify as a form of state aid as defined in Article 87 of the EC Treaty. The European Commission's existing decision practice does not offer clear guidelines on the applicability of the state aid regime to asymmetric auctions, however. The Commission's decisions on the granting of licences for GSM radiotelephony in Italy and Spain[10] stated that a Member State breaches Article 86 (public enterprises) in conjunction with Article 82 (abuse of dominant position) of the EC Treaty when it discriminates between the incumbent dominant provider and the new second operator to the disadvantage of the latter. However, these decisions do not shed light on the applicability of the state aid rules to auctions that grant certain advantages to newcomers.

Existing EC law on related subjects suggests that asymmetric auctions are likely to fall under the scope of the state aid rules. The following three examples, taken from decisions of the Commission and of the Court of Justice, may illustrate this.

(1) Transactions leading to the sale of land and buildings owned by public authorities are considered to contain elements of state aid when the sale is not concluded on the basis of an *open and unconditional bidding procedure*, accepting the best or only bid, or when, in the absence of such procedure, it is made at less than market value as established by independent valuers.[11]

(2) In privatisation operations, the Commission only considers those operations to fall outside the scope of the state aid rules when the terms and conditions of the sale are *non-discriminatory and transparent* and state property is sold to the highest bidder.

(3) Regarding the application of the state aid rules to procedures leading to the selection of the provider of services of general interest, the Court of

---

[10] Commission's Decision of 4 October 1995, OJ L 280 of 23 November 1995; Commission's Decision of 18 December 1996, OJ L 076 of 18 March 1997.
[11] Commission's Communication on state aid elements in sales of land and buildings by public authorities, OJ C 209 of 10 July 1997.

Justice has ruled that where a benefit granted to an undertaking entrusted with the operation of such a service (in this particular case, the wholesale distribution of medicinal products for human use) merely offsets the additional costs caused by public service obligations, the recipients do not enjoy an advantage within the meaning of Article 87(1) and the measure in question therefore does not constitute state aid.[12] In his conclusion on a case that is currently pending before the Court, advocate-general Jacobs argued that, in such cases, 'to dispel any doubts in a particular case Member States will have an incentive to grant compensation for the provision of general interest services on the basis of unequivocal and transparent arrangements, and perhaps even on the basis of public service contracts awarded after *open, transparent and non-discriminatory public procurement procedures*'.[13]

However, so far it remains uncertain whether these principles will actually apply to asymmetric auctions.

### 4.3     Assessment of asymmetric auctions under the state aid rules

To assess the possible impact of the state aid regime on a particular (type of) asymmetric auction, one will have to analyse on a case-by-case basis

(i) whether the asymmetries introduced in the auction in question can be regarded as state aid, taking into account the definition of this notion and its components; and

(ii) whether the asymmetric auction – when it falls under the scope of the state aid regime – qualifies for one of the exceptions in Article 87(2)–(3) or belongs to one of the categories of aid the Commission has exempted by regulation.

We now discuss these two questions.

*Does a specific asymmetric auction qualify as state aid?*   A state measure is qualified as a form of state aid within the meaning of Article 87 when it meets all of the following four criteria.

(1) *The measure confers on certain undertakings an advantage which they would not enjoy from their own commercial endeavours or which would relieve them of charges that are normally borne from their budgets.*

---

[12] Judgement of the Court of Justice of 22 November 2001 in Case C-53/00, Ferring/ACOSS, [2001] ECR 9067.

[13] Opinion of advocate-general Jacobs of 30 April 2002 in Case C-126/01, Ministère de l'économie, des finances et de l'industrie/GEMO, not yet reported.

*(2) The measure is specific or selective in that it favours only certain undertakings or the production of certain goods or services.*

Asymmetric auctions will probably, by their very nature, meet these two criteria. By contrast, symmetric auctions will not qualify as state aid because of the absence of any selectivity in the auction design.

*(3) The advantage is granted by the state.* This may take the form of any transfer of state resources to private undertakings, be it in the form of an actual payment by the state (e.g. through grants or subsidies) or in the form of a loss of revenue by the state.

In the case of asymmetric auctions, which are intended to increase government's revenue, it may be argued that these 'escape' the definition of state aid to the extent that there is no transfer from the state's resources towards certain private undertakings. In the case of set-asides, the argument could be that no such transfers occur since incumbents will have to pay a higher price for the licences and newcomers would not have had any possibility of acquiring a licence in a symmetric auction. The case of bidding credits may be more difficult: if a party receives a licence at a lower price than he would have had to pay without such a benefit, one could argue that there is a money transfer from the state towards a certain undertaking.[14] This argument may be valid despite the fact that the asymmetric auction may increase the overall revenue of the state. For the legal analysis, the decisive criterion does not seem to be the total revenues of the state but rather the amount of the payment made by an individual undertaking profiting from an advantage granted by the state. At this point, it is striking to notice that symmetric auctions, which clearly do not fall within the prohibition of state aid, may decrease a government's revenue. If bidders are in asymmetric positions licences will be sold below their highest value. As a consequence, the government loses money and no legal rule can avoid this outcome. There thus seems to be a tension between the rules on state aid and the need to organise asymmetric auctions. Even if it could be argued that affirmative action creating a level playing field will lead to higher bids rather than to a decrease of the state's revenue, it may remain difficult to legally prove *ex ante* that the auction will indeed have this effect. Therefore, the outcome of potential state aid cases remains uncertain. As argued in section 3, the difficulty consists in setting the appropriate types and levels of asymmetries to guarantee a positive result. If the level of set-asides or bidding credits is chosen wrongly, the revenue of the state may decrease. In any

---

[14] However, in most cases, it is likely that all winners will pay more.

case, since there are no precedents in the Commission's decision practice supporting the argument that asymmetric auctions increasing state revenue escape the prohibition of Article 87(1) of the EC Treaty, it will prove difficult to conclude that an asymmetric auction falls outside the scope of the prohibition on state aid.

(4) *The measure must affect competition and trade between Member States.* Under settled case law, this criterion is usually met if the aid strengthens a firm's position relative to that of other firms that are competitors in intra-Community trade and, *a fortiori*, when the recipient firm itself carries on an economic activity involving/connected to any trade between the Member States.

In the case of asymmetric auctions, it may be argued that the distortion of competition, in the sense of Article 87, during the auction is offset by the enhanced competition after the auction. Indeed, one has to distinguish the competition in the auction and the competition in the post-auction market. This brings us to another tension in current policy-making: there may be a trade-off between the prohibition of state aid and the rules on competition. Giving benefits to certain bidders (for instance, by excluding incumbents enjoying market power) may be defended on the ground that this will improve competition in the post-auction market. This would then lead to the conclusion that the state measure, on balance, has a pro-competitive effect that may justify excluding it from the scope of Article 87(1). However, it is again difficult to make a hard case out of this argument since the *ex ante* economic analysis on how competition in the post-auction market will develop will probably not meet the legal burden of proof. Because of these uncertainties and the lack of precedents supporting such reasoning, the validity of this argument remains uncertain.

*Does the auction qualify for one of the exceptions to the state aid prohibition?*   In the event that a state measure such as an asymmetric auction is regarded as a form of state aid, the possibility of treating it as one of the exceptions needs to be considered. Three of these exceptions may be of relevance here:

(1) *The exception of Article 87(3)b of the EC Treaty for aid intended to promote the execution of a project of common European interest (or to remedy a serious disturbance in the economy).* To benefit from this exception, one would first have to demonstrate that the aid is in the interest of a project of common European interest. There is no clear definition of this notion. While it is clear from the Commission's decision practice that this exception is not limited to projects in which all Member States are

involved, it will nevertheless be necessary to demonstrate that the aid would lead to the achievement of a community objective and would not be limited to benefiting the interests of one particular Member State. It is also doubtful whether aid directed at specific firms in one specific sector would be considered to be justifiable by this exception.[15]

Second, it would have to be demonstrated that the state aid measure is necessary to achieve this result and that it could not have been obtained otherwise (for instance, through the market process).

Furthermore, one would have to demonstrate in advance that the duration, intensity and scope of the aid are proportional to the importance of the intended result.

It is clear that it would be very difficult to legally prove *ex ante* that all of these requirements are met in the case of an asymmetric auction. Furthermore, one has to bear in mind that aid qualifying for an exception under this provision would in any case still have to be notified to the Commission, and the Commission would ultimately decide whether the exception applies.

(2) *The exception of Article 87(3)c for aid intended to facilitate the development of certain economic activities . . . where such aid does not adversely affect trading conditions to an extent contrary to the common interest*. To benefit from this exception, it would have to be demonstrated that the aid is directed at the development of an economic activity in general and not just the development of specific undertakings. It is improbable that aid to weaker undertakings in a market that overall is considered 'healthy' would be allowed under this exception. Here too, it would have to be shown in advance that the state aid measure is necessary to achieve this result and that its duration, intensity and scope are proportional to the intended result.

Again, it will prove difficult to establish legally that an asymmetric auction meets all of these requirements. Aid qualifying for an exception under this provision would also still have to be notified to the Commission who would ultimately decide whether the exception applies.

(3) *The exception for* de minimis *aid*. On the basis of the powers granted to it by the Council, the Commission has issued a regulation in which it defines so-called *de minimis* aid.[16] This is aid which is sufficiently small that no appreciable effect on trade and competition among the Member States is anticipated.

---

[15] Commission's Decision of 15 November 1988, OJ L 106 of 18 April 1989.
[16] Commission's Regulation (EC) No. 69/2001 of 12 January 2001 on the application of Articles 87 and 88 of the EC Treaty to *de minimis* aid, OJ L10 of 13 January 2001.

To be qualified as *de minimis* aid, the aid granted by a state measure to a particular undertaking must not exceed €100,000 over a three-year period from when the first *de minimis* aid is granted. This limit is expressed as a cash grant of €100,000. In cases where assistance is provided in a form other than a grant, it has to be converted into its cash grant equivalent value for the purposes of applying the *de minimis* limit.

For an asymmetric auction to escape the prohibition on state aid, it would have to be shown that the value of the benefit attributed to the participating undertakings does not exceed the €100,000 limit when converted to a cash equivalent.

State measures that can be qualified as *de minimis* aid are thought not to fall under the scope of Article 87(1) and do not have to be notified to the Commission under Article 88(3).

## 5     Case study: the British UMTS auction

A case study can illustrate the principles developed above. To this end, we analysed the auction of UMTS licences in the UK. Our analysis will focus exclusively on the conformity of the set-aside, which was introduced in this particular auction, with the EC rules on state aid. We first give a brief economic evaluation.

The UK government used a simultaneous ascending auction to auction five 3G licences, termed A–E. The bandwidth for each licence is shown in table 4.1. Licence A was set aside for a new entrant. Only potential new entrants were allowed to bid for this licence.[17] All bidders (four incumbents and nine potential new entrants) could bid on any of the remaining licences (B to E), and each bidder could win at most one licence. Furthermore, a measure was used to ensure that the new entrant(s) had access to roaming on 2G networks. This was by means of a roaming condition inserted in an incumbent's Telecoms Act licence, which would be triggered if the incumbent won a 3G spectrum licence.[18] The UK government defined its objectives for the auction as to:

(1) utilise the available spectrum with optimum efficiency ('efficiency');
(2) promote effective and sustainable competition in the provision of 3G services ('competition'); and
(3) subject to the overall objectives above, design an auction that is best able to realise the full economic value to customers, industry and the taxpayer of the spectrum ('revenue maximisation').

---

[17] 2G service providers, like Virgin Mobile, were also considered as potential new entrants.
[18] As indicated in section 2, we will not analyse this form of asymmetry.

Table 4.1. *Bandwidth in MHz for each licence*

|  | A | B | C | D | E |
|---|---|---|---|---|---|
| Paired spectrum | $2 \times 15$ | $2 \times 15$ | $2 \times 10$ | $2 \times 10$ | $2 \times 10$ |
| Unpaired spectrum | 5 | 0 | 5 | 5 | 5 |
| Total | 35 | 30 | 25 | 25 | 25 |

In a report of the UK National Audit Office (2001, p. 5), one can read that the UK government and the Radiocommunications Agency essentially reserved licence A (the largest one) for a new entrant because of goal 2, in spite of the fact that reserving more spectrum for an entrant would be at the expense of goal 1:

The Government recognised that the incumbent companies' existing networks and customer base are major barriers to new entrants, who would have to build their own networks over several years during which their service could be inferior and unattractive to consumers. The Agency allocated more spectrum for the new entrant in order to strengthen its business. Extra spectrum allows operators to reduce their investment in infrastructure, and to sell surplus capacity to other companies who wish to offer telephone services under their own brands. This is inefficient in technical terms because the new entrant, Hutchison 3G UK (TIW), starts with no existing base of customers, and the extent to which its spectrum will remain under-utilised depends on how quickly the company attracts customers and gets them using advanced, non-voice services. The Agency and OFTEL however, saw efficiency in wider terms, considering that a new entrant would roll out 3G services quickly and exert competitive pressure on the four incumbent companies to do likewise. This reduced the risk that the incumbents might otherwise defer their investment in 3G services while exploiting their spectrum only for less intensive voice telephony.

Cramton (2001, p. 53) argues that, on balance, setting aside the largest licence for a new entrant probably was a desirable trade-off between 'competition' and 'efficiency'. His argument is as follows:

The only potential source of inefficiency was setting aside a large 15 MHz license for a new entrant. The bidding revealed that BT valued the extra 5 MHz more than the new entrant TIW. However, guaranteeing that the entrant would win a 15 MHz license and not be forced to pay BT's incremental value for 5 extra MHz likely was pro-competitive, both in the auction and in the post-auction market. The set-aside surely stimulated participation by potential entrants. Post-auction competition was also stimulated, since the new entrant (TIW) will be stronger and less capacity constrained as a result of the extra 5 MHz block.

The auction resulted in unprecedented proceeds of £22.5 billion, which was not only more than had been raised by previous allocations of spectrum licences in the UK, but also more than the proceeds of similar auctions in other countries.

A closer inspection of the events in the British UMTS auction suggests, however, a slightly more cautious evaluation, for two reasons. Firstly, the British design (which favoured outsiders) created incentives for potential entrants to act as arbitrageurs, that is to bid in the auction in their own name, and later to sell licences to non-entrants. It is widely rumoured that arbitrage did occur. The set-aside was won by a Canadian company called TIW, which, as it turned out, was not interested in a licence. TIW sold its licence immediately after the auction to Hutchison Whampoa.[19] This appears to have been a pre-arranged deal. Why was it done in this way? The UK government said after the auction that Hutchison Whampoa, had it tried to bid in its own name, would not have been allowed to join the auction. This was because Hutchison Whampoa did not dispose fast enough of its shares in Orange. It also had close board links with Vodafone, although these, apparently, would not have constituted any problem. Secondly, the British design created incentives for bidders to become outsiders artificially. It is likely that Hutchison Whampoa's 1999 sale of Orange was motivated by its desire to be admitted as an outsider to the auction. This failed for Hutchison Whampoa, because it did not sell Orange fast enough, but it is widely believed that this was its aim.[20]

From a legal point of view, the asymmetries present in the British UMTS auction were deemed compatible with the provisions of the European Licensing Directive, which was applicable here. The Licensing Directive requires licences to be granted on the basis of open, non-discriminatory and transparent procedures unless there is a reason for 'objective differentiation'. The Radiocommunications Agency believed that the decision to reserve a licence was justified in this case, while realising that, as with any licensing decision, it could still have been subject to a legal challenge. The Agency considered that, if there had been five incumbents, a legal challenge might have been more difficult to counter. In that case, it might have been hard to convince the courts that the set-aside was a proportionate measure, since one incumbent would have been excluded from getting a licence.

While this reasoning might lay the basis for an interesting theoretical legal discussion, we focus, as indicated in section 1, on the question of whether the EC state aid rules were applicable. One has to bear in mind that the provisions of the EC Treaty override any instruments of secondary EC law such as regulations and directives. This means that, even

---

[19] More precisely, it sold the subsidiary, which owned the licence.
[20] The manoeuvres described above are documented in more detail by Börgers and Dustmann (2003).

if the auction was in line with the provisions of the European Licensing Directive, one would still have to comply with the state aid rules where they apply. According to our information, the question of the legality of the auction in the light of these rules was considered during the preparation of the auction, but the European Commission was not contacted on the issue.

Nevertheless, it may prove difficult to deny the applicability of the state aid rules to the UK auction, taking account of the four criteria described above (see section 4.3).

The first two criteria would without any doubt be met. In its 'Vademecum – Community rules on state aid', the European Commission (2002) states that an economic advantage is being conferred upon undertakings 'when a company enjoys privileged access to infrastructure without paying a fee', a situation which is comparable to the one at hand (criterion 1). Since a certain category of undertakings was excluded from bidding for licence A, the measure is inherently selective (criterion 2).

A more difficult – and crucial – question is whether this advantage can be considered to imply a transfer of state resources (criterion 3). In its decisions regarding sales of assets by Member States or state companies, the European Commission argues that their behaviour 'should correspond to the rationale of a private vendor operating under normal market economy conditions . . . In these conditions, a private vendor would examine the possibility of alternative purchase offers and sell the asset to the person making the highest offer.'[21] When the sale of assets by a Member State yields a lower profit than would be the case under normal market conditions, the Commission will consider this as state aid.

When applying this legal standard to the UK auction, one would have to establish *ex ante* that the chosen auction mechanism guarantees higher revenue than without affirmative action. It seems to be difficult to build up a solid *ex ante* legal reasoning in this particular case. Firm estimates of the value of the licences proved difficult since 'there had been no previous auction to provide a benchmark, and the [Radiocommunications] Agency's financial advisers found it difficult to obtain any valuations from the industry itself' (National Audit Office, 2001, p. 17). Furthermore, the Agency and its advisers 'had considered before the auction that the huge variances in financial market conditions, and between the operators, made it very difficult to predict the likely total revenue from the auction' (National Audit Office, 2001, p. 17). These uncertainties make it very difficult to exclude with certainty the applicability of the state aid

---

[21] Commission's Decision of 21 July 1991 (Derbyshire County Council/Toyota Motor Corporation), OJ L 6 of 11 January 1992.

rules on the basis of this third criterion. Even *ex post* it is difficult to tell whether overall revenues would have been higher or lower without the set-aside. Revenues could have been lower as the two strongest incumbents (Vodafone and BT) were not competing for one large licence, but for two. The price for the large licences would have been set by the third strongest incumbent (Orange). Whether overall revenues would have been higher or lower without the set-aside depends on how high Orange would have been willing to bid for the extra 5 MHz of paired spectrum. According to Cramton's (2001, p. 52) analysis of the bid data, overall revenues would have been slightly lower without the set-aside.

As far as the effect on competition and trade between the Member States (criterion 4) is concerned, it is clear that the auction had the effect of enhancing the position of an undertaking or a selected group of undertakings (the newcomers) relative to that of their competitors (the incumbents) who, according to the National Audit Office (2001, p. 39) report, have all 'built nationwide mobile networks in the United Kingdom and either own, or are linked to, companies with an international customer base'. The fourth criterion, as described above, would therefore probably be met.

The question remains of whether the argument that the auction was intended to increase competition in the post-auction market, thus offsetting the distortion of competition and having an overall pro-competitive effect, is valid. First, one has to remember that the applicability of the state aid rules to a certain state measure depends on its foreseeable effect and not on its causes or aims: the objective of the measure is irrelevant and will not suffice to put it outside the scope of Article 87.[22]

Second, it remains to be seen whether it was possible to prove and quantify *ex ante* what the pro-competitive effects of the auction would be in order to 'escape' the applicability of the state aid rules. It is clear that the new entrant will be stronger and less capacity-constrained as a result of the extra 5 MHz block. However, it is difficult to tell *ex ante* how much the post-auction competition will be stimulated by this, and whether it will be enough to offset the distortion of competition, in the sense of Article 87, during the auction.

Third, as stated above, there are no precedents supporting such an argument. On the contrary, in its communication on the application of the state aid rules in the aviation sector,[23] the Commission suggests that

---

[22] Judgement of the Court of Justice of 2 July 1974 in Case 173/73, Italy / Commission, [1979] ECR 709, recital 13.

[23] Commission's Communication on the application of Articles 92 and 93 (now 87 and 88) of the EC Treaty and Article 61 of the EEA agreement to state aid in the aviation sector, OJ C 350 of 10 December 1994. In this communication, the Commission lays down, among other things, the principles applying to sales of shareholdings by Member States or state companies.

operations in which the government disposes of certain assets will in certain circumstances be subject to the pre-notification requirements of Article 87(3) of the EC Treaty because there is a presumption that they contain aid. This would be the case when they are 'sales *by way of restricted methods* or where the sale takes the form of a direct trade sale' (emphasis added).

Since it would be difficult to argue *ex ante* that the fourth criterion is not met, it seems that one cannot rule out with certainty the applicability of the state aid rules.

Furthermore, one can hardly see how any of the possible exemptions would apply to the auction. The exception of Article 87(3)b for aid intended to promote the execution of a project of common European interest would not apply, since the positive effects of the auction would most probably be limited to the UK. The exception of Article 87(3)c for aid intended to facilitate the development of certain economic activities would probably not apply either since the auction was not, as such, aimed at the development of an economic activity in general. Besides, in both cases, the state measure would still have to be notified to the Commission. The exception for *de minimis* aid would be very difficult to apply, since it would not only be very hard to estimate the cash value of the advantage that was being granted, but also very unlikely that this value would be below €100,000.

## 6    Conclusion

This chapter has illustrated that there is a tension between asymmetric auction design and the prohibition of state aid. Even though arguments can be advanced to allow affirmative action by governments to be exempted from the prohibition of state aid, legal certainty on this issue does not exist. The main argument allowing asymmetric auctions is the following. It may be shown, at least theoretically, that affirmative action yields additional revenues for the state. If all bidders either pay more for the licence, rather than less, or would have had no chance to obtain a licence in a symmetric auction, the basic requirement for state aid that there must be a transfer of state resources would not be satisfied. It may be more difficult to argue along these lines if the effect of an asymmetric auction is that an individual firm has to pay less for a licence, even if the overall revenue of the state increases. However, even assuming that the argument that the auction design increases overall state revenue is legally acceptable, there will never be absolute certainty. The prohibition of state aid could be avoided only by accepting theoretical arguments and reasonable forecasts of auction results. However, these may not meet the legal burden of proof. Hence, the tension between asymmetric auction design and the prohibition of state aid remains. Another example of the uneasy relation between auction design and state aid rules is the fact that symmetric auctions, which may decrease state revenues if bidders are in asymmetric positions, will be deemed legal.

It has also been shown in this chapter that there is another tension – between the prohibition of state aid and the promotion of competition. To enhance competition in the post-auction market, affirmative action to exclude dominant firms from participating in the auction may be desirable. This argument in favour of asymmetric auctions is also fraught with legal uncertainties. Economic analysis on how markets would have developed with other players may again not meet the legal burden of proof. Moreover, ordinary rules of competition law may cope with possible abuses. Hence, the question remains of whether asymmetries are a proportional remedy to the expected restrictions of competition in the post-auction market.

Given all the legal uncertainties surrounding affirmative action by the Member States, it seems wise to notify asymmetric auctions to the European Commission. This does not necessarily imply that they will be forbidden. Rather, it will enable the Commission to gather experience and collect the necessary information to develop rules concerning asymmetric auctions. This should ultimately lead to a Notice or a Group Exemption specifying the rules under which Member States can introduce asymmetries in auction design. Such a measure would at the same time bring about more legal certainty and mitigate the tensions discussed in this chapter.

In our view, these tensions should be resolved. If this cannot be achieved within the framework of the EC competition rules, specific regulatory action is required. Member States should not be hindered in choosing the auction design appropriate for maximising producer and consumer surplus.

## References

Ayres, I. and P. Cramton 1996, 'Deficit reduction through diversity: how affirmative action at the FCC increased auction competition', *Stanford Law Review*, 48(4): 761–815.

Börgers, T. and C. Dustmann 2003, 'Awarding telecom licenses: the recent European experience', *Economic Policy*, 36: 216–68.

Cramton, P. 2001, 'Lessons learned from the UK 3G spectrum auction', in National Audit Office (2001), Appendix 3.

Damme, E. van 1998, 'Asymmetrisch veilen: waarom geen sprake is van staatssteun?' ('Asymmetric auctioning: why should it not be considered as state aid?'), mimeo, Netherlands Ministry of Finance.

2002, 'The European UMTS-Auctions', *European Economic Review*, 46(4–5): 846–58.

European Commission 2002, 'Vademecum – Community rules on state aid', Directorate-General for Competition, Brussels.

Klemperer, P. 2002, 'What really matters in auction design', *Journal of Economic Perspectives*, 16(1): 169–90.

McMillan, J. 1994, 'Selling spectrum rights', *Journal of Economic Perspectives*, 8(3): 145–62.

Myerson, R. 1981, 'Optimal auction design', *Mathematics of Operations Research*, 6(1): 58–73.

National Audit Office 2001, 'The auction of radio spectrum for the third generation of mobile telephones', Report by the Comptroller and Auditor General, HC 233 Session 2001–2.

Onderstal, S. 2002, 'Level playing field in the design of auctions', mimeo, CPB (Netherlands Bureau for Economic Research).

# 5 Allocation mechanisms and post-allocation interaction

*Maarten Janssen and Benny Moldovanu*

## 1 Introduction

In many traditional auctions, the seller or auctioneer is only interested in the price obtained for the auctioned objects. That is, the sole objective is to raise revenue. But, whenever a government sells some rights, it is often the case that it is also interested in *who* will get the rights, and *how* the rights will be used. Generally speaking, when a market arises after an allocation mechanism is implemented (as is the case with mobile telephony frequencies, radio frequencies or the right to exploit petrol stations along highways) a government is also interested in welfare issues related to the functioning of the industry and the economy as a whole. Hence, the seller may try to establish at the allocation stage conditions that ensure a future competitive market. Thus, whenever an auction affects the way a market functions, the seller (government) may have multiple objectives rather than the single one of maximising revenue. One of the questions that arise is: how should these multiple objectives be ranked?

For potential bidders there are also fundamental differences between participating in a regular auction[1] and participating in an auction which gives the winner(s) an entry ticket to the market that arises afterwards. When there is a market after the auction, bidders may care about who (else) wins the auction and with what rights. This implies that their valuations are endogenous: they depend on the entire partition of objects among potential bidders. As a consequence of the ensuing strategic aspects, some of the fundamental results of traditional auction theory may fail to hold. In particular, the reasons for favouring auctions over Beauty Contests are no longer clear-cut.

The above issues are particularly relevant in privatisation exercises. Large privatisation exercises (such as licence auctions and Beauty

We would like to thank Eric van Damme for helpful comments.

[1] For accounts of the traditional theory, see Börgers and van Damme (this volume, chapter 1) or, for a more elaborate overview, Krishna (2002).

130

Contests) do not only allocate scarce goods, but also determine the nature of whole industries. The initial allocation is just the beginning of a prolonged interaction among firms, consumers and regulators. Potential acquirers of licences, say, will try to anticipate their respective profits in the possible future scenarios as a function of the auction's outcome, i.e. as a function of who wins licences, who receives what capacity, what prices are paid, etc. This means that the values of the acquired items cannot be exogenously determined; rather, they depend on the auction's outcome. This is a novel aspect that differentiates large privatisation exercises from other more standard allocation situations. A good recent example that involved huge monetary stakes was the German UMTS auction where the number of licensed firms could vary between four and six. Prior to the auction, a major investment bank (see Deutsche Bank, 2000) estimated per licence values of €14.75 billion, €15.88 billion and €17.6 billion for a German symmetric market with six, five and four firms, respectively. Whatever these numbers are worth, they clearly illustrate the perceived endogeneity of valuations, and suggest that firms should try to reduce the number of sold licences in order to increase future profits. It is obvious that strategic behaviour directed at influencing the number of licences may also affect various goals such as attaining an efficient allocation or maximising revenue (in fact, firms collectively paid at that auction about €20 billion (!) in order to reduce the number of licences from six to five or four, but were ultimately unsuccessful).[2]

As suggested by the above example, during an allocation procedure with endogenous valuations, firms will condition their behaviour on their expectations about future scenarios, and will act strategically in order to achieve the best possible scenario from their point of view. But this may not always be in the interest of a government which also has preferences over the various scenarios that go beyond the monetary revenue that is raised. These preferences must also represent the interests of future consumers, other future users of the scarce resources, other current users, etc. Hence, a government may want to be careful in designing allocation mechanisms by which rights are privatised.

This chapter focuses on the many ways in which allocation mechanisms and post-allocation events interact. The chapter is organised as follows. Section 2 looks more closely at several common seller objectives. In section 3 we briefly look at strategic bidding behaviour in

---

[2] See, also Maasland and Moldovanu (this volume, chapter 7). In the German case, this number can be easily measured as follows. At the moment when only six bidders were left competing for six licences, total bids amounted to €30 billion. But bidding continued as some bidders wanted to have bigger licences and fewer parties in the market. The auction ended with revenue of almost €50 billion, but all six bidders were licensed.

auctions with 'external effects' – these effects allow us to describe situations in which bidders care not only about their own allocation, but also about the entire distribution of rights among the relevant agents, i.e. they care about who (else) wins what.[3] Next, in section 4 we describe the main features of allocation procedures that are followed by interactions among the agents. We point out that these strategic effects may completely blur the relations between some standard and well-known design goals. The main new strategic effects are illustrated via several simple examples. In section 5, we summarise the resulting main lessons for the design of allocation procedures that influence future market outcomes.

Before proceeding, we want to mention that the influence of future interaction on competitive 'bidding' situations is widespread, and is not confined to privatisation exercises. Here are a few other interesting examples (see also Jehiel and Moldovanu (1996) and Jehiel, Moldovanu and Stacchetti (1996)):

- In takeover or merger deals, the structure of an industry may dramatically change and even firms that are not part of the transaction may be positively or negatively affected. We often see prolonged waves of restructuring in the same industry, as firms react to the merger of some competitors by merging themselves, exiting, etc.
- Any acquisition of an 'input' that is crucial for future competition (e.g. a licence to operate, a new major customer, a project that leads to the creation of an industry standard, etc.) will affect competitors in a significant way. This means that there are externalities between competitors that go beyond the competition for the object at stake.
- A large firm locating in a certain community may also create new jobs in nearby areas, and/or environmental damage to a larger region. Note that the location of large firms can be seen as a competitive bidding situation in cases where communities compete with tax rebates and other infrastructure sweeteners in order to attract large employers.
- The sales of weapon systems have clear adverse effects on countries or groups that have a serious conflict with the acquirer.

## 2   Auctions and future interaction: the seller's objectives

Efficiency in the economy at large or in a particular sector is generally enhanced when markets are competitive and when the most cost-efficient

---

[3] We focus here on physical external effects (agents care about the entire distribution of physical goods), and not on informational external effects arising when valuations also depend on the distribution of information available to other agents (see, in this context, Jehiel and Moldovanu (2000b, 2001a) and Maskin (1992)).

firms are active. Thus, in addition to monetary revenue,[4] a government may be interested in other objectives. In the Introduction to this book, other objectives are mentioned and defined, such as an efficient allocation process and efficiency of the market that appears after the auction. In a 'traditional' auction for one object there need not be a conflict between these different objectives: the criterion of an efficient market is not relevant since there is no market after the auction, while efficiency of the allocation process may fit very well with maximising revenue. This picture changes if there is a market after the auction. For example, it may be possible to raise high revenues by creating a privatised monopoly (since monopolistic profits tend to be higher than total oligopoly profits), but such an outcome is undesirable if it means that, owing to the absence of competition, consumers will have to pay high prices in the future.[5] That is, revenue maximisation is at odds with the objective of achieving a competitive market. We argue below that the relations among goals such as 'market efficiency' (which includes the government's and consumers' preferences), 'value maximisation' or 'efficiency of the auction allocation' (which focuses on the efficiency of the acquiring firms) and 'revenue maximisation' become complex and less transparent. Failing to take into account the effect of future interaction may have harsh consequences for governments and/or consumers.

For another prominent example, consider several of the questions related to the incumbent–entrant asymmetry in the UMTS licensing exercise. Should the government create a level playing field? Should licences be reserved for newcomers? Should handicaps be imposed on some bidders? Newcomers usually have lower valuations than incumbents and this is what we assume in what follows. An immediate observation is that if the government wants to 'put the licences in the hands of those who value them the most',[6] i.e. if it wants to *maximise the value generated by the auction*, it should not reserve a licence for a newcomer. On the other hand, reserving a licence for a newcomer may or may not increase *the revenue* that is raised through the auction, depending on how much competition there is for the remaining licences and how fiercely these same firms

---

[4] In what follows we will say that a mechanism is a revenue-maximising mechanism if, in the class of possible mechanisms, it is the one that yields the highest expected revenue.

[5] This is the case when the bidders are quite similar and expect identical profits in monopoly and oligopoly settings. When there is one strong bidder and many weak bidders, the strong bidder has to bid slightly more than the value of one of the weaker bidders in order to obtain the monopoly right. In this case, revenue may be increased by creating an oligopoly.

[6] This phrase is often used to explain the benefits of auctions to laymen. See Milgrom (2000).

would compete if no licence was reserved.[7] Finally, in terms of *after-market efficiency*, reserving licences for entrants usually increases market competition, as the newcomers have to fight to obtain market share. This increase in competition has to be weighed against the potential duplication of fixed costs.

Given that the three goals may diverge or even be inconsistent with each other, it is important to ask whether these objectives can be ranked from an economic point of view. Using the notion of total surplus, several interesting observations can be made.[8] First, the auction's revenue should not be a (very) important objective for the government, as total surplus is independent of the revenue raised through an auction: whatever amount the government raises through the auction comes at the expense of the winning firms (i.e. their shareholders). To be fair, one should take into account the possibility that the government will decrease taxes, since auction revenues can substitute for tax revenues. Since taxes are usually collected in such a way that they distort the economic process while auctions impose non-distortionary lump-sum taxes, revenue-raising through auction may enhance welfare. Unlike revenue maximisation (the welfare effect of which depends on the magnitude of the tax substitution), value maximisation and market efficiency always influence total surplus to a great extent.

## 3     Auctions and future interaction: buyers' strategies

We often think about traditional auctions as being populated by people who demand the good solely for their own consumption purposes. In particular, the agents do not care about the allocation of goods among the rest of society. As we explained above, such traditional thinking about auctions cannot accurately encompass situations arising where agents interact after the allocation procedure in a way that is influenced by the allocation procedure itself. Therefore, we need to consider extended models that allow us to capture the various ways in which agents care about how goods are allocated to others. It is common to call such

---

[7] An important issue in this context is whether newcomers will bother to participate in the auction if no licence is reserved for them and if the number of licences equals the number of incumbents (see Jehiel and Moldovanu (2001) and Klemperer (2002)).

[8] When considering the welfare implications of policy proposals, economists work either with the notion of Pareto efficiency or with the notion of total surplus. An allocation is Pareto-efficient if there does not exist another allocation in which some agents are better off, while nobody is worse off. Pareto efficiency does not compare the surpluses of different agents. The measure of total surplus simply adds all the surplus (welfare) of all agents in society. For our purposes, Pareto efficiency is too weak a notion since many outcomes are Pareto-efficient.

effects 'externalities', and to differentiate between 'positive' and 'negative' externalities.[9] In our context, the externalities represent the individual effects of each future scenario resulting from a particular allocation of goods among the agents. Firms, who are the buyers in these auctions, may impose externalities upon each other, but also on consumers and on the seller (government). One important externality arises from the fact that consumers are not active players in these auctions. In what follows we consider examples in which we assume that the seller is also interested in consumer welfare. Hence, we will focus upon externalities that the bidding behaviour of firms may impose on other firms and on the seller.

The presence of externalities creates a multitude of new and surprising strategic effects. We illustrate a few important ones through some simple examples. The first example illustrates how externalities can strongly affect the identity of the winner and the resulting price. In particular, with negative externalities, agents are willing to pay more than their intrinsic valuations in order to prevent the good falling into in the hands of another, i.e. there is a value attached to pre-emption. The opposite phenomenon occurs when there are positive externalities – agents are willing to pay less than their intrinsic valuations if they can expect a positive payoff in the event of another one winning. This is usually called 'the free-rider problem' and often plagues the private provision of public goods.

**Example 1:** There are two buyers. Buyer A values the object at 10 , while buyer B values the object at 8. In a standard auction, buyer A will get the object and pay approximately 8. But now consider the situation where buyer A suffers a loss of 4 if buyer B gets the object, while buyer B suffers a loss of 7 if buyer A gets the object. Now buyer A will be willing to pay as high as 14 (10 + 4) in order to prevent the good going to buyer B. Similarly, buyer B will be prepared to pay as high as 15 (8 + 7). Hence, at a standard auction, buyer B will win the object at a price of approximately 14. Note that, relative to the status quo before the auction, B is actually incurring a loss of 6. But this is better than the alternative where A gets the object, in which case B incurs a loss of 7. Note that valuations here are endogenous since, for example, if A publicly commits not to buy the object (say, by not filling the auction registration forms), the valuation of B immediately drops from 15 to 8. □

---

[9] Positive externalities are present when the payoff of one agent goes up when another agent consumes an item or bundle, while negative externalities are present when the payoff goes down.

The example shows that winning players may consciously take a loss. If taking such a loss seems curious, consider the following quotation from *The Economist* (28 June 1997, p. 97), which describes a bidding war among producers of aircraft engines.

The good sales at Rolls-Royce began 18 months ago when it snatched a huge order to supply Singapore Airlines . . . Its hard-nosed American rivals, Pratt & Whitney and General Electric, were prepared to take a loss to land such a prestigious deal. So they assumed Rolls-Royce won the bid by taking an even greater loss.

The idea behind this quote is that a failure to get the Singapore deal would put the firm in a disadvantageous position when bidding for later deals. The need to avoid this disadvantage in future market interactions drove firms to sacrifice current profits.

Example 1 gives some insight into one of the reasons that have been put forward in order to explain why telecom companies have paid such enormous sums of money for acquiring UMTS frequencies in some European countries: if incumbents feared that their current GSM frequencies would become worthless without the new UMTS services, they would be willing to pay more than their respective intrinsic valuations for the UMTS frequencies.[10]

When there are more than two buyers it can also be shown, with either positive or negative externalities, that some agents may prefer not to participate at an auction if they perceive that their mere presence (via the externalities) will influence the identity of the winner or the price to be paid (as in Example 1). For example, the French food conglomerate BSN quit a bidding war over Perrier in order to allow Nestlé to take over. It simply feared Nestlé less than other bidders.[11]

## 4    Buyers' strategies and sellers' objectives

We have discussed how a seller's possible objectives are related to each other, and how bidders may adapt their bidding behaviour in environments where externalities are important. We will now discuss the seller's objectives and the bidders' strategies simultaneously via several simple examples.

The first example in this section shows that value maximisation (for buyers) and efficiency (which also takes into account the seller's utility)

---

[10] Considerations like this may also have played a role in the strategic decisions of telecom operators to participate (or not) in different European auctions. After many newcomers did not win a licence in the first auction in the UK, they may have decided that their value of a licence in other European countries had gone down considerably.

[11] See *The Economist* (1992).

may diverge when there are externalities. In particular, this implies that a government interested in market efficiency may want to handicap some bidders while favouring others.

**Example 2**: Consider the same situation, with externalities as in Example 1, but imagine that the seller also incurs externalities. Assume that, besides getting the revenue from the auction, the seller incurs a loss of 2 if buyer A gets the object, and a loss of 4 if buyer B gets the object (for example, imagine that the buyers are taking over a public firm which is being privatised, and that they both have restructuring plans which include firing different numbers of workers; the government would, *ceteris paribus*, like to see as little firing as possible). In a standard auction (see above) the object is sold to buyer B, yielding a payoff of 10 (revenue of 14 minus loss of 4) for the government. But the government prefers to sell to buyer A: he is also willing to pay up to 14, but creates a smaller loss of 2 (e.g. by committing to fire fewer workers). This yields a payoff of 12 for the government.

The following straightforward calculations show that value maximisation and 'efficiency of the allocation process' may diverge. The value created for buyers is 3 when buyer A gets the object (this is obtained by subtracting from A's valuation of 10, B's loss of 7), while the value created for buyers is 4 when B gets the object (subtract from B's valuation of 8 the loss of 4 incurred by A). Hence, buyers' values are maximised by selling to B, and this outcome will indeed be achieved by a standard auction. Consider now the entire society, which includes the seller and regards revenue as a zero-sum transfer.[12] Total welfare is 1 when A gets the object (buyers' value of 3 minus seller's loss of 2), and 0 when B gets the object (buyers' value of 4 minus seller's loss of 4). Hence, if the seller is interested in 'efficiency of the allocation process' he should sell to A, which also agrees in this particular case with his own preferences.

In the example, it is possible to achieve 'efficiency of the allocation process' through a non-anonymous auction. One way to do this is by tilting the auction in A's favour or by handicapping B, e.g. by stipulating that A gets the object unless B bids at least 2 more than A.[13] But in practice many of the relevant valuations are not known *ex ante* and it will often be difficult to set efficient handicaps precisely. Thus, such non-anonymous auction procedures may be inefficient because of incomplete information, or because the handicaps and favours are set via a process that is subject to lobbying activity.                                              □

---

[12] Compare the discussion in section 2.

[13] For a discussion on asymmetric auctions, see Maasland, Montangie and van den Bergh (this volume, chapter 4).

We can learn from the above example that if a seller cares not only about revenue, but also about who wins the auction (because the seller believes that after the auction one bidder will behave in a way that better serves society's interest than another bidder) a standard auction may not produce an efficient outcome even though buyers' valuations are maximised.

In the next example we want to show that the goal of market efficiency may be in conflict with the goal of revenue maximisation. In section 2, we illustrated this issue with an example where the question was how many licences to auction. In Example 3 below we assume the number of licences cannot be chosen (and is here fixed at one) and show that revenue maximisation in the presence of negative externalities may imply that agents have to pay even if the object is not sold (bidders pay for the avoided losses). The same logic, applied to the case of positive externalities, implies that some agents should be compensated in order to induce them to provide a public good.

**Example 3:** Consider the same situation, with externalities as in Example 1, but assume now that there is another buyer C, to whom the seller prefers to sell. C values the object at 31 and does not perceive a loss or gain if someone else gets the object. Both A and B suffer a loss of 20 each if C gets the object. One instance in which this may be realistic is when A and B are incumbents who can also operate with their old licences, while C is a very efficient new entrant, able to take existing customers from A and B. The seller can be a government which thinks that the prices for consumers will be significantly lower after the entry of the efficient firm C and therefore prefers to sell to C.

A standard auction will award the object to C (who is willing to pay up to 31) at a price of about 30 (this is what A is maximally willing to pay, taking into account the need to pre-empt C). Is such an auction revenue-maximising? The answer is 'No!' The seller can get a higher revenue by committing not to sell the object at all, and by requiring payments of 19, say, from both A and B (who should be induced to believe that refusing to pay will lead to a sale to C). This yields total revenue of 38. Note that A and B are indeed each willing to pay 19 in order to avoid a sale to C, which would cause losses of 20 for each of them.

Is this outcome, where the object is not sold, also efficient? If the seller actually sells to C the buyers' valuations sum up to $-9$ (C's valuation of 31 minus two times 20, the disutility of buyers A and B when C gets the object). So, if the seller gets a payoff of more than 9 by selling to C instead of not selling at all, we find that the goal of efficiency (which calls for a sale to C) is in conflict with the goal of revenue maximisation (which

Table 5.1. *Bidder valuations*

|                    | Bidder $A$ | Bidder $B$ |
|--------------------|------------|------------|
| For object $p$     | 10         | 8          |
| For object $q$     | 7          | 12         |
| For both objects   | 17         | 20         |

calls for not selling the additional licence, while extorting payments, say a tax, from both incumbents).                                                          □

A Machiavellian scheme similar to the one illustrated above was in fact implicit in the German UMTS design. In that design the number of licences was endogenous, with four as a lower limit and six as an upper limit (there were four incumbents). The trade-off was between having a competitive market with more than four firms and obtaining high revenue from bidders who would pay to restrict the number of winners and thereby future competition. In fact, the winning firms were trapped and paid a lot without being able to reduce the number of licences.[14]

   The last example will show that in auctions where each buyer can buy more than one unit, even value maximisation for buyers and revenue maximisation are not correlated (as is usually the case in one-object auctions without externalities). For this illustration we do not need external effects (see Jehiel and Moldovanu (2001b)).

**Example 4:** Consider an auction for two objects, $p$ and $r$, with two bidders A and B. For both agents, the valuation of the entire bundle $\{p, r\}$ is given by the sum of their valuations for the individual objects in the bundle. These are shown in table 5.1.

   The *value-maximising* auction (which puts the objects in the hands of those who value them most) is simply given by two separate standard auctions, one for each object. Object $p$ goes to A for a price of 8, while object $q$ goes to B for a price of 7. Total revenue is therefore 15 and the total value of the winners that is generated through this auction for both objects is 22.

   Consider now a single auction for the entire bundle $\{p, r\}$. Note that B is willing to pay up to 20 for the bundle, while A is willing to pay up to 17.

---

[14] Other examples of such schemes abound in the world of weapon deals: China got the United States to lift its embargo on satellite exports by agreeing not to sell missiles to some countries in the Near East; Ukraine agreed to destroy its nuclear arsenal (thus preventing proliferation) after it received hefty payments from the United States, Russia and the European Union.

Hence, the bundle will go to B for a price of 17 and the total value that is generated through this auction is 20. Thus, auctioning the bundle yields higher revenue than the two separate auctions, but generates a lower total value. The *revenue-maximising* auction misallocates object $p$ to B, since A values it higher. If we add externalities to the example, the wedge between allocative value maximisation and revenue maximisation becomes even larger.                                                                    □

This example shows in a simple way that the precise definition of the sold objects matters for the auction outcome. If two physically separable objects have to be sold as a bundle, then the outcome (in terms of who gets what for which price) will be very different from the one where the objects are sold separately.

## 5     Main lessons for auction design

When there is interaction after the auction, bidders may not have a fixed valuation for the objects to be auctioned, and the seller may have preference over *who* wins the auction with *what* rights. Taking these effects into account, we have shown that several relations among objectives that hold for standard auctions may not hold for auctions with externalities. We now list the main implications of our analysis.

(1) In auctions followed by interaction, bidders are driven by aspects other than the intrinsic value of the auctioned objects (which may not even be well defined.)[15] These aspects can significantly affect the outcome (see Examples 1–3), and therefore, in order to avoid unpleasant surprises, must be well understood and taken into account at the design stage. This insight also applies to the lobbying activity that accompanies Beauty Contests.

(2) 'Put the licences in the hands of those who value them most' may not be a sensible goal (see Example 2) in view of overall economic efficiency – a criterion that takes into account the preferences of all economic actors (such as government, various consumer groups, other potential users, etc.). In an auction, firms take only their own interests into account. In particular, allowing too much flexibility to bidders (in order to facilitate value maximisation) may run contrary to the designer's objectives. As an

---

[15] Janssen (2003) considers the case where winning an auction gives the right to play a co-ordination game with two Pareto-ranked equilibria. The intrinsic value of winning the auction is not well defined in such a case as the value depends critically on how the co-ordination game is played.

example, consider auctions of radio spectrum to commercial operators. If the government cares about the content of the programmes that are broadcast, it may need to give up some revenue in order to reach the desired programming variety.

(3) Another widespread idea is that 'value maximisation for buyers and revenue maximisation go hand in hand.' The intuition is as follows: if a large pie is created (by maximising value for the bidders), it may be possible to extract more revenue, as bidders are willing to pay up to their valuation; conversely, a large willingness to pay (reflected in high bids and revenues) means that a large value has been created. Based on this belief, it seems possible to use revenue maximisation as a handy proxy for the more fickle objective of value maximisation. Moreover, revenue maximisation may be a legitimate goal in itself in cases where this form of taxing firms is less distorting for the sector or the economy as a whole than other, more traditional taxation schemes.

However, the above argument is based on intuitions from one-object auction theory with exogenous valuations. There is no general relation between value maximisation and revenue in auctions where the valuations are endogenous because of external effects caused by market structure considerations, or in multi-object auctions with either exogenous or endogenous valuations (see Examples 3–4). This means that multi-object auctions that maximise revenue will not necessarily put the objects in the hands of those that value them most, and auctions that maximise value may not maximise revenue. It is important to be aware of these conflicts, and to choose the appropriate weights for the various goals in each particular application.

(4) With endogenous valuations due to future interactions, standard auctions lose many of their appealing properties (see Examples 1–3). Even post-auction bilateral re-trading may not be able to restore efficiency (see Jehiel and Moldovanu (1999)). More complex mechanisms (such as the so-called Vickrey auctions, where agents pay proportionally to the external effect they impose on society) are in some cases able to achieve efficient allocations. Revenue-maximising mechanisms are not generally known. For multi-object auctions with exogenous valuations an important lesson is the need to bundle some of the auctioned objects (see Jehiel, Meyer-ter-Vehn and Moldovanu (2002)). With endogenous valuations, revenue maximisation may require that the auction rules incorporate some 'threats' to impose unpleasant outcomes if bidders do not pay enough (see Example 3 and Jehiel, Moldovanu and Stacchetti (1999), and recall the German UMTS design).

Frequently 'Vickrey auctions' or revenue-maximising auctions do not take the form of simple bidding procedures, and may be cumbersome to implement in practice. Hence, for practical purposes one often has to make a trade-off between a simpler auction format that may not be optimal and a more complex optimal format whose practical implementation may be problematic.

(5) A particularly important application of the above points concerns the behaviour of incumbents (see also Gilbert and Newbery (1982)). When new scarce goods are allocated, incumbents will be driven both by their valuations for the resources and by the need to 'protect their turf'. Understanding the interplay between these pre-emptive motives and the standard demand motives is essential in order to achieve a good, balanced design (the same applies, of course, to Beauty Contests, which are often accompanied by intense partisan lobbying).

For example, at one stage of the process,[16] the design for allocating spectrum for national radio services in the Netherlands stipulated that some 'designated' frequencies (for stations broadcasting classical music, news, etc.) could be allocated to regular commercial stations if nobody had bid on them during the first few stages of the auction. This was thought to allow more flexibility and to avoid the creation of money-losing enterprises. But it might also drive some incumbent stations to buy these designated frequencies in addition to their main one (this was allowed by the rules) precisely in order to prevent the entry of new commercial national stations. It is possible that such considerations are irrelevant (since the achieved value of such a strategy may be low) but it is necessary to consider them carefully at the design stage in order to assess the probability of their occurrence.

(6) Since all incumbents are partially driven by a common pre-emptive goal (see Example 3), there is a strong motive for collusion among them (in addition to the standard motive of keeping prices down). Perfectly legal collusion-like behaviour without illegal money transfers becomes feasible if there is a symmetric method for sharing the cost of pre-emption (see Jehiel and Moldovanu (2000a)).

Consider as an example an auction for one new licence among two incumbents and several potential entrants. Each incumbent prefers to preserve the cosy duopoly, but also prefers that the cost be borne by

---

[16] The process of allocating radio frequencies to commercial stations has taken many years and the design has changed many times. The design mentioned here was discussed in the summer of 2001.

the other incumbent (this is a 'free-rider' problem). If the new licence is not very valuable *per se* to incumbents, there is a reasonable probability that an entrant will acquire it, since each incumbent hopes that the other will buy it.[17] But consider now the same situation with two licences: it appears that entry would be even more likely. But entry may not occur at all since the two incumbents can now easily and legally share the cost of pre-emption by buying one licence each. This last example shows why a design such as the one for the Dutch UMTS auction (with five licences and five incumbents) was problematic, and why it was possible to anticipate its outcome.

(7) We have seen that in asymmetric situations, efficiency may be achieved by handicapping some firms while favouring others (see Example 2). The feasibility of such operations depends on the particular legal system in place. For example, the US Federal Communications Commission favoured certain small or minority-owned firms and the UK design for the UMTS auction did not allow incumbents to bid on the largest available licence.[18] An asymmetric design must be based on transparent and well-defined 'hard' criteria (this applies also to Beauty Contests). Such a designed asymmetry will create new strategic incentives, and it is necessary to assess whether these new effects will indeed combat the ones they mean to alleviate.

### References

Caillaud, B. and P. Jehiel 1998, 'Collusion in auctions with externalities', *Rand Journal of Economics* 29: 680–702.

Deutsche Bank 2000, 'UMTS, the third generation game', Deutsche Bank Equity Research, London.

*The Economist* 1992, 'BSN and the Agnellis: friend or foe?', 29 February.

1997, 'Aircraft engines: Rolls Royce flies high', 28 June.

Gilbert, R. and D. Newbery 1982, 'Preemptive patenting and the persistence of monopoly', *American Economic Review* 72: 514–26.

Janssen, M. 2003, 'Auctions as collusion devices', *Tinbergen Institute Discussion Papers*, 2803-017/1.

Jehiel, P., M. Meyer-ter-Vehn and B. Moldovanu 2002, 'Mixed bundling auctions', Discussion Paper, University of Bonn.

Jehiel, P. and B. Moldovanu 1996, 'Strategic non-participation', *RAND Journal of Economics* 27: 84–98

---

[17] We abstract here from illegal side payments among incumbents.

[18] See also Salmon (this volume, chapter 6) on the FCC case and Maasland, Montangie and van den Bergh (this volume, chapter 4) on asymmetries.

1999, 'Resale markets and the assignment of property rights', *Review of Economic Studies* 66: 971–91.

2000a, 'License auctions and market structure', Discussion Paper, Mannheim University and CEPR.

2000b, 'Auctions with downstream interaction among buyers', *RAND Journal of Economics* 31: 768–91.

2001a, 'Efficient design with interdependent valuations', *Econometrica* 69: 1237–59.

2001b, 'A note on efficiency and revenue maximisation in multi-object auctions', *Economic Bulletin* 3(2): 2–5.

Jehiel, P., B. Moldovanu and E. Stacchetti 1996, 'How (not) to sell nuclear weapons', *American Economic Review* 86: 814–29.

1999, 'Multidimensional mechanism design for auctions with externalities', *Journal of Economic Theory* 85: 258–93.

Krishna, V. 2002, *Auction Theory*. Academic Press, San Diego.

Klemperer, P. 2002, 'What really matters in auction design', *Journal of Economic Perspectives* 16: 169–89.

Maskin, E. 1992, 'Auctions and privatizations', in H. Siebert (ed.), *Privatization*, Institut für Weltwirtschaft der Universität Kiel.

Milgrom, P. 2000, 'Putting auction theory to work: the simultaneous ascending auction', *Journal of Political Economy* 108: 245–72.

*Part II*

# Case studies

# 6 Spectrum auctions by the United States Federal Communications Commission

*Timothy C. Salmon*

## 1 Introduction

In 1985 the then chairman of the Federal Communications Commission (FCC), Mark Fowler, first asked permission from the US Congress to use auctions in the assignment of spectrum licences. This request was denied. In fact, successive FCC chairmen asked Congress for this authority every year until it was finally granted in 1993. In the Omnibus Reconciliation Act of 1993, Congress finally provided the FCC with the statutory authority to conduct spectrum auctions. This led to the FCC's first spectrum auctions being conducted in 1994. Since then the FCC has conducted over thirty-seven auctions with net high bids summing to over $40 billion.

Over the course of these auctions there have been many successes but also a few failures, with some of these failures being quite serious. In this chapter, we detail the reasons for both the successes and the failures, with the aim of using the FCC's experience in designing and running auctions to show how auctions can be designed to solve highly complex allocation problems.

Section 2 discusses the regulatory background of spectrum allocation methodologies in the United States in order to describe how the auctions programme came to be. Section 3 presents the structure of a simultaneous ascending auction including the specific version used by the FCC as well as some modifications to the design that might be used under different circumstances. Section 4 discusses some of the successes and failures of specific FCC auctions to see what lessons can be learned. Section 5 discusses the different approaches the FCC has taken to ensure that the markets that result from spectrum auctions remain competitive.

## 2 Regulatory history of spectrum allocation

As with most spectrum regulatory authorities, the FCC has a long tradition of assigning licences through the use of comparative hearings, or

Table 6.1. *Bidder values*

|        | Firm 1 | Firm 2 | Firm 3 | Firm 4 |
|--------|--------|--------|--------|--------|
| Item A | 100    | 40     | 95     | 25     |
| Item B | 45     | 85     | 120    | 65     |
| Item C | 10     | 95     | 35     | 60     |

Beauty Contests as they are sometimes called. In the early 1980s the FCC tried a brief experiment in which lotteries were used to assign licences, before finally settling upon the use of auctions. It was a long and drawn-out process to get to this point but it is useful to look into the reasons why it took so long as well as why it was the right thing to do.

The problems with comparative hearings are well known but they were particularly difficult in the United States. To understand why, it is useful to understand more clearly the fundamental nature of the allocation problem facing the FCC. To illustrate this problem we use a simple example of three licences needing to be allocated among a group of four potential operators. The goal of the government should be to ensure that the licences end up in the hands of those operators who can use them in the most economically valuable manner for society. If this is accomplished, then we can say that the efficient outcome has been reached. The value each operator has for winning each item is shown in table 6.1. We can think of these values as the economic value to society the licence would have if it were in the hands of that firm, or we can think of them as the value each firm places on owning the item. Under certain assumptions, both ways of viewing these values are the same. For simplicity we assume that the value each firm has for winning multiple licences is the sum of the individual values. This simplified example also ignores other important issues with values being dependent across bidders and/or being derived from external market interactions as described in Janssen and Moldovanu (this volume, chapter 5). Before adding such complications, it is important first to understand the simple case. We will discuss many of these additional complicating factors below.

The government's problem is to decide who among the four firms should be assigned each of the items. The efficient assignment, as stated before, would assign the items to the firms who have the highest value for them. In this case firm 1 should get item A, firm 3 item B and firm 2 item C. This allocation results in a total value to society of $100 + 120 + 95 = 315$. We can measure the level of efficiency of any other possible allocation according to this benchmark. Consider the value achieved by assigning firm 1 item B, firm 2 item A and firm 3 item C. The value achieved here is $45 + 40 + 30 = 115$ and the ratio of value achieved to value possible is $115/315 = 0.365$. If the government made this second assignment, it would have achieved 36.5 per cent of the possible value and we term this the efficiency level of the assignment.

This explains what the government wants to do. Now we need to decide how it should go about it. In order to make the right decision, the government needs to know the values each firm has for each item. One possible way to extract this information might be simply to ask each firm what its value is and then assign the object to the one stating the highest value. This can be thought of as a loose approximation to the comparative hearing process. The process involves each firm presenting a case to the regulator of why it is the most deserving candidate or why society is best served if it is awarded the item. If we frame the problem in this example context and simply ask each of these four firms what they value each licence at and assign the licence to the firm stating the highest value, it is clear to see that they will all have an incentive to overstate their value as there is no penalty for doing so. The problem for the regulator in the comparative hearing process then is to try to uncover the true values from the potentially misleading signals being sent in by each firm. This is not likely to be an easy task. One possible advantage of such hearings, though, is that if there is thought to be some social value to awarding an item to a particular type of firm, such considerations can be explicitly taken into account during the hearing process.

In the FCC's case of allocating licences to provide wireless telephony, the problem was significantly more difficult. The number of items was very large and the value structure of the firms over these licences was much more complex than the simple one contained in the table above. These complexities will be explained in more detail later. Using a hearing process to uncover these values would have been a long, difficult and probably inaccurate process. Such processes in the United States have been known to take many years to allocate even single licences. During those intervening years, the public does not receive service and the firms spend large sums of money on legal bills to have teams of lawyers argue their cases to the regulator. In the end, the probability of the regulator making the efficient assignment is quite low. If, however, the situation is less complex, involving only a few potential firms and a few licences, then the problem may be of low enough dimensionality that these problems can be overcome. Even in the simple example above, however, the task is already appearing difficult unless the regulator has very good information on the firms.

Because of these issues, the FCC decided to allocate cellular telephone licences in the 1980s through the use of a lottery mechanism. This resulted in hundreds of thousands of applications being submitted for around 1400 licences and we can use our example above to get some idea of the likely efficiency level of such a process. If we consider each of the bidders equally likely to win each licence, we can compute the expected value realised by the lottery, 193.75, which results in an expected efficiency level of $193.75/315 = 0.615$. This is the efficiency level that is expected to be achieved on average although the actual level could be above or below. The level is obviously quite low, but these are just arbitrarily chosen values. If the values of the applicants were closer, then the randomly achieved expected efficiency would be higher. It is an open question as to what the differential would be in practice, but in the FCC's case, many were applying who had no value for the licence themselves and wanted to win a licence purely for resale. If the FCC had restricted the lotteries only to 'serious' applicants, we might look at the recent UK UMTS auction for an idea of the practical spread in values. This was revealed to be at least £2 billion since the first bidder dropped out of the auction when the prices reached the £2 billion level while the final sale prices were in the neighbourhood of £4 billion. Similar estimates could be made based on spectrum auctions in the United States, but the simplicity of the structure of the British auction makes it easier to infer approximate values from prices at which bidders dropped out.

Given the likely inefficient allocation that would result from a lottery, some argued that the efficiency of the initial assignment was unimportant as secondary resale markets could work out any misassignments. This is certainly possible, but because of the complexity of the resulting market, it took many years after the lottery assignment for operators to obtain enough contiguous cellular licences to form legitimate businesses. The fundamental problem is that if a business needs three licences to operate, once they have committed to buying two they face an exposure problem should they not be able to obtain the third licence. It would be possible for another firm to offer the lottery winner more money for that third licence leaving the first firm with only two licences that may be of little use to them now. Also, the lottery winner of that licence has a very large amount of bargaining power and might be able to extract significant extra money from the operator. The combination of these two effects tells us that all lottery winners would prefer to be the last one to sell, while all operators would prefer to be able to buy all of their licences simultaneously. These motivations as well as the size of the market result in an exceedingly complex sequential bargaining problem, the practical solution of which is likely to require a large amount of time, money and patience from any firm wishing to operate a business.

Experience in the United States showed that neither comparative hearings nor lotteries were effective means of assigning spectrum. The key to understanding why auctions are expected to be more effective requires us to go back to our simple example. In order for the government to make a good assignment they need to know the entries in that value table. This requires some mechanism for eliciting those values from the firms and it is important to elicit those values correctly. This is precisely what auctions are designed to do and why they should be expected to allow the government to make more efficient assignments. Properly designed auctions, or more generally 'mechanisms', work by having bidders send in signals and then using those signals to assign objects and generate payments. The payment schemes are designed to ensure that bidders find it in their best interest to send in their true value as their signal. If they do so, the efficient assignment is made.[1]

This explains the economic reasons why it was a good idea to adopt auctions in the United States for assigning spectrum. As with most cases, the political reasons for which they were adopted were not exactly identical. For a more detailed description of the political process that led to auctions being adopted, see Kwerel and Rosston (2000) and Hazlett (1998). As noted before, the FCC began asking for the authority to conduct spectrum auctions in 1985 and this authority was finally granted in 1993. During this time, Congress was reluctant to grant auction authority because of the political lobbying power of broadcasters, who were strongly opposed to auctions. The explanation of why auction authority was eventually approved by Congress is derived from the large budget deficits that existed in the United States in the late 1980s and early 1990s. In 1993, the political rhetoric about reducing these deficits reached a peak and this led Congress to look for any source of revenue it could find. Their need for revenue sources was what finally overcame their resistance to the idea. This also explains why the auction authority was granted in a Balanced Budget bill. Curiously enough, though, in the initial legislation, the FCC was forbidden from using revenue maximisation as part of its goals for the design of the auctions. They were charged with making the auctions a 'fast, fair and efficient' means of allocating licences.

Once the FCC had been granted authority to conduct auctions, its approach to designing the auctions was particularly effective. The process followed the FCC's standard approach to the design of policies, which is that they released various 'Public Notices' and 'Reports and Orders' that outlined the FCC's plans for the auction. They allowed time for public

---

[1] As a technical note, this is precisely the purpose behind the design of the second-price (or Vickrey) auction, and the ascending (or English) auction strategically mimics this auction. Traditional first-price sealed-bid auctions work a little differently, but the same general ideas are embedded into why and how they should be expected to achieve efficient allocations.

comment, followed by additional periods for parties to comment on the comments of other parties. The somewhat unusual part of the process was that during these comment periods, many of the major telecommunication industry firms hired academic auction experts to write detailed auction design proposals as well as comments and critiques on the proposals of others. The FCC had itself hired a few academic experts to help it in sorting the proposals and comments.[2] Over the course of this process, many designs were put forward, some were tossed aside, and improvements were made to others. Also included in this process was a period of experimental testing, detailed in Plott (1997) and Ledyard, Porter and Rangel (1997). Based upon this record of proposals by academic auction theorists as well as the empirical testing of experimental economists, the FCC not only was able to decide upon a methodology, but also had some empirical verification that it had a chance of working. Rarely has there been such close co-operation between the academic community and a regulatory authority and in this case things worked out quite well. The high level of success achieved by the FCC in their auction programme over the years can probably be traced back to their willingness to work with experts on auction design.

Another part of the lesson that can be learned from this process is the value of experimental testing of auction mechanisms. During the process there were many designs proposed but there was typically no way to compare the designs rigorously on theoretical grounds. Comparing auction designs through field-testing was not feasible either, as most rational government regulators are reluctant to engage in field-testing of different mechanisms by using them for multi-billion dollar auctions. These are the two traditional means economists use to evaluate different policy options, and without them we might be left with having only each proponent of an auction design trying to make a convincing argument that their design seems like it would work the best. Using economic experiments, however, it is possible to compare empirically the performance of different mechanisms prior to field implementation. The use of experiments in policy studies such as this has been going on since the early 1980s, and the 2002 Nobel Prize in economics was awarded to Vernon Smith in part for his role in researching experimental economics, which was later developed by himself and others into a tool for 'testbedding' economic policies in the laboratory. The information obtained by the FCC through the experimental tests that were conducted was quite useful in helping

---

[2] A number of papers containing summaries of the experiences of some of those involved can be found in a special edition of the *Journal of Economics and Management Strategy* 6(3) (1997).

it to decide on and have confidence in a design, and serves to show that this is both a valid and a useful tool for such purposes.

## 3      Overview of the simultaneous ascending auction

The auction format used in all but two of the FCC's auctions was a version of a simultaneous ascending auction (SAA) that is sometimes referred to as a simultaneous multiple round auction. It is important to realise that the form used by the FCC is just a specific parameterisation of a larger class of mechanisms. In this section, we explain the reasoning behind the design of the specific version used by the FCC and also discuss the contexts in which other designs may be more appropriate.

To understand why the SAA was the chosen methodology, it is useful to consider the basic problem with which the FCC began. We use the AB-block PCS auction (FCC auction 4) as an example. For this auction, the FCC divided the United States into fifty-one licence areas called MTAs (major trading areas) and then divided 60 MHz of spectrum in each MTA into two blocks of equal size, the A block and the B block. Their task was to find an auction methodology that would be capable of placing these 102 licences in the hands of the firms best able to use them. This task is made difficult because of the complexity of the preferences firms have for items like these. There are three main characteristics of these preferences that complicate the design process.

(1) *Synergies across items.* Two licences close together will generally be worth more if won as a package than the sum of their values if they were won separately. For example, a New York licence is likely to be more valuable if an operator also has the Philadelphia, Boston and Washington DC licences. In fact, there could be a minimum efficient scale that dictates the size of operation necessary to be profitable. For example, a firm might need to win at least three contiguous licences for them to have any use value at all.

(2) *Cross-bidder complementarities.* The value one operator has for a licence can depend on who else has won a licence around them. If they are a provider intending to use CDMA technology, then there may be little reason to bid for an A-block licence in a market where another CDMA provider is on the B block, since the two firms would be able to set up collaborative roaming arrangements after the auction. Similarly, if other CDMA operators are winning in areas around another licence, that licence may be more valuable than if only TDMA or GSM providers were bidding on the surrounding licences.

(3) *Affiliated values.* Values are likely to be affiliated, rather than common or independent, across bidders. That is, while bidders may not know exactly what a licence is worth to them, they do know that their value is unique to them and that their value is related to the values of other bidders. The relationship between the values of two bidders is that if one bidder has a high value for a particular licence, it is more likely that the other does as well.

These and other factors lead to very complex and highly contingent preferences on the part of bidders. Complicating things even further is that, quite often, the bidders themselves will have difficulty articulating and quantifying exactly how some of these issues affect their values. Any allocation mechanism intended for use in a context like this must be designed with all of these considerations in mind.

The first choice to be made in the design of the auction mechanism is whether to auction the licences simultaneously or sequentially. The most obvious possibility would be to use sequential auctions as is done in Sotheby's or Christie's auction houses when there are multiple items for sale. This would involve putting each of the 102 licences for sale in separate auctions conducted sequentially. Benoit and Krishna (2001) argue that this approach would generate more revenue than a simultaneous auction if bidders are budget-constrained, as they are likely to be. Sequential auctions would be quite easy to run, but bidders would have a very difficult time figuring out reasonable bidding strategies in them. As an example, since bidders' preferences and values for the New York licence might depend on who wins the Boston licence it is quite difficult for them decide on an effective bidding strategy for the New York licence if it is auctioned first. If they bid on the New York licence expecting a particular bidder to win the Boston licence and they turn out to be wrong, this could mean that they under- or overbid on the first licence. Solving for theoretically optimal bidding strategies in sequential auctions is only tractable in limited cases and finding even reasonable bidding strategies in real cases will be more difficult. A sequential auction is therefore highly likely to result in inefficient assignments in cases such as this because of the inability of bidders to perfectly forecast results in future auctions. Sequential auctions are more likely to be successful when the objects being auctioned are independent of each other.

This indicates that it might be beneficial to conduct a simultaneous auction in which the market for each item in the auction is simultaneously opened and closed. The next step is to decide on what format to use. In the standard theory of single-unit auctions, there are four frequently analysed formats that we might use here: the first-price sealed-bid;[3] the Dutch, or descending clock, auction;[4] the second-price sealed-bid auction;[5] and the English, or ascending clock, auction.[6] Which should be used? If our goal is efficiency, the theory of single-unit auctions suggests that in simple environments all of these should be efficient in equilibrium. This gives us no means of selecting between them.

One result that some are tempted to apply from single-unit auction theory in deciding which format is best is that when bidder values are affiliated, as they seem to be in this case, the English auction is expected to raise the most revenue. This is derived from what is known as the 'linkage principle' proved by Milgrom and Weber (1982). There are, however, two problems with this result that make it less applicable and useful than is commonly thought. First is that the linkage principle does not generally extend to multiple unit auctions, as shown by Perry and Reny (1999), and therefore nor does the result suggesting that the English auction always raises the most revenue. Second is that the actual increase in revenue in single-unit affiliated value auctions from using the English auction over a sealed-bid auction is not large even in theory, as shown by Riley and Li (1999), and the result can be overwhelmed by other effects. Kagel, Harstad and Levin (1987) show that in experimental comparisons of single-unit auctions with affiliated values, first-price auctions can generate more revenue than English auctions because bidders typically bid above the level predicted by a risk-neutral Nash equilibrium model in first-price auctions. So both theory and empirical evidence tell us that the linkage principle is not a very strong argument for using ascending auctions. Further, since the auction authority legislation prohibited the FCC from using such considerations in their decision anyway, were this argument valid, it could still not be the official reason for adopting an ascending format.

To determine if there are other reasonable arguments in favour of the ascending auction, it is useful briefly to consider the other three. The main problem with the first-price sealed-bid and the Dutch auctions is that trying to determine a reasonable bidding strategy is again highly difficult for many of the same reasons that bidding in sequential auctions

---

[3] Each bidder submits a bid, the highest bidder wins and he pays the price he bid.

[4] A price clock starts very high and then counts down. The first bidder to accept the price wins the item at the price he accepts.

[5] Each bidder submits a bid, the highest bidder wins but he pays a price equal to the second highest bid received.

[6] The price starts low and increases until only one bidder is left. He wins and pays the price at which the last bidder dropped out.

is difficult.[7] Consider a relatively simple environment consisting of two objects and four bidders in which each bidder sees the objects as almost perfect substitutes. Each bidder would therefore like to win only one of the two objects and may have a preference ordering over the objects. On which object(s) should a bidder bid? Should they bid on only one and risk not winning anything? Should they bid on both and risk winning more than they want? It is possible that bidders mis-coordinate and all bid on only one of the objects allowing the other to go unsold. Solving for such bid functions, even theoretically, in environments of much greater complexity is typically intractable, and trying to approximate such things in practice would, of course, be even harder. Consequently, we should expect serious mistakes and misallocations from such methodologies.

In the second-price format, the well-known result from single-unit auction theory is that it is a dominant strategy to submit a bid equal to one's true value. In moving to multi-unit auctions, in which bidders may demand more than a single item, this is no longer true without modifying the design. The basic version of a second-price auction would have similar problems to the first-price and it would no longer be a dominant strategy for a bidder to bid their true value. In order for a bidder submitting their true value for the objects to be an equilibrium in the multi-unit context with interdependent preferences, the FCC would have to use a generalised Vickrey–Groves–Clark mechanism[8] that would require individuals to submit their values for all $2^{102} - 1$ possible combinations of licences in the AB block auction. Such an auction has many desirable characteristics, but forcing bidders to send in a bid detailing what they would bid for all possible combinations is simply unworkable. This leaves us with the English or ascending auction.

To find a version of an ascending auction that will work requires still more effort though. Simply taking the auction-house approach and placing 102 auctioneers in a room would also not be workable. Bidders would not have the information processing capabilities to keep up with such a design. Instead of using a straight analogue of the auction-house style of English auction, we can consider a discrete process. The way the discrete

---

[7] It is worth noting, though, that Che and Gale (1998) argue that in single-unit auctions with financially constrained bidders, first-price auctions will yield more revenue than second-price or ascending auctions under certain circumstances.

[8] In this mechanism, bidders send in their bids as one bid for each possible combination of items. If there are two items, this means a bid for {AB}, one for {A} and one for {B}. Items are assigned by finding the set of mutually exclusive bids that sum to the highest total. Each winning bidder pays an amount equal to the cost they are inflicting on society. This is found by computing the total value achieved in the actual allocation, leaving out that bidder's value, and then subtracting the value achieved in the allocation that would have resulted had that bidder not sent in any bids.

version works is that bidding consists of several sequential rounds. In the first round of the auction, bidders are allowed to send in sealed bids so that no one can see anyone else's bids during the round. When that round has been completed, the results are published, including the high bidders from that round and the bids necessary to top them. Bidders are given time to analyse the results of that round and then a new round opens in which bidders are allowed to submit new bids if they choose.

The primary benefits of this version is that bidders obtain significantly more information about the relative prices for the licences as the auction progresses, which allows them to alter their bidding strategy as needed. If, for example, in a two-item auction all of the bidders in round 1 happen to bid on one object, in the second round the bidders who did not send in the highest bid on the first item can move to the second. While working out a full equilibrium bidding strategy in such an environment is usually not feasible, there are simple rules of thumb and heuristic strategies that should work in many cases. One such simple approach is called straight-forward bidding and involves a bidder being willing to bid on the set of objects in each period that would maximise their total surplus at the current prices. If all bidders bid according to this strategy, the auction will produce an approximately efficient result, as proven by Demange, Gale and Sotomayor (1986) and Milgrom (2000).

There are other benefits from an ascending auction structure, as explained by Compte and Jehiel (2000), derived from the fact that it can be difficult and costly for bidders to determine exact values for all combinations of items. Their environment supposes that bidders begin an auction with unrefined and imprecise estimates of their values for the items in the auction. The ascending structure allows them to observe for which sets of licences refined value estimations are worth obtaining, to help the bidders guide their allocation of resources to such tasks. Sealed-bid auctions provide no such cues. In such cases, the ascending auction yields higher welfare to the participants than a sealed-bid auction and can yield more revenue as well.

This then is the basic structure of the FCC's auction process. There are, however, many additional rules used to accomplish certain specific goals. These are now discussed under four headings.

*Simultaneous closing rule*   In a single-unit English auction, the closing rule is simply to close after people stop bidding. What is the most reasonable multiple unit analogue? Many suggested an item-by-item closing rule by which, after people have stopped bidding on, for example, a Kansas licence, bidding on this licence is closed even if people are still bidding on, for example, a New York licence. The problem with such a closing rule is that it limits the ability of bidders to arbitrage between markets and pursue alternative options when they realise they can no longer compete in one particular market. If markets are closed individually, the back-up market in which a bidder might want to bid could be closed by the time the bidder decides to start bidding in it. This would lead to loss of efficiency and revenue. A simultaneous closing rule, however, avoids the problem by allowing bidding on all items until bidding has ceased on every item. In the FCC's rules, this is implemented by closing the auction after the first round in which there has been no new activity.

*Increment requirements*    As a mechanism for pacing an auction, an auctioneer will typically impose some requirement that a new bid should meet a minimum-increment requirement. The FCC uses a variable increment that varies across licences and usually ranges between 10 and 20 per cent depending on the level of activity on the licence. The greater the recent bid activity, the higher the bid increment. Bidders submit bids in integer multiples of this minimum increment.

*Activity and eligibility rules*    One problem in ascending auctions is that, given the option, bidders normally prefer to wait to bid as long as they can. This allows them to keep their intentions and information secret while observing the activity of others. Since everyone has this same incentive these auctions could take a very long time to complete, without something to spur on activity. The uncertain closing rule serves this purpose to some extent but in auctions as large as the FCC's, more is needed. As a means of accomplishing this, prior to each auction the FCC assigns a certain number of bidding units to each licence in the auction. This number varies positively with the population covered by the licence so that licences covering more populous and therefore more valuable areas have a higher number of bidding units associated with them. Also prior to the auction, bidders must submit an initial payment that buys them a certain number of bidding units. This money is refunded at the conclusion of the auction if a bidder wins no licences and is applied to his total amount owed if he does win. The initial payment also serves as at least a partial demonstration of a bidder's ability to pay at the conclusion of the auction. In order to place a bid on an item during the auction, a bidder must have a number of unused bidding units at least as great as the number associated with the licence. Upon placing a bid, a number of bidding units (BU) equal to the number for the licence become 'active'. For example, if there are two licences in an auction, A and B, such that licence A has 100 BUs and licence B 75 BUs and if a bidder were to buy 125 BUs with an initial payment, in any given round this bidder could be active on either licence A or B but not on both. In order to be active on both in the same round, the bidder must purchase 175 BUs. These constitute the eligibility rules, which dictate on which licences a bidder is eligible to bid.

The activity rules work by first separating the auction into three stages. In stage 1, a bidder will typically be required to be active on 70 per cent of his bidding units. In the example above, if the bidder only places a bid on B, he is considered active on $75/125 = 0.60$ or 60 per cent of bidding units and would not meet the requirement. In that event, the bidder's total number of bidding units would be reduced such that he would meet the requirement, or he would be reduced to having $75/0.7 = 107$ BU's. Thus, if a bidder is not bidding actively, his ability to continue bidding is jeopardised. As the auction progresses to stages 2 and 3, this requirement is increased to perhaps 85 per cent and then 95 per cent. Bidders are, however, allowed five activity rule waivers, which means that they can waive the requirement during five rounds of the auction if they choose and not lose eligibility even if their activity is insufficient to meet the requirement.

*Withdrawals*   This last set of rules exists because bidder values are interdependent. Assume there is a bidder interested in two licences such that his value for either A or B independently is 100 but if he can get both, his value for the package is 300. Now imagine the situation in which the auction is progressing and this bidder is bidding on both licences and the price of each reaches 100. What should the bidder do? If he ends up winning both, he can bid up to a total of 300. What happens though if he bids up to 125 on both and then some other bidder comes in and bids 400 on B? This means that the first bidder can no longer profitably win A and B and he is 'stuck' with paying more for A than it is worth to him unless someone outbids him. This is known as the 'exposure problem'. In order to give bidders a way to deal with such situations, the FCC allows bidders to withdraw standing-high bids. When one bidder withdraws a high bid, the minimum required bid drops back to the second highest bid received on the licence. To deter frivolous withdrawals, the withdrawing bidder runs the risk of incurring a withdrawal payment. This payment is equal to the difference between the price they had bid and the price for which the FCC eventually sells the licence, assuming the final sale price is less than his bid. If the final sale price is greater, no payment is required. Bidders are also restricted to making withdrawals in only two rounds of the auction although each bidder can choose the two rounds for himself.

The particular set of rules used by the FCC is by no means the only way one might construct an SAA. There are several different ways one might structure the increment, activity, eligibility and withdrawal rules but perhaps the most important part of the specification used is the multiple round structure. This structure is necessary because of the large number of items and the complex information processing that must occur after each set of bids has been announced. The problem with the multiple round format though is that it can lead to very prolonged auctions. Some of the early FCC auctions lasted 3–6 months although most of its recent auctions have finished within 1–2 months. For some cases this is an acceptable trade-off but in smaller auctions where there is less complexity, there is little reason to use this format.

An alternative is to consider using a continuous SAA. In this version of the auction, bids are announced as soon as they have been submitted and other bidders can respond immediately with a new bid. A reasonable closing rule for such an auction is to use a countdown clock over a certain period, perhaps 15 minutes. Every time a new bid is submitted this countdown clock is reset, but should the clock reach zero, the auction closes. This is a direct analogue of the simultaneous closing rule discussed above. A more detailed description of such an auction can be found in Plott and Salmon (2001). A mechanism of this sort was designed and intended for use with some broadcast licences the FCC was scheduled to auction in 2000, but for various unrelated reasons these auctions were cancelled and the mechanism was not implemented. Otherwise, the only known field use of this mechanism has been in several real estate and other auctions run by the authors of the cited paper. It has functioned quite well and can be used to complete in a few hours an auction that might take weeks or months in the multiple round format.

## 4    Lessons learned from auction results

Overall the FCC has enjoyed what is generally considered to be a successful series of auctions using the described methodology. There have, however, been a few spectacular failures in the FCC's past and thankfully the reasons for these failures are easy to identify and to avoid in future auctions. There were other more minor problems in some of the FCC's auctions, which are more difficult to eliminate. We discuss many of these issues including some ideas on how to ensure such problems do not appear in future auctions.

## 4.1    IVDS and C block

The auctions for IVDS and C block are considered to be the worst two failures in the FCC's auction programme and the main reason for failure was the same for both. We should also note that the IVDS (Interactive Video Data Service, FCC auction 2) auction was one of the two auctions for which the FCC did not use the simultaneous multiple-round format. This auction was conducted as a sequential series of ascending auctions, but this was not the prime cause of failure.

As part of the FCC's mandate when given auction authority, it was charged with making sure that 'designated entities' would have a fair chance to win licences in the auctions. The phrase 'designated entities' was used to refer to groups, thought to be disadvantaged, that Congress wanted to ensure would be given a chance to compete, and initially included new and small businesses as well as businesses owned by women or members of minority groups. As a consequence, when the FCC was planning its large PCS auctions, it split the first part of the spectrum into three blocks, A, B and C, each having 30 MHz of spectrum per licence. The A and B blocks were auctioned first and any firm was eligible to bid in this auction. This auction attracted the well-established and large US telecommunications firms such as AT&T and Sprint. The total of the high bids in this auction was $7 billion for a total of 60 MHz of spectrum covering the entire United States. The C block auction (FCC auction 5) was held later and entry to it was restricted to 'entrepreneurs' (defined for this auction as entities, together with affiliates, having gross revenues of less than $125 million and total assets of less than $500 million at the time the FCC Form 175 application was filed) and 'small businesses' (defined for this auction as entities, together with affiliates, having gross revenues of less than $40 million at the time the FCC Form 175 application was filed). The total of the net high bids in this auction was just under $10 billion for 30 MHz of spectrum covering the entire country. The fact that a group of 'small' businesses was offering to pay significantly more money for less spectrum than the large firms was a clear sign that something strange was occurring.

That 'something strange' was related to the provisions the FCC had adopted in the C block auction to 'help' the designated entities. In addition to reserving the auction just for them, the FCC had a belief that the main hurdle to these firms in acquiring spectrum was access to capital. Consequently, the FCC instituted a system of very generous instalment payments on winning bids from this auction. This allowed ten-year financing with no requirement for repayment of the principal in the first six years and at an interest rate based on the ten-year Treasury note. The

FCC used a similar scheme for the IVDS auction. The key detail was that these credit options were available to any high bidder in the auction and there was no credit screening at all to determine if firms would be able to pay. As is predicted by Wilkie (1997) and Zheng (2001), such credit terms gave bidders an incentive to bid significantly higher than they otherwise would and the bidders with the riskiest business plans were generally the winners. Many of the firms that did win in this auction were intending to put out an IPO (initial public stock offering) as soon as the auction was completed to obtain financing for their business plans or as a means to quickly turn around and sell the rights to use the licences they won in the auction. Unfortunately, the auction lasted six months (18 December 1995–6 May 1996) and during that time the market for telecommunications stock suffered a significant downturn, making this no longer a viable option. Soon after the auction was completed, many firms began declaring bankruptcy and defaulting on their instalment payments. Although the scale of the problem was much smaller, winners in the IVDS auction suffered similar problems at the conclusion of that auction.

The resolution of the bankruptcies for C block has been a very long and tortuous process for the FCC. Many firms, after declaring bankruptcy, sought refuge in bankruptcy courts to protect the licences and in some cases the courts forced the FCC to accept significantly reduced payment for the licences. In one such case, GWI PCS, which was the third largest winner in the auction, was able to have a bankruptcy court reduce the amount they owed the FCC by 84 per cent, from approximately $1 billion to $169 million. Other bidders voluntarily returned their licences, which led to two additional auctions of licences for this spectrum. One was held immediately after the initial auction (FCC auction 10, 3 July 1996– 16 July 1996) and one several years later (FCC auction 22, 23 March 1999–15 April 1999).

Perhaps the most problematic case from this auction was Nextwave Communications. They were the largest winning bidder in the auction, winning fifty-six licences with total net high bids of $4.2 billion and were one of the firms declaring bankruptcy. After extensive court proceedings, but before they were concluded, the FCC decided to have yet another C block re-auction to sell Nextwave's licences in late 2000 (FCC auction 35, 12 December 2000–26 January 2001). The total of the net high bids in this auction was $16.9 billion. Unfortunately, in August 2001, the court made its ruling and found that the FCC did not have the right to conduct the auction as the licences belonged to Nextwave.

There is no doubt that this auction was an unmitigated disaster for the FCC, and it did not at all help small businesses, as the financing options encouraged many to overbid and led to their bankruptcies. This should not have been surprising as any simple economic analysis would have revealed the incentives embedded in such generous financing plans were problematic and also that the programme was unneeded when combined with the set-aside. It is important to realise that although this auction was a failure, the problems were not a result of the auction design itself but of the peripheral rules relating to payment schemes. The lesson learned, then, is that instalment payments are not a good way to try to help small businesses. Why the FCC decided that these firms needed not only a block of spectrum set aside for their exclusive use but also instalment payments is a question that does not appear to have any satisfying answer. Section 5 will deal in more detail with how one might structure an auction design and a regulatory environment to help small firms.

### 4.2    WCS and LMDS

The WCS (Wireless Communication Service, auction 14) and LMDS (Local Multipoint Distribution Service, auction 17) are two more auctions that are generally considered to have been failures for the FCC. The WCS auction involved the sale of blocks of 5 and 10 MHz of spectrum in the 2300 MHz range. The LMDS auction involved the sale of 1150 and 150 MHz licences in the 2.8 GHz range. In both cases, revenue estimates prior to the auctions were quite large with both being in the billions of dollars. The actual revenue totals were $13.6 million and $579 million respectively, and the most publicised example of these revenue totals was that many licences in the WCS auction sold for $1 and one of the San Francisco licences sold for $6. This led many, especially those in Congress after the WCS auction, to believe that the FCC had made a serious mistake in these auctions. The question is: what was the mistake?

In both cases, the FCC had been forced to rush the auction through in order to satisfy Congressional and other political pressures. These pressures were largely based on Congress' desire for additional revenues. At the time of the WCS auction, there was no existing equipment that was designed to operate at that frequency and the military, which operates around that part of the spectrum, had indicated that its operations would probably interfere with anyone choosing to operate in this band and placed stringent out of bandwidth emission limits on winners. In the case of LMDS, the high wavelength meant there were a number of problems with the service such as the equipment that existed at the time not being very effective during rain or even high humidity. An analysis of the post-auction results shows quite clearly that the prices of the licences and the probability that a licence was sold were significantly negatively correlated with the level of rainfall in the licence area.

The LMDS auction is a particularly clear example of this problem since in a re-auction (FCC auction 23), which was held approximately one year after the initial auction, many licences that went unsold during the initial auction were now sold and several licences which had been returned after a default by a winner were resold. In the intervening months, there had been a technological innovation in the industry that resolved many of the problems with the service. For this reason and also because the minimum opening bids in this auction were set at a much lower level than in the initial auction, competition in the re-auction was significantly higher. In the end, this collection of licences, which had been deemed to be of least value by the market in the previous auction – to the extent that no one was willing to purchase them – ended up selling for more in terms of $/MHz*pop than the licences in the initial auction. This is a clear indication that the initial auction was held earlier than it should have been. There is also an indication that the very high minimum opening bids in the initial auction reduced the number of bidders entering the auction, while the 'bargain basement' minima in the second auction led to a significantly greater level of entry.

One is tempted to believe that this is a trivial and obvious lesson, but it is one that appears difficult for the US Congress to learn and therefore worth pointing out. There are signs, though, that members of the Congress may be making progress. In response to Congressional attempts to push through more auctions prematurely, HR 4560, also known as the Auction Reform Act of 2002, was proposed in an attempt to eliminate deadlines for certain pending spectrum auctions. The issue is summed up quite well in a May 2002 statement by Congressman John Dingell, ranking member of the Committee on Energy and Commerce that oversees the FCC, in reference to HR 4560:

We've seen this train wreck before. In May 1997, the FCC auctioned the so-called 'WCS' frequencies due to a statutory mandate that was neatly tucked into an appropriations bill as a spending offset the year before. The Congressional Budget Office (CBO) predicted the WCS auction would raise nearly $2 billion. When the dust settled, the receipts totaled only $13 million – that's less than one percent of CBO's projection. The lucky bidders literally paid less than a penny on the dollar. Even fire sales do better than that. One WCS bidder actually won the right to serve four large states for the whopping sum of $4.00 – that's about the price of a Happy Meal at McDonald's. But a happy meal it was when many of these WCS licenses were later sold on the secondary market, generating millions of dollars in profits for these spectrum speculators and their shareholders. (Dingell, 2002)

In both of these cases, we see the problem that arises from rushing an auction to the market before the market knows quite what to do with what is being auctioned. In such a case, bidders will not have time to form business plans around the spectrum offering and will not have time to obtain financing. Although it is generally considered to be a good thing to get the spectrum into the hands of the firms as soon as possible, the caveat to that should be that the spectrum should be allocated as soon as possible after the industry knows how to use the spectrum. It is important to a successful auction that bidders are given enough time to prepare for it. Otherwise the result is lower revenue and efficiency. It is important to note again, though, that the reason for the failure of these auctions was nothing to do with the design of the mechanism but rather with the regulatory environment in which the auctions were conducted.

## 4.3    DEF block

The DEF block auction (FCC auction 11) represents something of a mini-failure on the part of the FCC. This was the last of the large initial PCS auctions held by the FCC. It consisted of three blocks of 10 MHz licences and is generally considered to be the auction with the highest level of collusive activity of all FCC auctions.[9] It is the only FCC auction that resulted in prosecuted collusion cases.

To assess the extent of the problem from collusion in this auction, we might look at the revenue achieved by the auction compared to that from the AB auction. The DEF block auction raised $2.5 billion, while the AB block auction raised $7 billion. A straight extrapolation from the AB results would have predicted an approximate revenue total of $3.5 billion for the DEF block auction, since half the total amount of spectrum was offered. A more accurate extrapolation would need to account for the fact that each of the licences might be less valuable on a per MHz basis in 10 MHz blocks rather than 30 MHz blocks, and the fact that the DEF was conducted after most firms had obtained their core licences. These licences were mainly used to fill minor holes in a carrier's coverage area. Also, there were restrictions in place to allow only small businesses to bid on F block licences. These issues suggest that the revenue total from the DEF auction should have been less than from the initial offering of AB licences. Consequently, it is not obvious what proportion of the $1 billion in lower revenue was due to collusive activity and what proportion was due to the differences in the demand structure. There were, however, a large number of documented cases of bidders attempting to send collusive signals in the auction, prompting many to suggest that this had the

---

[9] Chapter 3 in this volume by Salmon contains a more extensive treatment of the problem of collusion in auctions.

effect of lowering revenue, although no one has been able to provide a convincing estimate of the level of the effect. Even without a precise estimate, it seems reasonable to conclude that some non-trivial proportion of the revenue decrease was due to collusive activity.

As discussed by Salmon (this volume, chapter 3), not long after this auction, the FCC closed many of the avenues bidders had used to send collusive signals in this auction, and subsequent auctions have not resulted in anywhere near at least the obvious levels of collusive activity. The problems have probably not been eliminated completely, but there is some evidence for the suggestion that they have been significantly reduced. The lesson from this auction, then, is that in designing an auction, it is important to limit the potential for collusive activity.

## 4.4    Withdrawals

The final problem with the FCC's auctions is not necessarily specific to any one auction but has probably caused at least minor difficulties in almost every auction, and more noticeable problems in others. These problems arise from the ability of bidders to withdraw a standing-high bid as a means of alleviating the 'exposure problem'.

As has been explained above, the exposure problem is something that can occur in multiple unit auctions when bidders possess values for the items that are interdependent (meaning that bidders view some of the items as either substitutes or complements) but bids are only allowed to be made for individual items. If a bidder is bidding on the assumption that he will win a group of licences and be able to realise the synergy value obtained from owning the entire group, but then manages to win only a part of the group, then he is exposed to a possible loss. This possibility of loss can lead to a number of problems including efficiency and revenue losses as well as post-auction defaults. These problems are explained in more detail by Bykowsky, Cull and Ledyard (2000). To minimise this problem, the FCC allowed bidders to withdraw standing-high bids during the auction.

To illustrate this point more clearly we can return to the example we discussed earlier of the bidder who valued either licence A or B separately at 100 but the combination at 300. The extra 100 that is added to the total value when the two licences are won together is referred to as the synergy value of the package. When the prices on the individual items reach 100, this bidder has a problem: does he continue bidding, splitting the synergy value across the items, or does he stop bidding? If the bidder continues bidding, he could end up winning only a single item. This will cause the bidder to make a loss on the item he does win and could lead him to defaulting on payment or bankruptcy. This is the essence of the exposure problem.

If he is worried about this possibility, then he might stop for fear of being left with only one of the items and having committed to paying a price greater than 100. If this bidder could have won the items by pursuing them, then his refusal to continue bidding hurts both efficiency and revenue. If the bidder would have lost, then only revenue is reduced. The idea of the withdrawal rule, then, is clear. It gives bidders an option that if they end up winning only parts of a package they can withdraw their bids on the remaining items and limit their possible losses. With this safety net, bidders should be more willing to pursue aggregations aggressively instead of ceasing to bid once the individual item values have been reached. Should this bidder end up withdrawing, the hope on the part of the FCC is that another bidder will be able to place a bid on the licence at the lowered price instead of leaving the licence unsold. The intention of this rule is to improve both revenue and efficiency for the government and to reduce losses for the bidders.

There is evidence that bidders have been successful in forming packages of licences they desire in the FCC's auctions, but there is also evidence that the interests of some bidders have been harmed by the exposure problem. The possibility of withdrawals has, however, led to a number of problems. One is that it makes a strategy of 'parking' early in the auction easier to implement and more damaging to the FCC. Parking involves a bidder bidding on items he has little interest in winning during the first part of the auction to draw attention away from the licences in which he is interested, and then moving to his real interests late in the auction. Without withdrawals, a bidder has to consider the possibility he could be stranded on a licence in which he has little interest if no one outbids him, and this reduces the incentive to park. If the bidder can make withdrawals, however, he can mitigate the damage of such an occurrence by withdrawing his high bid on the licence he does not want and shifting his eligibility over to the licence he does want.

This exact sequence of events has occurred in many auctions with bidders bidding on licences they did not want and then withdrawing their bids to move to others late in the auction. The real problem occurs when they do this very late in the auction at a point when no other bidders have the eligibility necessary to place bids on those licences from which the bidder withdrew. This causes those licences to remain unsold at the conclusion of the auction. Since withdrawal payments are assigned on the basis of the final sale price, and no sale has been made, the bidder causing the problem is not even assigned a withdrawal payment, though 3 per cent of his withdrawn bid is usually held in anticipation of a final withdrawal payment being assigned. With the licences unsold at the end of the auction, service cannot be provided to the public with them until a re-auction has been held. For some services this can take a very long time, if one is ever held.

It is obvious that something has to be done to correct for the exposure problem but allowing withdrawals is not a suitable solution because of the other problems that this option can cause. The alternative is to use a combinatorial auction that allows bidders to place bids on combinations or packages of items. If a bidder has the values of {A, 100}, {B, 100} and {AB, 300} then they can place a package bid of 250 on the group AB and have no risk of only winning one. To do this in a standard auction, they would have to place bids of 125 on each and risk winning only one. A detailed discussion of such auctions is not possible here, but explanations of the issues involved, as well as possible auction designs, can be found in Plott (2000), Ledyard, Porter and Rangel (1997) and Ledyard *et al.* (1999). Such auction designs will be most appropriate for cases in which bidder values for items are interdependent. For auctions where all items are unrelated, or bidders are only allowed to win a single item, there is no need for combinatorial auctions as the exposure problem is not an issue.

The FCC is intending to use a combinatorial auction for the first time in the auction of returned VHF television licences in the 700 MHz range (FCC auction 31). The process of designing this auction has led to a great number of comments and suggestions from the academic community of auction theorists and experimentalists,[10] with perhaps the key comments being found in Plott (2001), Plott and Salmon (2000) and Harstad (2000). While large-scale combinatorial auctions are by no means easy to design or administer, they should be expected to lead, for certain applications, to significantly better outcomes. In the past few years, there has been significant progress in the design of such auctions and they have begun to see limited field use. The results are encouraging and indicative of the fact that there is now enough knowledge about how these mechanisms work to support their use in the right circumstances.

## 5    Competitive effects

One issue that should be clear from the last section is that a successful auction requires more than just a well-designed auction mechanism. It is at least equally important to ensure that the auction is being conducted within a generally well-designed regulatory framework. As was seen

---

[10] They can be found in their entirety on the FCC's webpage at http://wireless.fcc.gov/auctions/31/releases.html.

before, most of the serious problems with FCC auctions have come through a failing in this area rather than in the auction design itself. One area of general regulatory concern for any industry is the degree to which the market is competitive. This issue is of key importance in the design of licence auctions since each licence is a grant of some degree of market power to the licensee. Ensuring the market for service remains competitive after the auction requires more than just designing an auction and obtaining an 'efficient allocation' from the auction itself, as this may be a much more complicated matter than was described in section 2.

The concern about the anti-competitive effects of auctions is that auctions might allow large firms or incumbent operators to buy all licences in a single area to keep out new entrants and maintain a monopoly, or collusive oligopoly, in that region. In a comparative hearing process, this possibility can be eliminated as the administrative court can exclude a particular firm from being allocated more than a certain amount of spectrum. The FCC has tried four main methods of accomplishing similar results in the auction process. One of these approaches was the offering of instalment payments to designated entities to allow them financing on favourable terms, which could help them to compete against larger firms. This has already been discussed with reference to the C block auction and shown to have been an abysmal failure for the FCC. The other three approaches have fared somewhat better.

## 5.1    Spectrum cap

If the goal is to ensure that no single firm can dominate any market, one way to do this would be expressly to limit the amount of spectrum a firm can win in an auction or across auctions. This was the basis for the imposition of a cap on the amount of spectrum for which any single firm could have licences in any given region. The rule applied to frequencies classified as licensed broadband Personal Communications Service (PCS), cellular and Specialised Mobile Radio (SMR) spectrum. Under the spectrum cap rule, no entity could hold more than 45 MHz of spectrum, or 55 MHz in rural areas.

This rule has made certain that there is more than one carrier with usable spectrum in each region, and in many regions there are seven or more different service providers for wireless telephony. As a means of tracking the level of competition in the industry, the Wireless Telecommunications Bureau in the FCC compiles a yearly competition report in which they carefully analyse any trends of increasing or decreasing competition in the industry. Figure 6.1 is from the 7th Annual CMRS Competition

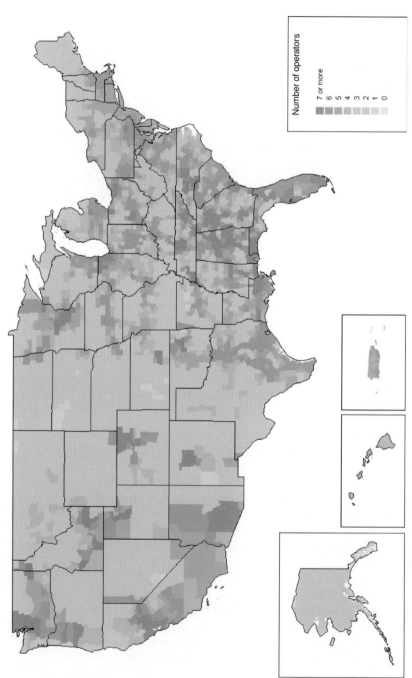

Figure 6.1. Mobile telephone operator coverage by county. Cellular coverage based on the service area boundaries reported to the FCC by cellular operators. Coverage by broadband PCS and digital SMR operators based on publicly available sources. (*Source:* FCC's 7th Annual CMRS Competition Report.)

Number of operators

7 or more
6
5
4
3
2
1
0

Report and shows the number of carriers in each part of the United States. A summary of what the figure shows, as stated in the report, is that 'Over 229 million people, or 80 percent of the US population, live in counties with five or more mobile telephone operators competing to offer service. And 151 million people, or 53 percent of the population, live in counties in which six different mobile telephone operators are providing service.' These pieces of evidence are strong indicators of what the rest of the report argues in more detail, which is that there is a healthy level of competition in this industry in the United States.

Competition in the industry was deemed healthy enough by the FCC that it decided to eliminate the spectrum cap from 1 January 2003. The belief on the part of the FCC was that the cap had done its job by inducing a large number of operators to enter the industry and now that there seemed to be enough to sustain competition, it was no longer necessary. There were, of course, some who strongly disagreed with this viewpoint as evidenced by the dissenting statement released by Commissioner Michael J. Copps alongside the majority ruling on the issue. His view was that the spectrum cap was working and repealing it was dangerous when there was no compelling reason to do so. While it is uncertain whether the FCC's decision to repeal the spectrum cap will help or hurt the industry, by most accounts it seems to have been an effective tool in encouraging competition in the industry.

## 5.2    Bidding credits

Another provision the FCC has used to help out designated entities in its auctions is bidding credits. These are percentage discounts on the final payment given to qualifying bidders. In each auction the qualifications to receive a bidding credit will change slightly as will the level of the bidding credits themselves. Typical requirements for bidding credits might be the firm having gross revenues less than $5 million/year to qualify for a 'very small business' credit and receive a 25–35 per cent discount, or gross revenues less than $25 million/year to qualify for a 'small business' credit and receive a 10–15 per cent discount. If a qualifying bidder wins a licence in the auction, the price they pay is reduced by the amount of the bidding credit.

Assessing the success of this programme is difficult. As already explained, the overall level of competition in the industry is healthy and perhaps some of this can be attributed to the existence of bidding credits. Bidders qualifying for these credits have won a significant number of licences in the FCC's auctions but it is not clear that the same firms would not have won without them. It is also not clear that all of the companies claiming small or very small business status to obtain the credits were legitimately small or very small businesses. Many were potentially 'shell' companies serving as fronts for larger firms. The inability reliably to detect such arrangements at the application stage of an auction is probably the most serious problem with implementing a programme of this sort. Clever accountants and lawyers can usually create a company that would at first glance satisfy the FCC's requirements even though the real entity behind the firm does not.

What is more clear about the use of bidding credits is that they have caused little harm to the FCC's auctions process, and certainly not the same level of harm as the instalment payment programme. The main problem with implementation is in deciding the appropriate level for the credits. A principled approach would involve a careful study of the degree to which small firms are disadvantaged in credit markets as well as the degree of inefficiency in the original allocation that the regulatory agency is willing to accept if it allows the level of competition in the industry to increase. A discussion of the effects of credits of this sort on bidding behaviour and on the efficiency and revenue of an auction can be found in Salmon and Isaac (2002). The FCC has more typically set the bidding credits more arbitrarily. This can induce more inefficiency than desirable and tilt the results too much in favour of one side or the other. In the end, there seems little evidence that either effect has been terribly severe in FCC auctions thus far. As is discussed by Salmon (this volume, chapter 3), bidding credits of this sort may also help to fight collusion problems in auctions by encouraging smaller firms, that might otherwise believe they have little chance of competing, to enter an auction.

## 5.3    *Spectrum set-asides*

This is the final method the FCC has used in trying to help out smaller firms and it involves setting aside certain licences that can be won only by firms meeting certain size restrictions at the time of the auction. The success of this policy has been hindered by the fact that the two occasions on which the FCC has used this policy were the C block and DEF block auctions.

The C block result has already been shown to have been a failure, but the failure was not due to the fact that only designated entities were allowed to enter the auction. One thing that should be clear is that once a band of spectrum has been set aside for small businesses there should be no need for instalment payments or bidding credits. If the problem for small firms winning licences is to obtain financing, as long as the small firms are competing only against other small firms, they all face exactly the same constraint. Thus there is no reason to use instalment payments to level the playing field, as it is already level. One would expect prices to be lower in a small business set-aside auction, but if the idea is to use the set-aside to increase competition, this is not as important an issue.

In the DEF block auction, the F block was set aside so that only designated entities could win licences, while any firm could win the D and E block licences. Not surprisingly, the highest bids on the F block licences were lower than those on the D and E block licences, but again this was not necessarily a significant issue. The real problem was that the F block licences contained only 10 MHz of spectrum. If this was all a small business had won, it was unlikely to be enough for it to be able to compete with firms all owning 30 MHz or more.

These complicating factors make it very difficult to assess the degree of success of spectrum set-asides on the part of the FCC. Theoretically, these will be more effective than either instalment payments or bidding credits in helping small firms to compete as they ensure that if there are any small firms that desire licences, they will be able to obtain them. The only issue of concern is the possibility that in industries in which economies of scale exist, too many licences might be set aside for small firms and these firms might not be able to provide service as cost-efficiently as larger firms. So long as that possibility is balanced against the potential for increased competition, it seems that this may be the most effective approach.

## 6    Conclusion

The FCC was a pioneer in the use of complex multiple-unit electronic auctions and its history of using these auctions is an interesting one from which to learn. By and large, it has achieved great success with its programme, but its few failures have been severe. There are a number of lessons that the FCC's experience has taught us about auction design but there are two that are pre-eminent.

First, it is important to design the auction correctly. Designing a complex auction mechanism is a difficult task. There is certainly a great deal of insight that auction theory can give when designing auction mechanisms for novel situations. Since real bidders might not always bid as our models predict and since theoretical results based on real environments are often unattainable, it is also important to incorporate experimental testing into the design process as a means of comparing alternative designs to determine which works best.

Second, while the design and implementation of the auction is important, it must take place within a generally sound regulatory structure.

When the FCC has had a failed auction, it has generally been because of rules and regulations outside the scope of the auction itself. Either the FCC has tried to use some misguided approach to helping small firms or, on account of Congressional pressures, it has rushed a band of spectrum to auction before the industry has been ready to absorb it.

There are also other, more specific lessons that can be learned from the FCC's experience with regard to how to accomplish these two broader goals. One of the key regulatory issues on which the FCC's programme has performed well is the maintenance of a competitive marketplace after the adoption of an auction programme. Since the auction of licences for the exclusive use of a resource grants a certain degree of market power to the winner, there is a risk that using auctions to assign such licences could generate too little competition in an industry. The FCC has shown that there are ways in which competition in the resulting market can be successfully facilitated through the auction itself, for example through licence set-asides and bidding credits for new entrants. It has also shown that external regulations such as spectrum caps or limits on the number of licences a single firm can win may be successfully used to establish cross-auction limits on the grant of market power to individual firms.

Perhaps the most useful lessons one can draw from the FCC's experience concern the design of large multiple-unit auctions. The FCC's experience has shown the power and ability of simultaneous ascending auctions to be used for large-scale resource allocation problems and paved the way for conducting such auctions through electronic markets. This is a model that has been successfully copied in Canada, Australia, Mexico, the UK and other countries around the world. While the specific design used by the FCC should never be viewed as a 'one size fits all' design, it is possible, by examining the reasons for its construction explained above, to learn a great deal about how to modify the general design to fit other situations.

## References

Benoit, J. and V. Krishna 2001, 'Multiple object auctions with budget constrained bidders', *Review of Economic Studies* 68: 155–79.

Bykowsky, M., R. Cull and J. Ledyard 2000, 'Mutually destructive bidding: the FCC auction design problem', *Journal of Regulatory Economics* 17: 205–28.

Che, Y. and I. Gale 1998, 'Standard auctions with financially constrained bidders', *Review of Economic Studies* 65: 1–21.

Compte, O. and P. Jehiel 2000, 'On the virtues of the ascending price auction: new insights in the private value setting', Working Paper, University College London.

Copps, M. 2001, 'Dissenting statement on 2000 Biennial Regulatory Review spectrum aggregation limits for commercial mobile radio Services', WT Docket No. 01-14, http://www.fcc.gov/Speeches/Copps/Statements/2001/stmjc123.html (accessed at 8 November 2001).

Demange, G., D. Gale and M. Sotomayor 1986, 'Multi-item auctions', *Journal of Political Economy* 94: 863–72.

Dingell, J. 2002, 'Statement in reference to HR 4560', http://www.house.gov/commerce_democrats/press/107st110.htm (accessed at 7 February 2003).

FCC 2002, '7th annual report and analysis of competitive market conditions with respect to commercial mobile services', Staff Report, July, http://wireless.fcc.gov/cmrs-crforum.html (accessed at 7 February 2003).

2003, 'FCC announces wireless spectrum cap to sunset effective January 1, 2003', Press Release, WT Docket No. 01-14, http://wireless.fcc.gov/spectrumcap.html (accessed at 7 February 2003).

Harstad, R. 2000, 'A blueprint for a multi-round auction with package bidding', Comment submission to the FCC, Rutgers University, Piscataway, NJ.

Hazlett, T. 1998, 'Assigning property rights to radio spectrum users: why did FCC license auctions take 67 years?' *Journal of Law and Economics* 41: 529–75.

Kagel, J., R. Harstad and D. Levin 1987, 'Information impact and allocation rules in auctions with affiliated private values: a laboratory study', *Econometrica* 55: 1275–304.

Kwerel, E. and G. Rosston 2000, 'An insider's view of FCC spectrum auctions', *Journal of Regulatory Economics* 17: 253–89.

Ledyard, J., D. Porter and A. Rangel 1997, 'Experiments testing multi-object allocation mechanisms', *Journal of Economics and Management Strategy* 63: 639–75.

Ledyard, J., C. DeMartini, A. Kwasnica and D. Porter 1999, 'A new and improved design for multi-object iterative auctions', Social Science Working Paper No. 1054, California Institute of Technology, Pasadena.

Milgrom, P. 2000, 'Putting auction theory to work: the simultaneous ascending auction', *Journal of Political Economy* 108: 245–72.

Milgrom, P. and R. Weber 1982, 'A theory of auctions and competitive bidding', *Econometrica* 50: 1089–122.

Perry, M. and P. Reny 1999, 'On the failure of the linkage principle in multi-object auctions', *Econometrica* 67: 885–90.

Plott, C. 1997, 'Laboratory experimental testbeds: application to PCS auctions', *Journal of Economics and Management Strategy* 6: 605–38.

2000, 'A combinatorial auction designed for the Federal Communications Commission', Report to the FCC, California Institute of Technology, Pasadena.

2001, 'The FCC rules for the 700MHz auction: a potential disaster', Working Paper, California Institute of Technology, Pasadena.

Plott, C. and T. Salmon 2000, 'Comment sought on modifying the simultaneous multiple round auction design to allow combinatorial (package) bidding', Comment submission to the FCC, California Institute of Technology, Pasadena.

2001, 'The simultaneous ascending auction: dynamics of price adjustment in experiments and in the UK 3G spectrum auction', Working Paper, Florida State University.

Riley, J. and H. Li 1999, 'Auction choice', mimeo, University of California Los Angeles.

Salmon, T. and R. Isaac 2002, 'Revenue from the saints, the showoffs, and the predators: comparisons of auctions with price-preference values', Working Paper, Florida State University.

Wilkie, S. 1997, 'Explaining price anomalies in the PCS license auctions', Working Paper, California Institute of Technology, Pasadena.

Zheng, C. 2001, 'High bids and broke winners', *Journal of Economic Theory* 100: 129–71.

# 7    An analysis of the European 3G licensing process

*Emiel Maasland and Benny Moldovanu*

## 1    Introduction

In the years 2000 and 2001, several European countries issued licences for third-generation (3G) mobile telecommunications, usually referred to as UMTS. In the context of the present book, where auction methods are analysed and compared to their alternatives, the UMTS case is of particular interest since it is one of the few cases in which countries have chosen different allocation mechanisms to allocate similar goods. Several papers have already been written on the European 3G licensing process.[1] This chapter is structured around the two main research questions of the present book, namely:

(1) What mechanisms can be used to allocate rights to operate in a market, and under what set of circumstances should one allocation mechanism be preferred over others?
(2) What are the important design issues once a particular mechanism is chosen?

Section 2 addresses the first question. It categorises the different allocation mechanisms used by European countries and offers a comparative analysis. It is important to note at the outset that the usual distinction between auctions and Beauty Contests is too simplistic. Section 3 addresses the second main research question. It offers a general survey of the main issues pertaining to efficiency and revenue maximisation in licence auctions. In section 4, we look in more detail at the most flexible design – the German (and Austrian) one. Section 5 concludes.

## 2    Licensing methods

In the recent allocations of spectrum for UMTS mobile telephone services, European governments had to make decisions on two main issues:

We are grateful to Tilman Börgers for his contribution to a previous version of this chapter.
[1] For survey articles, see for example Börgers and Dustmann (2003), Jehiel and Moldovanu (2003), Klemperer (2002a, b, c), Pratt and Valletti (2001) and van Damme (2002).

Table 7.1. *Classification of licensing methods*

|  |  | Number and size | |
|---|---|---|---|
|  |  | G | M |
| Allocation | B | I | — |
|  | A | II | III |

(1) How many licences should be awarded, and with what spectrum capacity?

(2) Which companies should win licences and at what prices?

Different European countries have adopted very different methods for making these decisions. Table 7.1 classifies the different licensing methods.

The columns of the table refer to the way a country settled the first question: how many licences should be awarded, and with what spectrum capacity? In some European countries the number and size of licences was simply chosen by the government (G). In other countries, the market (M) played a role in determining the number and size. In these countries, the available spectrum was divided into a fixed number of identical blocks (by the government), and the companies decided for how many blocks of spectrum they wanted to bid. The rows of the table refer to the way a country settled the second question: which companies should win licences and at what prices? Some countries selected a Beauty Contest with a fixed licence price (B);[2] other countries chose an auction (A).[3]

In every country that used a Beauty Contest, the number and size of licences was determined by the government. Therefore, we are left with three different licensing methods. We will call method I a *Beauty Contest,* method II a *fixed prize auction,*[4] and method III a *variable prize auction.*

The licensing methods used by the various European countries were as follows:

I Finland, France, Ireland, Luxembourg, Norway, Portugal, Spain, Sweden;

---

[2] Note that, in general in Beauty Contests, prices do not have to be exogenously fixed (see Dykstra and van der Windt (this volume, chapter 2)).

[3] The main difference between auctions and Beauty Contests is that the latter contain an element that cannot be easily quantified or otherwise made objective (see Dykstra and van der Windt (this volume, chapter 2)).

[4] Note that the 'fixed prize' refers to the number and size of licences. It does not refer to the valuations. The valuations may be variable if pay-offs are identity-dependent (see Janssen and Moldovanu (this volume, chapter 5)).

II Belgium, Denmark, Greece, Italy, Netherlands, Switzerland, United Kingdom;

III Austria, Germany.

The boundary between methods II and III is somewhat flexible. Italy and Greece, which are assigned to method II, left the number of licences up to the number of participants. If there were fewer bidders than licences, the number of licences would be reduced.

It is important to note that, within each category, variations between countries are possible. For example, countries that used a Beauty Contest to allocate licences took into account different criteria and weightings. Sweden awarded the licences to those who guaranteed the best coverage and roll-out rate.[5] In France and Spain there were many more criteria than in Sweden, and many criteria were relatively vague. Some countries, like Finland and Sweden, awarded the licences at no cost to the operators. Others, like France, Portugal and Spain, asked substantial initial fees. There were also substantial differences among the countries that used a fixed prize auction. Some chose an open auction format (e.g. the United Kingdom), while others chose a sealed-bid auction format (e.g. Denmark).

Which licensing method (Beauty Contest, fixed prize auction or variable prize auction) should be preferred? Here we restrict ourselves to a brief comparison between a Beauty Contest and an auction (without distinguishing between a fixed prize and a variable prize auction). For the pros and cons of fixed prize and variable prize auctions we refer the reader to subsection 4.3, where we analyse the German (and Austrian) design *vis-à-vis* less flexible designs.

There seems to be a wide consensus among economists that an auction is the preferred selling mechanism. Maskin (1992, p. 115) argues that with respect to both efficiency and revenue 'auctions tend to fulfill these objectives better than do most common alternatives to auctions'. McMillan (1995, p. 191) claims that 'of the alternative spectrum allocation methods . . . auctioning works best'.

Beauty Contests are often criticised for the fact that they lead to (the perception of) favouritism and corruption. Indirect signs of favouritism, such as the lack of transparency about selection criteria and the reasoning behind allocative decisions were indeed present in the European 3G licensing process.[6] Another argument against Beauty Contests is that the implicit commitments made by firms are not enforceable: 'How could

---

[5] For a detailed description of the Swedish licensing process, see Hultén, Andersson and Valiente (2002).

[6] A good overview of these signs of favouritism is given by Börgers and Dustmann (2003).

government monitor and enforce any commitments made by those companies?' (Klemperer, 2000, p. 8). Lack of commitment endangers efficiency because, if commitments are not enforced, promises are not informative, and therefore a Beauty Contest does not generate the information needed to allocate licences efficiently. In the European 3G licensing process, Spain and France indeed eased the burden on the licensed operators on account of dramatically deflated expectations for 3G. As Beauty Contests are subjective and not transparent, they are likely to generate legal challenges. In Spain, newcomer France Telecom, which failed to secure a licence, has challenged the outcome in the courts. In Sweden, incumbent Telia (which did not win a licence) started a legal procedure too.[7]

A potential disadvantage of auctions is that only minimum requirements are taken into account regarding the use of a licence. An auction reduces the competition to the price dimension, given certain minimum quality requirements. In contrast, Beauty Contests are more flexible: business plans are being judged not only on the price, but on quality aspects as well. If the market can be expected to provide a socially optimal set of prices and qualities, this potential disadvantage should not be taken too seriously.[8] Note that objectives like a speedy roll-out and the extent of coverage can easily be made explicit and built into the scoring function of a multi-attribute auction. Performance guarantees can also be built into the auction process by imposing appropriate rules and licence conditions.

We have assumed that quality is objectively measurable. In the case where quality considerations play a crucial role, but quality is not objectively measurable, then a (weighted) Beauty Contest might be preferable (see Dykstra and van der Windt (this volume, chapter 2)).

## 3     The main aspects of licence auction design

The most important issues in the design of licence auctions are located at the intersection of industrial organisation and mechanism design. Licence auctions (or other procedures such as Beauty Contests) not only allocate scarce goods but also determine the nature of whole industries where entry is otherwise very difficult. Hence, the outcome of any allocation procedure influences the future interaction among winning firms, the regulator (i.e. government) and consumers. This effect should be taken

---

[7] Auctions may also be prone to legal fights. In the Netherlands and Italy (which used auctions), there were legal challenges too. But the motive behind legal action is usually different: it relates either to the auction design or to the behaviour of the other participants in the auction.

[8] Bjuggren (2002), who analysed the Swedish Beauty Contest, has the same opinion.

into account in applications of auction theory to licence auctions since valuations (which depend on expectations about future market structure) are determined by the allocation procedure itself, and are therefore endogenous. Thus, potential acquirers of licences will anticipate the future scenarios as a function of the auction's outcome, and they will condition their behaviour before and during the auction on those expectations (Jehiel and Moldovanu 2000, 2003). Failing to take into account these basic strategic motives at the design stage can have harsh consequences for governments and/or consumers.

## 3.1    The main goal: economic efficiency

The main goal of most licence allocation procedures is economic efficiency, which, correctly interpreted, means the maximisation of a (possibly weighted) sum of consumer and producer surplus. This maximisation exercise must necessarily consider several alternative future market scenarios. In particular, future firm profits and consumer rents are determined by the number of licensed firms. A secondary goal in most licence auctions has been raising revenue for the government.

A serious hurdle on the way to economic efficiency is the fact that consumers do not directly participate in the spectrum auctions or Beauty Contests. Moreover, an *ex ante* measurement of expected consumer surplus in various market constellations is very difficult. Therefore, consumer surplus does not usually play a role, unless special provisions are made in a careful auction design. Unfortunately, at the design stage, the regulators are operating in the dark since information about consumer welfare in various future scenarios cannot be easily measured or anticipated. Only after a regulatory scheme which satisfactorily deals with this problem has been chosen is it possible to concentrate on an auction format that aims at maximising the value for firms or the government's revenue.

There is a myriad of oligopoly models which make various predictions about the relations among concentration measures (that aggregate the number of firms and their respective outputs), industry profits and welfare. There is no conclusive theory. Several standard oligopoly models predict that, in reasonable ranges, both consumer surplus and overall efficiency increase with increased competition among firms. This justifies the pursuit of a goal to 'create sufficient market competition' as a proxy for economic efficiency. But creating sufficient competition means that entry should be encouraged as long as it is economically viable. Obviously, the duplication of fixed costs and other factors specific to network industries implies that new entry cannot be forever welfare-increasing. Entry encouragement must come at the licensing stage since, unlike standard industries, which do not require a tedious licensing process, entry is either impossible or very difficult at later stages (owing to spectrum scarcity, strong network effects, regulatory constraints, etc.).

## 3.2    Asymmetry between incumbents and entrants

Why should one choose a design where entry is encouraged? Why is it not enough to choose a design that gives all firms equal chances to acquire licences? Because entry is encumbered by a basic asymmetry in licence valuations between the firms that already operate a GSM network in a given country (incumbents) and those that do not (entrants).

For any bidder, the 'pure' economic value of a licence with a fixed capacity is obtained by subtracting from the value of expected profits the fixed cost required to build a network and start operations. Note that the value of expected profits increases if the licence is endowed with more capacity, and decreases if more firms are licensed.

The asymmetry between entrants and incumbents has three main sources:

(1) The fixed cost of setting up the infrastructure required for 3G services is very large, but some of the 2G incumbents' fixed costs are already sunk, since they can use parts of their existing facilities (e.g. base station sites).

(2) Many incumbents enjoy large customer bases and strong brand names, and have accumulated significant marketing know-how. In particular, they will also enjoy a positive cash flow during the years until the full deployment of 3G services.

(3) Since per-firm industry profit tends to decrease with the number of active firms, incumbents are also driven by entry pre-emption motives (e.g. the need to avoid cannibalisation of their existing profits by additional entrants) which translate into increased willingness to pay for licences and capacity (see also Gilbert and Newbery (1982), and Katz and Shapiro (1986), in the context of patents).

To sum up, incumbents will tend to have higher valuations for licences than new entrants even if the respective firms are otherwise comparable in terms of operating costs, technical know-how, managerial skill, etc. (see also the commercial evaluations made by investment banks such as Deutsche Bank (2000), UBS Warburg (2000), and WestLB Panmure (2000)). Hence, incumbents will be willing to bid higher than entrants, and we should always expect all GSM incumbents to win 3G licences. In other words, entering the market by directly overbidding a GSM incumbent seems possible only if the new entrant is much more efficient and therefore expects much higher profits in the future.

If potential entrants understand this logic, they either will choose not to participate in the auction, or will try to form consortia with incumbents. Both types of behaviour have been observed frequently in the UMTS auctions, with adverse effect on competitiveness (and, hence, ultimately on efficiency) and on revenue. Hence, a main question for practical design exercises is how to alleviate the incumbent–entrant asymmetry and encourage entry.

Special circumstances may lead to an entrant having a higher value than an incumbent. For example, a particular country's licence may be the 'last piece in the puzzle' for a global firm which, consequently, may be willing to pay more than a small incumbent with only local interests; or again, because of idiosyncratic circumstances (e.g. after buying expensive licences elsewhere) an incumbent may have a tight budget constraint. But such features are hard to predict, and are subject to constant change since firms form and break alliances and change their business plans, and stock exchange valuations fluctuate, etc. In our view, considerations based on such transitory features should not play a major role in auction design.

### 3.3    Entry considerations in practice

*The number of licences*    The most important variable for controlling entry is the number of licences. Since the 'right' number must also take into account the future consumers, its determination is, in practice, very difficult. Note that this is, primarily, an issue of industrial organisation, not of auction design!

Most countries which opted for Beauty Contests adhered to a rule-of-thumb formula in order to determine the 'right' number of licences. Also several countries that organised auctions (most notably the UK) adopted the same formula, which made entry almost inevitable:[9]

Number of 3G licences = Number of GSM incumbents + 1.

The number of new 3G licences was a hotly debated issue during the UK auction design stage (see, for example, Binmore and Klemperer, 2002). The eventual design (an ascending auction) tried to level the playing field for the four GSM incumbents and new entrants. Its main feature was the reservation of the largest licence for a new entrant (there were five licences, one more than the number of incumbents).[10] This design

---

[9] In cases where the plan was to auction even more licences, intense pressure was applied by industry to reduce the number.

[10] This asymmetric design feature is studied by Maasland, Montangie and van den Bergh (this volume, chapter 4) from a legal perspective.

attracted, besides the four incumbents, nine potential entrants. Four licences were, not surprisingly, acquired by the four GSM incumbents. The final bids of all thirteen bidders clearly shows that the average incumbent bid was much higher than the average entrant bid. An initial plan that called for an auction of four licences was abandoned after many deliberations about the 'right' number and after a change in the view about the technical feasibility of five licences had taken place.

The Dutch organised an ascending auction for five licences in a market with five GSM incumbents. We have argued above why this is problematic, and why the unsatisfactory outcome (no serious entrant participated and total revenue was a relatively low €2.7 billion) could have been (and was!) anticipated.[11] Of course, it might be argued that five licences was the 'right' number for the Netherlands as well. But then it is not clear why an auction without serious reserve prices was thought to be appropriate given the circumstances.[12]

The German regulatory agency thought that a directed intervention to help new entrants was unnecessary (nor would be fair to incumbents). The German design was flexible, and it allowed both for an endogenous number of licences (up to six) and for endogenous capacity endowments (see a detailed description in subsection 4.1). An earlier design, which prescribed a fixed number of five licences, had been abandoned because the flexible design was thought to offer 'a fair, undiscriminating and efficient market solution to the problem of finding the optimal number of licences' (REG-TP, 2000). Moreover, general principles of competition policy 'require allowing the highest possible number of firms to enter the market'. Hence, the regulator sought to solve the difficult problem of finding the right number of licences by shifting the 'burden' to the participating firms. In section 4 we assess this design in greater detail.

The Italian design had a somewhat naïve feature: it stipulated that, after the bidders had qualified for the auction, the number of licences could be reduced to ensure that there were no more licences than bidders. In Italy there were six bidders, four incumbents and two new entrants. Hence, according to the rules, the number of licences was not reduced and remained fixed at five, and at least one new entry was inevitable. But one firm (Blu) very quickly dropped out of the auction, apparently because of conflicts among its main shareholders, and only the relatively high reserve prices avoided a 'Dutch outcome'. Accusations (yet unproven)

---

[11] See, for example, Maasland (2000) and the May 2000 version of Klemperer (2002a), available at http://www.paulklemperer.org.

[12] For a detailed evaluation of the Dutch UMTS auction, see Janssen, Ros and van der Windt (2001).

say that Blu was 'asked', and maybe 'paid', by the other firms to ficti-
tiously take part in the auction in order to keep the number of licences
at five!

It is also worth mentioning in this context the experience of the auctions
held in 2001, one year after the major wave of European 3G auctions, and
at a time of deflated share prices and expectations about the 3G market.
Belgium and Greece used the 'Incumbents + 1' formula in their auctions
but failed to attract bidders other than the incumbents, who obtained the
licences at the reserve price. Denmark wanted to auction four licences
in a market with four incumbents, a situation similar to the Dutch one.
Having learned from that experience, the Danes chose a pure sealed-bid
design. Given the timing of their auction and the industrial organisation
situation, this was probably a good decision (see below), even if it meant a
very high-risk situation for the firms. It is remarkable that one incumbent
failed to get a licence, which shows that the greater uncertainty in a
sealed-bid design may be favourable to entry.

*Sealed-bid auctions and the hybrid auction as a panacea*   In open
ascending auctions, bidders have an incentive to stay in the auction until
the price reaches their true valuation. If the number of licences to be
auctioned is less than or equal to the number of incumbents, entrants
(having lower valuations than incumbents) clearly do not have a chance
to win a licence. Sealed-bid auctions, on the other hand, may encourage
participation by outsiders. Economic theory predicts that under a first-
price sealed-bid format, bidders who are known to have high valuations
will sometimes place bids which risk being overbid by bidders known to
have lower valuations. This possibility makes it worthwhile for bidders
with lower valuations to participate.[13]

A possible drawback of first-price sealed-bid auctions is, however, that
they hamper the exchange of information among the bidders. Information exchange is important as it may enhance efficiency. This can be seen
as follows. If information flows unhampered, bids will be based on better information, and thus the auction may come closer to assigning the
licences to those bidders who will use them most valuably.[14] Precisely because of this reason the economic advisers of the UK government did not
propose a first-price sealed-bid auction in the early stages of the preparation period (when it was still thought that only four licences could be
sold in a four-player market), but a mixed ascending-sealed design. In this

---

[13] This argument is based on Klemperer (1998).
[14] Of course, not every form of information exchange is desirable. Where information
exchange could facilitate collusion, it is clearly undesirable. Collusion will be discussed
further below.

hybrid construction an open, ascending auction would take place until all but five bidders had dropped out of the auction. The remaining five bidders would then participate in a sealed-bid auction. The minimum bid in this auction would be the price at which the sixth bidder had dropped out of the auction. This hybrid construction was called an 'Anglo-Dutch auction' because the open, ascending auction format is also known as the 'English' auction, and the sealed-bid format implements the same outcome as the descending clock auction, known as the 'Dutch' auction. Theoretical results for this Anglo-Dutch design are not available. It has been experimentally tested, though, by Abbink *et al.* (2001). They conclude that, given their assumptions on the value distributions, the Anglo-Dutch design and the ascending format are comparable in their efficiency properties.

*Facilitating entry by reducing infrastructure costs*     There are several other features, not directly pertaining to the rules of the allocation procedures, that influence the probability of entry. The adoption of all or some of the following rules has the effect of decreasing the infrastructure costs (including financing costs), with a stronger relative effect on entrants. They can play an important role in levelling the playing field for entrants and incumbents.

(1) *Mandatory roaming.* This stipulation requires GSM incumbents to grant an entrant access (for an appropriate fee) to their networks while the entrant builds its own infrastructure. This means that a new entrant can immediately start to offer 2G services and generate a positive cash flow for the several years it takes to build a new network. The UK design originally included this feature, but it was removed following a suit brought by an incumbent (Deutsche Telekom's subsidiary OneToOne). A 'voluntary' agreement between the government and two other incumbents will now guarantee free roaming. In Germany, the incumbents complained that a free-roaming stipulation would infringe their existing rights, as defined by the terms of their GSM licences, and the idea was abandoned. The regulatory agency argued that roaming agreements could and would be achieved by bilateral bargaining. Other countries (such as Finland) allowed even the 3G networks to be based on roaming, in the sense that each winner was requested to cover with its own network only a relatively small fraction of the population, while relying on roaming for the remainder.

(2) *Licence fee payment by instalments.* Another way to ease the financial constraints is to spread the licence fee over several years. While this rule benefits all firms, it is particularly important for new entrants whose

cash flow is going to be negative in the first years because of the large infrastructure investment. The UK adopted such a plan, but the required interest rate was so high that firms chose not to use this opportunity. In contrast, Germany required full payment just ten days after the auction. As it became clear that the fees were going to be enormous, adverse effects on share prices and bond ratings were triggered. These reactions were partly responsible for the timing of the auction's end (see the details in subsection 4.3). At the moment, several firms are in serious financial difficulties and share prices have plummeted.

(3) *Mandatory site-sharing*. This stipulation requires GSM incumbents to grant access to their antennae and relay installations, so that several firms can use the same facility. Note that 3G networks will require a denser cell structure than existing 2G networks. Moreover, it is increasingly difficult to obtain authorisation for new sites, on account of planning and environmental restrictions. Dealing with this issue is thought to constitute a sizable share of the infrastructure costs. Hence, mandatory site-sharing can considerably reduce these costs. Not surprisingly, incumbents have argued that, because of technical constraints, site-sharing is not feasible on a large scale. In Germany there are new considerations about the feasibility of such plans, and it is now conceivable that not all licensed firms will build independent networks.

## 3.4    Revenue maximisation

Up to this point we have discussed efficiency aspects. Another important goal has been revenue maximisation. Often this goal has been (erroneously) regarded as the main one by the media, the public, and even by some academic commentators, who tend to compare auction outcomes on the basis of the associated revenue. Revenue maximisation seems a legitimate goal, particularly in the cases where it is believed that this form of taxing firms is more efficient (i.e. less distortionary) than other, more traditional taxation schemes.

The revenue-maximising format for multi-object auctions is not known at a good enough level of generality (see Janssen and Moldovanu (this volume, chapter 5) for some theoretical results). Pure revenue maximisation often calls for bundling of objects, which, in the context of licence auctions may lead to unacceptable monopolisation (see Jehiel and Moldovanu (2001)). But there are several simple insights that may be used in order to obtain satisfactory revenues.

(1) Besides the value of the objects, the most important factor determining revenue is the amount of competition during the auction. As

we argued above, the design itself may affect the firms' participation decisions (i.e. if entrants see no chance of winning licences, they will stay out). In this respect the ratio of new to old licences is crucial, and the Dutch experience shows what can happen when this ratio is equal to 1.

(2) Proper reserve prices that reflect the scarcity of spectrum and its other potential uses should be imposed. Such a feature can avoid catastrophic results even if, ultimately, there is not enough competition coming from the bidder side.

(3) An important aspect is collusion avoidance.[15] Collusion during the auction must be based on some exchange of information (note that the open, ascending design is rather favourable to such exchanges). Hence, a restrictive disclosure policy during the auction will make collusion harder, but it will also hamper the flow of information that may be relevant in order to achieve a value-maximising outcome (see above). In instances where there are strong common elements in the valuations of different firms the exchange of information can significantly increase revenues. This is because information exchange among bidders reduces in expected terms the amount by which bidders shade their bids to protect themselves from the winner's curse. The winner's curse affects winners who win an auction only because they have had partial, excessively optimistic information. There is also a relation between collusion and the incumbent–entrant asymmetry mentioned above. From the point of view of incumbents, who want to prevent entry, sustaining the collusive outcome is more difficult if there is no focal, symmetric method which allows the incumbents to share the pre-emption cost without exchanging side payments, which is usually illegal. In such a case there will be free-riding among incumbents (leading to increased entry) since each one of them prefers to let other incumbents pay the cost of pre-empting the entrants.

## 4    The German and Austrian auctions

In this section we look in more detail at the German (and Austrian) auction design, which was the most flexible one. We give the benefits

---

[15] Economic theory predicts that collusion in an auction with many participants is more difficult to achieve than collusion in an auction with few participants. This is another reason why it is important to have fierce competition during the auction (see point 1 above).

and disadvantages and make an assessment. We first briefly describe the design and the outcomes of these auctions.

## 4.1   Design

The rather complex design (which was common to the two countries) involved two consecutive auctions. The first auction allocated licences together with so-called 'duplex' or 'paired' spectrum frequencies. The second auction allocated paired spectrum that had not been sold at the first auction, together with additional 'unpaired' spectrum. Both auctions were of the 'simultaneous multiple-round ascending' type.

At the first auction, bidders did not submit bids for licences directly. Instead, the auctioned objects were twelve abstract blocks of paired spectrum (i.e. their location in the spectrum range was not known prior to the auction). A bidder obtained a licence if he acquired at least two blocks, and was allowed to acquire (at most) three. The number of licensed firms was therefore variable (between zero and six). If all blocks were sold, then there were bound to be at least four licences (equaling the number of GSM incumbents in both Germany and Austria).

Each block had a reserve price of DM100 million in Germany and €50 million in Austria. In each round a bidder had to bid on at least two blocks. Strangely enough, although the blocks were abstract and identical, bids carried name-tags! Bidding on only two blocks in one round precluded bidding on three blocks in later rounds. After each round, only the temporary winning bids on each block were announced (together with the identity of the temporary winners). In particular, it was not always known immediately whether a firm did bid on two or three blocks, but partial reconstructions were possible after observing activity in a few rounds.

A block could have remained unsold either because there were no bids for that block above the reserve price, or because the bidder who submitted the last highest bid on that particular block ultimately failed to acquire two blocks, in which case he was not required to make a payment.

The purpose of the second auction was to allocate additional capacity among the bidders who were licensed at the first auction. This meant that only those bidders that previously acquired at least two paired blocks of $2 \times 5$ MHz were allowed to participate.

Besides unsold paired blocks from the first auction, the second auction allocated an additional five unpaired blocks of $1 \times 5$ MHz each. Bidders could acquire any number of unpaired blocks, but were not allowed to acquire more than one paired block (if any were left from the first auction). Each unpaired block had a reserve price of DM50 million in Germany, and €25 million in Austria.

## 4.2    Outcomes

In Germany there were seven bidders (including four GSM incumbents), after six other qualified bidders ultimately withdrew from the auction. The auction lasted for three weeks and 173 rounds of bidding, and resulted in six licences being awarded (four of them to the existing GSM operators). The licensed firms were the four incumbents and two new entrants (one of them already operating as a service provider). Each licensed firm acquired two blocks of paired spectrum, paying approximately €8.4 billion (or €4.2 billion per block).

The most interesting thing occurred when one of the potential entrants, Debitel, left the auction after 125 rounds and after the price level had reached €2.5 billion per block. Since six firms were left bidding for a maximum of six licences, the auction could have stopped immediately. Instead, all remaining firms (and in particular the two large incumbents, Deutsche Telekom and Mannesmann) continued bidding in order to acquire more capacity. But no other firm was willing to quit. One by one, firms stopped trying to acquire more capacity, and bidding stopped in round 173. Compared to round 125, there was no change in the physical allocation, but firms were, collectively, €20 billion poorer! Luckily for the government, the outcome produced both high revenue and two new entries.

In the second auction, five firms (three incumbents and two entrants) each acquired an additional block of unpaired spectrum. There was no serious bidding in which firms tried to acquire more capacity – note that the pre-emptive motive was greatly reduced at this stage since the number of licences had already been determined. It seems that the enormous price paid at the first stage did not allow further flexibility (in particular, the smallest incumbent Viag Interkom was so budget-constrained that it could not afford serious bidding at all).

In Austria there were exactly six bidders (four of them GSM incumbents) for a maximum of six licences. Hence, in principle, the licence auction could have ended immediately, at the reserve price (€100 million per licence). Nevertheless, the auction continued for another sixteen rounds before stopping with six licensed firms (four of them being the existing GSM operators), each paying on average about €118 million per licence. Hence, about €108 million was again spent for nothing. There have been allegations that bidding occurred only to create a public impression of some 'real' competition. In any case, it seems that observing the alarming German outcome enabled the Austrian bidders to learn and reduce their demand much more quickly.

## 4.3      Benefits and disadvantages

A perceived advantage of the German auction was its flexibility. It has been argued that *ex ante* carving of spectrum into fixed chunks of capacity cannot be efficient, since the regulator is less informed about the precise operational needs of the involved firms (see Grimm, Riedel and Wolfstetter (2002) and Börgers and Dustmann (2003)).[16] In the same vein, since the regulator does not really know how many firms are efficient, why not let firms themselves determine the number of licences in a competitive bidding process? These arguments are not entirely correct, since they confuse value maximisation (for the involved firms) with efficiency, thus neglecting consumers. From the point of view of value maximisation, a design which allows for a variable number of small and large licences seems more desirable than those designs where the number of licences and their capacities are fixed *ex ante*. While this argument is correct, its implementation in the German and Austrian design mixed flexibility in that dimension with flexibility concerning the number of firms. Since per-firm profits probably fall with the number of firms while consumer surplus probably increases, letting the firms decide how many will be able to operate in the market is problematic for consumers' efficiency. Consider a hypothetical situation where the regulator proposes the following regulatory scheme to existing firms in the market: each firm has to pay a substantial fee to the state; depending on the fees paid, the regulator allows a number (possibly none) of new firms into the market, with higher fees meaning fewer firms. This was, roughly speaking, how the German and Austrian designs operated.

It is instructive to judge the design in terms of its ability to achieve value and/or revenue maximisation (for some of the relevant theoretical results, see also Janssen and Moldovanu (this volume, chapter 5)). Six points can be made.

(1) By introducing bidding on one, two or three blocks rather than directly on licences, the auction artificially created a situation with multi-unit demand, and therefore offered scope for demand reduction gaming effects. Demand reduction is a strategic option in auctions where bidders have multi-unit demand, and where all units are sold at uniform prices: since bidding for the last unit, say, raises the price for all other units, bidders will

---

[16] Börgers and Dustmann underpin their argument by an analysis of the UK and Dutch bid data. They show, for example, that unlike what the UK and Dutch governments thought before the auction, a licence of $2 \times 10$ MHz paired spectrum seemed a viable option.

artificially reduce their demand on that last unit. Such effects usually lead to inefficiencies, but here they may, in fact, have had some positive effect since they could partly have offset the opposing demand-increasing effect arising from the incumbents' pre-emptive motives (see point 3 below).

(2) Complementarities existed among blocks. The first block was worth nothing, the second a lot, and the third had a positive value. Complementarities among the auctioned goods are usually a hindrance to efficiency (see McAfee and McMillan (1996) and Cramton (1997) for some US experience) and also create exposure problems (see point 5 below).

(3) Since the number of firms was endogenous, the auction called for strategic behaviour in order to reduce the number of licences, and created an artificial demand-increasing effect. It was impossible to bid 'straightforwardly' in the German auction, since there were, for the same set of parameters, multiple equilibria with very different outcomes. The intrinsic value of a third block of capacity was greatly augmented in feasible scenarios, where acquiring such a block led to fewer firms in the market. The rules implied that in any possible outcome with entry (with five or six licensed firms) there would be at least one new firm with the minimum mandated two blocks. If that firm lost one block, it would lose the entire licence. Thus, besides getting 'pure' economic value by acquiring one block of capacity in excess of the minimum two, an incumbent might get substantial extra value by denying an entire licence to a new entrant. (In order to achieve an outcome with only four licences, some more co-ordination was needed among three incumbents; see also point 6 below).

(4) A revenue-maximising seller may extract revenue by 'threats' to sell exactly to those agents that create strong negative externalities on others (see also Janssen and Moldovanu (this volume, chapter 5)). It seems that this argument was well understood by the auction designers. By allowing four to six firms, a threat to sell to newcomers was in effect operative, and it was, in principle, avoidable for a sufficiently high price. Some commentators argued that the German design was therefore much better geared towards revenue maximisation. If the endogenous entry decisions prior to the auction are neglected, this argument is correct.

(5) The multi-unit-demand and complementarity features created an exposure and regret problem for the involved firms. The exposure problem arises in multi-object auctions where the objects are complements (i.e. the value of a bundle is higher than the sum of the values of its components)

and where combinatorial bids on entire bundles are not allowed. In such a scenario, a bidder bids high on two items hoping to win them both, but, since he does not know the others' valuations, ultimately he gets stuck with only one item for which he has a low valuation. The exposure problem in the German design was a direct consequence of the fact that dominant incumbents tried to push entrants out of the market, but were ultimately unsuccessful (see Ewerhart and Moldovanu (2002)). The attempt to create a more concentrated market structure drove prices up for all acquired frequency blocks without changing the final allocation (thus causing regret). There are several potential explanations for this failure. First, there was intense pressure from stock markets and bond-rating agencies to stop bidding. Second, since there were only two financially strong incumbents, and since prices were already high when Debitel stepped out, at least one entry looked plausible. As one entry was likely to occur, the value of preventing a second entry was reduced. Auctions that create exposure and regret phenomena are not attractive for bidders, who may rationally decide to avoid bidding altogether.

(6) The simultaneous ascending auction (through its dynamic, iterative structure) is well suited for incumbents who wish to co-ordinate in order to prevent entry, without the need of external monetary transfers. Towards the end of the auction there was clear signalling activity between the two large incumbents, who tried to sort out whether to continue bidding in order to reduce the number of entrants. Mannesmann made several bids where the smallest free digit (i.e. taking into account the rules that allowed bids only in multiples of DM 100,000) was 6, suggesting that it was finally ready to accept an outcome with six firms. Initially, Deutsche Telekom responded with bids ending in 5, suggesting that it was willing to bid even higher in order to reduce the number of licences to five. Only after further price increases and increased nervousness in the stock markets did bidding stop.

## 4.4    Assessment

The German design allowed both a flexible allocation of capacity and a flexible number of licences. This is a clear advantage *vis-à-vis* less flexible designs. But the pre-emption effects stemming from market structure considerations (combined with the presence of incomplete information) created a significant exposure for bidders, which affected the financial stability of the telecommunications industry. The Austrian bidders quickly learned to avoid this pitfall, and the Austrian auction generated little revenue.

Because the flexible design allows incumbents to fight entrants, the prices paid in the flexible design can be strictly higher than those resulting from a less flexible design yielding the same outcome. But the flexible design included the risk of creating a more concentrated market structure, with adverse effects on consumers.

For these reasons, we question the efficiency gains obtained by the flexible design as it was used. A small modification, with flexibility between five or six licences (which would ensure entry and therefore reduce the pre-emptive motives and exposure), seems to us preferable.

The outcome of the German auction can, however, be considered a great success: the German government ended up with both high revenues and an unconcentrated mobile-phone market!

## 5     Conclusion

In this chapter we have shown that in the European 3G licensing process three distinctly different methods have been used. The first licensing method is the *Beauty Contest*. The characteristic feature of this licensing method is that it always contains a subjective element: there is no pre-defined algorithm that determines who will have the best bid. In all the Beauty Contests, the number and size of the licences, as well as the licence-holder and prices, were determined by government bureaucrats. The second licensing method is the *fixed prize auction*. Like the Beauty Contest, this allocation mechanism determines the number and size of the licences bureaucratically; the licence-holder and prices, however, are determined in an auction. The third licensing method is the *variable prize auction*. In this allocation mechanism not only are the licence-holder and prices determined by an auction, but also the number and size of the licences (to a certain degree). This chapter argues that an auction is usually the best way to allocate 3G licences. Whether one should choose the second or the third licensing method is dependent on the goal of the allocation and the current market situation.

In this chapter we have also surveyed some important aspects of licence auction design. We have argued that in complex environments it is necessary to base practical auction engineering on a sound theoretical foundation that combines the insights of auction theory with those of 'industrial organisation'. Overlooking market structure details can have far-reaching consequences for the shaping of one of the most important future markets.

Besides allocating spectrum, licence auctions shape future market structure in almost irreversible ways. A successful design must level the playing field between incumbents and potential entrants. The asymmetry between incumbents and entrants is a constant feature of most licence auctions, while many other features (such as particular aggregation interests or particular alliances across countries) are of a more transitory nature. Designs that encourage entry will result in increased efficiency, but they will also generate more revenue since more bidders will be attracted by the auction if they perceive real chances of winning.

Licences should be defined unequivocally. The length of the contract, the minimum required speed of network roll-out, the minimum requirement for geographic and/or population coverage, limitations about resale, mandatory roaming agreements, number portability, etc. should all be specified *ex ante*. If these issues are not dealt with properly, even an 'efficient' assignment process may lead to a badly functioning industry *ex post*. It is important too that the government commits itself not to change the terms of the licences *ex post*.

Given the increased global nature of the telecommunications industry, it may be worthwhile thinking about the advantages and disadvantages of some kind of European 'super-auction' that allows the aggregation of continent- (or EU-) wide licences besides the national ones. Even if spectrum allocations remain national affairs for the foreseeable future, some harmonisation measures may be required. At the moment, many firms complain that Beauty Contests always favour national incumbents, while those incumbents (who often obtained licences almost for free in their own country) can freely compete with deep pockets in foreign auctions.

## References

Abbink, K., B. Irlenbusch, P. Pezanis-Christou, B. Rockenbach, A. Sadrieh and R. Selten 2001, 'An experimental test of design alternatives for the British 3G/UMTS auction', mimeo, University of Bonn.

Binmore, K. and P. Klemperer 2002, 'The biggest auction ever', *Economic Journal* 112: 74–96.

Bjuggren, P.-O. 2002, 'The Swedish 3G Beauty Contest: a beauty or a beast?', mimeo, Jönköping International Business School.

Börgers, T. and C. Dustmann 2003, 'Awarding telecom licenses: the recent European experience', *Economic Policy*, 36: 216–68.

Cramton, P. 1997, 'The FCC spectrum auctions: an early assessment', *Journal of Economics and Management Strategy* 6: 431–95.

Damme, E. van 2002, 'The European UMTS auctions', *European Economic Review* 46: 846–58.

Deutsche Bank 2000, 'UMTS: the third generation game', Deutsche Bank Equity Research, London.

Ewerhart, C. and B. Moldovanu 2002, 'A stylized model of the German UMTS auction', Discussion Paper, Mannheim University.

Gilbert, R. and D. Newbery 1982, 'Pre-emptive patenting and the persistence of monopoly', *American Economic Review* 72: 514–26.

Grimm, V., F. Riedel and E. Wolfstetter 2002, 'The third generation (UMTS) spectrum auction in Germany', *Ifo Studien*, 48: 123–43.

Hultén, S., P. Andersson and P. Valiente 2002, 'Beauty Contest licensing – lessons from the 3G process in Sweden', mimeo, Stockholm School of Economics.

Janssen, M., A. Ros and N. van der Windt 2001, 'De draad kwijt? Onderzoek naar de gang van zaken rond de Nederlandse UMTS-veiling' (Research into the proceedings of the Dutch UMTS auction), Erasmus University Rotterdam.

Jehiel, P. and B. Moldovanu 2000, 'License auctions and market structure', Discussion Paper, Mannheim University and CEPR.

  2001, 'A note on efficiency and revenue maximization in multi-object auctions', *Economic Bulletin* 3: 2–5.

  2003, 'An economic perspective on auctions', *Economic Policy*, 36: 270–308.

Katz, M. and C. Shapiro 1986, 'How to license intangible property', *Quarterly Journal of Economics* 101: 567–90.

Klemperer, P. 1998, 'Auctions with almost common values: the "Wallet Game" and its applications', *European Economic Review* 42: 757–69.

  2000, 'Spectrum on the block', *Asian Wall Street Journal*, 5 October 2000.

  2002a, 'What really matters in auction design', *Journal of Economic Perspectives* 16: 169–89.

  2002b, 'How (not) to run auctions: the European 3G telecom auctions', *European Economic Review* 46: 829–45.

  2002c, 'Using and abusing economic theory: lessons from auction design', Alfred Marshall Lecture, 2002 Meeting of the European Economic Association.

Maasland, E. 2000, 'Veilingmiljarden zijn een fictie' ('Billions from Auctions: Wishful Thinking'), *ESB* June 9: 479 and translation available at http://www.paulklemperer.org (accessed at 26 February 2003).

Maskin, E. 1992, 'Auctions and privatization', in H. Siebert (ed.), *Privatization*, Institut für Weltwirtschaft der Universität Kiel.

McAfee, R. and J. McMillan 1996, 'Analyzing the airwaves auction', *Journal of Economic Perspectives* 10: 159–75.

McMillan, J. 1995, 'Why auction the spectrum', *Telecommunications Policy* 19: 191–9.

Pratt, A. and T. Valletti 2001, 'Spectrum auctions versus Beauty Contests: costs and benefits', *Rivista di Politica Economica* 91: 59–109.

REG-TP 2000, 'Entscheidung der Präsidentenkammer vom 18.02.2000 über die Regeln für die Durchführung des Versteigerungsverfahrens zur Vergabe von Lizenzen für UMTS/IMT-2000; Mobilkommunikation der dritten Generation' ('Ruling of 18 February 2000 by the President's Chamber on the rules for conduct of the auction for the award of licences for UMTS/IMT–2000; third-generation mobile communications'), Aktenzeichen BK-1b-98/005-2, official declaratory document, Bonn.

UBS Warburg 2000, '3G Hysteria! Not everyone's idea of fun and games', mimeo, UBS Global Equity Research, London.

WestLB Panmure 2000, 'UMTS: the countdown has begun', mimeo, WestLB Panmure, Pan European Equity, London.

# 8 Auctions of gas transmission access: the British experience

*Tanga Morae McDaniel and Karsten Neuhoff*

## 1 Introduction

An essential component of most utility industries is the network that transfers the commodity (e.g. gas, electrons, data, water) between producers and consumers. Frequently the supply of the commodity cannot meet demand either because of constraints within the network or because of insufficient capacity at points where the commodity is inserted or withdrawn. At these times producers or demand may be rationed. Producers at transport-constrained locations may be replaced by producers at unconstrained locations. Rationing on the demand side can be voluntary, based on price signals or based on interruptible contracts, or it can be involuntary, as occurs during times of rolling blackouts and unanticipated crashes of departmental computer servers. To determine who is rationed first, or, alternatively, who bears the costs of rescheduling production in order to match transmission constraints, we have to identify who owns the rights to the use of the network. Such rights can be implicit, granting unlimited access, explicit, guaranteeing a certain amount of physical delivery, or financial, compensating for costs incurred due to transmission constraints.

The question of transmission rights is of relevance once vertically integrated gas, electricity or water utilities are unbundled such that competing enterprises want to use scarce parts of the network. The successors of previously integrated utilities frequently argue that historic flow patterns guarantee an implicit right to continue similiar use of the transmission network. On the basis of this line of reasoning, newly defined transmission rights have been granted to existing producers or distribution utilities, a process referred to as grandfathering. Alternatively, transmission rights

We wish to thank Professors David Newbery, Paul Joskow and Maarten Janssen for their comments and for research support from Transco plc and UK-Interconnector. Support from the UK Economic and Social Research Council under the projects R000 238563 *Efficient and Sustainable Regulation and Competition in Network Industries* and R42200034307, from the Gottlieb Daimler Foundation and from the CMI Electricity Project is gratefully acknowledged. Any remaining errors are our own.

have been granted in bilateral negotiations, a process particularly suited to buying the support for different utilities or their (regional public) owners. More recently, auctions have been introduced in the hope of increasing transparency, allocative efficiency and competition while decreasing user discrimination. In the United States some gas transport services are sold by auction, as are access rights to the national gas network in Britain and the use of electricity interconnectors between many European countries (e.g. Belgium–UK and Germany–Netherlands).

In this chapter we use the experience of the British gas industry to develop the following argument. In a vertically unbundled industry the allocation of access to scarce transmission requires well-defined rights. Grandfathering such rights is not transparent, biases against new entrants and fails to capture scarcity rents. Selling the rights at a posted price may work for some time, but fails as soon as more rights are asked for than there is transmission capacity available. Therefore, we conclude that auctioning of well-defined access rights is an efficient and non-discriminatory way to ration rights to a constrained transmission network, given that there is competition in both production and supply of the final product.

The use of auctions in the gas industry is the result of a progression involving changes in industrial structure and regulation, so the qualifiers in our argument are important. The fact that the gas market is liberalised in Britain and that both production and supply are not highly concentrated means that auctions are feasible. Moreover, the monopoly network owner, Transco, has been physically unbundled from gas supply and production since 1997, thus reducing if not eliminating the danger of discrimination between network users. Where competition is lacking, where transmission constraints are not binding or where there is significant vertical integration, auctions are not obviously preferable to regulated posted prices.

If rights are auctioned, then a reserve price or additional transmission charge might be required to cover network costs when transmission is not scarce – in which case an auction would provide zero revenue. A further motivation for a reserve price is that gas producers with market power will understate their demand for transmission rights to avoid scarcity and positive prices for transmission rights. Even in the British gas industry, where there is competition and vertical separation, there are some points on the network that are only used by a very small number of producers. These producers have local market power in auctions for location-specific transmission rights, and reserve prices ensure that network costs are still recovered.

In the next section we discuss features of the British gas industry and provide a brief introduction to the privatisation and liberalisation of the industry. The industry phases leading up to the current auctions are addressed in section 3 and a description of the auction design is given in section 4. Sections 5 and 6 offer an evaluation of the auctions and our conclusions. In this chapter our focus is the auctions of monthly system entry capacity that have been held since September 1999. In Britain, auctions are now also used over longer periods to inform investment decisions; we briefly discuss this use of the auctions in section 5. We do not separately address the question of gas storage or auctions for storage, as we believe that the additional complexity does not alter the basic economic arguments we present.

Our arguments assume the particular characteristics of gas transmission networks and the results are not directly transferable to the electricity industry. Transmission rights for gas are comparatively easy to define, gas flows are rather stable and the network itself can be used to stabilise intraday variations of demand and supply. In contrast, in electricity networks, demand has to match supply at any moment, loop flows complicate the definition and reallocation of transmission rights, and the variety of generation technologies creates large variations in the flow patterns during the day. Physical transmission rights on the electricity network therefore have to be defined for short time periods of less than an hour, with high locational resolution, and can only be retraded centrally. The resulting inefficiencies from illiquid markets and high transaction costs make physical transmission rights less suitable for dealing with transmission constraints in electricity networks.

## 2  Privatisation and Liberalisation

Utility networks have properties of natural monopoly and as such are usually owned by a single company. Creating competition in network industries therefore involves requiring the monopolist to give other companies the right to use the network. Much of the regulatory process involves deciding how rights should be given, monitoring this process and determining how much users should pay. The process of allocating rights also affects the costs to the network owner of alleviating system constraints when demand for access exceeds the physical capability of the system. If rights are not firm and are poorly defined or if users do not face financial disincentives to overstating their demand for capacity, then the network owner will incur unnecessarily large costs to get rid of constraints. Moreover, the information provided to the owner about demand for network services and the need for new investments will be distorted.

Property rights (or access rights) to a monopolised transmission network can be allocated in one of the following ways:

(1) by leaving the access rights with the existing monopolist who can negotiate with potential users;

(2) by allowing existing users to continue their transmissions at traditional volumes (grandfathering);

(3) by auctioning the rights.

The British experience from 1982 to 1990 shows that British Gas (BG), as a vertically integrated monopoly network owner and majority gas supplier was reluctant to create competition by granting access to its network. As BG was slowly vertically unbundled following its privatisation in 1986, and as its market share in gas supply began to decline, more market-oriented mechanisms were introduced. As we later discuss, these mechanisms were easily gamed by the network users – the result of which was large costs for eliminating network constraints. Grandfathering of rights discriminates against entrants thereby reducing competitive pressure. In contrast, when there are well-defined property rights, the transmission operator issues transmission access corresponding to the available transmission capacity in the system; appropriately designed auctions accompanied by secondary trading markets can apportion these property rights efficiently.

## 2.1     Background

We discuss the development of the British gas industry in order to motivate our argument that feasible transmission access design depends on the existing industry structure and concentration. There is now an independent owner and operator of the transmission network and competition in gas production and gas supply. The structure of the industry is now such that auctions are feasible. This structure was attained through a long legislative process following privatisation in 1986. Prior to 1986 the industry had been in public ownership for just under forty years.

The British gas industry was nationalised in 1949 with the creation of twelve area supply boards, which were later united to become the British Gas Corporation in 1972. In the nationalised framework an integrated high-pressure network was built to deliver natural gas directly from the North Sea in place of coal- and oil-based town gas and liquefied gas delivery.

The Oil and Gas Act of 1982 was the first step towards industry liberalisation. The Act permitted competing gas companies access to the transmission network in order to supply large industrial customers with demand above 25,000 therms. The Gas Act of 1986 transformed the British Gas Corporation into British Gas (BG) and in the same year

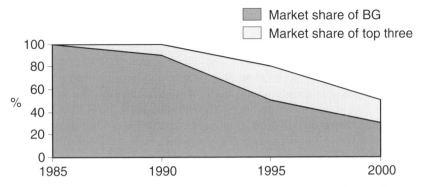

Figure 8.1. Competition in the gas supply sector, UK. (*Source:* Oxera, 2000.)

shares were offered for sale. Figure 8.1 shows that BG had at that time 100 per cent of the supply market share, which it retained throughout the eighties.

Following the 1986 Gas Act other industrial customers were legally allowed to contract with independent companies (or shippers),[1] and BG was required to provide transmission facilities. However, it was only after inquiries by the Monopolies and Mergers Commission (MMC) in 1988 and 1993 and several interventions of the Office of Fair Trading that competition truly began. In these inquiries it was found that BG was using its monopoly position to discriminate against independent shippers by applying high, non-transparent tariffs for the use of the transmission system and for the use of back-up gas. Moreover, the network owner had discriminated against shippers other than BG in the provision of system reinforcements and connection services. In 1998, the MMC panel required BG to publish information about the tariffs it charged to customers and not to contract more than 90 per cent of any new gas field. The Office of Fair Trading ruled in 1991 that BG's gas market share should not exceed 40 per cent; consequently, the monopoly tariff threshold was lowered in 1992 from 25,000 therms to 2,500 therms, allowing small businesses to contract freely with other suppliers.

Traditionally, transportation and storage formed part of BG's integrated gas supply business. The 1993 MMC report concluded that the lack of effective neutrality of the transportation and storage business 'may

---

[1] A shipper is anyone who requires capacity on the transmission network. Shippers are usually producers, but the term would also be applied to traders if they were bidding in the auction.

be expected to inhibit choice, restrict innovation, and lead to higher levels of gas prices to users' (paragraph 2.104). Based on the MMC recommendation the Secretary of State required BG to establish a separate business unit for transportation and storage with full physical separation of people, property and computer systems and information barriers between units.[2] Transco was established as the network owner/operator and a business unit of BG in 1994 and has been subject to a separate (RPI – X) price control since 1 October 1994. Subsequently, the ownership structure and market share of British Gas changed substantially. In 1997 a demerger created Centrica plc which became responsible for gas supply, retail services and production from the Morecambe gasfields. Transco remained a part of British Gas plc until demerging to join Lattice Group plc in 2000.

The Gas Act of 1996 created the framework to open the market even for small consumers, with full domestic liberalisation to be implemented by May 1998. However, during the 1997 MMC inquiry it became apparent that gas sales and trading, services and the retail business had to be separated. All of the demerged companies remained in the same group, Centrica plc, and separation of ownership was only achieved in October 2000 when Transco became part of Lattice Group plc and thus separate from gas supply. By 2000, 25 per cent of domestic and 72 per cent of industrial customers had switched gas suppliers (Oxera, 2000).

To summarise, British Gas was privatised as a vertically integrated monopolist in 1986, but it was not until 1997 that supply and (some) production were unbundled from transport. At that time, supply and production became the responsibility of Centrica, while Transco (and so the transport business) remained with British Gas. In October 2000 Transco demerged from British Gas and joined Lattice Group plc. A merger between Lattice Group plc and National Grid Company in October 2002 gave ownership of the gas and electricity transmission networks to the new company, National Grid Transco plc.

The major contribution towards a lower level of concentration in supply was an 85 per cent growth in gas demand in the UK between 1990 and 2000 (figure 8.2). Sixty per cent of the growth was due to new combined cycle gas turbines, which until 1990 had been prohibited under EU energy law (Department of Trade and Industry, 2001).

The concentration of upstream gas production was and is rather low. Oxera (2000) suggested that in 1985 British Gas accounted for 22 per cent of total UK gas production, a share that has dropped insignificantly to 21 per cent for the combined output of BG and Centrica (see

---

[2] To ensure that the trading business would not have access to information provided by its competitors to the transportation business. (MMC, 1997)

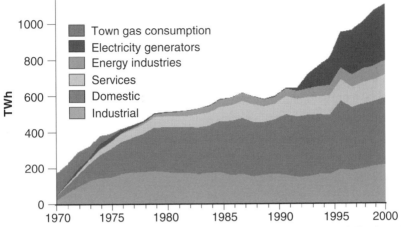

Figure 8.2. Gas consumption, UK. (*Source:* Department of Trade and Industry (2001), and national statistics.)

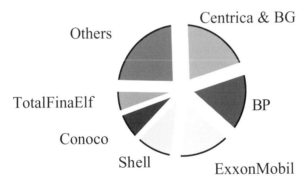

Figure 8.3. Shares of UK gas production. (*Source:* Leading UK Gas Producers, Platts 1998.)

figure 8.3). This low overall concentration should, however, not distract from the fact that the concentration of gas producers at individual entry terminals is typically significantly higher and therefore local competition for entry rights or balancing services lower or non-existent. This issue will be addressed again in section 5.

A consultation process started in 2001 by the industry regulator, Ofgem (Office of Gas and Electricity Markets), addressed questions raised by downstream suppliers, specifically that of whether upstream producers can and do exercise market power. Because of transmission constraints producers can have regional market power even though total concentration is low.

The above discussion shows the difficulties of introducing competition if a vertically integrated monopolist is in private ownership. We next describe the UK gas network and how the access regime has evolved with increased industry competition.

## 2.2    The gas pipeline network

Figure 8.4 illustrates the main gas pipeline network in the UK and the North Sea. Most underwater pipelines start from gas fields and transport gas of different consistencies that has to be processed at the coast before it can be inserted into the National Transmission System (NTS). The UK is responsible for 55 per cent of North Sea gas production, which is from either wet-gas or dry-gas fields. Wet gas is produced in the northern fields that are interconnected to St Fergus and can be considered a by-product of crude oil production. Producers with wet-gas fields respond to price signals in the oil market and do not adjust their output substantially according to changes in gas demand. The other fields are dry-gas fields which only produce natural gas and can be more easily adjusted to accommodate seasonal variations in gas demand.

The UK is connected to a number of other European markets via pipelines and interconnectors. The Frigg pipeline was initially constructed to allow gas from the UK-Norwegian Frigg field to be transported to the UK. The Frigg Treaty of 1997 allowed the use of the pipeline to import gas into the UK from additional Norwegian gas fields by interconnecting it with other pipelines and using it for new gas exploration. The UK–Belgium interconnector, opened in October 1998, was initially planned to allow for exports of UK gas to the Continent, but is also used for so-called reverse flows for imports into the UK during winter peak demand. Upgrades of compression facilities are to be completed in 2005 to increase the reverse flow capacity. Two further interconnectors are used for exports to Ireland. Given the level of abstraction of the current study, we simply classify use of interconnectors as additional demand on the NTS.

The NTS in Britain connects the gas landing facilities and storage facilities to gas customers. Demand for transmission services is volatile over the year and capacity is capital-intensive. Therefore, it would be inefficient to have a network that can satisfy all transmission requests. In recent years the St Fergus terminal in Scotland has been the most constrained. This continues to be the case, as currently binding constraints

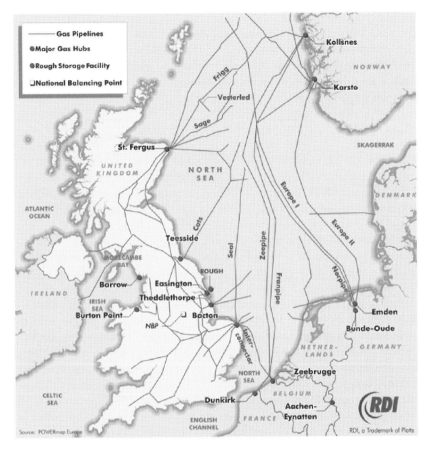

Figure 8.4. Gas pipelines in the UK and the North Sea. (Copyright Platts, 2001. Reproduced by kind permission.)

at Aberdeen, Moffat & Woller and Kirriemuir in Scotland restrict the transmission of gas towards England.[3]

## 3     Evolution of the access rights regime

Three general methods are available to resolve transmission constraints on the gas network: (i) inserting gas into the NTS at a different node on the network – usually from a different gas field; (ii) using storage facilities in import-constrained areas to provide gas at times of high demand;

---

[3] Jones (2001).

(iii) offering interruptible contracts to industrial consumers and electricity generators. Interruptible contracts allow Transco to stop supplying gas for up to forty-five days per year if system demand reaches 85 per cent of peak demand and transmission constraints prevent delivery. In exchange, industrial consumers pay lower capacity charges for access to the transmission network.

### 3.1    1986–1996

For most of this period BG was a vertically integrated monopolist and dominated the supply of gas as well as controlling the transmission network. Independent shippers supplied only large industrial customers, who usually have a low variance of energy demand during the year. As such, the initial regime for using the NTS did not address transmission constraints during operation, but required BG to resolve them autonomously. Shippers were only required to balance (i.e. to match the gas consumption of their customers with the gas shipments inserted at the coastal terminals) on a monthly basis. BG would balance the system on a daily basis and resolve transmission constraints using the three methods listed above: managing the volume and terminals at which gas was inserted into the network, storage and interruptible contracts.

Because BG dominated the industry, a protocol which left BG with sole responsibility for system balance and resolution of transmission constraints was feasible. However, the scope for discrimination and abuse of its dominant position were obvious drawbacks: '[BG] acknowledged, for example, that problems had occurred in some cases in estimating the capacity available for its competitors when they [had] sought to supply customers previously supplied by BG' (Monopolies and Mergers Commission, 1993). Subsequently it was decided that shippers could only be charged for costs of capacity expansion for the direct interconnection of the plant (shallow connection charges), but not for system-wide reinforcements (deep connection charges).

As the dominant position of BG declined with the lowering of the monopoly threshold, competitors began to serve customers with greater seasonal variation in demand, who required more balancing and accounted for more constraints on the system. As a result, the former constraint alleviation methods were compromised. In any case, this combination of industry structure and access regime was seen as an intermediate stage. The Monopolies and Mergers Commission (1993) concluded: 'In the longer term, however, we would regard the ability of competitors to access the transportation network and other facilities such as storage on non-discriminatory terms (including, for example, the balancing regime adopted by BG to ensure adequate availability of gas in the system to meet demands) as essential if competition is to be sustained.'

## 3.2    New Network Code, March 1996

The network operations of BG became the responsibility of Transco in 1994, and the Network Code ('the Code') was adopted in 1996. The Code was the industry's response to a number of factors including: the opening of the domestic market (with volatile demand profiles); the falling market share and therefore reduced balancing capabilities of BG; increased pressure for non-discriminatory pricing of transmission services; and the request of independent shippers to profit from providing balancing services. The Code required shippers to balance gas inserted at terminals and storage facilities with the gas delivered to their contracted customers. Transco would balance the system if deviations occurred and subsequently charge shippers the resulting costs.

Under the Code, Transco continued to use interruptible contracts to manage constraints but it also introduced a new mechanism for buying back excess entry capacity rights. Under this mechanism, shippers first had to book and pay for annual entry capacity for a specific terminal at a price related to Transco's capacity costs.[4] One day ahead, they would then nominate how much gas they would flow the following day.

This system did not *ex ante* incorporate transmission constraints. Shippers could book unlimited amounts of entry capacity, could nominate above their booked capacity for an additional fee,[5] and could insert gas above the nominated level at the risk of the 'overrun charges'. However, the system did provide Transco with day-ahead information on how much gas would be inserted at any terminal. Transco would then use information about large consumers' demand and estimates of domestic users' demand (based on weather forecasts) to simulate the next day's gas flows. If constraints were anticipated, then Transco would use a pseudo market instrument called the 'flexibility mechanism' to resolve the constraints. For example, if expected gas insertion at St Fergus exceeded transmission capacity in Scotland, then Transco would sell gas at St Fergus and buy gas at southern shore terminals closer to demand. Uncertainty about the functioning of the flexible mechanism meant that Transco retained additional storage at the beginning to allow for balancing, but the initial success of the Code allowed most of the storage facilities

---

[4] This cost was a regulated tariff based on the long-run marginal cost of expanding the network to accommodate additional flows at the terminal.

[5] Equal to 73/183 of the annual entry capacity.

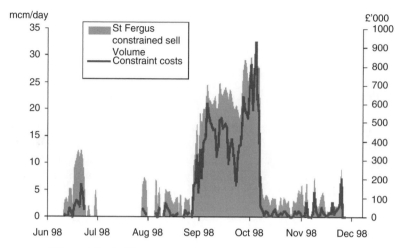

Figure 8.5. St Fergus and Bacton constraint costs. (*Source:* Ofgem, 1999a.)

to be made available to shippers on an annual basis based on regulated tariffs.[6]

For the first two years the Network Code and flexibility mechanism appeared to work well. Then, in the summer of 1998 significant capacity shortages occurred for entry at St Fergus due to delayed commissioning of additional capacity and construction on existing capacity. As a result 'The level of nominations was far in excess of the available capacity, or indeed the level of [additional] capacity originally projected by Transco to be available at St Fergus' (Ofgem, 1999a). Transco had to sell significant amounts of gas at St Fergus and acquire replacement supplies at other terminals, resulting in total balancing costs of £23.1 million during the period from late August to 8 October 1998 (see figure 8.5). In this situation, shippers faced perverse incentives. Even if they had otherwise not planned to ship gas, they could nominate gas insertions and subsequently submit bids via the flexibility mechanism to reduce the announced insertion. Such behaviour was individually rational: the shipper profited and was only exposed to a fraction of the costs he created since balancing costs were shared among all shippers.

The design of shipper licences, defined in the Gas Act 1986, equips the regulatory body with authority beyond usual competition law to intervene in the case of non-competitive behaviour. Condition 2(2) prohibits shippers from knowingly or recklessly pursuing a course of conduct that

---

[6] For a discussion of the storage market and the introduction of storage auctions in the UK, see Hawdon and Stevens (2001).

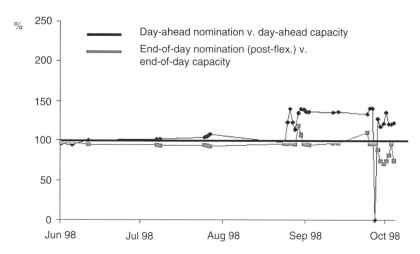

Figure 8.6. Elf Exploration's excess nominations. (*Source:* Ofgem, 1999a.)

is likely to prejudice the efficient balancing of the system. Condition 2(3) requires that the licensee shall not knowingly or recklessly act in a manner likely to give a false impression to a relevant transporter as to the amount of gas to be delivered by the licensee on a particular day to that transporter's pipeline. Standard condition 9 furthermore requires the shippers to furnish the director-general of the regulatory body (now Ofgem) with such information as he may reasonably require, even if this information is subject to confidentiality provisions; information is excluded only if a court in civil proceedings would not be able to compel the shippers to produce it.

Ofgem concluded in its 1999 inquiry that making excessive day-ahead nominations constituted a breach of the standard conditions 2(2) and/or 2(3). The most impressive part of the evidence was against Elf Exploration. Figure 8.6 illustrates how Elf nominated excessive capacity once it became apparent in September that Transco would have to use the flexibility mechanism to resolve anticipated constraints.[7] It would be interesting to see whether the evidence available to Ofgem would suffice for the conclusion to stand up to judicial review. In the event, shippers did not have to challenge Ofgem's conclusion because, owing to subsequent changes to the trading arrangements in September 1999, Ofgem did not take enforcement action.

---

[7] Traders of Shell gas were similarly ignorant of the capabilities of regulatory offices, whereas most other shippers behaved according to the spirit of the Network Code.

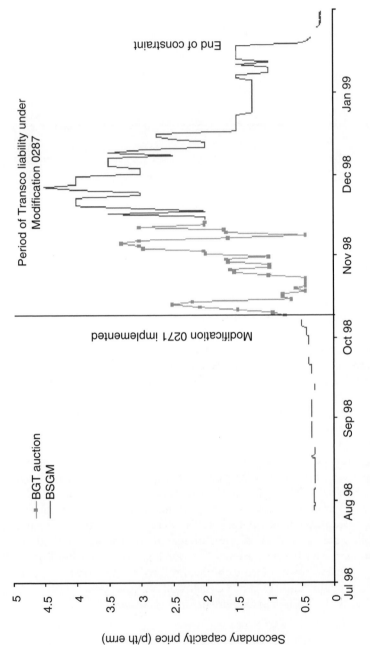

Figure 8.7. Price in secondary capacity auction. (*Source:* Ofgem, 1999a.)

### 3.3    Scaling back

As a reaction to the increasing costs of constraint resolution with the flexibility mechanism, as illustrated by figure 8.5, Ofgem modified the Code in October 1998. Modification 271 required Transco to (proportionally) 'scale back bookings to ensure that booked capacity equalled the amount of gas that could be physically evacuated from St Fergus entry terminal'. Obviously the result was that some shippers did not receive the capacity they required for their contractual requirements, while other shippers, in particular at that time BG, still retained unused booked capacity. BG made its excess capacity available in a day-ahead auction until November 1998 when Modification 273 introduced a day-ahead auction at entry terminals, allowing unsold or unused physically available capacity to be made available to shippers.

The value of entry rights in the day-ahead auction is illustrated in figure 8.7. The prices for entry rights match the price differences in the day-ahead spot market for gas at St Fergus and gas at the National Balancing Point (as shown in figure 8.13). This was a first indication that auctioning entry rights might be successful. The scaling-back approach was considered to be only a temporary solution, mainly because of complaints about the uncertainty shippers face up to the day ahead over whether they will have access to sufficient capacity. The Ofgem inquiry of December 1999 concluded that some shippers had breached their licence conditions during this period by nominating gas flows above the capacity which had been available after their initially booked capacity had been scaled back. The defence brought forward by shippers was that they faced significant uncertainty about available capacity and felt they had to honour commercial commitments to ship the gas. Even though these shippers could have resolved the conflict between commercial commitments and obligations following from the licence conditions by interacting in the spot market, such a solution would have required significant interactions. The corresponding transaction costs can be considered to be a major disadvantage of the scaling-back approach.

The conclusion to be drawn from the UK experience is that selling an unlimited amount of transmission rights at a posted price only works in an unconstrained network.

## 4    Auctioning entry rights

Charges to use the gas transmission system are split between use of the National Transmission System (NTS) and use of the Local Distribution System. Only the NTS is relevant for our purposes. Fees to use the NTS

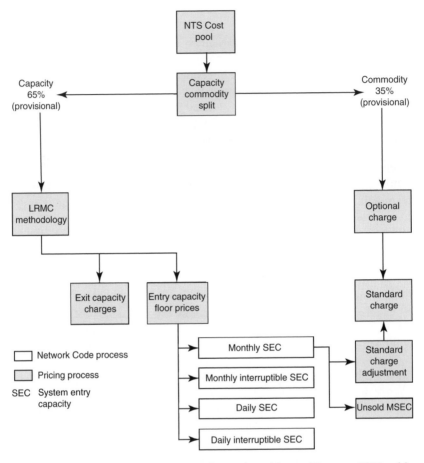

Figure 8.8. NTS charges and floor prices. (*Source:* Transco, 2000, table 3.2.1.)

are split between capacity (65 per cent) and commodity charges (35 per cent). Capacity charges include both an entry fee (charged at the auction price) and a regulated exit fee (based on a long-run marginal cost calculation). The commodity charge is a flat fee per unit of gas transported and is independent of the entry and exit zones. This description is shown schematically in figure 8.8.

Transco is a monopolist with regulated revenues and an allowed annual revenue. Provisions are made for the eventualities of over- and under-recovery of revenues and generally entail revisions to other regulated network charges. Revenues from the monthly system entry capacity (MSEC)

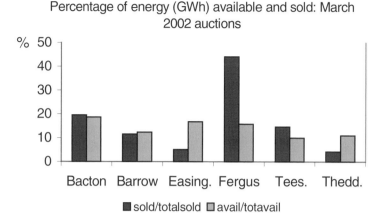

Figure 8.9. Energy availability and sales.

auctions are part of Transco's revenue target, and day-ahead and daily auctions (which do not contribute to the revenue target) form part of an incentive scheme whereby Transco is rewarded for increasing available capacity.

### 4.1    Description of the current auction approach

As can be seen in figure 8.4 there are six major coastal terminals in Britain where gas is put into the NTS: St Fergus, Teesside, Easington, Theddlethorpe and Bacton on the East Coast and Barrow on the West Coast. The auctions for rights to insert gas into the NTS began in September 1999 and originally only included these six terminals. The subsequent auctions also included a number of onshore fields, storage and constrained liquified natural gas facilities. St Fergus in Scotland and Bacton in the south-east are the terminals with most demand for capacity. Figure 8.9 shows the volumes of energy sold and available at these six terminals for the March 2002 auctions (as a percentage of total capacity sold and available at all terminals). St Fergus and Bacton account for only 16 and 19 per cent, respectively, of available entry capacity, but 44 and 20 per cent, respectively, of gas is produced and sold at these terminals. The importance of St Fergus may be understood by noting the number of gas pipelines connecting it to gas fields in the North Sea. Bacton is likewise connected to a number of major pipelines, but, more importantly, it is the terminal closest to the interconnector linking Britain to the Continent via Zeebrugge in Belgium.

The major characteristics of the auction design and product, the auction rules, and the evolution of the auction design since 1999 are outlined below.

## 4.2    Auction features

The product sold in the auctions is the right to enter a volume of gas at a given entry point for one month (referred to subsequently as monthly system entry capacity, or MSEC). Auctions of MSEC are held twice a year and are for six-month tranches; auctions held in March allocate rights for the period April–September, and auctions held in September allocate rights for the period October–March.

Transco considered whether to sell twelve-, six- or one-month capacity rights at each auction; it concluded that the monthly option would be best in principle since it would provide the most flexibility to shippers, but this option could not be realised in time for the September 1999 auctions. Six months were preferred to twelve since this would reduce shippers' risk from bidding mistakes and would take account of the different demand profiles of winter and summer (Transco, 1999).

Transco furthermore assessed how auctions would meet criteria with respect to allocative efficiency, ease of use, familiarity, accommodation of complements/substitutes and system readiness. The accommodation of complements and substitutes among different entry terminals is an important feature of any design of gas network auctions. Shippers will value the ability to adjust their demands at different terminals depending on maintenance, for example, or their need to have rights for consecutive periods, while Transco can shift available entry capacity between different terminals if the transmission constraints are not directly at the terminal but deeper in the transmission system. MSEC auctions are accompanied by daily auctions of firm and interruptible capacity rights.

*Auction rounds*    The total capacity available at each terminal is divided equally and sold over four rounds separated by one business day. Beginning with the March 2000 auctions, these four rounds were supplemented by a fifth 'flexible' round in which any unsold (aggregate) capacity could be auctioned and subsequently nominated at any entry terminal on the network. There is one proviso, however: Transco sets a maximum amount that can be allocated to each terminal in the MSEC auctions. Thus, if a shipper bought capacity in the fifth round and wanted to nominate at St Fergus, she would only be able to do so if that maximum was not binding. As the fifth round is a 'residual' round, the volumes sold are rather low. In the March 2000 auctions a very small amount of the aggregate residual capacity remained unsold because bids to nominate fifth-round capacity to St Fergus were rejected on the grounds that the maximum allowed MSEC for that terminal had been reached.

*Reserve prices*   Reserve prices reduce the risk that the network owner will be unable to meet its revenue requirement and are important for capacity auctions in the presence of either market power or excess capacity. Prior to October 1999, entry rights were booked on the basis of regulated prices that were estimates of the long-run marginal cost (LRMC). Reserve prices equal to LRMC would reduce the efficiency of the auction if these were above the marginal valuation of shippers. In determining appropriate reserve prices, the estimated LRMC has been used as a benchmark, with proportional discounts dependent on the concentration of bidders at each entry point. At Barrow, where there is essentially just one bidder, the reserve price equals the LRMC and the auctions always clear at this price.

*Auction quantities*   The amount offered for sale in the monthly auction will affect the amount of secondary trading and the number of rights that Transco must repurchase in the event of network constraints. This implies that the amount offered for sale in the auction will not necessarily correspond to the amount of physical capacity available either in total or at each entry point. Initially, the baseline level of demand that determined *total* capacity offered at MSEC auctions was calculated using historical information on the average amount of capacity that would be available each month under conditions of seasonal normal demand (SND). The total was then allocated among terminals on the basis of actual flows over the previous three years (Ofgem, 1999b). Ofgem was not satisfied with the use of SND as a measure of available capacity since it was 'backward-looking' and might not accurately represent the current state of the energy market. The approach was also criticised because the calculations were done by Transco. Through a number of Modifications to the auction rules the total amount of capacity made available at each auction has steadily increased.

If more capacity is auctioned than is warranted by downstream demand then Transco must buy back those rights from shippers, possibly at higher prices (see table 8.1 and section 5 for a discussion of the high buyback costs in October 2000).

### 4.3    Auction rules

We follow Ofgem documents and the Network Code published by Transco in the discussion of the auction rules and procedures (Transco, 2001). Capacity rights for six separate months are sold at each auction. The auctions are sealed-bid, pay-bid and concurrent by terminal and month.

Each bid has to include the shipper's identity, the entry terminal, the month for which capacity is sought and a minimum volume and bid price. Shippers' bid prices are given in pence/kWh/day, specified to four decimal places, and must not be below the reserve price. The minimum volume for which a shipper can bid is 100,000 kWh/day. Shippers can submit as many as twenty bids for each terminal and each month in each round.

The auctioneer ranks bids, ignoring the entry point, high to low. Bids with identical bid prices are ranked by bid volume. Then capacity is allocated in the order of descending bid prices. If the requested amount of the marginal bid exceeds available capacity, the last bidder receives the remaining amount.

Between auction rounds (before 9 a.m. on the next business day) bidders are informed about their winning volumes, the highest/lowest bid price of capacity that was allocated and the weighted average price of accepted bids.

### 4.4    Monthly interruptible capacity

Like the monthly firm auctions, interruptible capacity is made available each month and is sold in six-monthly tranches. These auctions are also pay-bid, but occur over two rounds instead of five. The monthly capacity available on an interruptible basis is:

$$C_m^I = \text{Maximum physical demand}$$
$$- \text{available monthly firm capacity}.$$

Capacity in each round equals $\frac{1}{2} C_m^I$. The reserve price is 90 per cent of the estimate of long-run marginal cost, and any unsold capacity is made available in the daily auctions.

### 4.5    Short-term auctions: daily and within-day

Day-ahead auctions are held for firm and interruptible capacity rights. Reserve prices for the daily firm auctions are 50 per cent of the estimate of long-run marginal cost at each terminal; for daily interrupt auctions, reserve prices are zero. Daily interruptible capacity is:

$$C_D^I = \text{Unsold monthly interrupt} + \text{'use it or lose it' capacity}.$$

'Use it or lose it' capacity consists of capacity previously bought by a shipper that has not been nominated for use on the day. The original owner of the rights can *ex post* decide to nominate or resell the rights herself. In this case the new owner would be interrupted. In June 2000 Transco began to hold within-the-day auctions for firm capacity rights. Reserve prices in these auctions are 50 per cent of the estimate of long-run marginal cost.

## 4.6    Evolution

While the essential auction design has remained the same, a number of changes have occurred in the auction process since September 1999. The most significant of these changes has been the increase in the total MSEC made available. The total MSEC available in the September 1999 auction was the SND for each month in the October 1999 to March 2000 period. For the March 2000 auctions, available capacity was increased from SND to SND + 10 per cent. Because total downstream gas demand in Britain is lower in summer than in winter, the total MSEC in September 1999 (equal to SND) was still greater than the total in the March 2000 auctions. The available monthly capacity was increased still further in the September 2001 auctions. More recently, Ofgem has changed Transco's licence to encourage a release of capacity that more accurately reflects system capability. Transco has incentives to reduce the cost (and so quantity) of buy-backs of capacity in the event of constraints.

As the MSEC has increased, the availability of daily and within-day capacity has declined. In particular, the result has been a substantial reduction in the amount of interruptible capacity. Reduced short-run capacity availability increases shippers' incentive to secure MSEC. Total capacity available at St Fergus between October 1999 and February 2002 is shown in figure 8.12.

Transco has an incentive to make available as much capacity as possible. As such, it is allowed to retain a proportion of revenues received from daily and within-day auctions. Additional capacity sales increase the likelihood of constraints; thus Transco has to be exposed to the resulting costs. The company is responsible for 20 per cent of the cost of buy-backs necessary to alleviate any constraints on the network due to overbooking of capacity. The total amount of Transco's responsibility is capped annually and monthly, and shippers are responsible for the remainder of these costs.

The need for a structured approach to deal with over-recovery became apparent only after the March 2000 auctions when revenues were 160 per cent above Transco's regulated target. To redistribute future over-recovery, Transco proposed introducing a fund that would reduce the amount that shippers are responsible for paying to alleviate network constraints.

## 5     Evaluation

From a theoretical perspective a comprehensive analysis of this auction design and the efficiency of its outcomes is problematic for a number of reasons. Most importantly, these are concurrent, sequential auctions with multi-unit demands and common values. As such, one does not *a priori* anticipate full efficiency.[8] However, inefficiencies will be reduced if the entry cost for traders is low and there are liquid spot markets, which serve as secondary markets and ensure that the party that values transmission capacity most will use it.[9]

When bidders in an auction have affiliated values (i.e. the value to any one bidder is correlated to the values of other bidders) and there is a possibility of a winner's curse, bidding is expected to be more conservative than in the case in which bidders have private values. Ascending auctions can mitigate the winner's curse (Milgrom and Weber, 1982) since observation of when others drop out of the auction reveals something about their values and so reduces the chance that the winner will pay too much. Conversely, open ascending auctions make collusive strategies feasible.

Also, in contrast to private-value auctions, increasing the number of buyers in common-value auctions can decrease the expected revenue for the seller. That is, increasing the number of bidders can lead to more conservative bidding when values are correlated. The fact that you win an object in a common-value auction suggests to you that you probably paid too much since you beat everyone else. The more bidders there are competing against you, the more likely you are to curse if you win.[10] These results suggest a trade-off between increasing competition on the one hand and preventing the winner's curse on the other.

We believe that the sealed-bid sequential auction, where bidders are given feedback between rounds, mimics the properties of the open-bid auction. The information obtained between rounds allows shippers to learn about the values of other bidders and therefore decreases the chance

---

[8] Dasgupta and Maskin (1998) show conditions under which multi-unit auctions with common values can result in efficient allocations. Bids are contingent on others' values in their model, however.

[9] At this time we do not have full data on the extent of shippers' secondary trades.

[10] See Bulow and Klemperer (2000) for a broader discussion. Bulow and Klemperer also suggest, however, that increases in supply can mitigate the winner's curse by increasing the number of winners and thereby removing or lessening the curse of being among the winners.

that they will be subject to the winner's curse. However, if there is market power at an entry point, multiple rounds can serve to maintain collusion. Given that these are repeated auctions, the emphasis should shift over time to give more weight to the problems associated with collusion.

Although entry capacity auctions are held for the six major terminals on the NTS, significant constraints occur only at St Fergus. Evidence of this is shown in figure 8.10 for the March 2002 auctions. Apart from St Fergus the mark-ups at the other terminals are always below 25 per cent and mostly below 15 per cent. This implies either that transmission constraints are not binding at these terminals or that gas producers are exercising market power at these terminals. They would reduce output to prevent transmission constraints binding, in order to buy entry rights at a low price or sell gas at higher prices to shippers who obtained cheap entry rights. We focus our subsequent analysis on the case of St Fergus.[11]

In figure 8.11 we present empirical results from the auctions. The circles give the price paid for entry rights in the monthly auctions. One notes the strong correlation between simultaneously auctioned months, which arises because similar information is available. Even more obvious in the data is the sharp difference between winter (October–March) and summer months (April–September). Figure 8.12 shows that during summer months less entry capacity is available at St Fergus, partly because higher outside temperatures reduce transmission and compression capacity but mainly because lower gas demand by consumers and industry reduces the off-take of gas in the North, while the transmission capacity to the south is constrained in Scotland and northern England.[12]

Most fields delivering gas to the St Fergus terminal are wet fields, and reducing the gas output would require a simultaneous reduction of oil production. Revenues from oil are greater than from gas and adapting output quantities is difficult. Therefore, most oil companies are willing to sell gas, even at a lower price, and are prepared to pay higher prices for entry rights at St Fergus.

The thicker line in figure 8.11 gives the 30-day moving average of the value attributed to entry rights in the day-ahead spot market. Unfortunately, results of the daily capacity auctions were not available, and would

[11] For some of the auctions, mark-ups were significantly higher than those shown here (except at Barrow). This is particularly true for the second auction where revenue over-recovery was so great. This auction's outcome is discussed further below. We attribute overbidding at terminals other than St Fergus in the early auctions to uncertainty about the level of rights to be made available in the spot market since the capacity made available for the first few auctions changed so frequently and with such magnitude.

[12] Network analysis by Jones (2001) showed that the relevant (binding) constraints in winter 2001/2 were expected in such diverse locations as Aberdeen, Moffat & Wooler and Kirriemuir.

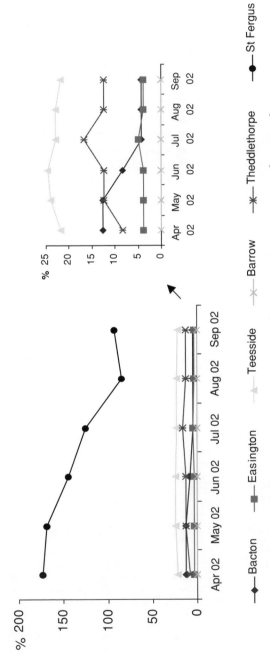

Figure 8.10. Percentage by which auction price exceeds reserve price: average over four rounds.

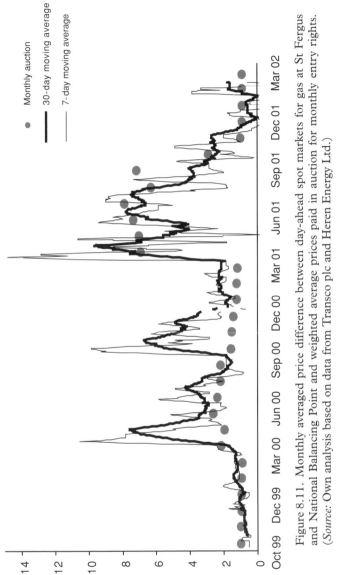

Figure 8.11. Monthly averaged price difference between day-ahead spot markets for gas at St Fergus and National Balancing Point and weighted average prices paid in auction for monthly entry rights. (*Source:* Own analysis based on data from Transco plc and Heren Energy Ltd.)

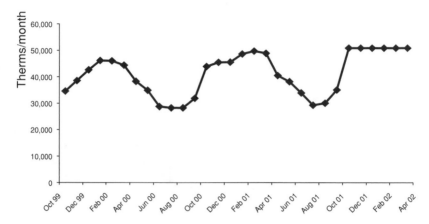

Figure 8.12. Available entry capacity in monthly auctions for St Fergus.

in any case only cover days with excess capacity. Therefore, it was necessary to calculate the daily value attributed to entry rights by comparing
the day-ahead spot market prices at St Fergus (before entering the NTS)
with the spot market prices at the National Balancing Point (NBP) (when
the gas is in the NTS) (see figure 8.13). The resulting price differences
are very volatile, so we present the 30-day moving average to allow comparison with the results from the monthly auctions. The graph shows that
anticipated entry prices in the monthly auctions are roughly matched by
the subsequent realisations of spot prices.

However, from April 2000 the day-ahead evaluation of entry capacity
was frequently above the price paid in the entry auction. To explain this
we look for events that occurred after the auctions for monthly entry rights
in March; events happening before the auction should already have been
reflected in the prices paid in the monthly auctions. The unexpected oil
price spikes of 2000 had a twofold effect on the value of entry capacity.
First, higher oil prices during the fuel crisis induced producers in the
northern fields to increase oil production and, correspondingly, their gas
production. However, constraints on entry capacity implied that gas sales
could not be likewise increased. Increasing supply while maintaining demand reduces prices, as the drop in the St Fergus spot price in summer
2000 proves (figure 8.13). At the same time, gas prices on the Continent
rose because they are coupled to oil prices. In Britain, gas contracts are not
directly linked to oil prices; therefore, shippers wanted to sell additional
gas on the Continent via the interconnection between Bacton and Zeebrugge, pushing up British gas prices (again observable in figure 8.13).
As access to the network was constrained, higher continental and British

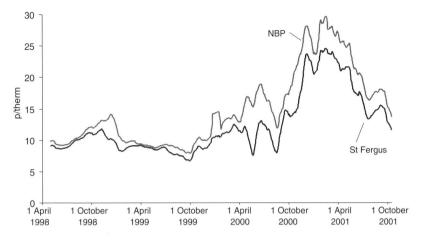

Figure 8.13. Monthly averages of spot prices at the National Balancing Point (NBP) and St Fergus. (*Source:* Based on Heren Energy Ltd data.)

gas prices could not feed through to St Fergus spot prices, and lower St Fergus spot prices could not balance higher NBP prices. The result was a wedge between prices at St Fergus and the NBP – and a high value attributed to entry rights.

The next spike for entry rights occurred from October 2000. Ofgem claims that because of warmer than expected weather demand for gas in Scotland and northern England was lower, reducing the available entry capacity below the volume of firm rights sold in the monthly auction. Transco had to buy back a significant volume of capacity rights and was paying prices of 18p/therm on average. This price is again greater than the wedge between spot prices at St Fergus and the NBP. The 'premium' paid in the buy-back market above the spot market can possibly be explained by the additional costs incurred by gas producers when they have to change their production at short notice during the day. Furthermore, shippers might have used their market power to obtain higher prices from Transco when selling back entry rights. In a subsequent investigation, however, Ofgem concluded that no action was required as 'shippers and Transco [had] to learn about the dynamics and operation of the capacity buy back market' (Ofgem, 2001a).

However, the main reason for the unexpected price spike for entry rights in autumn 2000 can be seen in figure 8.13. Wholesale gas prices in the British market almost doubled, but constrained entry capacity at St Fergus did not allow producers at St Fergus to react to higher demand at the NBP. Therefore, prices at the NBP did not feed through to prices at

Table 8.1. *Capacity buy-backs, April 2000–February 2001*

|  | Number of days requring buy-backs | Average daily buy-back volume (GWh) | Weighted average price (p/kWh) | Total cost of buy-backs (£) |
|---|---|---|---|---|
| April | 0 | 0 | — | 0 |
| May | 0 | 0 | — | 0 |
| June | 5 | 11.93 | 0.21 | 126,717 |
| July | 7 | 28.2 | 0.40 | 783,041 |
| August | 10 | 12.57 | 0.07 | 87,259 |
| September | 6 | 18.08 | 0.19 | 203,349 |
| Total | 28 | 17.54 | 0.24 | 1,200,366 |
| October | 20 | 76.71 | 0.55 | 8,514,192 |
| November | 8 | 47.78 | 0.45 | 1,723,850 |
| December | 5 | 28.63 | 0.61 | 869,433 |
| January | 0 | 0 | — | 0 |
| February | 1 | 128.53 | 0.37 | 475,158 |
| Total | 34 | 64.35 | 0.53 | 11,582,633 |

*Source:* Ofgem, 2000.

St Fergus, where spot prices stayed constant. The resulting wedge between prices was reflected in a spike in the value attributed to entry rights.

From 2001 the monthly auctions returned to being a good predictor of the average value attributed to entry rights. The benefits of auctioning entry rights can be seen by comparing the scarcity of entry rights during the high constraint period in September 1999, when the average difference between spot prices in St Fergus and NBP was 0.7p/therm, and October 2000, when the average difference between the spot prices was 6.7p/therm. Even though the scarcity of transmission capacity increased tenfold, the cost for buy-backs has fallen. Since the auctions began in September 1999, there has been one instance of seemingly substantial buy-backs by Transco to reduce network constraints. Table 8.1 shows the cost of buy-backs for the auctions to February 2001. For the five-month period, October 2000 to February 2001, these costs reached £11.6 million. This was high enough to prompt an investigation into shipper behaviour by Ofgem (2001a), yet it was still below the £23.1 million for the five-month period August–December 1998 shown in figure 8.5. This provides just one example to illustrate the general advantage of the auction approach, its greater transparency. Because Transco typically waits until the gas day to buy back entry rights, these costs are higher than the prices at which the rights were bought at the auction.

Another issue which arises in these auctions is Transco's revenue requirement. Deciding how to distribute over-recovery of auction revenues is a problem not normally confronted in private-sector auctions, yet it is important where the auctioneer is a regulated firm. The fact that over-recovery occurs should not be a problem *per se*, but a well-defined auction should address this issue at the beginning so that participants know the game they are playing. How to distribute 'surplus' revenues is not a trivial problem since reimbursements can impact shippers' bidding decisions in the monthly auctions. As such, participants should have recourse to a credible dispute resolution procedure in the event, for example, that well-founded assumptions regarding the use of extra revenue do not materialise. Transco's auction revenues for the period October 1999–March 2000 were £85.62 million (within −3 per cent of its revenue target). A similar situation was anticipated for the March auctions. In the event, Ofgem claimed that Transco's revenue was 160 per cent of its target (Ofgem, 2000).

The auction rules made allowances for under/over-recovery. Specifically, it was anticipated that adjustments would be made to the generic correction factor in Transco's price control, i.e. the price control contains a revenue under/over-recovery adjustment factor such that if the company over-recovers relative to its revenue target in a given year, the target is scaled downwards the following year. This would mean a general reduction in transportation charges for shippers in the following year.

Following the large over-recovery from the second auctions, Transco decided to make a one-off adjustment whereby commodity, capacity and transport charges were proportionately reduced. Fifteen per cent of the over-recovery went to reductions in transport charges, while the remainder reduced NTS capacity and commodity charges (Ofgem, 2000). It seems obvious that such a rebate mechanism would alter bidding behaviour if this type of surplus redistribution became the rule. If a portion of entry capacity charges is refunded to shippers they will not incur the full cost of their bids and therefore have skewed bidding incentives. This would bias estimates of the demand for capacity and lead to erroneous investment decisions if longer term capacity auctions were pursued. In the future, under- and over-recoveries will be assigned to a 'buy-back' fund that will reduce shippers' share of constraint costs.

Finally, in the international environment the auction mechanism seems to prevail as well. In October 2001 additional pipelines in the North Sea were taken into service to allow the export of gas from Norwegian fields to the UK, using the St Fergus terminal. Even though Norway complained that the constraint costs would reduce the Norwegian revenues in the project, it finally supported a project that retains the bottleneck and therefore the capture of scarcity revenues on British soil.

## 5.1    Long-term auctions

Until recently the time horizon of auctions was six months, but from January 2003 the use of auctions for allocating entry capacity to the network was extended to longer periods. The goal was to provide more information to Transco about future uses of the network and to guide its decisions on capacity expansion.[13] In a separate study (McDaniel and Neuhoff, 2002) we argue that, in the presence of market power, long-term auctions will provide distorted signals to the auctioneer, Transco, with a consequent danger of under-investment.[14]

In the long-term auctions, shippers can book quarterly access rights up to fifteen years into the future. The quantity made available in the long-term auctions is determined in a two-stage process. First, a baseline level of output representing the maximum physical capacity is determined for each auctioned terminal. This quantity is referred to as the transmission operator baseline output level. Second, 90 per cent of this baseline level (referred to as the system operator baseline level) is then made available for auctions – 80 per cent of this is being made available for long-term auctions and 20 per cent is being reserved for one year before the relevant gas year (i.e. one year ahead of when the capacity would actually be used).[15] Reserving a fixed quantity of capacity for short-term auctions (auctions with a time horizon of one year or less) is an important feature of the auction design because it ensures that some capacity will be available for entrants and traders.

The short-term auctions for transmission rights have had the comforting property that an inefficient auction outcome, in which shippers who do not value the rights most obtain rights, can be corrected by secondary trading or in the gas spot markets. In contrast, any distortions created by long-term auctions will be reflected in inefficient investment decisions, and can therefore no longer be corrected. Moreover, shippers can be expected to use their private information in order to distort the auction outcome to their benefit. A gas producer located at St Fergus benefits from excessive transmission capacity because it increases gas spot prices at St Fergus. On the other hand, a gas producer at another terminal might prefer insufficient transmission capacity from St Fergus because

---

[13] A description of early ideas for such auctions is given by Ofgem (1999b, 2001b). A discussion of the auctions that began in January 2003 is in Ofgem (2002).

[14] Discussions of 'long-term' auctions and their potential problems can also be found in McDaniel (2003) and Newbery (2003).

[15] The distinction between transmission operator and system operator output levels is not important for this discussion. We include it only for precision. These two aspects of Transco's duties are regulated separately.

it reduces national supply and increases national gas prices. Likewise, a trader who owns transmission rights from St Fergus prefers scarce transmission capacity so that his rights gain in value.

One of the purposes of having an auction is to extract shippers' private information about future use of the network: the network users know more about their future production decisions and their own customers' demand for gas than the network owner. McDaniel and Neuhoff (2002) show that the way shippers use their information depends on their type, and the incentive to over- or understate their demands for capacity is affected by how much capacity is reserved for short-term markets. The auction designer can choose the amount of capacity to hold in reserve in the long-term auction and can thereby correct the incentive for any one group of shippers to distort their revelation of private information in the long-term auction. However, the designer cannot choose a proportional split between long- and short-term markets that simultaneously removes distortions from market power, distortions from private information and distortions arising from 'network effects' (i.e. the fact that some shippers land their gas at different points on the network). The importance of private information is supported by the following statement from Transco:

Improved understanding of the potential interactions between demands at different terminals is needed if the ability of the NTS to respond flexibly to changing demands from shippers and producers is to be met in a way which ensures reliability and efficiency for gas consumers.[16]

Using auctions to guide investment is an interesting idea. One of the most difficult legal aspects of any design, however, is how to define and enforce property rights. The design proposed by Ofgem is very complex and it appears as though Transco will have discretion over how to use the auction results (Transco, 2002). On one hand, it is reassuring that it is not *only* the auction results that will drive investment decisions. On the other hand, either bidders will bid as if the auctions are the only driver, or they will have little incentive to reveal their demands for capacity truthfully; therefore, how does one interpret the auction outcome?

## 6    Conclusion

We began with the hypothesis that the auctioning of well-defined access rights is an efficient way to deal with significant transmission constraints in the presence of monopoly ownership of the network and competition in production and supply, while also allowing for non-discriminatory access

---

[16] *Periodic Review: Supply and Demand*, which can be found at http://www.transco.uk.com/publish/periodrev/periodrevsuppdmnd.htm

and entry. We have supported this view by describing the evolution of the liberalisation of the gas industry in Britain, discussing the shortcomings of the previous methods of allocating network access and illustrating the correspondence between auction and spot prices.

We provide a description, though not a thorough evaluation, of the specific auction design, as a full theoretical model is outside the scope of this chapter and the small number of auctions to date prohibits us from making a convincing statistical analysis. A number of events occurring outside of the auction mechanism have influenced auction results. These include, most notably, higher gas prices in continental Europe, the oil price spikes, with impacts on wet-gas fields, and changes in the allocation of excess revenues from auctions. Empirical comparisons between the auctions and previous methods of allocating network access rights would have to take account of the opening of the UK–Belgium interconnector in October 1998, which changed trade patterns, and a continuous increase in gas demand in the UK (in parallel with falling production at existing fields), which increased scarcity of entry capacity at St Fergus by up to a factor of ten. Nevertheless, the cost of resolving constraints has fallen significantly and the auction has made it possible to capture scarcity rents from producers – implying that the definition and auctioning of property rights for entry capacity has been successful.

We conclude that the current auction improves upon the previous methods used in the UK to allocate entry rights. We want to emphasise, however, that a crucial feature of the auction is the reserve price, which covers costs when transmission is not scarce or when producers with market power withhold output to keep auction prices down. Finally, although we are enthusiastic about the use of auctions to allocate entry rights when the network is fixed, we have reservations about the appropriateness of using auctions to decide on and fund network investments.

## References

Armstrong, M., S. Cowan and J. Vickers 1994, *Regulatory Reform, Economic Analysis and British Experience*, MIT Press, Cambridge, Mass.

Bulow, J. and P. Klemperer, 2000 'Prices and the winner's curse', Working Paper, http://www.nuff.ox.ac.uk/users/klemperer/papers.html (accessed at 8 February 2003).

Dasgupta, P. and E. Maskin 1998, 'Efficient auctions', *Quarterly Journal of Economics* 115: 341–88.

Department of Trade and Industry 2001, *UK Energy in Brief*, A publication of the Government Statistical Service, UK. Available at http://www.dti.gov.uk.

Hawdon, D. and N. Stevens 2001, 'Regulatory reform of the UK gas market: the case of the storage auctions', *Fiscal Studies* 222: 217–32.

Jones, R. 2001, 'MSEC network analysis', System Operation, Transco.

Milgrom, P. and R. Weber 1982, 'A theory of auctions and competitive bidding', *Econometrica* 50: 1089–122.

McDaniel, T. 2003, 'Auctioning access to networks: evidence and expectations', *Utilities Policy*, forthcoming.

McDaniel, T. and K. Neuhoff, 2002, *Entry Capacity Auctions and Investment Signals*, MIT Center for Energy and Environmental Policy Research Boston.

Monopolies and Mergers Commission 1993, 'Reports under the Gas Act 1986 on the conveyance and storage of gas and the fixing of tariffs for the supply of gas by British Gas plc', London.

1997, 'BG plc: a report under the Gas Act 1986 on the restriction of prices for gas transportation and storage services', London.

Newbery, D. 1999, 'Deriving long-run marginal cost tariffs using transcost', mimeo, Department of Applied Economics, University of Cambridge.

2003, 'Network capacity auctions: promise and problems', *Utilities Policy*, forthcoming.

Ofgem 1999a, 'St Fergus and Bacton investigation: a report under Section 39(4) of the Gas Act 1986', London.

1999b, 'The new gas trading arrangements: a review of the October 1999 NTS capacity auctions and consultation on developing the capacity regime', London.

2000, 'The new gas trading arrangements: a review of the new arrangements and further development of the regime', http://www.ofgem.gov.uk/ (accessed at 8 February 2003).

2001a, 'Ofgem's investigation into shipper conduct in the capacity market in October 2000: conclusions', http://www.ofgem.gov.uk/ (accessed at 8 February 2003).

2001b, 'Transco's national transmission system, system operator incentives 2002–7: final proposals', London.

2002, 'Long-term entry capacity auctions: modification proposals 0500 "Long-term capacity allocation" and 0508 "A method of long-term capacity allocation"', London.

Oxera 2000, 'Energy liberalization indicators in Europe: a consultation document based on a study carried out by Oxera for the governments of the UK and the Netherlands', London.

Platts 2001, 'Revised charges since October 2000', http://www.transco.uk.com/ (accessed at 8 February 2003).

Transco 1999, 'Option for the mechanism to allocate terminal capacity in October 1999', 1999-06-30, Solihull, West Midlands.

2000, 'Transport charges from 1 October 2000', http://www.transco.uk.com/ (accessed at 8 February 2003).

2001, 'The Network Code: version 2.26', http://www.transco.uk.com/ (accessed at 8 February 2003).

2002, 'Incremental Entry Capacity Release Statement: version 1.0', Solihull, West Midlands.

# 9 The design of Treasury bond auctions: some case studies

*Joseph Swierzbinski and Tilman Börgers*

## 1    Introduction

Bonds valued at many billions of dollars are sold in Treasury bond auctions each year. In terms of the total value of the items auctioned each year, Treasury auctions are among the world's most valuable auctions. The performance of these auctions in raising revenue has the potential to increase or reduce a government's cost of borrowing. Whether to use auctions to issue new government bonds, and, if so, which format to use, must therefore be a matter of great concern to governments.

The issues which Treasury auctions raise are of more general relevance to other auctions. In particular, as the use of auctions in government policy becomes more widespread, the issues which are raised by Treasury auctions will need to be faced in other contexts too. On the other hand, it needs to be acknowledged that certain government auctions are quite different from Treasury auctions, and the considerations which are important for the design of these auctions are different from the considerations affecting Treasury auctions. We therefore begin this chapter with a discussion of the main features of Treasury auctions and the extent to which these are shared by other government auctions.

A first important feature of Treasury auctions which determines the specific issues that need to be considered is that the typical bidder in a Treasury auction bids for very many identical units that are offered for sale rather than for just one unit. The existence of multi-unit demand raises many important questions in auction design that are not present if bidders bid for only a single unit, as they do in certain licence auctions, for example. There are other important allocation problems that resemble Treasury auctions in this respect. An example is the allocation of pollution permits. Auctions have been proposed as a method for establishing an initial allocation of pollution permits, and typically companies will seek to acquire many pollution permits, not just one.

Second, Treasury bond auctions are distinctive in that the bonds being auctioned will typically be traded in a very liquid market after the auction.

Moreover, close substitutes for the auctioned bonds are also usually traded in the bond market prior to the auction. In some cases, the auctioned bonds may actually be identical to bonds already traded in the bond market. Bond auctions are again not the only auctions with this feature. For example, the auctions for pollution permits mentioned in the previous paragraph also interact with the market for tradable pollution permits. The UK plans to use an auction as part of its programme for starting an emission-trading scheme for carbon. (See, for example, Department for Environment, Food and Rural Affairs (2001) and other documents available from DEFRA's website http://www.defra.gov.uk/.) Similarly, European governments are considering trading in radio spectrum, and, if allowed, the interaction between such trading and the spectrum auctions will be important. However, it may well be that permit markets and spectrum markets will, even in the long run, be much less liquid than bond markets. This will mean that the interaction with existing markets will be less important for these auctions than for bond auctions.

Treasury bonds are bought for many different reasons, but one prominent reason is that they provide a safe (and legal) form of investment for pension funds. The ability of a pension fund to operate depends on its ability to gain access to government bond markets. In a sense government bonds constitute an essential 'input' for pension fund operations. In a similar way, pollution permits constitute an essential 'input' for many businesses and licences to use spectrum are a required 'input' for firms providing wireless communication services. However, the importance of a spectrum licence for a mobile telephone company might be much greater than the importance of a pollution permit for some other business, or the importance of any particular bond issue for a pension fund. Thus, while a spectrum auction often shapes the future structure of an industry, the same cannot be said of Treasury bond auctions or of pollution permit auctions. Thus, the specific difficulties arising from the endogenous determination of industry structure do not arise in bond auctions.

This chapter reviews selected empirical case studies of auctions of Treasury bonds in a number of countries. The cases that we consider include Treasury auctions in the United States of America (Cammack, 1991; Simon, 1994; Nyborg and Sundaresan, 1996), Sweden (Nyborg, Rydqvist and Sundaresan, 2001) and Mexico (Umlauf, 1993).

As we consider the case studies of Treasury auctions, we focus on several issues that we expect are relevant for policy-makers. Below, we outline these issues, indicate our main conclusions and then comment on whether these conclusions are of wider relevance than just for Treasury bond auctions.

The first issue is the choice of auction format. This choice has received considerable attention in the United States and elsewhere and continues to be a topic of debate. There are two main formats for auctioning Treasury bonds, uniform price auctions and discriminatory auctions. Most Treasury auctions in the United States and in a number of other countries are of the discriminatory type. However, some economists, such as the Nobel Prize winners Milton Friedman and Merton Miller, have argued that the uniform price auction design would raise more revenue and so reduce the government's cost of borrowing. From time to time the US Treasury has experimented with uniform price auctions, and Simon (1994) and Nyborg and Sundaresan (1996) report on the results of some of these experiments. Umlauf (1993) reports on a similar experiment in Mexico. From a review of these studies, we conclude that the case for switching from a discriminatory to a uniform price auction remains arguable.

One reason for this conclusion might be that the auction price of Treasury bonds is so closely tied to the market price that the choice of auction format cannot matter much. However, as we indicate in the next few paragraphs, the evidence seems to suggest that important information is revealed in bond auctions which is not contained in market prices. It is then less clear why there is no significant difference between discriminatory and uniform price auctions. Theoretical analysis of these auctions is so incomplete that we cannot really compare our finding to theoretical predictions. However, as the explanation of our finding does not seem to be the existence of a liquid secondary market, the finding is potentially relevant in other circumstances where multiple identical units are sold to bidders with multi-unit demand, for example permit auctions.

A second set of issues concerns the interaction between the auction and the bond market and how this interaction might affect the choice of whether or not to use an auction, and the choice of the auction format. The first issue to consider is how the use of auctions to issue bonds influences the information flows in the bond market. This is a matter of importance to policy-makers, and indeed to anyone interested in or affected by the workings of capital markets. Indeed, a financial market is often called (informationally) 'efficient' if it quickly incorporates information into asset prices. We consider whether the conduct of a Treasury auction accelerates the revelation of information about future bond prices held by bidders. Cammack's (1991) study of US Treasury auctions provides positive support for the view that such auctions do release information, which affects the bond price. This finding supports the use of auctions to issue bonds. Of course, the argument for the use of auctions as allocation mechanisms is even stronger if the secondary market is not as liquid as it is for Treasury bonds.

The second issue which we consider under the general heading of the interaction between auctions and bond markets is how the degree of uncertainty in the market price affects the desirability of conducting an auction, and, in particular, whether auctions create 'sorry' bidders who suffer from the winner's curse. To explain this issue in more detail we first note that, if there were no transaction costs, the underlying value of the bonds being auctioned would be the same for all bidders since the future market price of these bonds is the same for everyone. Thus Treasury auctions are common-value auctions where the differences in bidders' valuations for the auctioned bonds result entirely from differences in information that produce different forecasts of the future market price. Although transaction costs may be important in Treasury auctions, the common-value assumption is often taken as an appropriate starting point for models of Treasury auctions.

The theory of common-value auctions for a single item warns that uncertainty in the bond market price can have a serious deleterious effect on the outcome of such an auction if bidders are not sufficiently sophisticated. If a bidder learns that his forecast of the future market price is higher than that of any of his rival bidders, he should probably conclude that his initial forecast was too optimistic. Unless a bidder correctly incorporates the potential information contained in rival bids into his own bidding strategy, a winning bidder may find himself 'cursed' with negative profits by bidding too high in the auction. In many of the case studies we surveyed, bidders on average do appear to react to the uncertainty in the bond market sufficiently to avoid the persistent negative profits associated with the winner's curse.

The possibility of 'sorry' winners due to a winner's curse arises in many other contexts as well. For example, spectrum licence auctions raise this possibility. It is important for the policy-maker to form a judgement on whether bidders will be sufficiently sophisticated and anticipate the winner's curse in their bids. It is reassuring that the literature finds that at least the highly sophisticated and experienced bidders who participate in Treasury bond auctions do anticipate the winner's curse.

A final policy question, which we briefly consider, is whether a Treasury auction opens up the opportunity for a bidder to 'corner the market' or otherwise manipulate the market price. Whether policy-makers need to be concerned about a cornering of the market depends on the answer to two questions:

(1) Is there a serious possibility that one or a few bidders might purchase most of the bonds in a Treasury auction?
(2) Can a bidder who wins a large share of the bonds in a Treasury auction use these bonds to successfully manipulate the market price?

The case studies we consider indicate that the answer to the first question is 'yes', at least for some auctions. The answer to the second question depends in large part on the size of transaction costs and the availability of close substitutes for a particular type of bond. Jordan and Jordan (1996) consider the extent to which Salomon Brothers was able to manipulate the price of a certain US Treasury bond after it successfully purchased more than 80 per cent of the amount being issued. Thus, this appears to be a potentially important issue. Policy-makers can address this by restricting the proportion of an issue which any individual bidder can purchase.

This issue will be even more important in the context of other auctions with a stronger potential impact on subsequent market structures. A bond trader who corners the market thereby creates a monopoly for himself in the secondary market. Similarly, a spectrum bidder who corners the market thereby creates a monopoly for himself. This monopoly could be a monopoly in the market for spectrum, where such a market exists, but it could also be a monopoly in the market in which spectrum users compete, such as the market for mobile telephone services. Here, too, it might be enough to restrict the proportion of supply which any individual bidder can acquire. But more sophisticated tools, such as those provided by general competition law, might be needed as well.

Our discussion of the issues listed above focuses on empirical case studies. However, these case studies are preceded by brief reviews of the relevant parts of economic theory. The purpose of these reviews is to provide an appropriate framework in which to view the empirical evidence. In considering both the theoretical arguments and empirical case studies discussed below, the reader should keep in mind the limited state of economic knowledge concerning multi-unit auctions such as Treasury auctions. This concerns both the state of economic theory of auctions with multi-unit demand, and also our experimental and empirical understanding of these auctions. At present, any conclusions concerning such auctions should be regarded as both preliminary and tentative. It is the limited nature of our knowledge of Treasury auctions that makes the format of case studies particularly appropriate for this chapter.

Most of the case studies which we review focus on information about the average prices paid in these auctions. However, a study of Swedish auctions by Nyborg, Rydqvist and Sundaresan (2001) forms an exception. These researchers had access to the bids submitted by individual bidders in a series of auctions.

In table 9.1 (p. 254) we provide an overview of the case studies discussed in this chapter. Many of the conclusions reported in these case studies involve some comparison of the average price in an auction, which we denote by $P_A$, with a measure of the market price for these bonds, $P_M$, near the time of the auction. In particular, the difference in these prices, $P_A - P_M$, can be interpreted as a measure of the average profit of bidders participating in the auction. It is interesting to know whether this difference is positive, indicating that bidders in the auction earn positive profits on average. It is also interesting to compare this difference as the auction format changes from a uniform price to a discriminatory auction. If the average profit of bidders decreases with a change in auction format, this suggests that the change in format results in higher revenue for the government. Other related comparisons include a comparison of the market price of a bond shortly before and shortly after an auction. Such a comparison figures prominently in Cammack's (1991) analysis of the information released in US Treasury auctions.

Table 9.1 collects comparisons of the average auction price and the market price gathered from a number of the case studies. When reading table 9.1, it is important to remember that the details of these comparisons differ considerably from study to study. Differences include the way in which the market price is measured and how the price difference is normalised. We discuss some of these differences in more detail as we describe the various case studies.

## 2      Which auction format, uniform price or discriminatory auction, is likely to lead to higher revenues?

Uniform price and discriminatory auctions are the most commonly used and discussed formats for Treasury bond auctions. However, before comparing them we should point out that it has been argued that other formats might have advantages over both uniform price and discriminatory auctions. These formats have not yet been used in practice for government bonds. Treasury bonds could, in principle, be sold in an open, ascending format where, for example, the auctioneer raises the price while bidders announce the number of bonds they would be willing to buy at each successive price. The UK plans to use an open auction as part of its procedure for setting up a trading scheme for carbon.

Uniform price and discriminatory auctions are examples of sealed-bid auctions, and their designs share a number of other important features. In both types of auction, each bidder submits a demand curve specifying the maximum price he is willing to pay for each successive bond that he is offered. For any given price, the number of bonds with a maximum price greater than or equal to the given price thus represents the bidder's total demand for bonds at that price. The auctioneer then adds up the bidders' demand curves to determine a total demand curve for the bonds. As long as the demand is sufficiently large, the clearing price for the bonds is simply the price at which the total number of bonds demanded by all bidders is equal to the supply of bonds on offer. In both types of auction, each bidder is allocated the number of bonds that he demands at the clearing price.

Uniform price and discriminatory auctions differ in the way that the price a bidder pays for the bonds which he receives is calculated. In the uniform price auction, a bidder simply pays the clearing price for each bond. Hence, a bidder's total payment in the uniform price auction is the clearing price multiplied by the number of bonds the bidder receives. In contrast, in a discriminatory auction a bidder pays the maximum price he is willing to pay for each bond, as indicated by the demand curve which the bidder has submitted. Hence, a bidder's total payment in a discriminatory auction is given by an area under the bidder's submitted demand curve. Since the price paid for each bond in a discriminatory auction is the maximum price specified by the bidder's demand curve, discriminatory auctions are sometimes referred to as pay-your-bid auctions.

For each bond which a bidder receives, the clearing price (which is also the price paid for each bond in a uniform price auction) is less than or equal to the price which a bidder pays for that bond in a discriminatory auction. Hence, for the same submitted demand curve, a bidder's total payment in a uniform price auction is always less than or equal to the bidder's total payment in a discriminatory auction. Why then do economists and Treasury officials continue to debate which of these auction designs raises the most revenue?

The comparison in the previous paragraph fails to take into account that a bidder may wish to shade the maximum prices specified in the demand curve submitted to the auctioneer below the bidder's true valuations. Once it is realised that the degree of bid-shading is likely to depend on the auction design, it is no longer obvious which auction design will produce the higher expected revenue.

A bidder in a discriminatory auction will typically wish to submit a demand curve with maximum prices that are below his true valuations. For, if a bidder in a discriminatory auction bids 'honestly' and submits his true valuation for each bond, then the bidder pays his full valuation for each bond that he is allocated and always obtains a net profit of zero. Since one can also obtain zero profit by simply not entering the auction, who would enter an auction if they had no hope of earning a positive profit?

Although it is not so obvious, a bidder in a uniform price auction may also have an incentive to shade his submitted demand curve below his true valuations. Hence, it becomes a matter of theoretical debate and empirical evidence as to which type of auction is likely to produce the higher average revenue.

### 2.1    Theoretical considerations

At least four types of theoretical intuition have been advanced in the debate comparing uniform price and discriminatory auctions. These intuitions unfortunately lead to different conclusions regarding the auction format which is likely to produce the highest revenue for the government. The gist of the four arguments is as follows.

(1) The greater strategic simplicity of the uniform price auction is likely to produce higher expected revenue by encouraging entry.

(2) Implicit collusion among bidders to maintain a low price is likely to be more difficult in the discriminatory auction, which thus may produce higher expected revenue.

(3) Bidders have a greater incentive to submit lower demands in an effort to reduce the clearing price in a uniform price auction. This argument suggests that discriminatory auctions may produce higher expected revenue.

(4) The uniform price auction is more likely to reveal information about uncertain common factors such as the future market price of bonds, and thus leads to greater competition among bidders and higher expected revenue.

Thus considerations of simplicity and entry and the revelation of information have been advanced in favour of the uniform price auction, while arguments involving implicit collusion and the incentives to manipulate the clearing price have been advanced in favour of the discriminatory auction.

In the rest of this subsection, we discuss the intuitions listed above in greater detail. But the reader is reminded that current economic theory concerning Treasury bond auctions is highly incomplete. Back and Zender (1993) and Ausubel and Cramton (2002) further discuss some of the economic theory relevant to the comparison of uniform price and discriminatory multi-unit auctions.

(1) Nobel Prize-winning economists Merton Miller and Milton Friedman have been among those who argue that the problem of choosing a profitable bidding strategy is simpler in a uniform price auction. In particular, the simple strategy of submitting your true demand curve, while not necessarily optimal, has at least the potential to produce positive profits in a uniform price auction. In contrast, bidding your true valuation for each bond will produce only zero profit in a discriminatory auction. Advocates

of a uniform price auction further suggest that the availability of such a simple, potentially profitable strategy is likely to encourage greater entry in a uniform price auction, especially among smaller, possibly 'unsophisticated' bidders. A greater number of bidders could, in turn, lead to more aggressive bidding and higher average revenue in a uniform price auction.

Friedman and others sometimes go one step further and claim that a bidder can do no better than to bid his true demand curve in a uniform price auction. If such a claim were true, it would certainly strengthen the case for the strategic simplicity of the uniform price auction. However, as shown by, for example, Back and Zender (1993) and Ausubel and Cramton (2002), submitting your true demand curve is not generally optimal in the uniform price auction. Friedman and others appear to have been misled by an incorrect analogy with the second-price, sealed-bid auction for a single unit, where it is often optimal to bid your true valuation.

How different auction designs affect the incentives for entry is clearly an important unresolved question in the economics of multi-unit auctions. However, the argument described so far in favour of the uniform price auction does not seem fully persuasive. Relatively simple strategies are also available for the discriminatory auction – for example, shade the valuations that determine your true demand curve downwards by a fixed percentage. Such strategies are potentially profitable, although probably not optimal, for a bidder in a discriminatory auction.

(2) In a uniform price auction, a bidder may find it optimal to submit a demand curve that is initially very steep and then falls to a relatively flat, low level. Demand curves with such a shape can facilitate implicit collusion while reducing the clearing price, and hence the revenue obtained, in a uniform price auction to a low level. Binmore and Swierzbinski (2000) study a very simple example with only two bidders using graphs. Back and Zender (1993) and Ausubel and Cramton (2002) compare the theoretical outcomes in uniform price and discriminatory auctions for a wider class of cases.

By submitting initially steep demand curves in a uniform price auction, bidders who wish to co-ordinate on a low price can limit the gains from cheating on a collusive agreement. For a bidder who wishes to cheat on a collusive outcome does so by raising his submitted demand curve slightly to increase the amount he can buy at the low collusive price. But when the other bidders' demand curves become steep at levels of demand not much below the levels tacitly agreed on, the prospective bidder runs risks of shifting the total demand such that demand equals supply where the total demand is steep and the clearing price is much higher than the intended low price.

The cost of submitting an initially steep demand curve is likely to be low in a uniform price auction. When a bidder submits such a demand curve, that bidder is bidding a high maximum price for the first units that he wishes to buy. But it is not likely that these initial high bids will be a factor in determining the clearing price – and it is the clearing price which the bidder actually pays. In contrast, a bidder in a discriminatory auction who submits a steep demand curve can be sure to pay a high price for the first units he buys.

(3) Compared to bidders in a discriminatory auction, bidders in a uniform price auction also appear to have a greater incentive to submit low bids for units when those bids may affect the clearing price in the auction. By submitting a bid that reduces the clearing price, a bidder in a uniform price auction reduces the price that he pays for every unit that he buys. In contrast, a bidder in a discriminatory auction who reduces the clearing price by bidding low for the last unit he purchases simply reduces the price he pays for that last unit.

Concerns about implicit collusion and the incentives for demand reduction seem most relevant when there are a relatively small number of large bidders. For large numbers of bidders, the difficulty of co-ordinating on a collusive agreement seems prohibitive, so that the enforcement of such an agreement becomes moot. Moreover, it also seems unlikely that any one bidder's demand can significantly affect the clearing price when there are many bidders, all of whom are small.

(4) As we have already observed, Treasury auctions are often modelled as common-value auctions where the differences in the valuations of different bidders are due to differences in the information available to these bidders when they forecast the future market price of the bonds up for auction. The theory of single-unit, common-value auctions predicts that if bidders bid in an unsophisticated way, they may fall prey to a winner's curse and earn negative expected profits. If the bidders bid as theory suggests, they may earn positive profits and these profits may be interpreted as a return to the private information which the winning bidder possesses.

Auction theorists such as Paul Milgrom (1989) have used the theory of single-unit, common-value auctions to propose the linkage principle as an informal guide to comparing designs for common-value auctions. If bidders' profits represent a return to private information, then auction designs that link the price paid to the information of other bidders might 'dilute' the effect of this private information, reducing bidders' expected profits and increasing the auctioneer's expected revenue. In a uniform price auction, the price paid by each bidder is 'linked' to the bids made by others through the clearing price. The linkage principle suggests that bidders' expected profits will be lower, and the auctioneer's expected revenue will be higher, in a uniform price auction than in a discriminatory auction. Chapter 1 explains that the linkage principle, while true in single-unit auctions, does not generally hold in multi-unit auctions.

## 2.2    *Empirical case studies*

We now turn to case studies. Typically, the case studies do not allow us to identify precisely which of the four intuitions, or possibly other effects, are at work; we can only observe the overall differences between the two auction formats. However, in some cases one can try to infer more detailed conclusions about individual effects, and we point out where this is the case.

The empirical case studies described in this section involve 'natural experiments' where the US or Mexican Treasury switched from one auction format to the other when conducting actual auctions. A serious difficulty complicates the interpretation of virtually all natural experiments. Many other factors that might potentially affect the performance of the auctions being studied are usually also changing at the time the auction format is switched. What fraction of any observed change in performance is due to the switch in format and what fraction is due to changes in other factors? One may attempt to model or otherwise account for the effect of factors other than the change in auction format. For example, the studies considered attempt to control for changes in the value of the auctioned bonds by using a measure of the difference between the auction and market prices as a basis for comparison. Nevertheless, isolating the effect of the change in format may be difficult or impossible.

A study which is not affected by the problems of natural experiments is Hortaçsu's (2001) innovative analysis of Turkish Treasury auctions. Hortaçsu considers only discriminatory price auctions. The data available to him are the complete demand functions submitted by bidders. Using econometric techniques he reconstructs from the demand functions the bidders' true valuation functions. He then conducts the counterfactual experiment of determining what the expected revenue would have been had the auction format been uniform price. He finds that a switch to a uniform price format would have caused average revenue losses of

14.23 per cent. This is surprisingly large. However, he indicates that the potential random error in these results is very large too.

Hortaçsu's analysis of the bidding functions relies on strong assumptions about bidders' behaviour. In particular, it is assumed that bidders bid rationally, and thus do not follow simple rules of thumb, as suggested by intuition (1) above. He also assumes that bidders do not collude, thus ruling out effect (2) above. The correct interpretation of his results is probably that he indicates the likely size of the effect described in intuition (3) above, if we are willing to assume that the other effects are not at work. His findings then suggest that effect (3) is present, although its statistical significance *ex ante* is not easy to establish.

*US Treasury auctions*  The US Treasury typically sells its bonds using discriminatory auctions. However, in the 1970s and again in the 1990s the Treasury experimented with uniform price auctions. Simon (1994) describes the results of experiments in the 1970s, while Nyborg and Sundaresan (1996) consider experiments that occurred in the 1990s.

Simon compares the results of five uniform price auctions and ten discriminatory auctions that took place from 1973 to 1976. Since the summer of 1974, a competitive bid in a Treasury bond auction consists of a combination of a desired number of bonds and a yield to maturity. Bidders can submit multiple bids and so effectively submit a demand curve by placing several bids with different yields to maturity. The yield to maturity, the coupon interest rate and the maturity and face value of a bond together determine the bond's price.

The face value, which is the amount the bond pays when it matures, and the maturity, which is the number of years until the bond pays its face value, are set in advance of the auction by the Treasury. The coupon interest rate is a percentage of the face value that is paid to bond-holders, typically on an annual or semi-annual schedule. For some of the auctions Simon considered, the coupon rate was also set in advance. In other cases, the Treasury used the results of the auction to set a coupon interest rate close to the average yield bid in the auction. The bonds Simon considered had maturities ranging from fifteen to thirty years.

Simon measured the average bidder's profit from an auction by using the difference between the average yield to maturity in the auction and the market yield to maturity near the time of the auction. Simon refers to this difference as the mark-up. In calculating this mark-up, Simon usually uses a market yield based on transactions in the when-issued market. In a few cases, where the auctions represented the sale of additional amounts of bonds that were already being traded and when-issued data was not available, Simon used the market yield of the traded bonds.

The when-issued market in the United States is a forward market that operates before and shortly after each Treasury auction. In this market, prospective bidders and other traders can trade claims to the bonds being auctioned. Trades in the when-issued market are settled after the results of the auction become known. For more information on the when-issued market, see Bikchandani and Huang (1993) and Nyborg and Sundaresan (1996).

Using data which Simon reports in table 1 of his paper, one can calculate that the quantity-weighted average mark-up in yield for the discriminatory auctions that Simon considers is 1.58 basis points of yield. (A basis point is 0.01 per cent.) The corresponding mark-up for the uniform price auctions he considers is 1.92 basis points. Hence, switching from a discriminatory to a uniform price auction format appears to have increased the mark-up by 0.34 basis points of yield. After attempting to control for various factors that may have affected the auction or market yields, Simon concludes that the switch to a uniform price format increased the mark-up by 7 to 8 basis points.

A higher yield to maturity corresponds to a lower bond price. Hence, the positive yield mark-ups reported by Simon correspond to positive average profits for bidders. For coupon rates and maturities similar to those considered by Simon, a small difference in yield must be multiplied by approximately a factor of ten to obtain the corresponding difference in the bond price measured as a fraction of the bond's face value. Using this approximation, the yield mark-up of 1.58 basis points for discriminatory auctions corresponds to a price mark-up of 15.8 basis points or an average profit for bidders of $1580 for every million dollars of face value purchased. The corresponding profit for the bidders in the uniform auctions was $1920 per million dollars of face value purchased.

Subtracting these two measures of profit indicates that the switch from a discriminatory to a uniform price format increased bidders' profit (and, therefore, reduced the Treasury's revenue) by $340 per million of face value. Controlling for other factors, Simon estimates that the switch from a discriminatory to a uniform price format resulted in a loss in revenue to the Treasury of between $7000 and $8000 per million of face value. These are relatively large loss estimates, but their plausibility depends on the degree to which Simon has adequately controlled for the effects of other factors. Simon's analysis does not allow us to distinguish the potential impact of the different intuitive effects discussed earlier.

Nyborg and Sundaresan (1996) study the auctions of two-year and five-year US Treasury notes that took place in 1992 and 1993. (It is a common convention in financial economics to refer to Treasury bonds with very short maturities (e.g. ninety days) as 'Treasury bills'. Bonds with moderate maturities such as those studied by Nyborg and Sundaresan are referred to as 'Treasury notes', while the term 'Treasury bond' is reserved for bonds with long maturities.)

As in Simon's study, Nyborg and Sundaresan calculate the average bidder profit in terms of the yield mark-up. Nyborg and Sundaresan also used the when-issued forward market to obtain an estimate of the market yield to maturity near the time of the auction. Their when-issued data consisted of all the transactions made by Garban Inc., one of the active participants in this market.

Table 8 of Nyborg and Sundaresan's paper lists the average yield mark-ups for their auctions. They find that the average yield mark-up depends sensitively on the maturity of the bond being auctioned and the exact time that the when-issued yield is calculated, as well as on the auction format. For discriminatory auctions of two-year notes, Nyborg and Sundaresan calculate an average yield mark-up of 0.527 basis points when the when-issued yield is measured at the time bids are submitted and a yield mark-up of −0.03 basis points when the when-issued yield is measured at the time the auction results are released. For uniform price auctions of two-year notes, the corresponding average yield mark-ups are −0.048 basis points and 0.695 basis points. For discriminatory auctions of five-year notes, the yield mark-ups are 0.44 basis points and 1.52 basis points, and for uniform price auctions of five-year notes they are 0.698 basis points and −0.601 basis points.

For the two-year and five-year maturities considered by Nyborg and Sundaresan, a small difference in the yield to maturity can be approximately translated into a small difference in the price of the bond by multiplying the yield difference by the bond's maturity. The result is a price difference expressed as a fraction of the bond's face value. Using this approximation, we obtain the following estimates for a bidder's average profit per million dollars of face value that the bidder buys at auction. (One basis point of price difference corresponds to $100 of profit per million of face value.) For discriminatory auctions of two-year notes, the estimated average profit is either $105 of profit or a $6 loss, depending on which when-issued yield is used. For uniform price auctions of two-year notes, Nyborg and Sundaresan's profit estimates are either a $9.6 loss or a $139 profit per million face value. For discriminatory auctions of five-year notes, the corresponding profit measures are either $222 or $762 of profit per million of face value purchased. For uniform price auctions of five-year notes, there is a $349 profit or a $300 loss, depending on the time at which the when-issued yields are measured.

Recall that an increase in a bidder's profit corresponds to an identical reduction in the government's revenue. By comparing the average bidder's profit listed above across auction formats, one can therefore conclude that the switch from a discriminatory to a uniform price format in the auctions for two-year Treasury notes resulted either in a gain in revenue of $115 or a loss in revenue of $145 per million of face value purchased. Similarly, for five-year Treasury notes, the corresponding changes in average revenue are either a $127 loss per million of face value sold or a $1062 gain, depending on when the when-issued yield is calculated. Thus, Nyborg and Sundaresan's analysis seems inconclusive.

*Mexican Treasury auctions*    Umlauf (1993) considers auctions of thirty-day Mexican Treasury bills (denominated in pesos) that took place from 1986 to 1991. These short-term notes did not have coupons. The auctions occurred weekly and followed procedures similar to those used in US auctions. A competitive bid in the Mexican auction consisted of an offer to purchase a given quantity of bills at a price specified in terms of a discount from a reference level. Bidders could submit multiple bids and so effectively submit a demand curve. Competitive bidders included government banks, private banks, stock brokerages and insurance companies. The auctions began in 1986. From 1986 until June 1990, the auctions used the discriminatory format. In July 1990, the Mexican Treasury switched to a uniform price format, which was used throughout the rest of the period considered by Umlauf. Umlauf's data include the results of 181 discriminatory auctions and 26 uniform price auctions.

One reason why Umlauf's data are interesting in the context of our discussion is that, according to Umlauf, it was widely believed that the six largest bidders in the Mexican auction formed a bidders' cartel. In this regard, it is interesting to note that although there was an average of twenty-five competitive bidders in each auction, the six largest bidders purchased an average of 72 per cent of the bonds. As we discussed above, theoretical intuitions suggest that the operation of a cartel should be easier in the uniform price auction than in the discriminatory auction. We now ask whether Umlauf's data confirm the above intuition.

In the Mexican auctions, bids were submitted on Tuesdays with the results announced on Wednesday mornings. According to Umlauf, the bulk of the auctioned bonds were resold in the market on Wednesday afternoon. Umlauf uses the difference between the Wednesday resale price and the average price paid in the auction as a measure of the average profits earned by bidders. Umlauf reports this difference as a fraction of the average price paid in the auction.

For the discriminatory auctions, the average profit earned by bidders was 1.84 basis points or $184 profit for every million spent in the auction. For the uniform price auctions, Umlauf reports a profit of $-0.3$ basis points, that is an average loss of $30 for every million spent in the auction. Subtracting the above two measures of profit indicates that the switch from a discriminatory to a uniform price auction reduced the average bidder's profit by $214 per million spent and, hence, appears to have increased the Mexican government's revenue by this amount.

Thus, Umlauf's data definitely do *not* confirm the theoretical intuition. However, the effect might be present and might just be outweighed by other effects which operate in the opposite direction. Moreover, it is interesting to note that Umlauf calculates that the average profit of the supposed bidders' cartel was $206 per million spent in the auctions with a discriminatory format and −$44 per million spent in the uniform price auctions, that is a loss of $44 per million. These average profits seem small and the existence of losses is surprising. If the six bidders did form a cartel, it does not seem to have been very effective at generating profits.

*Conclusions*  Regarding the effect of a switch from a discriminatory to a uniform price auction, Simon estimates that such a switch resulted in a relatively large loss in revenue for US Treasury auctions in the 1970s. Umlauf, on the other hand, estimates that such a switch resulted in a moderate gain for the Mexican Treasury. Finally, Nyborg and Sundaresan's results suggest that such a switch might result in either moderate gains or losses for the Treasury, with the estimates depending, among other things, on exactly when the when-issued yield is measured. Overall these results seem inconclusive.

It is difficult to find in these case studies direct confirmation of the four intuitive effects listed above. However, it does seem plausible that the straightforward effect, that uniform price auctions create stronger incentives for demand reduction, is present. On the other hand, we have not found direct evidence of the implicit form of collusion, which the uniform price auction in principle makes possible. We have also not found evidence that bidders would not know how to shade their bids correctly, and would therefore either use simple rules of thumb or fall prey to the winner's curse. These effects may be present, however, even if we cannot document them at this stage.

It is worth reiterating that the interpretation of natural experiments such as those reported here is complicated by the difficulty of accounting for the effects of changes in factors other than the auction format. In particular, Umlauf, Simon and Nyborg and Sundaresan all compare auction formats with a profit rate that uses the difference between the auction price and some market price. If we assume (1) that a change in auction format affects the auction price but not the market price and (2) that changes in factors which affect the underlying value of the bonds being auctioned influence both the auction and the market price in similar ways, then such a procedure can be a useful way to control for changes in factors other than the auction format. If, on the other hand, the market price is also sensitive to a change in auction format, then there is a problem. In this regard, it is troubling that Nyborg and Sundaresan's paper also suggests that when-issued yields may indeed be affected by the auction format.

## 3    How do interactions between Treasury auctions and the Treasury bond market affect policy choices?

### 3.1    *Does the conduct of an auction accelerate the revelation of information held by bidders?*

In a classic article, Fama (1970) highlighted the importance of the informational role of financial markets. He called a financial market (informationally) 'efficient' if the prices of assets traded in the market 'fully reflected' all available information. The importance of the 'informational efficiency' of financial markets (and the degree to which these markets are indeed informationally efficient) is a theme that has been taken up by many financial economists since Fama.

If the conduct of periodic auctions of Treasury bonds accelerates the release of information held by bidders, then auctions may have an important role in contributing to the informational efficiency of bond markets. Cammack (1991) examined this question in an influential study of US auctions for short-term Treasury bonds (often called Treasury bills because of their short maturity). Much of Cammack's analysis involved comparing the market price of these bills shortly before and shortly after each auction. Cammack also compared the market price to the auction price to calculate the profits earned by bidders.

Cammack studied auctions that were conducted on a weekly basis by the US Treasury during the period from 1973 to 1984. Each Monday in the early afternoon, competitive bidders could submit multiple price-quantity bids for Treasury bills maturing in 91 days or 182 days. The auctions were discriminatory auctions in which each competitive bidder paid his bid for the bonds won at auction. Although we have not emphasised this point up to now, in many Treasury auctions in the United States and elsewhere, including the auctions considered by Cammack, small investors can also submit 'non-competitive' bids which entitle them to buy bonds at a quantity-weighted average of the bid prices. The presence of non-competitive bids turns out to feature in Cammack's analysis.

The auction results were announced on Monday evening. By Tuesday the bills were being actively traded in the bond market. Although Cammack focuses on the auction for 91-day bonds, the presence of an auction for 182-day bonds was also important for her analysis. In addition to an active Tuesday market for bills with a 91-day maturity, the auction of 182-day bonds three months previously meant that on Monday, before the auction, there was already an active market for bonds with a 92-day maturity – and these bonds should be a very close substitute for the 91-day bonds being auctioned. (See Cammack (1991) for further detail on the exact timing of trading and delivery for the various bills she considers.)

Cammack studies three prices, as well as profit measures or mark-ups based on these prices. Following Cammack, let $P_A$ denote the mean auction price. Let $P_M$ denote the market price on Monday (before the auction results are announced) of the 92-day Treasury bill adjusted for the one day difference in maturity. Finally, let $P_T$ denote the Tuesday market price of the auctioned bonds.

Cammack calls the normalised difference between the Monday market price and the mean auction price, $(P_M - P_A)/P_A$, the 'Monday bidding adjustment'. Similarly, the normalised difference $(P_T - P_A)/P_A$ is the 'Tuesday bidding adjustment'. Finally, the 'Tuesday return' is the normalised difference $(P_T - P_M)/P_M$. All these differences are reported in percentages or basis points.

As a point of clarification that may be helpful to readers of Cammack's paper, she actually reports the natural logarithm of price ratios. For example, $\ln (P_M/P_A)$ is the Monday bidding adjustment. The interpretation of these price ratios as normalised price differences is obtained using the Taylor approximation that $\ln (1 + x) = x$, which should be highly accurate for the small values of $x$ that are relevant here.

Cammack finds that the mean Monday bidding adjustment is approximately equal to the mean Tuesday bidding adjustment and the two are equal when averaged over her entire sample to approximately 1 basis point. Hence, by buying in the auction and selling in the Tuesday market, bidders could earn an average profit of $100 for every million spent in the auction.

As a second point of clarification, Cammack often refers to the 1 basis point difference in the price as a 'difference of four basis points'. When she does so, she is converting price to yield measured on an annual basis.

Cammack also finds that 'the standard deviation of the Monday bidding adjustment is approximately one-half that of the Tuesday bidding adjustment'. Cammack attributes the additional variability in the Tuesday bidding adjustment to the arrival of information during the twenty-four hours from Monday to Tuesday. Some of this information may be from the release of the auction results on Monday evening. But some or even all of the additional variability may be due to the random arrival of other information.

In an attempt to isolate the effect of information contained in the auction on the Tuesday market price, Cammack regresses the Tuesday return, $(P_T - P_M)/P_M$, on variables that proxy for the information contained in the auction results. One such variable is the ratio of competitive bids placed to competitive bids accepted. A second variable is the ratio of non-competitive bids to the total amount of bills auctioned. These variables are measures of the demand for the auctioned Treasury bills by bidders and small investors. Finally, Cammack considers the logarithm of the difference of the mean and low auction prices, which she regards as a measure of the dispersion of opinion concerning the bonds' value.

For each independent variable, Cammack first uses a time series model to decompose the variable's value into an anticipated and an unanticipated component. 'News' from the auction is assumed to be conveyed primarily by the unanticipated component. Whether or not the unanticipated components of demand-related measures are significant in explaining the variability in the Tuesday return depends in part on how other variables are controlled in the regression. However, the unanticipated component of Cammack's 'dispersion of opinion' measure is significant in explaining the variability in the Tuesday return, suggesting that the results of the auction do release information to the market. This seems in principle to offer support for the use of auctions, as they increase informational efficiency.

### 3.2   Does the degree of uncertainty in the bond market affect the desirability of conducting an auction?

Since Treasury bonds are typically traded in an active aftermarket, the underlying value of these bonds must be nearly the same for all bidders. Moreover, differences in bidders' values for the auctioned bonds seem likely to be due in large part to differences in the bidders' forecasts of the future market price. As we have previously observed, these features of Treasury auctions suggest that the theory of common-value auctions may be relevant for explaining behaviour in Treasury auctions.

As was also mentioned in the introduction, the theory of single-unit, common-value auctions warns that there is a danger that bidders may bid too optimistically in such auctions. When a bidder in a common-value auction wins the auctioned item by bidding high, the very fact of winning is a signal that the bidder's initial forecast was too optimistic. Unless the bidder shades his bid downwards in a way that takes appropriate account of the information contained in the bids of other participants in the auction, he may fall prey to a winner's curse, paying more for items than they are worth and earning *ex post* negative profits.

As observed, for example, by Laffont (1997), the winner's curse in common-value auctions became a matter of great practical concern in the context of auctions for oil drilling rights in the Gulf of Mexico. In spite of the large amount of oil available in the Gulf, bidding companies appeared to be making low profits that did not produce an adequate return on investment. It was suggested that over-optimistic bidding was the cause. As Laffont also notes, later empirical work calls into question the degree to which the winner's curse was operating in these oil auctions. But a long debate ensued as to the appropriate way to bid in auctions for oil leases.

The degree of bid shading required to avoid the winner's curse increases as uncertainty about the underlying value of the auctioned items increases. In the context of Treasury auctions, this suggests that bidders are more likely to fall foul of the winner's curse and earn low or even negative profits when market uncertainty is high. Is there a threshold level of market uncertainty where an auction is not even advisable? Or do bidders learn to adjust their bids appropriately in response to market uncertainty?

Nyborg, Rydqvist and Sundaresan (2001) draw on an earlier analysis of Ausubel to observe that the appropriate response to uncertainty is more subtle when bidders can submit demand curves, as is the case in Treasury auctions. Unlike the discrete win–lose signal that occurs in a single-unit auction, there is a continuum of possible signals in a Treasury auction. The more a bidder wins in a Treasury auction, the stronger is the signal that the bidder's initial forecast of the future market price was too optimistic. When bidders submit demand curves, the appropriate response to uncertainty may involve not only a downward shading of the average price bid but also a change in the shape of the submitted demand curve, making it steeper.

One way to assess the practical significance of the winner's curse in Treasury auctions is to consider the average profits of bidders in such auctions. Many of the studies we consider attempt to measure these average profits by comparing the mean auction price to some measure of the market price. We summarise the information on average profit from these studies in table 9.1. At the crudest level, the profit estimates contained in this table do not suggest to us that the bidders in Treasury auctions bid so aggressively as to earn large negative profits on average. A few case studies do report relatively small average losses but we do not find these results persuasive. For example, in Nyborg and Sundaresan's US study, whether they estimate an average loss or an average profit depends on the fine details of how the market price is estimated.

Umlauf (1993) also reports a small average loss in uniform price Mexican auctions, but asserts that these losses occurred when a bidders' cartel was supposedly operating and earning negative profits. If there was a bidders' cartel, why was it earning a negative average profit? One explanation may be the degree of uncertainty characterising the Mexican economy during the time period of Umlauf's study. Umlauf reports that during this period there occurred a foreign debt crisis, hyperinflation and a presidential election that Umlauf describes as 'highly contested'. Thus, although in principle one could argue that Umlauf's results show that the cartel was incompetent in dealing with the winner's curse, the uncertainty with which the cartel was dealing might have been so unusual that this comment is unfair.

Although not shown in table 9.1, which reports only the average profit over all auctions – which was positive – Nyborg, Rydqvist and Sundaresan (2001) also find negative average profits in auctions involving Swedish bonds with certain times to maturity. However, Nyborg, Rydqvist and Sundaresan also note that their measure of profit is likely to be an underestimate because of the way the market price of bonds was calculated.

In considering the evidence presented in table 9.1, a reader should keep in mind that we have not discussed what level of profit provides an appropriate level of compensation for the risk involved in participating in the auction and later reselling in the bond market. The degree of risk surely varies from country to country. One wonders, for example, whether the $184 average profit which Umlauf estimates for discriminatory Mexican auctions is adequate compensation for the risk involved in these auctions. However, while noting this issue, we do not propose to consider it further here.

It is interesting to ask whether bidders in Treasury auctions respond to market uncertainty as the theory of common-value auctions suggests by lowering the average price bid and adjusting the shape of the submitted demand curve. To best address these questions, data on the behaviour of individual bidders are useful.

Nyborg, Rydqvist and Sundaresan (2001) report results from a series of Swedish Treasury auctions where data on the actual demand schedules submitted by individual bidders were made available (with the identity of the bidders protected). They find that the level of market uncertainty has a statistically significant effect on both the average price a bidder submitted and the shape of the bidder's demand curve.

Nyborg, Rydqvist and Sundaresan (2001) studied more than 400 auctions of Swedish bonds that occurred from 1990 to 1994. The auctions were discriminatory. The majority of the auctions considered involved Treasury bills with a maturity of fourteen months or less. Approximately one-third of the auctions were for Treasury bonds with maturities ranging from six to sixteen years from the original issue date. Since most of the auctions involved additional sales of already existing bonds, the actual time to maturity of the Treasury bonds ranged from one to eight or more years.

Although almost all the bonds considered by Nyborg, Rydqvist and Sundaresan appear to have been actively traded in the bond market, the transaction prices in this market are not made available to the public. These authors typically used the median prices quoted by a number of dealers shortly after the auction as a proxy for the transaction price in the secondary bond market.

Average bidders' profit in each auction was calculated as the difference between the post-auction market price and the quantity-weighted average of the winning bids in the auction. Averaged over all the auctions, the mean profit was 2 basis points of the face value of the bond. This corresponds to an average profit of Kr 200 per million of face value purchased. This mean profit is reported in table 9.1.

The average profit in these auctions increased with the remaining time to maturity of the bonds being auctioned. For bonds with short maturities, average profit in the auction was sometimes negative. For example, for bonds with a time to maturity close to one year, Nyborg, Rydqvist and Sundaresan estimate an average loss of Kr 140 per million of face value purchased (see table 4 of Nyborg, Rydqvist and Sundaresan (2001)). However, they also suggest that their measure of average profit is likely to be an underestimate because they were unable to use transaction prices to estimate the market price of the bonds.

To describe the demand curves submitted by individual bidders, the authors use three numbers. The 'discount' is the difference between the market price shortly after the auction and the quantity-weighted average price of the bids submitted by the bidder. The discount is a measure of bid-shading. The shape of a bidder's submitted demand curve was measured by the 'dispersion', which was the quantity-weighted standard deviation of the prices bid by the bidder. If demand is linear, then larger 'dispersion' corresponds to a steeper slope of the demand curve. The third variable is the 'quantity', that is the maximum number of bonds bid for by each bidder, measured as a fraction of the total size of the auction.

The average discount observed by Nyborg, Rydqvist and Sundaresan was 9.2 basis points of the face value of the bonds. If all a bidder's bids were winning bids, then the discount would be the profit that the bidder earned in the auction. Hence, bidders on average shaded their bids by

Kr 920 per million of face value compared to the (estimated) post-auction market price. Of course, not all the bids were winning bids, so the actual profit earned was less than Kr 920 per million of face value.

The average dispersion was also positive, with a value of 4.6 basis points. Hence, on average bidders submitted downward-sloping demand curves. This result is itself interesting in that it indicates that bidders typically do use the flexibility afforded to them by the opportunity to submit a downward-sloping rather than a flat demand curve. On the other hand, the minimum value of the dispersion was zero, indicating that at least some bidders did submit a flat demand curve. The average number of bids per bidder in an auction was 4.9 with a mode of 2 for the shorter maturity Treasury bills and a mode of 4 for the longer maturity Treasury bonds.

How do the discount and dispersion that describe an individual bidder's submitted demand depend on market uncertainty? Nyborg, Rydqvist and Sundaresan measure market uncertainty near the time of an auction by fitting a time series model to data on bond returns to estimate the one-day volatility in the market price. The average level of the estimated one-day volatility was 26.7 basis points and there was considerable variation in this number across auctions.

The authors regressed both the discount and the dispersion of bidder's demand curves against their estimated market volatility. In each regression, the coefficient multiplying volatility was positive and highly statistically significant. The regression coefficients were also significant in an economic sense. An increase of 10 basis points in market volatility caused an average increase in the discount of 4.4 basis points, which is a substantial increase in the level of bid-shading. An increase of 10 points in market volatility also increases the average dispersion by 2 basis points. The mean dispersion of the bidders' demand curves was 4.6 basis points, so an increase of 2 basis points in the dispersion is also substantial. Thus, the findings overall suggest that bidders in Swedish Treasury bond auctions are well adapted to the winner's curse, and that the possibility of a winner's curse does not constitute a valid argument against the use of auctions in issuing bonds.

### 3.3    Do auctions open up the possibility that a bidder can 'corner the market' or otherwise manipulate the market price?

Should policy-makers be concerned that a bidder can acquire sufficient bonds in an auction to manipulate prices in the bond market? One relevant fact is that the US Treasury remains sufficiently concerned about this possibility to limit the amount that a single bidder can purchase in one of its auctions to 35 per cent of the auctioned bonds. It is also noteworthy that in Swedish auctions, where there is no 35 per cent rule, Nyborg, Rydqvist and Sundaresan (2001) report that a single bidder purchased all the bonds at auction in about 10 per cent of the more than 400 auctions which they studied.

The observations in the previous paragraph suggest that one or a few bidders may be able to win most or even all of the bonds sold in an auction. Whether these bonds can then be used to manipulate the bond market also depends on the availability of close substitutes for the auctioned bond. In Sweden, for example, most of the Treasury auctions involve adding more bonds to an existing issue that is already actively traded. If the amount sold in any one auction is a relatively small fraction of all the outstanding bonds, it may not matter if a single bidder purchases the entire amount being auctioned.

In US Treasury auctions, there are three markets that are potentially vulnerable to manipulation. One is the bond market itself. The others are the when-issued forward market where claims to the bonds being auctioned are traded and a related market known as the 'repo [repurchase] and reverse market'.

Bikchandani and Huang (1993) describe how the when-issued market might be manipulated. A seller of a forward contract in the when-issued market guarantees to deliver a quantity of the bonds being auctioned after the auction occurs. According to Bikchandani and Huang, primary dealers often sell contracts in the when-issued market to institutional clients who wish to ensure that they will be able to purchase some of the bonds being auctioned. If many of the sellers in the when-issued market are unable to acquire the needed bonds in the auction, a 'short squeeze' may occur. In this case, the sellers must either pay a high price to repurchase their when-issued contracts or borrow the needed securities in the 'repurchase and reverse' market. Borrowing securities in this market can be costly for the borrower and profitable for the lender.

The frequency with which short squeezes occur and the extent to which they are caused by deliberate action or merely chance events is a matter open to question. See Bikchandani and Huang (1993) for further references that are relevant to this debate as well as a fuller description of the repo and reverse market.

In considering possible manipulation in US Treasury markets, it is interesting to note the case of an attempted cornering of the market by Salomon Brothers in 1991. Jordan and Jordan (1996) discuss the incident and attempt to measure the level of Salomon Brothers' profits. In May 1991, the US Treasury auctioned more than $12 billion of Treasury notes with a two-year maturity. In spite of the Treasury rule limiting the purchase of bonds being auctioned to no more than 35 per cent of the total, Salomon Brothers was able to purchase over 80 per cent of the

Table 9.1. *Summary of case studies*

| Study | Auction details | Profit measure | Discriminatory auction profits | Uniform price auction profits |
|---|---|---|---|---|
| Cammack (1991) | US, 1973–84, 3-month bills | $(P_M - P_A)/P_A$ | 1 basis point; $100 profit | n.a. |
| Umlauf (1993) | Mexico, 1986–91, 1-month bills | $(P_M - P_A)/P_A$ | 1.84 basis points; $184 profit | −0.3 basis points; $30 loss |
| Simon (1994) | US, 1973–6, 15- to 30-year bonds | $(P_M - P_A)/F$ | 15.8 basis points; $1580 profit | 19.2 basis points; $1920 profit |
| Nyborg and Sundaresan (1996) | US, 1992–3, 2-year bonds | $(P_M - P_A)/F$ | 1.05 basis points or −0.6 basis points (depending on measure of market price); $105 profit or $6 loss (depending on measure of market price) | −0.096 basis points or 1.39 basis points (depending on measure of market price); $9.6 loss or $139 profit (depending on measure of market price) |
| Nyborg and Sundaresan (1996) | US, 1992–3, 5-year bonds | $(P_M - P_A)/F$ | 2.22 basis points or 7.62 basis points (depending on measure of market price); $222 profit or $762 profit (depending on measure of market price) | 3.49 basis points or −3 basis points (depending on measure of market price); $349 profit or $300 loss (depending on measure of market price) |
| Nyborg, Rydqvist and Sundaresan (2001) | Sweden, 1990–94, 14-month bills and 6- to 16-year bonds | $(P_M - P_A)/F$ | 2 basis points; $200 profit | n.a. |

*Notes:* $P_A$ Average auction price; $P_M$ Average market price; $F$ Face value of bond.
In this table we calculate the average profit/loss for participants in auctions by comparing the average auction price to the average market price. The third column indicates the profit measure. It normalises the difference between auction price and market price by dividing either by the auction price or by the face value. The fourth and fifth column then report the value of the profit measure. The value is expressed in two ways: first, in basis points, where a basis point is 0.01 per cent; second, in dollars per million dollars of either auction payment or face value.

issue. According to Jordan and Jordan, Salomon purchased over 40 per cent of the bonds in its own name and purchased additional bonds by using unauthorised customer bids.

The Salomon Brothers incident received considerable public attention. Without admitting any wrong-doing, Salomon Brothers later reached a settlement with the Securities and Exchange Commission and other US agencies that, according to Jordan and Jordan, cost $290 million including $122 million paid to the Treasury to settle securities violations, $68 million paid to the Department of Justice, and $100 million paid to set up a fund to compensate injured parties. Evidently, at least some members of Salomon Brothers were willing to take substantial risks in the hope of profitably manipulating the bond market via the auction.

Jordan and Jordan note that one of the ways that Salomon Brothers was able to profit from its corner was by obtaining special deals in the repurchase and reverse market from firms that needed to settle contracts in the when-issued market. Jordan and Jordan also attempt to measure the degree of mispricing in the bond market itself that was caused by Salomon Brothers' manipulations. They conclude that the two-year note was significantly overvalued for approximately six weeks after the auction. Thus, Salomon Brothers seem to have manipulated the market, and imposing quantity bounds in bond auctions appears to be an important policy instrument.

## 4    Conclusion

One of the case studies reviewed in this chapter suggests that bond auctions can serve as information discovery mechanisms even in the presence of active secondary markets. This speaks in favour of using auctions for the sale of bonds. There is at most weak evidence that auctions create 'sorry losers' who suffer from the winner's curse. In general, bidders seem to adjust rationally to the presence of the winner's curse. The two most prominent auction formats for bond auctions, uniform price and discriminatory auctions, do not seem to lead to very large differences in governments' expected revenues. However, it does seem important in some cases to limit the proportion of any single issue which an individual bidder can purchase.

### References

Ausubel, L. and P. Cramton 2002, 'Demand reduction and inefficiency in multi-unit auctions', Working Paper, University of Maryland, http://www.cramton.umd.edu/ (accessed at 8 February 2003).

Back, K. and J. Zender 1993, 'Auctions of divisible goods: on the rationale for the Treasury experiment', *Review of Financial Studies* 6: 733–64.

Bikchandani, S. and C. Huang 1993, 'The economics of Treasury securities markets,' *Journal of Economic Perspectives* 7: 117–34.

Binmore, K. and J. Swierzbinski 2000, 'Treasury auctions: uniform or discriminatory', *Review of Economic Design* 5: 387–410.

Cammack, E. 1991, 'Evidence on bidding strategies and the information in Treasury bill auctions', *Journal of Political Economy* 99: 100–30.

Department for Environment, Food and Rural Affairs (DEFRA) 2001, *Draft Framework Document for the UK Emissions Trading Scheme*. This and other documents relating to the UK programme for trading carbon emissions are available at http://www.defra.gov.uk/ (accessed at 8 February 2003).

Fama, E. 1970, 'Efficient capital markets: a review of theory and empirical work', *Journal of Finance* 25: 383–417.

Hortaçsu, A. 2001, 'Mechanism choice and strategic bidding in divisible good auctions: an empirical analysis of the Turkish treasury auction market', unpublished draft, University of Chicago.

Jordan, B. and S. Jordan 1996, 'Salomon Brothers and the May 1991 Treasury auction: analysis of a market corner', *Journal of Banking and Finance* 20: 25–40.

Laffont, J. 1997, 'Game theory and empirical economics: the case of auction data', *European Economic Review* 41: 1–35.

Milgrom, P. 1989, 'Auctions and bidding: a primer', *Journal of Economic Perspectives* 3: 3–22.

Nyborg, K. and S. Sundaresan 1996, 'Discriminatory versus uniform Treasury auctions: evidence from when-issued transactions', *Journal of Financial Economics* 42: 63–104.

Nyborg, K., K. Rydqvist and S. Sundaresan 2001, 'Bidder behavior in multi-unit auctions: evidence from Swedish treasury auctions', *Journal of Political Economy* 110: 394–424

Simon, D. 1994, 'The Treasury's experiment with single-price auctions in the mid-1970s: winner's or taxpayer's Curse?', *Review of Economics and Statistics* 76: 754–60.

Umlauf, S. 1993, 'An empirical study of the Mexican treasury bill auction,' *Journal of Financial Economics* 33: 313–40.

# 10    Matching markets

*Benny Moldovanu*

## 1    Introduction

A basic goal of markets is to achieve a matching among buyers and sellers, or, more generally formulated, a matching between individual agents and physical objects or financial claims. In a commodity market (such as the market for gold) the price determines whether an agent decides to buy or to sell. But in many other markets (such as regulated labour markets, government-sponsored auctions or Beauty Contests for UMTS licences) the roles of the agents are relatively well defined: each agent operates on only one side of a bilateral market.

In auctions and in decentralised markets consisting of systems of overlapping bargained agreements the physical allocation of objects is accompanied by a determination of prices. In contrast, many other bilateral markets operate only on the matching dimension since, for various institutional reasons, money either does not enter the system or prices are determined exogenously. For example, many entry-level job markets focus on matching new graduates and potential employers at more or less fixed wages.

The theory of two-sided matching offers fundamental insights into the functioning of markets and identifies the main issues arising in the design of such markets. In particular, once money and prices are introduced in the models, this theory offers the basis of auction and market design. Moreover, there exist well-documented and successful large-scale applications that can guide further practical work. A broad conclusion is that markets require a good deal of organisation. This runs counter to the view implicit in much of the economic literature, which is that markets are largely self-organising entities that do not require thoughtful design.

This chapter will address the following main questions:

(1) What is a satisfactory matching in a bilateral market and when do such matchings exist?
(2) Which allocation mechanisms tend to produce satisfactory matchings?

(3) How does the choice of a matching mechanism influence the strategic incentives of agents on each side of the market, and how do strategic manipulations influence the final outcome?

(4) What are the main lessons for the design of auctions and Beauty Contests?

The chapter has the following structure. In section 2 we describe a famous case study, the US market for medical interns. In section 3 we survey the main theoretical models and results. We consider one-to-one and many-to-one matching models without money. A good textbook for this material is Roth and Sotomayor (1990). In section 4 we revisit the market for medical interns and explain the observed events in light of the theory. In section 5 we extend the model by introducing money, and connect the matching theory to auctions. We conclude with the main lessons for the design of auctions and Beauty Contests.

## 2    The matching market for US medical interns

One of the most famous applications of market design is the organisation of the US market for medical interns (or residents). Interns are students at the end of their studies who get an additional year of concentrated clinical exposure. By employing interns, hospitals get cheap labour. From the start of the programme at the beginning of the last century, the number of offered positions was much greater than the number of applicants, and there was intense competition among hospitals. A consequence of these conditions was that the date at which contracts were signed had advanced by 1944 to about two years before the student's graduation. Since this was considered to be ridiculous, the Association of American Medical Colleges (AAMC) decided that a student's grade transcripts and letters of reference would only be released in the summer of graduation. The entire matching of students to positions moved to the final summer preceding employment, and, more often than not, students were sitting on offers hoping to get better positions at hospitals where they were on the waiting list. In many cases, students reneged on agreed offers after obtaining better ones.

In 1945 the AAMC succumbed to pressure from the American Hospital Association (AHA) and ruled that students could sit on an offer for at most ten days. In 1946 this was shortened to eight days, in 1949 to twelve hours, and in 1950 to one minute (these offers were called 'explosive'). Since more time-squeezing was impossible, it became clear that a new approach had to be found.

In 1951 a centralised algorithm was proposed in which students and hospitals submitted rank order lists (ROL) of preferred hospitals and students, respectively. Students and hospitals were then matched taking into account the submitted preferences. After a trial run, students complained that the algorithm encouraged 'clever' manipulation of submitted preferences, and the procedure was slightly modified. The centralised market is still in use today and fills about 20,000 positions per year in about 3000 hospital programmes. Most tellingly, although participation in the centralised scheme is completely voluntary, until the mid-seventies the participation rate was about 95 per cent of eligible students and hospitals. Participation dropped in the later seventies to about 85 per cent. Another growing concern was the fact that rural hospitals were often left with empty positions. In the mid-nineties, the market began to suffer a crisis of confidence, and students (supported by vocal consumers' rights advocates such as Ralph Nader) complained that the outcome was unreasonably favourable towards hospitals. A new algorithm was devised by Alvin Roth, a distinguished economist, now at Harvard, and was used from 1998 onwards (see Roth and Peranson (1999)).

Several questions arise from this:

(1) Why did the frantic recontracting activity and the 'explosive' offers immediately disappear once the voluntary centralised market was introduced?

(2) Why was a participation rate of 95 per cent initially achieved by the centralised procedure, even if all agents were able to continue to contract privately?

(3) What prompted the drop in the participation rate in the late seventies?

(4) Is it possible to change the rules of the matching algorithm such that more positions get filled at rural hospitals? What other repercussions would such a change cause?

(5) Were the recent students' complaints justified, and does the new mechanism perform better?

(6) What are the main lessons for other matching markets?

In order to answer these questions, we first take a brief look at the basic theory of two-sided matching markets.

## 3 The theory of two-sided matching markets

### 3.1 The one-to-one matching model

The two-sided matching model is probably the simplest market model in the whole of economic science. It consists of two distinct groups of agents. In this subsection we will call the members of the first group 'men' and the members of the second group 'women'. An agent is characterised by a *rank order list* (ROL) over the members of the group to which it does not belong. The ROL describes the ordinal preference of the particular agent over potential matches, and it means: I prefer to be matched to the individual appearing first on my list; if this is not possible, then I prefer to be matched with the individual appearing second on my list, and so on. An individual ROL may not include all members of the other side of the market, with the implication that an individual with an incomplete ROL prefers to remain single rather than be matched to one of the non-listed agents.

A *matching* consists of several matched pairs and several unmatched (i.e. single) individuals. The basic economic problem is to find a 'satisfactory' matching between men and women. The main question is what 'satisfactory' should mean. A first easy criterion is one of 'no coercion' (or individual rationality): no individual should be matched to a non-listed (i.e. non-acceptable) partner. The second criterion is 'efficiency': a matching is efficient if there is no other matching where at least one agent is better off (i.e. matched to another, more preferred agent) while all other agents are at least as well off.

But, apart from efficiency and no coercion, another important criterion is needed. To illustrate this, consider first the following simple proposal that yields an efficient, individually rational matching:

Order the agents on one side of the market (say the women) alphabetically[1] (e.g. Ana, Betty, Britta, Carla, etc.). Match Ana with her most preferred man (say Maarten) in the set of men that she regards as acceptable and that regard her as acceptable. If such a man does not exist, let Ana be single. Then match Betty to her most preferred man (say Benny) among those remaining who are acceptable to her and who regard her as acceptable; otherwise let Betty be single, and so on. It is obvious that any other matching will make at least one woman less well off. Hence, the proposed matching is efficient and individually rational.

Nevertheless, the above proposed matching is not satisfactory. The following problem may appear: in the proposed matching Maarten and Betty are not together (since Maarten is matched to Ana). But consider preferences such that Betty prefers Maarten to Benny, and such that Maarten prefers Betty to Ana. Unfortunately, the above matching procedure did not make the pair Betty–Maarten possible. Hence, the members of this pair prefer to leave their proposed partners, in order to form a pair themselves. Such behaviour destabilises the entire proposed matching (since we must find new partners for Ana and Benny, etc.), and a 'matchmaker' using the above procedure will soon lose her reputation, and possibly her job.

---

[1] Any well-defined order will do here.

The above insight leads to the following important definition:

An individual *blocks* a matching $m$ if he/she is paired to an unacceptable partner. A woman–man pair *blocks* a matching $m$ if they are not matched to each other in $m$, but each prefers the other to their current partner in $m$. A matching is *stable* if no individual or pair blocks it.

The most important and surprising result in matching theory is due to Gale and Shapley (1961): a stable matching always exists.[2] The ingenious proof is constructive, by means of a *deferred-acceptance algorithm* (which, by the way, is a precursor of the simultaneous ascending auction). The algorithm functions as follows: to start, each man proposes to his favourite woman (of course there is an analogous procedure where women propose). Each woman rejects the proposal of any man who is unacceptable to her, and each woman who receives more than one proposal rejects all but her most preferred of these. Any man whose proposal is not rejected is kept 'engaged'. At any further step, any man who was rejected at the previous step proposes to his most preferred woman among those who have not yet rejected him (or does not make proposals if all remaining women are unacceptable). Each woman receiving proposals 'engages' the most preferred man in the group consisting of the new proposers together with any man she may have kept engaged at the previous step. The process stops after a step in which no man is rejected, and the matching obtained at this step is the final one.

It can easily be shown that the algorithm stops after a finite number of steps and that it always produces a stable matching. If a man $h$ prefers a woman $f$ to his final partner, then $h$ must have proposed to $f$ before proposing to that partner. Since $h$ and $f$ are not matched, $f$ must have rejected $h$. Hence $f$ cannot prefer $h$ to her final partner.

Gale and Shapley also show that there exists a stable matching which is optimal for the men in the sense that all men prefer this matching to any other stable matching and that the deferred-acceptance algorithm with men proposing yields exactly that matching[3] (analogously, when women propose, a women-optimal matching is obtained). Moreover, it can be shown that an individual who remains single in a stable matching necessarily remains single in all stable matchings.

An important feature that we have neglected so far concerns strategic considerations. Do agents have incentives to submit their true preferences

---

[2] It is interesting to note that stable matchings always exist only in bilateral markets (i.e. they do not always exist in unilateral, trilateral markets, etc.).

[3] This may explain the widespread custom where men (now in the literal sense) propose marriage to women, rather than vice versa.

to a matching algorithm (or, equivalently, to behave according to the rules in a 'dynamic' procedure such as the deferred-acceptance one)? For example, assume that a particular woman is known to be very popular: each man thinks that there is a slight chance of being matched to her. In that situation, maybe it is worthwhile for a man to manipulate the ROL by ranking another woman highest, thus increasing the chance of being matched to that second-best alternative.

If agents distort their reported preferences, a stable matching obtained from the reported preferences may not be stable for the true preferences, and hence the outcome will be destabilised by blocking pairs. It can be shown (Dubins and Freedman, 1981; Demange and Gale, 1985) that in any procedure that yields the men-optimal stable matching, it is optimal for all men to state their true preferences, i.e. any man optimises by submitting his true ROL, independently of what other agents are doing (and, vice versa, in any procedure that yields the women-optimal stable matching, it is optimal for all women to state their true preferences).[4] In addition, no coalition of men can improve their position by jointly distorting their reported preferences. There is generally no algorithm that makes it optimal for both sides of the market to state their true preferences. In particular, when the stable matching for one side of the market is chosen, members of the other side have the incentive to manipulate, and the easiest way to do so profitably is to submit a ROL where some acceptable partners are simply not listed.

## 3.2    The many-to-one matching model

An important extension to the above model is obtained by allowing agents on one side of the market (call them 'firms') to be matched to several agents on the other side (call them 'workers'). This corresponds to the situation where a hospital may employ several interns. As before, workers rank all acceptable firms from most to least preferred, but firms have preferences of entire subsets of workers. Since such preferences over entire groups are necessarily more complex than rankings of individual agents, the existence of stable matchings (see, for example, Kelso and Crawford (1982)) is now ensured only if firms regard workers as *substitutes*. This means that, if a firm prefers to employ a group that includes worker $w$, it will want to employ this worker even if other workers in that group become unavailable. For example, assume that a firm needs $n$ workers, that it can rank all workers using a ROL, and that it always prefers to hire

---

[4] As we will see, these results are the precursors of analogous results for the second-price auction and other similar mechanisms.

the highest-ranked available $n$ workers. Then this firm regards workers as substitutes since it will want to hire a sufficiently high-ranked worker even if other workers become unavailable. In contrast, consider an economics faculty that has a fixed budget and wants to build either a strong group in auction theory or a strong group in macroeconomics (but is not interested in two weak groups in each discipline). Then the desirability of a particular auction theorist crucially depends on the availability of other auction theorists, and professors are *complements* rather than substitutes. In this case, stable matchings may not exist. Most of the properties discussed above generalise to the many-to-one model, but there are exceptions. In particular, even if the firm-optimal matching is implemented, firms may have an incentive to manipulate their reported capacities.

## 4 The market for medical interns revisited

In light of the above theoretical results, we can now answer the six questions raised at the end of section 2.

(1) The frantic recontracting activity and the 'explosive' one-minute offers immediately disappeared and a voluntary participation rate of 95 per cent was achieved because the algorithm was making a stable matching. This implies that a student unhappy with the hospital he was assigned to was not able to find outside the centralised system another better hospital that was willing to employ him (and vice versa for hospitals). Alvin Roth analysed the algorithm in 1984 (about thirty years after it was devised) and discovered that, although it functioned differently from the deferred-acceptance procedure, it nevertheless achieved the hospital-optimal stable matching. Hence, the doctors and engineers that devised the algorithm had anticipated Gale and Shapley's seminal insight by about ten years.

(2) See (1) above.

(3) The drop in participation rates in the late seventies had a prosaic reason: more and more married couples (where both partners were doctors) began to apply for internships. Such couples necessarily have more complex preferences than are expressed in simple ROLs, since they usually prefer being together in one hospital or city. It was noticed that couples tended to avoid the centralised market, and tried to arrange a match privately. The original algorithm was changed in order to get better matches for couples, but to no avail. Is this a problem of the particular scheme that was used? The answer is 'no'. It can be shown that in a system with

complex preferences for couples, the set of stable matchings may be empty, and therefore no algorithm can produce a stable matching.

(4) The meagre allocation of interns to rural hospitals is unavoidable if students do not like going there, and if a stable matching is desired. Recall that the set of single individuals (or the set of unfilled positions) always remains the same, no matter what stable matching is chosen. Hence, it is impossible simultaneously to choose a stable matching and fill positions at rural hospitals which were not already filled by the original algorithm. Indeed, new routines were introduced in the matching algorithm in order to give certain priority to rural hospitals – but to no avail.

(5) Since we now know that the original algorithm was the hospital-optimal one, the students' complaints (that the system favours hospitals, and that clever students can successfully manipulate the system by submitting false ROLs) seem eminently reasonable. Therefore, the new algorithm introduced in 1998 was devised in order to achieve the student-optimal matching. This also makes sense from a welfare point of view, since hospitals probably do not differentiate too much between their seventh and tenth candidates, but students may care a lot whether they live in Miami or in Seattle, independently of the quality of the respective hospitals. The new algorithm was also optimised with respect to married couples (but, as mentioned above, a fully satisfactory solution for this problem does not exist). The designers of the new algorithm performed an intriguing experiment: they used the new matching rules on the ROLs submitted to the system in previous years, and focused on the resulting differences. To their surprise, these differences were very small: about one applicant in 1000 was affected by the choice of the algorithm (or, otherwise stated, the requirement that a matching be stable already determined 99.9 per cent of all student–hospital matches). The reason is that hospitals and students tend to list each other only following an interview. Since the number of feasible interviews is constrained by time and travel costs (to a generous maximum of about ten interviews per student), one can show that in a very large market where students' lists contain only a few acceptable hospitals there is almost always a unique stable matching, which therefore must be picked by any stable algorithm. In addition, we now know that the best advice to students must be, 'submit your true ROL', since possibilities of manipulations are almost non-existent, and since manipulation (which calls for deleting some acceptable hospitals from the submitted list) introduces the additional risk of not being matched at all.

(6) Although the original matching algorithm was not based on then existing theory, later theoretical developments (combined with simulation and experiments) completely explained the main features of the problem and its solution, and paved the way for a new, carefully devised algorithm (rather than the more or less 'blind' adjustments made previously). Moreover, it is now possible to use similar solutions in many other contexts. Roth and Sotomayor (1990) and Roth and Xing (1994) describe the history of many highly specialised markets where matching plays an important role (a few examples are professional athletes in team sports, Canadian lawyers, new professors, US football bowls, UK medical specialities, etc.) Although each and every one of these markets displays unique characteristics, it is possible to say, roughly, that only those market institutions that tended to produce stable matchings survived in the long run.[5]

## 5        Connections to auctions and market design

In almost all European UMTS licence auctions there was a fixed number of licences with a fixed capacity, and it was stipulated that no firm could buy more than one licence. We had, therefore, a classic one-to-one matching problem. In other situations, such as the US spectrum auctions of regional licences for mobile telephony or the allocation of regional radio licences in the Netherlands, one firm could buy several licences. These were many-to-one matching problems. Other interesting examples for many-to-one matching problems are the European market for football players and the market for pollution emission rights which is to be introduced soon. Of course, in such markets money also plays an important role.

In order to understand the implication of the two-sided matching theory for such situations, and in order to connect the above insights to auctions and market design, we need first to extend the basic model in order to allow for money. We do it here briefly for the one-to-one matching model, and refer the reader to Kelso and Crawford (1982), Roth and Sotomayor (1990), Gul and Stacchetti (1999), Milgrom (1999) and Ausubel and Milgrom (2001) for parallel results in the many-to-one case.

---

[5] Some unstable mechanisms survived if they were complemented by rules that made 'divorce' very costly (a good example are the cumbersome transfer rules in professional sports). But such rules create lots of friction and are often subject to prolonged legal battles (recall the famous Bosman case that led to a revolution in European football).

## 5.1    *The one-to-one matching model with money*

Consider two distinct groups of agents, called now 'buyers' and 'sellers'. Each seller $s$ owns an indivisible object, say a house, and has a reservation price for the house, say $r_s$ (i.e. the seller is prepared to sell the house for a price which is at least $r_s$). Each buyer has money, and is characterised by a list of reservation prices for the individual houses, i.e. a list of maximal prices that this buyer is prepared to pay for each house. Let $r_{bs}$ denote the reservation price of buyer $b$ for the house owned by seller $s$. Then, the pair $\{b, s\}$ can be characterised by the associated gains from trade, $v_{bs} = \max (0, r_{bs} - r_s)$. A matching $m$ consists of a set of buyer–seller pairs, a set of unmatched agents and a set of prices for each house, where $p_s$ denotes the price of the house owned by $s$. If $\{b, s\}$ are matched and trade at price $p_s$, then the buyer's pay-off is $r_{bs} - p_s$, and the seller's pay-off is $p_s - r_s$. A matching is *stable* if no matched buyer pays more than his reservation price for the house he buys, no matched seller gets less than her reservation price, and if, for any unmatched buyer–seller pair $\{b, s\}$, there is no price $p_s$ such that trading at that price makes both traders in the pair better off. A system of prices for which we can find a stable matching consistent with those prices is called a *competitive price system* (the reason will become clear below).

The main results for this model are as follows (see Shapley and Shubik (1972)). A stable matching always exists. The set of competitive prices has a minimal element which is optimal for the buyers (i.e. a price system such that all other competitive price systems yield higher prices for all houses) and a maximal element which is optimal for the sellers (i.e. a price system such that all other competitive price systems yield lower prices for all houses). This last result generalises the existence of men-optimal and women-optimal stable matches in an earlier section. For example, in a market where a single house is available, the set of competitive prices is precisely the interval between the highest and second highest reservation prices. The minimal competitive price (which is optimal for buyers) is the second highest reservation price, which may belong either to a buyer or to the seller.

The generalisation of the Gale–Shapley deferred-acceptance algorithm now takes the form of a *simultaneous ascending auction*. For the version where buyers are active, this works roughly as follows (see Demange, Gale and Sotomayor (1986) and Milgrom (1999)). At the first stage the auctioneer fixes the prices equal to the sellers' reservation prices. At these prices, each buyer announces which house (if any) he wants to buy. If no house receives more than one bid, the auction stops, and each bidder obtains the house for which he bid at the seller's reservation price.

Otherwise, the price of those houses that obtained more than one bid is raised by a small increment[6] (while other prices remain constant). Again, buyers announce which houses they want to buy, and so on. The auction stops at the price level attained after a step in which no house receives more than one bid.

For the matching model without money, the deferred-acceptance algorithm yielded the optimal stable matching for the proposing party. Members of the proposing party had an optimal strategy: to reveal their true preferences. The present model with money yields analogous results. Consider a direct revelation mechanism (i.e. where bidders simultaneously submit reservation vectors and the above algorithm is run by a computer) yielding the stable matching associated with the minimum competitive price system. Then, submitting the true reservation prices for each house is optimal for each buyer. If buyers bid in the ascending version, then the auction stops with the minimum (i.e. buyer-optimal) competitive price system if bidders behave *straightforwardly* (i.e., at each stage, buyers place bids on their respective most preferred houses given the current level of prices). Straightforward bidding ensures that a crucial feature of the deferred-acceptance algorithm is maintained: bidders make first offers they prefer most and proceed monotonically to offers they prefer least.

Recall that in a market with a single house, the minimum competitive price is exactly the second highest reservation price. Thus, the optimality of truthful bidding for buyers generalises to multi-object auctions Vickrey's famous result about the single-object second-price auction. Although buyers have an optimal strategy to state their true preferences, collusion becomes profitable here since buyers may make side payments among each other. For example, in a single-object auction, the highest bidder may want to bribe the second highest bidder to decrease her bid (this can effectively be achieved by a pre-auction organised among the potential buyers).

Let us now briefly illustrate some of the above insights in a simple example where all objects for sale are identical. Buyers are characterised by their maximal willingness to pay for any one object, $r_b$, and sellers are characterised by their minimal reservation price, $r_s$. The respective values are given in table 10.1.

At a first glance it seems that we can maximise trade volume by arranging transactions for all five objects. Indeed, consider the matching and the corresponding prices shown in table 10.2. At these prices, all matched

---

[6] Alternatively, bidders themselves may raise their bids on objects of which they are not 'provisional winners'. There are some subtle strategic differences among the various versions.

Table 10.1. *Reserve prices*

| Index | Sellers' reserve prices | Buyers' reserve prices |
|-------|------------------------|------------------------|
| 1     | 10                     | 24                     |
| 2     | 12                     | 23                     |
| 3     | 16                     | 21                     |
| 4     | 18                     | 19                     |
| 5     | 22                     | 17                     |
| 6     |                        | 14                     |

Table 10.2. *Possible matching*

| Seller-buyer Pair | Price |
|-------------------|-------|
| 1–5               | 13.5  |
| 2–4               | 15.5  |
| 3–3               | 18.5  |
| 4–2               | 20.5  |
| 5–1               | 23    |

agents are willing to transact since each price is lower than the respective buyer's reserve prices and higher than the respective seller's reserve price.[7] But will traders want to participate in a centralised trading system that yields the above matching and prices? The answer is obviously 'no'! There are indeed ill-designed markets conceived along similar ideas where, very soon, participants discover that it is in their interest to trade outside the centralised system (one example is offered by the early rules for the auction of sulphur dioxide emission rights in the United States).

Consider for example buyer 1 and seller 1: these two agents are not paired in the above matching and they would rather transact outside the system at a price, say, of 18. It can be easily seen that such destabilising opportunities always arise as long as similar objects are sold at different prices. Hence, stable matchings may exist only if we impose a unique market price. As the reader can easily check, any matching between sellers 1–4 and buyers 1–4 based on a unique market price between 18 and 19 yields here a stable matching: no pair then has any incentive to trade outside the centralised market. Note also that these prices are also exactly those where demand equals supply (four units). Thus, the prices

---

[7] Prices were chosen exactly in the middle of this range.

sustaining stable matching coincide with those sustaining the well-known competitive equilibria. Obviously the lowest price in the range, 18, is the optimal stable price for the buyers, while the highest price, 19, is the optimal stable price for the sellers. An auction where each buyer places a single bid and the market price is chosen to be the minimal one such that demand equals supply yields incentives for buyers to bid their reservation prices truthfully (this generalises the insight of the second-price auction). Similarly, an auction where sellers make bids but the market price is the highest such that demand equals supply gives sellers incentives to bid truthfully. In general, there are no procedures that simultaneously give all agents on both sides of the market incentives to bid truthfully.

## 6    Extensions and main lessons

Any practical implementation of centralised market mechanisms (with or without money transfers) needs to yield stable matchings. Otherwise, agents will choose to transact outside the system. This consideration is often more important than other details (e.g. informational assumptions) on which traditional auction theory, with its emphasis on one-object auctions, tends to focus.

The chosen auction procedures in many recent applications have been variations of multi-stage ascending auctions. When well designed, such procedures constitute natural monetary analogues to Gale and Shapley's deferred-acceptance algorithm, and inherit many of its desirable properties. This basic relation offers the most solid theoretical basis for the widespread faith in the virtues of ascending multi-object auctions.

In many contexts, bidders are allowed to buy several objects – these are many-to-one matching problems. Flexible auction formats call then for allowing bidders to express preferences on entire bundles – in auction parlance, such procedures are called *combinatorial* auctions.[8] An application of the deferred-acceptance algorithm naturally yields a *combinatorial ascending auction*. Ausubel and Milgrom (2001) offer a detailed study of such an auction (in the light of matching theory) and they survey the advantages over static procedures such as the Clarke–Groves–Vickrey mechanisms. Obviously, the rules of combinatorial auctions are relatively complex for both auctioneer and bidders (e.g. how to determine which prices get adjusted upwards at each step becomes more delicate). Generalisations of the main results obtained for the one-to-one matching problems

---

[8] In this context, it is interesting to note that the US Federal Communications Commission (which has long favoured the simultaneous ascending auction because of its simplicity) is now considering the use of combinatorial auctions in a forthcoming event.

hinge, roughly, on the absence of *complements* (i.e. the willingness to pay for a bundle should not be higher than the sum of the willingness to pay for the individual objects in the bundle). The presence of complements induces many practical problems related to the non-existence of stable matchings and market-clearing prices.

We have assumed so far that agents care only about their own match. But, in many contexts, competing firms may also care about other aspects of the entire matching (e.g. who else gets what). In other words, there are external effects (for more on this topic, see Janssen and Moldovanu (this volume, chapter 5). Such features tend to destroy most of the theoretical results we have presented so far (in particular, the existence of stable matchings is not ensured). For example, the allocation of landing and take-off slots at airports displays both strong complementarities and strong externalities stemming from the desire to pre-empt competitors. Much care is required when devising satisfactory auctions for instances where complementarities and externalities are present.

There are generally no stable matching mechanisms that make it optimal for both sides of the market to reveal their true preferences – this means that the final outcome may not be a desirable one for the true preferences. This problem is particularly severe in thin markets with few agents. It then makes sense to combat the strategic incentives by implementing the optimal stable matching for the market side whose members stand to gain most from manipulations.

The above observation also implies that in auctions where buyers are active and make bids, the seller(s) can increase revenue by the choice of reservation prices. Fixing reservation prices becomes an important strategic issue for the seller. Using a simultaneous ascending auction is not an insurance policy against low revenue (as some recent UMTS auctions which closed near the reservation prices amply showed), unless appropriate reservation prices (that reflect the degree of scarcity implied by alternative or future uses) are chosen. In this context it is also useful to recall the fate of the unmatched rural hospitals. The lesson is that unattractive objects may get 'matched' only if additional sweeteners are offered. One may consider negative reserve prices (i.e. subsidies) if the designer desires a particular match. Good examples are the Dutch 'designated' radio stations that are strongly constrained in their programming.

If the optimal matching for one side of the market is chosen, the agents on that side do not have incentives to collude in the model without money. The situation changes in the model with money, and this implies that ascending auctions are not immune to collusion among bidders. In particular, in most applications bidders raise prices themselves. This flexibility (e.g. jump bids) can be used as a signalling device which co-ordinates collusion. Hence, it sometimes makes sense to restrict the bidding operations (e.g. by introducing strict activity rules and maximal bids at each stage) in order to get closer to the situation where the auctioneer raises prices on over-demanded objects by a pre-set minimum increment.

Beauty Contests that allocate objects to firms at fixed prices (which may be zero) can be seen as simple matching problems. If the allocated objects are heterogeneous (e.g. licences with different capacity, different geographic coverage, etc.) firms will be able to rank objects or bundles in order of preference. Sometimes these preferences are obvious (and are the same for all firms). In other instances, preferences are subtler, and it makes sense actually to ask for them (while explaining how this information will be used by the regulator in order to obtain an allocation). This will also give some information about the degree of scarcity inherent in the situation. The resulting allocation needs to be 'stable' in the sense that no firm should feel entitled (by the implicit rules of the contest) to a bundle that it likes more than the one it actually obtained. If an unstable allocation is chosen, unnecessary tensions accrue in the system, and legal battles may follow. In addition, if several firms are unhappy, resales and swaps may follow the allocation procedure, thus undermining the purpose of the entire exercise.

## References

Ausubel, L. and P. Milgrom 2001, 'Ascending auctions with package bidding', Discussion Paper, Stanford University.

Demange, G. and D. Gale 1985, 'The strategy structure of two-sided Matching markets', *Econometrica* 53: 873–88.

Demange, G., D. Gale, and M. Sotomayor 1986, 'Multi-item auctions', *Journal of Political Economy* 94: 863–72.

Dubins, L. and D. Freedman 1981, 'Machiavelli and the Gale–Shapley algorithm', *American Mathematical Monthly* 88: 485–94.

Gale, D. and L. Shapley 1962, 'College admissions and the stability of marriage', *American Mathematical Monthly* 69: 9–15.

Gul, F. and E. Stacchetti 1999, 'Walrasian equilibrium with gross substitutes', *Journal of Economic Theory* 87: 9–24.

Kelso, A. and V. Crawford 1982, 'Job matching, coalition formation and gross substitutes', *Econometrica* 50: 1483–504.

Milgrom, P. 1999, 'Putting auction theory to work: the simultaneous ascending auction', *Journal of Political Economy* 108: 245–72.

Roth, A. and E. Peranson 1999, 'The redesign of the matching market for American physicians', *American Economic Review* 89: 748–80.

Roth, A. and M. Sotomayor 1990, *Two-sided Matching*, Econometric Society Monograph No. 18, Cambridge University Press.

Roth, A. and X. Xing 1994, 'Jumping the gun: imperfections and institutions related to the timing of market transactions', *American Economic Review* 84: 992–1044.

Shapley, L. and M. Shubik 1972, 'The assignment game I: the core', *International Journal of Game Theory* 1: 111–30.

Vickrey, W. 1961, 'Counterspeculation, auctions, and competitive sealed tenders', *Journal of Finance* 16: 8–37.

# 11 Competitive procurement of reintegration services in the Netherlands

*Maurice Dykstra and Jaap de Koning*

## 1    Introduction

Recently, the delivery of reintegration services to the unemployed and the disabled in the Netherlands – formerly a public task – has largely been privatised. The government still funds these services, but implementation is left to private agencies that have to compete for the contracts. Considerable improvements in these services in terms of both effectiveness and efficiency are expected from the privatisation. The purpose of this chapter is to give a description and an evaluation of the initial period following the introduction of the new system. Before we do that, we first discuss a number of points that may not be familiar to readers who are not specialists in labour market issues. Thus, why does the government provide or at least subsidise reintegration services? What do we understand by reintegration services?

Reintegration services are a particular form of employment service. The general aim of employment services is to help unemployed people find a job and employers fill their vacancies. There are several reasons why jobseekers and vacancies do not instantly match. An obvious reason is that both jobseekers and firms have imperfect information. However, we can also observe that some unemployed or disabled people have more fundamental problems in finding a job. They may lack a good strategy in searching for work or a network to help find them a job, or their skills may be insufficient.

In most European countries the provision of employment services is largely a public task. Usually a special public organisation, the public employment service (PES), carries out this task. Its most important services are job brokerage and reintegration services. The latter consist of activities such as job counselling, training and placement in subsidised jobs. Reintegration services are more intense forms of help to unemployed and other jobless people. These services tend to be concentrated on the more disadvantaged groups.

Until recently, the traditional system also prevailed in the Netherlands. In the second half of the 1990s, however, the Dutch government decided to privatise the provision of reintegration services. Gradually, the funding for reintegration services was transferred from the PES[1] to the social security agencies (SSAs) responsible for unemployment and disability benefits[2] and to the municipal organisations responsible for social assistance. At the time, five SSAs existed: CADANS, GAK, GUO, SFB and USZO. The different SSAs operated in different sectors of industry. In turn, each SSA was also organised regionally. Initially, both SSAs and municipalities were obliged to involve the PES as the only service provider, but this obligation was only temporary; later, private providers could also be involved. At a later stage, the part of the PES dealing with reintegration services was privatised. It became known as KLIQ and is now one of the private reintegration firms that have to compete for the contracts that are tendered by the SSAs and the municipalities.

The process resulting in the privatisation of considerable parts of the PES had already started in the early 1990s. Up to 1991 the PES was a part of the Ministry of Social Affairs and Employment. In that year it was transformed into a tripartite organisation, administered by the social partners and the government jointly. Furthermore, the state monopoly in job brokerage was abolished. This development was in line with the general societal trend to give more scope to the private sector. The impact of this step was rather small, however, because the activities of the tripartite PES were still completely funded by government. Because of this situation, private providers had few opportunities to compete with the PES, with the exception of temporary work agencies. A 1995 evaluation of the tripartite structure revealed serious shortcomings, which induced the government to go further on the road to privatisation.[3]

It is important to note that in the new system the delivery structure for public employment services is not completely privatised. Public employment offices still exist. One of their main tasks is to improve the transparency of the labour market by collecting and diffusing information on jobseekers and vacancies. Another important task is the profiling of the people entering unemployment. These are divided into four groups according to the degree of risk of their becoming long-term unemployed. Those not at high risk can only make use of the services provided by the employment offices (mainly information on jobs and benefits), which are

[1] In Dutch: Arbeidsvoorziening.    [2] In Dutch, the so-called 'uitvoeringsinstellingen'.
[3] See Dercksen and de Koning (1995) for a summary of the results.

now called Centres for Work and Income.[4] Those at high risk of long-term unemployment are sent to the SSAs and the municipalities and are entitled to reintegration services. As already indicated, the SSAs and the municipalities contract the service delivery to private agencies.

Many of the larger reintegration firms are offshoots of public organisations such as the SSAs and the former PES. Other reintegration firms were founded by temporary work agencies. In addition to these organisations a large number of new private firms offering reintegration services have sprouted up.

At the time another player in the field of social security was LISV, the National Institute for Social Insurance, which functions as a kind of regulator.[5] LISV developed a set of rules for the competitive procurement of reintegration activities. The SSAs were compelled to follow this procurement procedure when purchasing reintegration trajectories. This set of rules is a type of Beauty Contest. In the year 2000 the first round of Beauty Contests was held.

Since then a number of changes have occurred. The five SSAs together with LISV have merged into one organisation, UWV. Furthermore, cooperation within groups of smaller municipalities was introduced, since the latter do not have the capacity to deal with tendering procedures adequately. Therefore, the number of actors on the demand side of the reintegration market has reduced significantly.

In table 11.1 the various organisations involved in the old and/or the new system are listed, and their status (public or private) and function indicated.

In this chapter, we evaluate the 2000 round for the procurement of reintegration services in the Netherlands as conducted by the SSAs. Based on information from previously conducted evaluations, we try to shed some new light on the various findings by looking at it from the perspectives of the theory of auctions and Beauty Contests and the theory of industrial organisation in general. The chapter is structured as follows. In section 2 we give a description and an evaluation of the Beauty Contest design and its implementation. The outcomes of the Beauty Contest are the subject of section 3. Then, in section 4, we discuss the difficulties in assessing the quality of reintegration services and their implications for tendering procedures in this field. Finally, section 5 contains the conclusions and recommendations.

---

[4] If after six months they are still unemployed, they then become entitled to reintegration services.

[5] LISV: in Dutch, Landelijk Instituut Sociale Verzekeringen.

Table 11.1. *Organisations involved in social security and active labour market policy in the Netherlands*

| Organisation (in Dutch) | English equivalent | Task | Status |
|---|---|---|---|
| Arbeidsvoorziening | Public employment service (not in existence anymore) | Increase labour market transparency; job brokerage; implementation of active labour market policy | Public |
| CWI: Centrum voor Werk en Inkomen | Centre for Work and Income (public employment agency) | Profiling; increase labour market transparency; assistance with submitting applications for unemployment benefits | Public |
| UVI: Uitvoeringsorganisatie sociale zekerheid | SSA: Social Security Agency (now merged into UWV). Organised on a sectoral basis | Provide benefits to the unemployed and the disabled; outsource reintegration services to private providers | Public |
| LISV: Landelijk Instituut Sociale Verzekeringen | National Institute for Social Insurance (now merged into UWV) | Former regulating body for social security | Public |
| UWV: Uitvoering Werknemers-verzekeringen | Employee Insurance Programs Agency (EIPA) | Provide benefits to the unemployed and the disabled; merger of former UVIS; Outsource reintegration services to private providers | Public |
| Gemeentelijke sociale dienst | Municipal social service | Provide social assistance benefits; outsource reintegration services to private providers | Public |
| Reïntegratiebedrijf | Reintegration firm | Offer services such as training and/or placement services for the unemployed and the disabled | Private |

## 2        Beauty Contest design

### 2.1        Basic design features

LISV developed a set of rules for the competitive procurement of reintegration services. The SSAs were compelled to follow this procurement procedure when purchasing individual reintegration programmes. The first procurement round was held in the year 2000.

The reintegration firms bid for lots consisting of clients who had to be reintegrated. In their bids, they described the services they would deliver in order to reintegrate these clients and the price for these services. The procedure contained no specific requirements for the description of the lots. In the lot descriptions the SSAs only defined the groups of clients and the number of clients per lot. The clients were in most cases classified by industry sector and region and by whether they were unemployed or disabled. Generally, therefore, the composition of the lots was very heterogeneous. This made it next to impossible to make fine-tuned bids for niche markets. Only in a few cases did the lots consist of a narrowly defined group of clients. However, in order to make such lots sufficiently large, they were not classified by region.

LISV defined a number of criteria for judging the bids. These referred to both the price and the quality of the services (see subsection 2.3). Therefore, the procurement procedure can be seen as a Beauty Contest. In the case of an auction, a detailed set of quality requirements by LISV and the SSAs would have been needed, particularly in terms of the output (minimum standards for placement results of more or less homogeneous groups).[6] Then, the bidding would have referred to the price alone. Later in the chapter we come back to the question of whether an auction is to be preferred over a Beauty Contest.

### 2.2        Procedure

The LISV approach to procurement, generally speaking, followed that of the European Service Directive. The SSAs could choose between two procedures, an open one and a restricted one.[7]

---

[6] Furthermore, sub-categories can be distinguished within both the class of auctions and that of Beauty Contests. For a detailed review, see Janssen (this volume, Introduction).

[7] Additionally the LISV procurement approach opens the possibility for an experimental procedure. In this procedure it is possible to grant a maximum of two contracts to bidders who, by the rules of the game, do not fulfil all the criteria or come out as winners. LISV wanted to give the SSAs the possibility for experimentation in the procurement of individual reintegration programmes for clients who are extremely difficult to place in the labour market. The value of these contracts may not be more than €201,000. As about €300 million are involved in the procurement procedure, this experimental procedure plays a very small role in the course of affairs.

In the open procedure the reintegration firms could directly make a proposal based on the call for tenders which was publicised in the Dutch national newspapers. The SSA had then to choose the winning bid from all proposals offered. The bids were first evaluated according to certain qualifying criteria. The purpose of the qualifying criteria was to weed out those firms which – so the SSAs expected – could not handle the individual programmes successfully. The bids that passed this test were then evaluated according to the bidding criteria.

In the restricted procedure there were two phases: pre-qualification and the contest itself. In the first phase the reintegration firms could show their interest for one or more lots. Based on the qualifying criteria, which were made public, each of the SSAs selected a minimum of five reintegration firms, which were granted the opportunity to make a competitive bid. From these bids each SSA chose the winning bid, based on the bidding criteria.

Two SSAs (GAK and CADANS) used only the open procedure, while GUO, SFB and USZO used only the restricted procedure. Because GAK and CADANS were by far the largest SSAs, this resulted in more than 80 per cent of the competition for the individual programmes being conducted according to the open procedure.

LISV prescribed certain qualifying criteria to the SSAs. These were basically the same as the bidding criteria. The SSAs were free to add more qualifying criteria. In most cases, only very formal criteria were added. GAK, for instance, added several dozen formal criteria. If a bid failed on one of these criteria it was ruled out. In addition GAK also took a very formal stance. If the slightest piece of information was missing from a bid, it could not be added later.

The procedure as implemented by GAK missed the goal it was intended to serve, namely to select the credible bids. It is questionable how far there was a correlation between having one's paperwork in tip-top shape and the credibility of one's bid. We expect that the marginal value of information gained through adding additional criteria diminished quickly. Applying many formal criteria, then, became an inefficient procedure in assessing the credibility of bids. The procedure also carried high administrative costs for bidding firms as well as for GAK.

Other SSAs took a much more relaxed view. Certain omitted items could be added to the file later in the process. The widely differing procedures meant that similar bids were treated in very different ways. These differences were harmful for the transparency of the market. This is illustrated by the fact that more than 80 per cent of firms that did not prequalify believed that the SSAs committed errors in the pre-qualification procedure (Vinke and Cremer, 2001).

The open procedure has the advantage of generating a large number of bids, which in itself enhances competition. With each additional bid the chance of finding a very high quality one increases. The opposite side is that the chance of winning a bid is relatively low for an individual firm, so it makes sense for a bidder not to put too much effort into the bid. This will reduce the quality of the bids made. An additional disadvantage of the open procedure is that the process is much costlier. This applies for both the reintegration firms and the SSAs. The reintegration firms have to make more complete bids than is the case for a restricted process. In addition, for the bids to qualify, all formal requirements have to be fulfilled. This results in an extra administrative burden. The SSAs, in turn, have to examine more bids fully. This also results in higher administrative costs.

All the lots were put up for sale simultaneously. This resulted in a large amount of work to be done in a short period of time by the reintegration firms as well as by the SSAs. One could thus expect a tendency for both bids and evaluations to be quick and dirty, resulting in low-quality bids and low-quality evaluations.

Even though the SSAs explicitly asked for bids for specific sub-lots, the reintegration firms rarely made such offers. Nearly all the bids were for the entire lot. Attempts to show a certain affinity with specific groups of clients within a lot could hardly be discerned from the bids made.[8]

## 2.3    Criteria and score function

The LISV procedure defined five bidding criteria: four quality criteria ('professional qualifications of staff', 'results achieved in the past', 'throughput time' and 'percentage of clients placed in job') and price. The SSAs were not permitted to add extra criteria. However, they were allowed to stipulate the bidding criteria more specifically. Each SSA wrote additional specifications into the bidding criteria. Despite LISV stating that the addition of extra criteria not in line with the criteria set out by LISV was not allowed, GAK and GUO did add one criterion, namely the drop-out rate.

It is highly improbable that the ranking of the bidders on each criterion is the same. Some bidders might offer higher quality, while others might try to compensate for a (somewhat) lower quality with a lower price. Therefore, one needs to have some kind of weighting procedure or score function to come to a decision.

[8] KPMG/BEA (2001).

We now discuss the criteria and the score function in greater detail. We group the criteria into four categories: structural criteria ('professional qualifications of staff' and 'results achieved in the past'), process criteria ('throughput time' and 'drop-out rate'), performance criteria ('placement results') and price.

*Structural criteria*    The criteria 'professional qualifications of staff' and 'results achieved in the past' refer primarily to the reintegration firm which is making the bid. These criteria are signals of quality rather than actual quality. They signal whether or not the reintegration firm can do the job if it wins the bidding competition.

When assessing the structural features the SSAs placed very different weights on 'professional qualifications of staff' and 'results achieved in the past'. According to KPMG/BEA (2001) CADANS put much more value on the professional qualifications of staff, while at the other extreme GAK did not value qualifications at all, and looked only at results achieved in the past. The other three SSAs held intermediate views.

*Process criteria*    The criteria 'throughput time' and 'drop-out rate' provide characterisations of how the firm would handle the reintegration process of its clients in the event of being successful.

The LISV procedure contained no specific definition of the criterion 'throughput time'. Consequently, both the SSAs and the reintegration firms defined it in various ways. Some SSAs and reintegration firms defined throughput time as the entire time between registration of the client and the placement of the client in a paid job, excluding time spent on education and training. For others, however, it related to the waiting time between the various stages of the process. To us the most straightforward definition of throughput time is the length of the period during which the SSA is dealing with the client, i.e. the time it takes to place a client. To say the least, it is remarkable that this criterion was not defined. This makes comparison of bids difficult.

The drop-out rate is the percentage of clients who for some reason leave the programme *prematurely*. Two of the SSAs, GAK and GUO, used this criterion, which was not included in the list specified by LISV. Therefore, GAK and GUO acted against the rules as developed by LISV. It is not clear why this criterion was added. From previous evaluations of labour market programmes we know that participants often leave a programme because they have found a job. This is particularly so in the case of training measures. Therefore, drop-out does not always indicate a problem.

*Performance criteria*   The procedure defines only one performance criterion: the percentage of people placed in a job. LISV defined placement to be the case where the programme results in the client working in paid employment for a period of at least six months. From the supplemental explanation given by LISV it became clear that the definition referred to the signing by a client of an employment contract for that period rather than actually working for that amount of time.

In a bid the reintegration firm had to specify the percentage of clients it believed it would place within one year.[9] The bidder had to state that he could place a minimum of 35 per cent of the clients in paid employment.

*Price*   In the LISV procedure price is defined rather loosely as the price of an average individual programme. In their bids, most bidders simply presented a list of products and services which could be used in the individual programmes of clients. The number and kind of products and services would vary by client. LISV expected the SSAs to make an educated estimate of the quantity and quality of the necessary products and services for the clients in the particular lot. The bidders did not have to quote an average price. They only had to quote price per product and service.

*Score function*   The decision procedure was typical for an unweighted Beauty Contest:

- The score per attribute and the overall score were determined judgmentally. Ratings reflected the subjective views of the awarding authority.
- There was no exact representation of the relationships between the attributes.
- Bidders did not know the exact algorithm used by the awarding authority to calculate the total score.

LISV determined the winner on the basis of the most economic bid. What 'most economic bid' means or how it should be made operational was, however, not prescribed or described. The evaluations also do not make clear how the SSAs tackled this problem. The evaluation by KPMG/BEA (2001) suggests that the SSAs had some sort of weighting for the attributes. From the evaluations, however, it is not clear whether or not the SSAs used weights and, if so, what these weights were. In each case, the bidders did not know them at the time of bidding.

---

[9] The period of one year is counted separately for each individual client. The period starts at the moment that the reintegration programme of an individual has been approved by the SSA. Also the period does not include time spent on educational activities.

## 2.4     Bidding

*The format*     The format of the competition was a simultaneous sealed-bid type. In this format each bidder places only one bid. The bidders present their bids in sealed envelopes, which are opened publicly at a pre-specified time by the awarding authority. The bid includes offers on both quality and price. The winning bidder is obliged to supply the services at the offered level of quality and price.

In general, the more information that is provided in the bidding competition, the more transparent is the contest and the better informed the bids which can be made. A disadvantage of the simultaneous sealed-bid format is that it precludes bidders learning from one another.[10] Bidders have no information on other bidders' estimates of the value of a particular lot. This can give rise to the so-called winner's curse. The winning bidder is the unfortunate one who, out of ignorance, underestimates the costs of the lot. In order to decrease the possibility of making a loss on a particular lot, bidders will adjust their quality bids downwards and their price bids upwards.[11]

If bidders are inexperienced, they may be less likely to correct for the winner's curse, and this may yield a high-quality and low-price bid. An additional reason why inexperienced bidders may offer high quality and low price is that newcomers have little experience to show of working in the area of reintegration. Working experience is one of the criteria on which the bids are judged. In order to make competitive bids, newcomers will have to compete particularly on quality criteria other than working experience and on price.

However, an internal note within the Dutch Ministry of Social Affairs and Employment suggests that bidders were quite well informed about the prices of their competitors. It says that the smaller reintegration firms were simply following the price set by the market leaders, that is the former public reintegration firms. Therefore, the problem of the winner's curse might not have been so important in this case. If the Ministry's note is right, we might doubt whether price played an important role in the procedure at all.

*Other possible formats*     The only format used by the SSAs was the simultaneous sealed-bid format. Alternatives, such as the sequential format, may be possible. In this format, a quality bid is made first and

[10] In the restricted procedure the SSA makes a short list of bidders. If the awarding authority informs the bidders which firms have been shortlisted, this can be of some aid to the bidders. They at least know against whom they are bidding. In the open procedure this information is lacking.

[11] A lower-quality bid implies a lower placement rate, a higher throughput time and a higher drop-out rate.

then, in a second stage, a price bid is made. The second stage can be conducted in two ways: as a one-off financial bid or following a procedure in which sequentially higher price bids can be placed. The version with the one-off financial bid resembles a sealed-bid auction with a bid handicap, while that with the sequentially higher price bids resembles an English auction with a bid handicap. In both versions, one's quality score in relation to the highest quality score bid determines the bid handicap.

The main advantage of these formats is that they provide much more information to the bidders. Besides knowing which parties are partaking in the bidding, the bidders also know how the others have scored on the quality dimension. This knowledge can be used in the financial bid. An additional advantage is that these formats should reduce the risk of the winner's curse arising. In comparison to the simultaneous sealed-bid format, this will lead to higher quality and lower prices being bid for the individual programmes.

An advantage of sealed-bid formats over open-bid formats is that sealed-bid formats are generally considered less prone to collusion among bidders. A bidder's defection from a collusive agreement (that is the submission of a bid with a higher quality and/or a lower price than in the collusive agreement) is harder for other bidders to prevent in a closed format than in an open bidding system. The risk of collusion arising is probably quite low. The reason is the sheer number of lots (several hundred) put on the market, in combination with the large number of bidders. This combination makes it highly unlikely that stable collusive agreements will come about. In the case where the open tender procedure is used the likelihood of collusion occurring will be even smaller than when the restricted procedure is used, owing to the larger number of bidders per lot.

A possible disadvantage of sequential formats in comparison to the simultaneous one is the costs involved. The costs of conducting the sequential open format for both the SSA and the reintegration firm are likely to be higher than the costs of using the simultaneous format. The costs of the simultaneous sealed-bid format and the sequential sealed-bid format will presumably not differ greatly. For some bidders the sequential format may, in fact be cost-saving. When informed of the quality scores of their competitors they might quickly make the decision to opt out and not make a price bid.

### 2.5    *Evaluation of the design*

The various quality criteria are very different by nature. The structural criteria relate to the supplier and only indirectly to the product or service, while the performance criteria relate directly to the product. Put differently, structural features are means by which a goal can be achieved. It is the performance, one could argue, that matters. However, it is also important to assess whether the promised performance is credible. If one bidder promises better outcomes than a second, but the latter seems to be more reliable on the basis of its experience and track record, one might choose the more reliable candidate.

However, if too much weight were put on structural features, new-comers would stand no chance. The very purpose of the procurement procedure is to increase competition by offering new providers a chance. From this perspective it is odd that the largest SSA, GAK, put so much emphasis on previous results achieved by reintegration firms. This effec-tively shut out newcomers. The CADANS approach, which focused more on the experience of a reintegration firm's staff, seems to have been more reasonable. Newcomers can, and in fact did, attract experienced staff from former public and private providers. Therefore, the last-mentioned approach seems to offer the best compromise between, on the one hand, introducing effective competition, and, on the other, ensuring that a win-ning firm has the capacity to operate successfully.

The fact that competition was only increased to a limited extent was one drawback of the design used. A second drawback was unclear definitions of criteria. Particularly unclear is what was meant by throughput time. As to the placement results, a minimum figure of 35 per cent within one year was required. However, this figure seems to be extremely low. In the case of unemployed people, even clients who do not take part in a reintegration programme have a higher chance of finding a job.[12] Therefore, the minimum percentage of 35 does not mean a lot. The third drawback was that it was unclear how the SSAs weighted the scores on the various criteria.

There were also weak points in the implementation of the procedure. First, in the rules that LISV developed, the qualifying and bidding criteria were mixed up. SSAs could add qualifying criteria to the ones prescribed by LISV, but in practice only formal ones were added. The largest SSA did this to the extent that formal qualifying criteria received more weight than bidding criteria.

A second weak point in the implementation was the fact that with a few exceptions the lots were defined for heterogeneous groups of clients, such as 'the unemployed' or 'the disabled'. It was therefore not possible to make finely tuned bids for niche markets. With these heterogeneous lots

---

[12] An evaluation of measures co-funded under the European Social Fund (ESF) reveals that in the period 1997–8 placement rates were 50 per cent or higher (de Koning *et al.*, 1999). It should be noted that in the years following 1998 the labour market improved further.

the risk of cherry-picking seems to have been real. Making pay dependent on placement results might have reduced this risk, but the contracts contained few, if any, such incentives for the reintegration firms. The more heterogeneous the content of a lot, the greater was the uncertainty of the bidder about the value of the lot. In order to avoid the winner's curse, a reintegration firm would bid lower on quality and higher on price. As a result, bids might actually yield a lower quality and higher price, and thus higher costs for the SSAs, than if relatively homogeneous lots were offered for sale.

All in all we are bound to conclude that the Beauty Contest design and implementation had serious flaws.

## 3    Results

### 3.1    Outcome of the bidding process

*Professional qualifications of staff*   Whether or not a certain affinity with a specific sub-group of clients could be shown barely influenced the final score in the bid assessment of four of the five SSAs (all but GUO). This point was never set out as an explicit criterion. The professional qualifications of staff or results achieved in the past were raised in a few instances. These minor points were, however, insufficient for a bidder to distinguish himself clearly from a competitor on these grounds. An innovative niche player thus had little opportunity to identify himself as such. This made it difficult to achieve the objective of increasing the number of innovative niche players.

*Eliciting information*   The SSAs put several hundred lots up for sale. This should have given them ample opportunity to acquire information from the bids. This kind of information increases the transparency of the market, and SSAs obtain more insight into the costs of integration services for various types of client. However, because the contents of the individual lots were very heterogeneous and ill-defined it was difficult to compare bids between lots. Bids could then only be compared one lot at a time. This limited the amount of information that could be elicited from the bids. More information could have been elicited from the bids if the lots had been defined more tightly and made more homogeneous. With more closely defined product combinations the costs for each such combination would have become better known. Instead of being a rich data source, the large number of lots then became a costly, low information affair. The poor definition of the lots was thus a missed opportunity for increasing the transparency of the market.

*Fallacious comparisons*   The procedure is rigged against firms specialising in difficult market segments, i.e. with clients who are difficult to place. The results for these difficult market segments are low while the costs are high. When these offers are compared to other bids, which involve a mix of easy and difficult groups of clients, and these different mixes are not allowed for by the evaluator, the bids of specialised firms will be turned down. Taken at face value the results of the specialised firms are worse while their price is higher. This is obviously a fallacious comparison.

*Lack of a quality specification*   The absence of a quality specification results in cherry-picking. Since the reintegration firms are accountable on an overall percentage of all individual programmes within a lot, it makes sense from a cost perspective if reintegration firms devote as little effort as possible to the high-cost individual programmes. As little as possible may be a minimum specified in the contract or it can be some self-imposed minimum which makes them credible to the SSAs.

*Difficulties for entrants*   It can be easily argued that entrants to this market for reintegration services have less information about which groups are more difficult and which are relatively easy to reintegrate into the labour market. Incumbents have more experience in this respect. This makes it easier for incumbents to pick the cherries than for entrants. Accordingly, newcomers tend to have higher prices, so that innovation does not come about so easily.

*Tackling cherry-picking*   The present approach to cherry-picking is by means of regulation and monitoring. A simpler approach would be to ensure that cherry-picking simply could not happen. This is the case for perfectly homogeneous groups: in homogeneous groups there simply are no cherries to be picked; all group members are identical. Of course, some degree of heterogeneity will always exist within a group. In forming lots on which bids can be made, it is essential to strive for clients having the same background characteristics. These could be, for example, education, age, sex, profession, physical handicap or psychological handicap. In order to achieve homogeneity it may be necessary to form small groups. The question, of course, is whether it is possible to identify and measure all the relevant factors that determine job chances. We come back to this point in section 5.

## 3.2    *Market outcomes*

Until 1998 GAK-Labour Market Integration (GAK-LMI, a branch of GAK) conducted the reintegration of disabled people with a new employer. In 1998 GAK-LMI was separated from GAK and placed within the PES. The SSAs were compelled to buy a minimum of 80 per cent of the individual programmes from the PES. The other programmes could be bought from private reintegration firms.

We do not know the exact market shares in 1999 of each reintegration firm. It is nevertheless obvious that major shifts in shares have taken place. A few years ago, KLIQ, which then was part of the PES, was virtually a monopolist. Its drop in market share continued in 2000. The other formerly public reintegration firms Argonaut (ex-GAK) and ABP witnessed increasing market shares in 2000. Most of the firms operating in the market in 1999 won a number of individual programmes in 2000.

In total, 36 per cent of programmes were contracted to the formerly public reintegration firms. The degree to which SSAs contracted programmes to the formerly public reintegration firms varied from 10 per cent for CADANS to 57 per cent for USZO.

The fear that reintegration firms which were formerly part of the SSAs would be favoured was partly justified. In the case of GAK, USZO and GUO the reintegration firms receiving the largest number of individual programmes were the former partners (Argonaut, ABP Reïntegratie and Relan respectively). SFB and CADANS did not allocate programmes to their former partners.

Remarkable newcomers were Alexander Calder, Serin, Fourstar and Creyfs Interim. CADANS, by a long way, contracted the most newcomers, which is not surprising given the fact that this SSA attached little weight to past results.

## 4    **Beauty Contests, auctions and quality measurement**

### 4.1    *Would an auction have given better results?*

The purpose of outsourcing placement activities to private agencies is to improve the efficiency of the services or to raise their quality, or to achieve both of these improvements. Although we lack information on the impact of the procurement procedure on the effectiveness and the efficiency of reintegration services, the previous sections make it at least improbable that such improvements occurred. We have pointed to a number of weaknesses both in the design of the procurement procedure and in the way it was implemented. This leads to the question of whether making use of an auction instead of a Beauty Contest could have prevented these problems.

The main difference between an auction and a Beauty Contest is that, in the former case, quality is taken as given and the bidding is solely on price, while in the latter case both quality and price determine the choice made by the contracting agency. In the case of an auction, bidders should fulfil two requirements:

• they should guarantee that the quality of the services exceeds the minimum level as specified by the contracting party;
• their staff should be sufficiently experienced to make their bid credible.

The contract could then be given to the bidder with the lowest price. Such a procedure seems to be much more simple and transparent. One does not need a score function. However, on a closer look, things are not that easy. The problem lies in ensuring a minimum service quality level. As we will show now, it appears to be extremely difficult to measure quality in the field of reintegration services.

### 4.2    *What is quality in relation to reintegration services?*

The purpose of reintegration services is to increase the transition rate from inactivity to employment for the target groups of these services. In the Netherlands, the target groups for these services are the disabled, the long-term unemployed and the short-term unemployed at high risk of long-term unemployment. What is aimed at is a positive *net* effect, the difference between the transition rates with and without the services. We know that even without the provision of the services at least some people from the target groups would find a job.[13] Therefore, reintegration services must be judged on their net effectiveness; placement figures as such are meaningless.

We know quite a lot about the net effectiveness of reintegration services or measures. It has been investigated in many studies covering many countries. From a methodological point of view, two types of studies can be distinguished. The first type tries to assess the impact of reintegration by estimating econometric models using aggregate data. A summary of the literature can be found in de Koning (2001). The second type uses a control-group design based on micro data. For this part of the literature

---

[13] Particularly in the United States, experiments have been conducted in which a measure is applied to a randomly selected group of unemployed participants, which is then compared to a control group (also randomly selected) of unemployed non-participants. Invariably we observe that a considerable percentage of the latter group also finds a job. For further reading we refer to Heckman, Lalonde and Smith (1999).

we refer to Heckman, Lalonde and Smith (1999). In both cases, the overall conclusion is that the net impact of reintegration measures is small. In some cases, participation in a programme appears to prolong unemployment rather than shortening it. The net effects on job entry chances tend to be higher for disadvantaged groups such as the long-term unemployed, but even here the average impacts found are of limited size and the variation in the effects considerable.

The design of the procurement procedure discussed in the previous sections does not give any guarantee of positive net effects. The only requirement in terms of placement results is that reintegration firms must place at least 35 per cent of the clients handed over to them. A recent report by UWV, the organisation into which both LISV and the SSAs merged, states that the realised placement figure will not differ much from the required 35 per cent. We have already pointed out that these results are poor in comparison to previous evaluations of similar measures. Apparently, reintegration firms devote just enough effort to realise the minimum requirements, an approach which could be expected of private, profit-maximising agencies.

### 4.3    How could we get a reasonable chance of positive net effects?[14]

How should the procedure be altered in order to get a reasonable chance of positive net effects? What we need is a good estimate of the job chances that the clients would have had without the benefit of reintegration services. On the basis of data from the recent past, such estimates could be made. Separate estimates could be made for different groups of clients, taking account of the fact that job chances depend strongly on characteristics such as age, gender, education, ethnic origin and handicap. From this information, sensible minimum requirements could be derived for each group of clients. For each group, treatment should result in job chances that are as least as good as in the case without treatment. Surely, on average, these would be considerably higher than 35 per cent. Such a procedure would acknowledge that for particularly disadvantaged groups, placement figures less than 35 per cent may already be satisfactory, while in other (presumably most) cases much higher placement figures should be expected. So far, client heterogeneity with respect to the previously mentioned characteristics has not been taken into account at all in the procurement procedure.

Although the individual characteristics mentioned account for some of the variation between individual unemployment spells, a considerable

---

[14] Partly based on de Koning and van Acht (2000).

part remains unexplained by them. Probably, psychological factors and other factors that are difficult to measure are also important determinants of the length of unemployment. To some extent the latter factors are taken into account in the profiling procedure conducted by the employment offices. On the basis of this procedure, which is mainly qualitative in nature, a decision is taken on which new unemployed clients should be sent to the SSAs. However, nothing is known about the validity of the risk assessment made by the employment offices. It would be better if the risk assessment was made on the basis of a statistically validated model including a whole range of factors varying from age and education to psychological factors.

Estimates of job chances can only be made on the basis of data from the (recent) past. However, after the contracts with the reintegration firms have been made, the labour market situation may change. It is possible to include contingency arrangements in the contract to deal with this problem. On the basis of past data the job chances can also be related to the general labour market situation. Then, the contracts made with the reintegration firms might include rules on how the minimum requirements regarding job chances are to be adjusted with the state of the labour market.

If we altered the system in this way, we would still leave it to the SSAs to decide which services to provide for a specific group of clients. Quality would be better ensured if we knew in advance which services are most effective for a given group of clients. Then, the SSAs could prescribe to the reintegration firms which services should be used. In that case an auction would become possible in which the reintegration firms would bid only on the basis of price. The question is: how can the SSAs find out what is best? In principle, an experiment could provide the information needed. In the United States, several examples of such experiments can be found in the field of reintegration measures. In such an experiment, a group of participants and a control group are randomly selected from the target group. Specific services (training, for example) are provided to the participants and not to the control group. Then, both groups are monitored for a sufficiently long period to see whether the participants have higher job entry rates than the controls. If needed, several types of service could be tested for several groups. On the basis of the outcomes, a decision could be taken on which types of service are most appropriate for the various groups. Furthermore, the experiment would also indicate the expected placement rates, which could then serve as the minimum requirements in the bidding process. A disadvantage of SSAs prescribing the types of services may be that there are then few possibilities for reintegration firms to develop new products.

So far, experiments in the field of labour market policy involving random assignment have not been applied in the Netherlands. The most important reason seems to be that it is legally impossible to exclude individuals from participation. So, we would have to choose the control group from the ones that did not wish to participate in a reintegration programme or are not selected for participation by the authorities. However, this would most likely be a non-random group, making the comparison with the participants difficult if not impossible. Although methods have been developed to deal with this type of selectivity, these are far from reliable. A second reason for not conducting an experiment is that it takes too much time. Although both arguments against conducting experiments do not seem convincing to us, they do seem to be so to the authorities. Thus, the approach mentioned earlier could be a reasonable alternative.

### 4.4    *Assessing quality* ex post

For several reasons it is important to make an *ex post* evaluation of service delivery. First, even if – from an experiment – an *ex ante* estimate of the net effectiveness was available, the *ex post* results could differ from it. Second, *ex post* placement figures are at least needed to determine whether reintegration firms have fulfilled the placement criterion. Such information is also important for future tendering procedures in which credibility will probably be one of the criteria. And last but not least, an *ex post* evaluation may throw light on different implementation strategies as used by the various reintegration firms. Information about which strategies lead to the best results may contribute to the overall effectiveness of the reintegration services. The Ministry of Social Affairs and Employment is considering offering a contract for such a study. In principle, for each contract between an SSA and a reintegration firm, information on costs, service content, number and characteristics of clients and placement results is available. A comparative analysis based on this data seems to be highly relevant. We do not know, however, whether the available data is adequate for a solid analysis.

The available information makes it possible to compare the results of the various service providers. It is also important to compare the job entry rates of the clients of the reintegration firms with those of unemployed and disabled persons who were not clients. Such a comparison would give us an *ex post* estimate of the net placement effects. We do not know, however, whether it is possible to form such a comparison group and whether sufficient data is available. Clearly, the authorities did not envisage such an analysis.

# 5     Summary

## 5.1     Conclusions

A few years ago the Dutch government decided to outsource the delivery of reintegration services for the unemployed and the disabled to private agencies on the basis of a tendering procedure. The government's expectations were that by introducing competition the effectiveness and the efficiency of the services would be enhanced. On the basis of the available information, however, it seems unlikely that this goal has indeed been achieved.

Particularly unsatisfactory are the minimum requirements which were set regarding the job entry rates of the clients. The reintegration firms had to guarantee that at least 35 per cent of their clients would be placed in the labour market. However, as an average score this is very low. It is likely that the same or even a higher percentage of the clients involved would have found a job without participating in a reintegration programme. Recent information about the actual placement figures indicates that these will probably not be much higher than the required 35 per cent.

The lots were in general heterogeneous, which makes the transparency for bidders, with regard to what they are exactly bidding on, low. Because lots are heterogeneous, little can be learned about the costs of different types of clients and whether it is cost-efficient to specialise in certain client groups rather than adopting a non-specialist approach. The procurement design offers a lot of opportunities to reintegration firms for cherry-picking, or 'creaming' as it is usually called in the evaluation literature on active labour market policies. One might fear that under the present conditions the outsourcing of reintegration services to private companies has led to *lower* chances for the most disadvantaged clients. Investigating this point should be an important aspect of an *ex post* evaluation of the procurement procedure.

The criteria used by the SSAs to evaluate the bids as well as the weights attached to the criteria were unclear. We do not know to what extent the SSAs used a structured decision-making procedure. In any case the reintegration firms were not informed about it. In the hypothetical case that the same group of firms is bidding on two identical lots offered by two SSAs, there is no guarantee that the same firm will win both lots. For a contest to be efficient this is essential.

In addition to obscuring the market rather than making it transparent, the procedure also leads to unnecessary costs for bidders. SSAs used different procedures and criteria and bidders had to fine-tune their bids to each separate SSA. Even for identical lots, bidders would have to provide different bids to different SSAs. In certain cases, bidders were asked for information with very low relevance to the Beauty Contest.

All in all we conclude that instead of enhancing transparency the procedure chosen obscured the market. It is difficult to imagine how the procedure could have contributed to a more effective and efficient delivery of reintegration services. What is also disappointing is that little thought was given to the possibilities of learning from the new procedure. The awarding authorities did not make the necessary preparations for an *ex post* evaluation that would throw light on the net effectiveness of the service provision. Although a study comparing content, quality and costs of the various service providers is envisaged, the available information may not be sufficient to come to reliable conclusions.

### 5.2    Recommendations

In this subsection we make a number of recommendations to improve the procurement of reintegration services. Before we do that it is important to note that in the mean time the SSAs and LISV have merged into one organisation, UWV. Therefore, in the future we can expect that one standard procurement procedure will be used, which will solve some of the problems identified in this chapter.

In our view a restricted procedure must be preferred. Such a procedure consists of two stages: a qualifying stage and a bidding stage. It is important that the awarding authority, UWV, defines quality as precisely as possible. In order to do that it should make an *ex ante* assessment of the job chances of the various client groups. On the basis of such an assessment, requirements regarding placement results could be set that would give a reasonable guarantee of positive net effects of the reintegration services. Bidders should, of course, be informed about the outcome of this assessment. Although it might be envisaged that bidding would then focus completely on price (in which case we would have an auction), we tend to prefer a Beauty Contest in which quality and price both determine the outcome. The reason for that is that by taking quality into consideration, reintegration firms would be stimulated to innovate in their provision of services. In view of the generally disappointing results of activation and reintegration services, there is a need for such innovation.

The question of credibility should be considered fully in the qualifying stage and should then be left to rest. The criteria used in the qualifying stage should be such that newcomers are not excluded almost by definition. The procedure should result in a sufficient number of competitors (say, five to seven) for each lot.

It is important that the awarding authority makes arrangements from the outset for the collection of the necessary data for an *ex post* evaluation. This evaluation should provide information on the net placement results and the performance of the various service providers, and on the variation in quality and implementation strategies (as determining factors of the placement results).

Clearly, a satisfactory design and implementation of a procurement procedure in the field of reintegration services is highly demanding for the awarding authority. It would be sensible to make use of external expertise on procurement and evaluation. However, the question remains of whether the awarding authority itself has sufficient incentive to get the best possible result out of the procurement procedure. This is at least unclear. The incentive structure would be clearer if the delivery of both benefits and reintegration services were outsourced to private companies. The role of the government could then be restricted to developing sets of rules, such as the entitlement criteria for a benefit. In the United States, examples of such a system can be found. However, the question is whether in such a system reasonable guarantees can be given that sufficient effort is made to help the most disadvantaged groups. In theory such a system may work, but in practice this will depend importantly on how the government manages the process. On the basis of past experiences, high hopes are not justified here.

A final observation is that in the Dutch situation there seems to be no room for clients to choose between service providers. In Australia, where public employment services have also been privatised, this freedom of choice is a cornerstone of the system. The Australian system is a licence system in which service providers have to meet certain criteria in order to get a licence for service provision. The government determines to what type of reintegration service each unemployed person is entitled. The client can then choose between the different providers. Payment is based partly on placement results. In this system, providers really have to compete for clients. In principle such a system could be combined with an auction for the licences. The problem of quality or impact measurement is also present here, however.

## References

Algemene Rekenkamer 2001, 'Reïntegratie arbeidsongeschikten' (Reintegration of incapacitated workers), Tweede Kamer der Staten-Generaal, Vergaderjaar 2001–2, 28131, Nr 2.

Cordia, L., A. Lucas, M. Buurman and E. Kruisbergen 2001, 'De kunst van het aanbesteden. Onderzoek naar werking van de aanbestedingsprocedure bij inkoop van reïntegratieactiviteiten' (The art of tendering. Research into the proceedings of the tendering procedure for the purchase of reintegration activities), CTSV, Zoetermeer.

Dercksen, W. and J. de Koning 1995, 'The new public employment services in the Netherlands (1991–1994)', WZB Discussion Paper, Berlin.

Fermin, B. 2001, 'Evaluatie aanbestedingsprocedure reïntegratiecontracten: rol sectorraden in de aanbestedingsprocedure' (Evaluation of the tendering procedure for reintegration contracts: the role of sector councils in the tendering procedure), TNO-rapport 5441/2510106, TNO Arbeid, Hoofddorp.

Haan, H.F. de (ed.) 2001a, 'Evaluatie Aanbestedingsprocedure Reïntegratiecontracten: Zelfevaluatie LISV, Juridische aspecten' (Evaluation of the tendering procedure for reintegration contracts: self evaluation LISV, legal aspects), TNO-rapport 5441/2510106, TNO Arbeid, Hoofddorp.

Haan, H.F. de 2001b, 'Evaluatie Aanbestedingsprocedure Reïntegratiecontracten: De rol van de SSAs' (Evaluation of the tendering procedure for reintegration contracts: the role of the SSAs), TNO-rapport 5441/2510106, TNO Arbeid, Hoofddorp.

Heckman, J., R. Lalonde and J.A. Smith (1999), The economics and econometrics of active labour market programs, in O. Ashenfelter and D. Card (eds.), *Handbook of Labour Economics*, vol. 34, Elsevier, Amsterdam.

Koning, J. de (2001), Aggregate impact analysis of active labour market policy: a literature review, *International Journal of Manpower* 22: 707–35.

Koning, J. de, and J. van Acht 2000, *De rol van incentives, marktwerking en regelgeving in de sociale zekerheid* (The role of incentives, competition and regulation in social security), SEOR bv, Rotterdam.

Koning, J de, J. Gravesteijn-Ligthelm, K. Jonker, R. Olieman and C. van der Veen, 1999, 'Tweede monitoring en interim evaluatie van het ESF-programma voor doelstelling 3' (Second monitoring and interim evaluation of the ESF programme for objective 3), NEI, Rotterdam.

KPMG/BEA 2001, 'Evaluatie Aanbestedingsprocedure, deel 2 Eindrapport, LISV' (Evaluation of the tendering procedure, Part 2 Final Report, LISV), Hoofddorp.

Vinke, H. and R. Cremer 2001, 'Evaluatie aanbestedingsprocedure. Ervaringen van reïntegratiebedrijven en hun branche-organisaties' (Evaluation of the tendering procedure. Experiences of reintegration companies and their branch organisations), TNO-rapport 5441/2510106, TNO Arbeid, Hoofddorp.

# 12 The provision of rail services

*Luisa Affuso and David Newbery*

## 1 Introduction

The main feature of the rail industry is that, unlike most other industries that were successfully privatised, it relies on government funding. Few (if any) enhancement projects can be funded on a purely commercial basis without public subsidies. Does this imply that auctions are not suited for rail capacity? What are the characteristics of this network that make auctions a mechanism for which the advantages are very unclear?

'Competition for the market' is the only model that has been tried for rail privatisation around the world. Franchises of vertically separated operations were adopted in Britain and concessions for vertically integrated operations was the adopted option in many countries in America and Africa (Thompson, Budin and Estache, 2001). Although many of these contracts were awarded on the basis of competitive tenders, these were typically administrative processes of a Beauty Contest type rather than proper auctions.

The allocation of contracts for rail service operation is an extremely complex and controversial process because of the particular economic characteristics of the industry. Railway infrastructure and rolling stock are long-lived assets. Perhaps more importantly, they are sunk to a large extent since most of the capital equipment is highly specific. The number of alternative uses (or routes for the rolling stock) to which assets could be redeployed may be quite small and in some instances non-existent. This gives railways particular features which are not present in other transport sectors, such as bus or air transport, where outside markets exist for secondhand assets, and auction mechanisms can more easily be adopted. Furthermore, scale and scope economies are pervasive in the railway industry (integrated railways experience large economies from traffic density). Another key feature of this industry is the high degree of interdependency among its different components, which gives rise to numerous externalities (e.g. delays and congestion on the track), technical complementarities (e.g. interdependencies between infrastructure and rolling stock) and potential conflicts in the allocation of scarce capacity among slow freight trains, commuter services and fast long-distance passenger services. These technical and economic complexities can be taken into account in a vertically integrated structure. When the industry is vertically separated, however, accounting for these factors becomes much more difficult. Contracts between firms could to some extent internalise some of these externalities, but this would entail large monitoring and enforcement costs.[1] The transaction costs involved might offset any expected gain from vertical separation and from the competitive tendering of rail service operations.

The aim of railway restructuring is to provide appropriate incentives for investment in railway infrastructure and rolling stock, as well as product innovation, while reducing the budgetary burden on the public sector. That raises the question of how best to design and allocate contracts to achieve these objectives. Solving this major problem is seen as critical to achieving an efficient transport system, but is anything but straightforward. Given the technical and economic characteristics of the railway track, auctioning individual train paths to service operators would still require a high degree of government regulation, not to mention considerable cost. Auctions or Beauty Contests for allocating franchises or concessions of rail service operations appear more practical, while allowing room for some degree of political manoeuvring. Slot (or train path) auctions remain as yet an untried mechanism in this industry.

This chapter discusses the experience of allocating rail franchises and concessions in several countries. Section 2 examines the railway systems resulting from the reforms implemented in Sweden, Argentina and Britain. Section 3 discusses in more detail the mechanism adopted for the allocation of rail passenger franchises in Britain and in other countries. Finally, section 4 draws conclusions.

## 2    Different models of rail restructuring

### 2.1    The Swedish and the Argentinian models

Railway restructuring experience across the world has provided two alternative viable models: the Swedish model of vertical separation and the Argentinian model of geographically separated integrated companies. The Swedish model relies on vertical separation of infrastructure

---

[1] In Britain, delays must first be attributed either to Railtrack or another train operating company, and then those at fault pay those affected. Identifying the causes of delay requires a considerable workforce. Similarly, trading track access to make better use of scarce timetabling slots is both slow and costly.

ownership and service operation. The approach adopted in Sweden was to retain track in public ownership and offer trains access priced at marginal cost, with the considerable fixed costs paid by a government deficit grant. The idea is that passenger services can be competitively provided at a profit by the private sector. Furthermore, the charges regime for railways mirrors road vehicle taxation arrangements in order to harmonise competition between these two transport modes.[2] The Argentinian model, instead, relies on a rail network divided geographically line-by-line into a series of vertically integrated exclusive franchise units. In this model the subsidy is injected through the franchising mechanism.

Each model has distinctive virtues and drawbacks. The Swedish model emphasises allocative efficiency. It also has the merit of addressing the problems of inter-modal competition between road and rail and of facilitating intra-modal competition in the provision of rail service by the private sector. The Argentinian model, on the other hand, promotes cost efficiency through the periodic competition process. By restricting rail competition it makes a surplus available to franchisees, thereby minimising the subsidy bill. Furthermore, by retaining a vertically integrated structure it avoids the cost burden of internalising externalities by the contract mechanism. The British system has adopted a mixture of features from both vertically and geographically separated models.

## 2.2    *The new industry structure in Britain*

The British restructuring took the important step of separating the ownership of railway infrastructure from the operation of train services. EU countries have to respond to the 1991 Directive 91/440/EEC of the European Commission, which requires Member States to separate operations from infrastructure and to provide infrastructure access to operators from other countries. This was intended to encourage non-discriminatory access to foreign rail service providers and hence unify the European railway market. It does not require ownership separation, or even privatisation.

In Britain, the decision to separate service operation from infrastructure was dictated by the need to separate the natural monopoly element (track) from the potentially competitive elements (service operation) in order to introduce competitive forces into the industry where possible.

Passenger train operations were separated into franchises lasting from five to fifteen years, with the majority of franchises lasting for seven. Operations to be franchised were set up as separate companies with their

---

[2] In practice, local authorities can subsidise unprofitable routes, and choose the most cost-effective allocation of funds between bus and rail transport (Baumstark, 2001).

own staff, assets and supporting contracts, and were then offered to open tenders. The loss-making franchises running services under public service obligation were awarded on the basis of a least subsidy payment required while the profitable franchises were allocated to the highest bid. The payment profile consisted of a schedule including a price for each year of operation. Tight restrictions were incorporated into the franchise specifications, as it was feared that the loss-making nature of many franchises would mean that franchisees would resort to lowering the quality of service or increasing fares to improve profitability. Franchisees were required to conform to punctuality, cancellation and crowding requirements, and to participate in certain inter-operator agreements. These conditions were enforced by a financial penalty or by the threat of the removal of the franchise itself. Restrictions were made even tighter by constraining certain fares to rise by no more than the Retail Price Index (RPI) for a three-year period and then by RPI − 1 per cent thereafter.

In order to facilitate competitive entry into service operation, Train Operating Companies (TOCs) were prevented from owning their rolling stock.[3] Three rolling stock leasing companies (ROSCOs) were created. These companies owned and leased out passenger locomotives and rolling stock to franchisees. Leases were determined on purely commercial terms, making the ROSCOs profitable in their own right. This arrangement reduces the risk of short-term franchises and makes it possible to transfer the franchise to a new TOC at the end of the franchise, as the original operator would then relinquish its leases and be left with no sunk assets.

The privatisation of the monopolistic network owner, Railtrack, required the introduction of a rail regulator. The Office of the Rail Regulator (ORR) was given the responsibility for regulating Railtrack's charges for track access, preventing abuse of its dominant position and approving access agreements.

The Office of Passenger Rail Franchising (OPRAF), later reformed to become the Strategic Rail Authority (SRA), was set up to award passenger service franchises, to determine the minimum service and quality standards to be met by franchisees, and to allocate and pay subsidies to franchise operators.

The approach taken in Britain of retaining the national infrastructure, as a single entity but separating it from train operations is based on the assumption that competition in rail services is best facilitated by franchises competing to run train operations on that infrastructure, given that many

---

[3] In order to acquire a fleet of new tilting trains, Virgin Rail had to set up a separate company (GL Railease).

franchisees share the same infrastructure. If one of these franchisees also owned the infrastructure this could give rise to problems of market foreclosure, especially in view of the introduction of open access competition as originally planned. Giving a train operator the ownership of the infrastructure upon which he operated might prevent the development of competition either on the track or for other operators who need access to some part of the track. The franchisee as owner of the infrastructure would also be responsible for carrying out long-term investment in the tracks. This would be at odds with the need to periodically re-tender the franchise.

## 3     The experience of allocating rail franchises in different countries

### 3.1     *Franchise allocation in Britain*

Separation of the infrastructure from service operation is not sufficient to guarantee competition in the rail industry. In Britain twenty-five franchises were created, roughly corresponding to the different profit centres in the former British Rail system (e.g. regional, intercity). These franchises were allocated by a mixture of competitive bidding and Beauty Contest in three main tranches between 1994 and 1997.

In general terms, franchising involves the granting of a licence, usually to the winner of a competitive bidding process, to operate a defined service and to receive associated revenues. Typically franchises are introduced in natural monopoly situations, where competition *for* the market constitutes an alternative to the unviable competition *in* the market. In other words, franchising may be the only means of introducing competitive pressures, by creating an incentive to reduce costs and improve quality, and the periodic refranchising process is intended to ensure that such pressures are maintained over time.

None the less, exclusive franchises are in some instances also adopted for operations that are not natural monopolies. For example, in the case of railways, the government can adopt exclusive franchises in order to maximise the proceeds from privatisation. In the British example the exclusivity was limited only to an initial short period, and open-access competition was to be introduced gradually from 1999, to be completed by 2002. The original time-limited exclusivity was believed necessary in order not to depress interest from the private sector and their potential bids.

When it was decided to restructure the railway industry, the original idea was to allocate rail service operation by a second-price sealed-bid

Vickrey auction where each operator would submit a bid for a timetable. All the bids would then be combined and the timetable with the highest overall value would be chosen. The winners would then pay the second highest price. This option however was regarded as too complex and it was therefore rejected in favour of a simpler competitive system.

The twenty-five franchises tendered are very heterogeneous. Some of them are profitable, while some have to be subsidsed. The bidders compete on 'minimum subsidy requested' or 'maximum payment offered' for running the bundle of services included in the franchise. It was thought that franchise bidding would guarantee that the subsidised franchises would be given at the lowest subsidy, while the profitable franchises could raise the highest returns for the government. The approach adopted in Britain included pre-qualifying discussions during which OPRAF discussed the bids with all potential bidders. Potential bidders had to supply a bid including a price schedule for each year of operation, and could also suggest some investment plans additional to those required, if any, by the conditions of the franchise to be awarded. As a result, very heterogeneous bids were received. The franchise agency, OPRAF, did not have clear information on the value to be expected from these franchises, nor did it announce any method by which it intended to compare the different dimensions of the bids, and specifically how quality enhancements would be balanced against higher subsidies required/lower payments offered. In that sense the resulting allocation was arguably more like a Beauty Contest than a simple auction, although clearly the subsidy element of the bid played a very important role.

The winning bids often did not seem to reflect the underlying economics of the operations. Some bids were over-optimistic, and led to early renegotiation, while some are believed to have generated very high returns to the bidders. The latter was especially the case on account of unpredicted increase in demand of about 30 per cent since privatisation.

Since franchise arrangements are contractual, they involve the need for a certain degree of monitoring to ensure compliance. Franchisees assume – to varying degrees – the risks associated with unanticipated events on both the revenue and the cost sides. As a result, a number of franchise renegotiations have occurred, especially in cases where the services provided by the franchisees were of public/strategic interest and thus gave the franchisee a strong bargaining position with the government to obtain better conditions. Hence the Strategic Rail Authority (SRA), which succeeded OPRAF, entered a phase of contract 'replacement' (basically, renegotiation with a more neutral name) with the aim of changing some contractual conditions. The entire replacement plan is reported by the SRA website.[4] The franchisees typically requested that franchises should be extended to last for a minimum duration of 15–20 years and a maximum of 30 years during this process of negotiation, and the SRA initially appeared sympathetic to such extensions.

One of the crucial choice elements in the specification of franchise contracts for rail operation is the duration of the contract. Longer franchises generally guarantee higher returns to the franchising agency, but at a cost of reducing the incentives towards improved efficiency which are generated by the re-procurement process. The British government initially was prepared to consider pleas from some bidders to extend contract lengths in exchange for investment. However, long franchises might enable the incumbent franchisee to establish barriers to entry that would undermine competition for the market at the time of re-tendering and the ultimate plan of introducing further competition in the system.[5] In a subsequent volte-face the SRA released its Franchising Policy Statement on 6 November 2002 stating that 'Generally the SRA envisages franchise lengths of between 5 to 8 years . . . If franchises meet key performance indicators and deliver on their plans, there is a provision for franchise extension.'[6]

The main problem with the franchises has been the difficulty in predicting demand, capacity and the cost of replacement rolling stock. Passenger demand grew rapidly and quite unexpectedly after almost static demand for many decades. Almost immediately the network showed signs of congestion at critical bottlenecks, making it difficult to meet the demand without increased crowding and initially some deterioration in reliability. The costs of expanding network capacity proved extremely high (and probably uneconomic), while the marginal track access prices were revealed to be too low. Managing maintenance in a now highly fragmented industrial structure in which Railtrack no longer had any in-house maintenance or even engineering capability proved difficult. What was to be the beginning of the end of Railtrack plc with its 250,000 shareholders came with the Hatfield derailment of 17 October 2000. On the face of it, this was a minor accident involving a broken rail and four deaths, but it

---

[4] See the news releases at http://www.sra.gov.uk/sra/news/ (accessed at 7 February 2003).

[5] Affuso and Newbery (2000) find evidence that shorter franchise lives can, in fact, increase incentives to invest. Their explanation for this finding is that shorter franchises mean that TOCs, facing re-procurement sooner, tend to invest in order to signal their commitment to the regulator and thus increase the probability of the franchise being re-awarded. Public threats of fines and non-renewal of franchises from the regulator have served as a strong incentive. Moreover, investing near the end of a contract also signals aggressive behaviour to potential entrants that raises their entry costs.

[6] See the news release at http://www.sra.gov.uk/sra/news/ for that date (accessed at 7 February 2003).

revealed the yawning gap between those responsible for rail safety, Railtrack, and the now separate rail maintenance companies that monitor track condition and repair faults. The whole railway timetable was abandoned for six months while the rail network was inspected and extensively renewed, causing delays, cancellations, a fall in passenger revenues, and distress to the TOCs as well as huge expense to Railtrack. That, coupled with escalating costs for contracted new investment, meant that Railtrack was unviable without additional subsidy or renegotiated track access charges. The end came when Railtrack was put into administration (i.e. effectively declared bankrupt) by the Transport Secretary in October 2001, and subsequently turned into a not-for-profit company, Network Rail.

It is therefore not surprising that many of the franchises had to be renegotiated after the contracts were first awarded. Part of the problem was that the Beauty Contest/auction took place under highly imperfect and asymmetric information about the real value of the operations being tendered. The more important problem is that there is an incentive for the franchisees, once they have been awarded the contract, to try and renegotiate some conditions in order to obtain more favourable terms, and asymmetric information exacerbates this problem. In the case of the SRA the renegotiation stage brought outcomes further removed from the original target of introducing increasing degrees of competition over time, and fluctuating views on what was the ideal length of a franchise, and how it should be extended or re-tendered.

### 3.2    Experience in other countries

The railway reforms that have taken place in other countries over the last couple of decades have aimed to combat excessive government spending and to improve the service quality and the cost effectiveness of its provision. In this section we outline the processes implemented in some countries that have adopted tender processes for the award of contracts for the operation of rail services.

By 1989 the Argentinian state-owned railway company, Ferrocariles Argentinos (FA) had an operating deficit of US$2 million per day. Restructuring began in mid 1990 and by the end of July 1994, FA was no longer running trains. Six commercially viable freight concessions were defined and were allocated to successful bidders for a period of thirty years with a ten-year renewal option. The concession holders were responsible for operations, maintenance and the investment to which they had committed themselves in the bidding. Responsibility for the intercity passenger services, which were thought to be commercially unviable, was passed to the provinces, who could either decide to support them through subsidies or terminate them. Commuter services in the Buenos Aires region became the responsibility of FEMESA, a state-owned corporation separate from FA. However, not long after the creation of FEMESA, it was decided to offer the commuter services as concessions as well. These concessions were very similar to the freight concessions, with the government owning the rolling stock, infrastructure and facilities but the concessionaire placed with the responsibility for train operations and maintaining the infrastructure. Concessions were granted for ten years with ten-year extension periods.

In fact, in both Latin America and Africa, many railway systems have been privatised by means of long-term concessions. In most instances an outsider, generally an agency, was given total control of the tender process. The concessions awarded were mainly for freight operations. Their duration tended to be long, about thirty years on average (Chile chose a twenty-year duration, while Mexico preferred a fifty-year option given the presence of alternative networks that generate effective competition).

The process for the allocation of the concessions varied. However, three main approaches adopted for the award of the concession/sale of the shares in companies holding the concessions were (i) sealed bids, (ii) public auctions (Brazil), and (iii) direct negotiation.

Sealed-bid auctions were adopted in the majority of the cases, with the concessions being awarded to the best offer. Only a few countries determined a minimum acceptable price for the bid process, the remainder leaving it to the market to identify the economic value of the operation. The auction in Brazil had to set a minimum price according to their legal requirements; the determination of this price was, however, very costly. In other cases, governments had a (private) value which determined their minimum acceptable price. This information was not disclosed to the bidders, with the result that some auctions did not reach this minimum value and the concessions were withdrawn (as, for example, in Mexico). As in Britain, Latin American and African countries preferred to adopt a pre-qualifying stage for the selection of bidders who would be allowed to bid for the concessions. This pre-qualification stage was also a way to take account of issues and competencies that were not easily quantifiable and so were difficult to include in the final bids. Only those parties who satisfied these criteria were admitted to the bidding stage.

The system for the identification of the winning bid varied. Different forms of 'points formulae' were adopted. In table 12.1 we illustrate the example of Argentina, which is interesting in its choice of the relative weights for the different elements of the bids.

The main objective of the formula adopted was to include all of the most important features of the bid and quantify them, with monetary

Table 12.1. *The bid-scoring system in Argentina*

| Factor | Maximum points |
|---|---|
| Bidder's experience, personnel and business plan | 23 |
| Basic investment plan amount and quality | 33 |
| Additional investment proposed | 5 |
| Annual payment to government for infrastructure concession | 10 |
| Toll to be charged to other operators for use of the track | 5 |
| Number of former railway employees to be hired | 15 |
| Argentine presence in concession | 9 |
| Maximum total points | 100 |

*Source:* Thompson, Budin and Estache, 2001.

values where possible, so as to limit arbitrariness in the final choice; however, different weights were given to various aspects of the bids depending on circumstances.

The formula of table 12.1 was adopted in one of the early concessions awarded in Argentina. Their experience with the performance of these concessions, however, demonstrated that the formula encouraged unrealistic and unpredictable bidding. This led to subsequent renegotiation of some concessions. An interesting case was that of Bolivia, where the highest bid won, and the winner was expected to make the payment of the total price on the day of the award. This money, however, was not retained by the government but was instead used to invest in rail assets to be used by the company.

An interesting bidding system was adopted for the Buenos Aires Metro, where the bidders were asked to bid (1) the monthly amount of subsidy required for their operation, and (2) the timing for a detailed capital programme requested by the government, subject to maximum fares and minimum service requirements. The winning bid was determined on the basis of the minimum present value of the sum of the subsidy and investment.

The sums raised by auctioning long-term concessions were quite substantial. The Brazilian Federal Railway (RFFSA) was losing around US$500 million annually; this was transformed into a payment to the government of US$1.7 billion. In Mexico, annual losses of around US$400 million were transformed into a positive payment of US$2.4 billion (see Thompson, Budin and Estache (2001)).

The winners of the concessions saw a quite large participation by local consortia. It was originally felt that local participation in the tender process should be encouraged because of political concerns over the privatisation of state-owned assets. Some concessions were declared critical to 'national interest' and required government approval, particularly for bidders including a majority participation of foreign companies. Moreover, local participation was encouraged by the fact that there was no immediate capital requirement on the bidders' side to build a new capital asset base, and in some cases this still remained a responsibility of the government. As a result most winning consortia had local majority ownership, with foreign participation limited to specific expertise, mainly on the commercial aspects. Thompson, Budin and Estache (2001) suggest that the consortia have functioned quite well.

### 3.3    *Auctions remain an untried allocation mechanism for allocating rail slots*

The allocation of each individual service by auction remains an untried option for rail.[7] The design of current contracts (franchises or concessions) implies the presence of internal cross-subsidies. Peak-time trains subsidise required off-peak services.[8] Profit-making services subsidise loss-making ones. An auction system for the separate allocation of each individual service could minimise the subsidy required for each loss-making service and maximise revenues from profit-making ones. Although efficient, it was widely believed that such a system would be far too complicated to implement. Some experiments conducted within the EU 'Europe-trip'[9] research project obtained algorithms able to:

- allocate capacity to maximise revenue;
- allocate costs; and
- generate efficient timetables in a vertically separated system.

Although feasible in experiments, this system is very demanding on computing capacity and the skills of rail operators. It can become almost intractable if, as could often be the case, some companies face economies from operating more than one service. That would tend to make a combinatorial auction the most efficient system. There is some research evidence to demonstrate combinatorial auctions for public service obligations can be both feasible and desirable, even in complex situations. Whether similar auctions would be feasible or cost-effective in the rail industry remains an open question.

---

[7] For more details on the complexities of rail capacity auctions, see Affuso (2003).

[8] The British solution was to make track access charges two-part tariffs, with extra paths at (originally understated) avoidable cost. Nevertheless, the original franchise commitments included services that were almost certainly individually non-commercial.

[9] http://europa.eu.int/comm/transport/extra/ (accessed at 1 July 2003).

## 4    Conclusion

From this brief review of the restructuring of railways in various countries it is clear that one of the key elements in deciding upon the amount of horizontal or vertical separation to introduce was the degree of perceived and desired competition within the railway industry and with other modes of transport in the country. This fundamental decision, together with the characteristics of the specific rail operation, dictated the choice of allocation mechanism.

In Sweden, road and rail transport decisions are part of the same harmonised policy. Public transport authorities were given the freedom to purchase train operations from any suitable contractor. Two operators, BK-Tåg and Linjetag, attempted to enter the market, though only BK-Tåg was successful in winning a contract. SJ responded to the competition by cutting tender prices by an average of 30 per cent. It has since secured all contracts and has displaced BK-Tåg from its two contracts.

The Argentinian system, unlike most EU systems, is dominated by freight rather than passenger traffic. Here, six freight concessions were given exclusive use of the tracks apart from the requirement to grant access to passenger operations in return for a compensatory track fee. This structure is of interest, as the concessions awarded were of long duration and some renegotiation occurred. The risk in awarding long franchises without competition is the inability of the regulator/government to determine when the companies are performing adequately or when they are abusing their market power. If there is a fixed unit of demand and firms submit bids to supply that unit, as with franchise bids, then allocative, productive and distributional efficiency all increase as competition, measured by the number of rival firms, increases. It is likely that there will be more rivals if the franchise is for a short period since it reduces the ability of the incumbent franchisee to erect barriers to entry by exploiting its informational advantage.

In addition, limiting the number of participants in an industry compounds the problems of asymmetric information and leaves the regulator less able to establish whether firms are behaving efficiently. Thus competitive pressure, or at least the presence of 'yardstick' competition, may actually lead the franchisees to increase their investment, since they do not intend to risk losing their franchise if they are seen to underperform. Concessions, like franchising, were used to maintain competition at each tendering. However, competition from road freight in Argentina was so intense that it led to a consequent failure by some concessionaires to undertake their specified investment programmes.

Long concession periods, like the thirty years in Argentina, combined with vertical integration could result in diminished incentives towards efficiency and large incentives towards opportunistic behaviour. Longer contracts make it progressively more difficult to establish whether the incumbent franchisee is abusing its monopoly position when asking the government for a renegotiation of its financial terms in the presence of unforeseen events.

We conclude with four remarks.

(1) The most suitable structure for the provision of railway services and, therefore, the best mechanism for allocating the resulting contracts or franchises will depend on the characteristics of the industry and the country. The choice will depend on the geography of the country, the composition of traffic, its distribution between freight and passenger, the average distance travelled, whether dominated by commuting, as in Europe, or by longer-distance travel, the degree of competition faced by rail from other modes like air and road, and the number of potential bidders for rail service operations.

(2) The British experience demonstrates that the competitive tendering of franchises has delivered positive results in terms of higher efficiency than under British Rail. As information is very incomplete at the first tender stage, there will inevitably be some informational rents being passed on to some franchisees. However, a short-term contracting framework, with repeated tendering for the franchises, enables the government to gain information and reduce the size of this rent at re-procurement stage, unlike a long-term concession framework. In the latter the risk of renegotiation is higher, but so are the returns that such concessions generate for the government.

(3) Rail restructuring systems used in different countries cannot readily be ranked against each other on merit. The restructuring process is inherently situation-specific and should be developed to suit each particular country. In some cases, though, political agendas can prevail over economic principles. None the less, the underlying principle of introducing a competitive system for allocating rail passenger services where possible undeniably represents a step towards using market forces. Whether this will lead to higher degrees of unbundling and an ultimate preference for auctions of rail paths over Beauty Contests for the allocation of bundles of services remains an open question.

(4) Perhaps the main problem lies in deciding what the size and shape of the railway system should be in the twenty-first century, 170 years after

the invention of the railway and 100 years after the internal combustion engine revolutionised road and air transport. Is the main objective a minimal and cheap railway, maintaining current capacity, where it is recognised that the cost of expansion is unlikely to be justified given the costs of increasing capacity on competing modes, or is the intention to expand capacity in the hope that rather ill-defined social benefits justify the cost? The answer to this question is likely to determine the size of investment needs, and hence the price of, supply of and demand for rail use. That will affect the value of franchises, the risks associated with various structural solutions, and hence the choice of the type of market mechanism to use in allocating responsibilities for service provision.

## References

Affuso, L. 2003, 'Auctions of rail capacity?', *Utilities Policy*, 11: 43–7.

Affuso, L. and D. Newbery 2000, 'Investment, reprocurement and franchise contract length in the British railway industry', Centre for Economic and Policy Research (CEPR) Discussion Paper, 2619.

Affuso, L., A. Angeriz and M. Pollitt 2002, 'Comparative efficiency of train operating companies in Britain', Regulation Initiative Working Paper Series, No. 48, London Business School.

Baumstark, L. 2001, 'The pioneering Swedish experiment in railway regulation', in C. Henry and A. Jeunemaitre (eds.), *Regulation of Network Utilities: The European Experience*, Oxford University Press.

Kelly, F. and R. Steinberg 2000, 'A combinatorial auction with multiple winners for universal service', *Management Science* 46: 586–96

Thompson, L., K. Budin and A. Estache 2001, 'Private investment in railways', Mimeo, The World Bank.

# Index